I Have Hidden Your Word in My Heart

Written by Dr. Shirley Anne Carson, Ed.D.

Poetry by Marilyn Kay Paddack Gage

May the Lord bless as you hide His word in your heart.

In Christ,

Dr. Shirley A. Carson

PRESS

Table Of Contents

Dedication

I lovingly dedicate *I Have Hidden Your Word in My Heart* to my Family:
To my husband, Dale, the encourager, the wonderful father of our daughters.

To Dayla Anne Blair and Lora Lynn (Lolly) Taylor, and to their husbands, Stephen Ray Blair and Edward Eugene Taylor.

To our grand- and great-grandchildren: Kyle Carson Blair, wife, Sara Paige, and son, Carson Ross; Toby Ray Blair, wife, Sarah Brooke, daughter, Landry Kate; and son, Henry Ray; Brooke Anne Taylor; Jordan Lynn Taylor and daughter, Londyn Grace Taylor; and Halle Grace Taylor.

Also, to my brothers, Dr. Ronald Lloyd Paddack and James Alfred Paddack, and my sister, Marilyn Kay Gage and their spouses, Hwa Hun Paddack, Sharon Kay Paddack, and George Edward (Bud) Gage.

To my nieces and nephews and your families, whom I love so dearly. I pray that the Lord will encourage and/or change your life as you read and memorize His Word.

And to my mother, Marjorie Amner Hubbard Paddack, who instilled a love of God's Word in all of us, and to my father, Lloyd Arlie Paddack, who taught us the vigilance of hard work.

Also, I dedicate this writing to our church family, the members of the Wayne First Baptist Church and to our special life-time friends and to all who hunger for God's word.

To <u>Xander</u>, the 11-year-old grandson of my cousin, who went to Heaven August 22, 2013. Xander Moore influenced numerous lives through his constant Christian witness during the 9 years he battled cancer. His grandfather, Rick Brown, said of the 2-year-old, when he was diagnosed, "This isn't about Zander. It's about God." And it was, and still is.

And especially, I humbly dedicate this writing to our Lord and Savior, Jesus Christ.

Foreword

D r. Shirley Carson has written a book that will aid in addressing one of the most serious problems that faces America today. No matter what revisionist historians have attempted to portray, our Founding Fathers intended that every citizen of these United States should become biblically literate, and our public school systems, including the vast majority of our nation's colleges and universities, were initially designed to promote primarily biblical curriculum. Tragically, with the passing of time, the lack of vigilance on the part of the church, and the misinterpretation of the United States Constitution, the citizens of this nation have been led astray from the truths of Scripture, and have become, for the most part, biblically illiterate and morally bankrupt! Without knowledge of the Word of God, the citizens of this, or any nation, have no working moral compass with which to accurately judge the actions of its leaders.

Dr. Carson has fully grasped the gravity of the situation, and drawing upon her godly family heritage and life-long devotion to Jesus Christ and His Word, she has successfully gathered and designed, within one volume, probably the easiest and quickest way any individual can come to understand and appreciate the Bible in its entirety. Every Christian will not only benefit from reading the book themselves, but should also consider making a gift of this work to those they know who are struggling with their understanding of the Word of God.

Dr. Rick McGee
Pastor - First Baptist Church
Wayne, Oklahoma

Acknowledgements

I am grateful to the Fellowship of Christian Athletes (FCA) for all they do for our youth in our schools. When I coached, I depended upon them for help with my athletes, and now they are active in our community school.

Wayne High School Local FCA at
Fields of Faith at Norman, Oklahoma

This week, our FCA attended Fields of Faith, and many of our youth gave their lives to the Lord. I was very thrilled when our School FCA director, Jim Paddack, gave me their study Bible called *God's Game Plan: The Athlete's Bible*. Most of the Themes for the Books of the Bible and parts of some of the summaries were taken from the FCA Bible. I highly recommend *God's Game Plan* to everyone, especially to young people!

Throughout the one and one-half years that I spent writing *I Have Hidden Your Word in My Heart*, my family and my church family has been very supportive. I thank those who contributed favorite Bible verses and those who read and gave suggestions for my writing. My pastor, Dr. Rick McGee, has aided in my growth more than he might realize because his lessons, sermons, and writings have been a constant inspiration.

I am very grateful to my sister, Marilyn Kay Paddack Gage, who wrote the poetry for the books of the Bible. Our daughter, Lolly Taylor, the computer expert of the family, has been indispensable. Thanks to Dayla Blair, my daughter, with whom I discuss ideas, and to my brother, Ronald, who was the inspiration for me to write in the first place. Thank you, Dale, for preparing wonderful meals for me while I've researched and written and for enduring my Parkinson Disease with me. I especially thank everyone for your prayers for the book, that God's Word will go forth and that people will see God's whole plan of redemption for their lives through Jesus Christ, our Lord,

About the Authors, Shirley Anne Carson and Marilyn Kay Gage

"We are sisters. And we are thankful for our parents who taught the Bible and the value of hard work. Our goal has been to pass the baton of faith to the next generation and to give them 'Memories That Wrap Their Arms around Them' like our mother and father did for us."

A long time school and university teacher, Marilyn Kay is now an adult Sunday School Teacher, sings in the choir, plays the piano, goes to painting institutes, takes many classes, and loves going to Southern Gospel Concerts. Mrs. Gage has written poetry for every chapter of the Bible. She has made dozens of quilts for special occasions and enjoys nieces and nephews.

Shirley was saved when she was 9 years old. She was already memorizing the Bible. Also, at age 9, she purchased a piano, and learned to play from the hymnal. She has hidden the words of the Bible and the hymnal in her heart for many purposes. She loves the Lord Jesus, her home and family, her church, and children.

Dr. Carson received her Doctorate in Language Arts in Education. She has written many articles in educational magazines, has spoken at Professional Conventions across the USA, counseled and taught Youth, and has sung in the choir at Falls Creel Youth Camp, many years. At age 12, Shirley began teaching in Bible School and Sunday School.

PART ONE

Why Hide God's Word in Your Heart?

Psalm 119:11, KJV: Thy word have I hid in mine heart, that I might not sin against thee.
Psalm 119:105, KJV: Thy word is a lamp unto my feet, and a light unto my path.

I've often thought that if our Bibles were confiscated during persecution as is happening all over the world, or if I were ever imprisoned for my faith, I would want to have God's word hidden in my heart. I would wish for a writing pad and pen so I could reconstruct from memory as much of the Bible as possible. I fear I would be ashamed that I could not recall some of all the books of the Bible and all the most important verses and doctrines, especially those that would uplift and give praise to God. Perhaps you and I together could recall these wonderful Words of Life.

We could now resolve to re-memorize everything we have memorized in the past. We could keep a journal of our memory work. We could also team up with a friend or family member and decide on worthy verses that would, in a concise way, include God's entire plan of redemption for us and for others.

This book began as a personal journal of my memory work in the Bible, along with a resolution to re-memorize everything that I have memorized in the past. Though I knew this would be a worthy goal, I began to think about my age and poor health and knew I would not have a long time to share with people the Word that was hidden in my heart. So I recorded these most wonderful words of life for my descendants and loved ones. Then I made this into a book for you to read. I pray that readers will see God's whole plan for redemption through Jesus Christ for your lives and that you will learn your purpose on this earth as you read the whole Bible from Genesis to Revelation in a short, concise way.

I also determined that I would record the favorite verses that relatives, church members, and friends had memorized. This was the greatest of blessings to me. I love the King James

Version. But, dear Ones, please begin the blessed journey of hiding God's Word in your heart, using your favorite version!

I pray that Section Five, *Scriptures for Special Occasions*, will be perfect for you when you have special needs.

Why hide God's Word in your heart? The person who knows the Bible has a much better prayer life because God answers our prayers by allowing us to call to memory God's Word when we pray! Also, we can "pray the Bible" for our children, others, and ourselves.

Why hide God's Word in your heart? So that when the Devil tempts you to do wrong, you can answer him with the scripture, like Jesus did when He was tempted. You will be able to make good decisions because God's word will be a light to your path. You will know absolutely what is right and wrong.

Why hide God's Word in your heart? So you can praise God using the wonderful words sung by David, by Jesus, by Isaiah, by Abraham, and by all those of the Hall of Faith.

Why hide God's Word in your heart? So you can pass your faith to the next generation. We do, as my Grandpa Paddack admonished us at family gatherings, want an unbroken circle of family in Heaven. I have often thought of a CD that our daughter and her husband played in their home, entitled "I Have Hidden your Word in My Heart." The chorus was followed each time with scriptures that I know have guided our precious grandsons all of their lives.

As we hide God's word in our hearts, we find God's purpose and plan that we were created by Him and for His glory. We learn that the only thing that lasts is our relationship with God and that life is preparation for eternity.

Why hide God's word in your heart? So you will know Jesus who takes away the sin of the world as the central theme of every book of the Bible. Also, a careful examination of *the characters* of the Old Testament shows they are each a picture or a foreshadowing of the Coming Messiah, Jesus Christ. From these wonderful characters of the Bible who were tempted, who sinned, who repented, who were persecuted for righteousness sake, or who were Giants in the Faith, we glean help for our everyday lives.

Why memorize the Bible? So you will be able to share Jesus with others without fear. You will be prepared at all times to tell others of the hope that is within you. You will be able to win others to Christ, to shepherd others, to disciple others, and to mentor and counsel with others if you have God's word in your heart.

Why hide God's word in your heart? To help save our Nation, America. God blesses the Nation that follows Him. In order for a nation to sustain freedom, the masses have to act morally and lawfully, and the Ten Commandments and the Sermon on the Mount are how we have judged good and evil, right and wrong.

Why abide in the Word? So we can claim God's Promises. Jesus said, "If you abide in me and my words abide in you, you shall ask what you will and it will be done unto you." John 15:7 (KJV)

Why hide God's Word in your heart? So you can see the world through the Biblical Worldview, rather than the Worldly World View. The Bible is unique: It is the only Book that is all Truth. God is the author of the Bible.

God speaks to us in various ways—through his beautiful creation, through his Holy Spirit, and through his Word, the Bible. Let God speak to you!

PART TWO

Scriptures about the Bible

The Word of God is quick, and powerful, and sharper than any two-edged sword, piercing even to the dividing asunder of soul and spirit, and of the joints and marrow, and is a discerner of the thoughts and intents of the heart. Hebrews 4:12: KJV

Heaven and earth will pass away, but my words will never pass away. Matthew 24:35: KJV

Study to shew thyself approved unto God, a workman that needeth not to be ashamed, rightly dividing the word of truth. II Timothy 2:15 KJV

All scripture *is* given by <u>inspiration of God</u>, and *is* profitable for doctrine, for reproof, for correction, for instruction in righteousness: that the man of God may be perfect, thoroughly furnished unto all good works. II Timothy 3:16-17 KJV

The law of the Lord is perfect, converting the soul: the testimony of the Lord is sure, making wise the simple. The statutes of the Lord are right, rejoicing the heart: the commandment of the Lord is pure, enlightening the eyes. Psalm 9:7-8

Jesus answered and said, "It is written, Man shall not live by bread alone, but by every word that proceeds out of the mouth of God." Matthew 4:4

Take the helmet of salvation and the sword of the Spirit, which is the Word of God. Ephesians 6:17 (The Bible is the only offensive weapon of the whole Armor of God.)

(God's word is all truth. Everything that comes into our lives must be filtered through the Truth.) John 8:32 and 36, KJV: And ye shall know the truth, and the truth shall make you free. If the Son therefore shall make you free, ye shall be free indeed.

James 1:23-25, KJV: For if any be a hearer of the word, and not a doer, he is like unto a man beholding his natural face in a glass: For he beholds himself, and goes his way, and straightway forgets what manner of man he was. But whoso looks into the perfect law of liberty, and continues therein, he being not a forgetful hearer, but a doer of the word, this man shall be blessed indeed.

Preach the word; be instant in season, out of season; reprove, rebuke, exhort with all long suffering and doctrine. 2 Timothy 4:2, KJV

Evidence of the Infallibility of the Bible as God's Word
(From *Rising Millennials Face Worldview Conflict*, Carson, 2002)

- There is more evidence that the Bible is a reliable source than for any other book of the ancient world.
- The Bible has proven to be historically accurate.
- Archaeological discoveries have <u>never</u> contradicted the Bible. They confirm many of the stories, events, places, and peoples of the Bible.
- No one has ever claimed the reward for finding a scientific blunder in the Bible.
- The sacred writings of all other religions are plagued with scientific blunders.
- The Bible has a history of victory over attack.
- 191 predictions in the Old Testament of the coming of Christ were fulfilled.
- Prophecies of Jesus' crucifixion and burial and 12 aspects of the passion are fulfilled.
- The Bible is inspired by God. Though 66 books were written by 40 men during 2000 years, there are no contradictions. Unity exists because it is God's word.
- The Bible is superior over all other writings in that it is all truth.
- The Bible changes lives.
- The Bible is the only religious book confirmed by documented miracles performed.
- Other writings are authored by people or prophets of God, but every word of the Bible is inspired by God.
- The Bible was written by people who were willing to die for its truth. The early disciples were in a position to know whether their message was true or false.
- The Bible <u>claims</u> to be the Word of God and <u>proves</u> to be the Word of God.

The grass withers, the flower fades:
But the word of our God stands forever (Isaiah 40:8).

Pass the "Baton of Faith" to the next generation

Picture taken at the 80th birthday of the author's Husband, Dale. Top Row (left to right): Kyle Carson Blair, Sara Paige Blair, Brooke Anne Taylor, Toby Ray Blair, Jordan Lynn Taylor holding Londyn Grace Taylor, Edward Taylor. Middle Row (left to right): Steven Ray Blair, Dayla Anne Blair, Lolly Taylor. Bottom Row (left to right): Landry Kate Blair, Shirley Anne Carson holding Henry Ray Blair; Dale Carson holding Carson Ross Blair, and Halle Grace Taylor. Not pictured is Sarah Brooke Blair, who was seriously ill at the time, but is now recovered.

PART THREE

Favorite Scriptures of Family

*T*he Bible is a very personal book because God speaks through His Holy Spirit to each of us in unique ways through our varying experiences.

My mother's favorite of her many beloved passages is Philippians 2:5-11, KJV. This is because it describes how Jesus humbled himself and was willingly sent from the glories of heaven to pay the price for our sins. Then we see Jesus glorified when every knee shall bow and every tongue confess that Jesus Christ is Lord. Mama memorized it, and so did I.

[5] Let this mind be in you, which was also in Christ Jesus: [6] Who, being in the form of God, thought it not robbery to be equal with God: [7] But made himself of no reputation, and took upon him the form of a servant, and was made in the likeness of men: [8] And being found in fashion as a man, he humbled himself, and became obedient unto death, even the death of the cross. [9] Wherefore God also hath highly exalted him, and given him a name which is above every name: [10] That at the name of Jesus every knee should bow, of things in heaven, and things in earth, and things under the earth; [11] And that every tongue should confess that Jesus Christ is Lord, to the glory of God the Father. My mother, Marjorie Amner Hubbard Paddack

Proverbs 6:6-8: Go to the ant, you sluggard! Consider her ways and be wise,

Which, having no captain, overseer or ruler, [8] provides her supplies in the summer, And gathers her food in the harvest. [9] How long will you slumber, O sluggard? When will you rise from your sleep? A little sleep, a little slumber, A little folding of the hands to sleep— [11] So shall your poverty come on you like a prowler, And your need like an armed man. My father, Lloyd Arlie Paddack: This was his philosophy – always. He valued hard work – and rising early.

John 3:16, KJV: For God so loved the world that he gave his only begotten Son that whosoever believeth in him should not perish, but have everlasting life. My encourager, my faithful husband for 58 years, Wendell Dale Carson

Isaiah 40:31: But they that wait upon the Lord shall renew their strength; they shall mount up with wings as eagles; they shall run, and not be weary; and they shall walk, and not faint. Our daughter, Lora Lynn (Lolly) Carson Taylor

I Corinthians 1:4-9: I give thanks to my God always for you because of the grace of God that was given you in Christ Jesus, that in every way you were enriched in him in all speech and all knowledge, even as the testimony about Christ was confirmed among you so that you are not lacking in any gift, as you wait for the revealing of our Lord Jesus Christ, who will sustain you to the end, guiltless in the day of our Lord Jesus Christ. God is faithful, by whom you were called into the fellowship of his Son, Jesus Christ our Lord. Lolly's faithful husband, Edward Eugene Taylor

James 1:21-25: Do not merely listen to the word, and so deceive yourselves. Do what it ays. [23] Anyone who listens to the word but does not do what it says is like someone who looks at his face in a mirror [24] and, after looking at himself, goes away and immediately forgets what he looks like. [25] But whoever looks intently into the perfect law that gives freedom, and continues in it—not forgetting what they have heard, but doing it—they will be blessed in what they do. Our granddaughter, Brooke Anne Taylor

John 16:33, KJV: These things I have spoken unto you, that in me ye might have peace. In the world ye shall have tribulation: but be of good cheer; I have overcome the world. Our granddaughter, Jordan Lynn Taylor

I Samuel 1:27-28, KJV: For this child I prayed. And the Lord hath given me my petitions which I asked of him; therefore also I have lent her to the Lord, as long as she lives she shall be lent to the Lord. Daughter of Jordan Lynn, Londyn Grace Taylor, born August 14, 2012.

I asked Halle Grace, a new kindergartner at Community Christian School, what her favorite verse was. She said, "My favorites are A, B, C, and D." Then very loudly and with wonderful expression and confidence, she quoted from the King James Version:

"A. All have sinned and come short of the glory of God. Romans 3:23. B. Believe on the Lord Jesus Christ, and thou shalt be saved. Acts 8:31 C. Children, obey your parents in the Lord, for this is right. Ephesians 6:1 D. Delight thyself in the Lord, and He shall give you the desires of your heart. Psalm 27:4", KJV, Granddaughter, Halle Grace Taylor, age 5 ½, daughter of Edward and Lolly Taylor, who told her Pop and me on September 28, 2012, "I asked Jesus into my heart night before last." At Christmas, she was baptized and had memorized many verses and songs!

John 14:1-6, KJV: Let not your heart be troubled: ye believe in God, believe also in me. [2] In my Father's house are many mansions: if it were not so, I would have told you. I go to prepare a place for you. [3] And if I go and prepare a place for you, I will come again, and receive you unto myself; that where I am, there ye may be also. [4] And whither I go ye know, and the way ye know. [5]Thomas saith unto him, Lord, we know not whither thou goest; and how can we know the way? [6]Jesus saith unto him, I am the way, the truth, and the life: no man cometh unto the Father, but by me. Chester Taylor, Edward Taylor's Father, and grandfather of Brooke, Jordan, and Halle.

Jeremiah 11:9: For I know the plans I have for you," declares the LORD, "plans to prosper you and not to harm you, plans to give you hope and a future." Ruby Taylor, Edward's Mother and grandmother of Brooke, Jordan, and Halle.

II Chronicles 7:14: [14]If my people, which are called by my name, shall humble themselves, and pray, and seek my face, and turn from their wicked ways; then will I hear from heaven, and will forgive their sin, and will heal their land." *And also.* Romans 12:2, KJV: And be not conformed to this world: but be ye transformed by the renewing of your mind, that ye may prove what is that good, and acceptable, and perfect, will of God. Our daughter, Dayla Anne Carson Blair, who has used Biblical wisdom to raise her boys to not conform to this world.

Romans 10:9, KJV: That if thou shalt confess with thy mouth the Lord Jesus, and shalt believe in thine heart that God hath raised him from the dead, thou shalt be saved. Our son-in-law, Steven Ray Blair, a loving, staunch Christian father and husband.

Ephesians 4:29: Let no corrupt communication proceed out of your mouth, but that which is good to the use of edifying, that it may minister grace unto the hearers. Our Grandson, Toby Ray Blair, quoted many favorite passages from memory. He may have more memorized than the older folks in our family.

Psalm 46:1: God is our refuge and strength, an ever-present help in trouble. Toby's wife, Sarah Brooke Blair

Jeremiah 29:11: For I know the plans I have for you," declares the Lord, "plans to prosper you and not to harm you, plans to give you hope and a future." Landry Kate Blair, age 3. Toby said her mother, Sarah, wrote Jeremiah 29:11 on the correspondence concerning Landry's birth.

Proverbs 22:6: Train up a child in the way he should go and when he is old, he will not depart from it. Henry Ray Blair, son of Sarah and Toby, born May 3, 2013.

I Corinthians 10:13: No temptation has overtaken you except what is common to mankind. And God is faithful; he will not let you be tempted beyond what you can bear. But when you are tempted, he will also provide a way out so that you can endure it. And also, Proverbs 1:7; 8: The fear of the Lord is the beginning of knowledge: but fools despise wisdom and instruction. My son, hear the instruction of your father, and forsake not the law of your mother. Our grandson, Kyle Carson Blair. Kyle always had great respect for his parents, Steve and Dayla.

Matthew 11:28-30: "Come to me, all you who are weary and burdened, and I will give you rest. [29]Take my yoke upon you and learn from me, for I am gentle and humble in heart, and you will find rest for your souls. [30] For my yoke is easy and my burden is light." Sara Paige Blair, Kyle's wife

Psalm 139: 13b – 14, KJV: Thou hast covered me in my mother's womb. I praise you because I am fearfully and wonderfully made; your works are wonderful; I know that full well. Carson Ross Blair, son of Sara and Kyle, born April 2, 2013.

Psalm 71:18, KJV: Now also when I am old and grey headed, O God, forsake me not; until I have shewed thy strength unto this generation, and thy power to everyone that is to come. Sue Blair, Mother of Steve Blair and grandmother of Kyle and Toby.

John 10:27-29: I give them eternal life, and they shall never perish; no one will snatch them out of my hand. [29] My Father, who has given them to me, is greater than all; no one can snatch them out of my Father's hand. My brother, James A. Paddack, a teacher of the Word, who shares the Bible with great wisdom and leads people to the Lord.

Philippians 4:13: I can do all things through Christ, which strengthens me. Jim's wife, Sharon Paddack, who beautifully shares the Word through the Praise Team at our church.

Philippians 4:5-7: Let your gentleness be evident to all. The Lord is near. Do not be anxious about anything, but in every situation, by prayer and petition, with thanksgiving, present your requests to God. And the peace of God, which transcends all understanding, will guard your hearts and your minds in Christ Jesus. My niece, Marilyn Kay (Katy) Paddack DeArman

James 1:2: Consider it pure joy, my brothers and sisters, whenever you face trials of many kinds, Katy's husband, Ricky Shon DeArman, Homeland Security Agent, who said this is his verse when he faces hardships and trials of any kind.

John 3:16, KJV: For God so loved the world that He gave his only begotten Son that whosoever believeth in Him should not perish, but have everlasting life. Wonderful son of Katy and Shon, Joshua Shon DeArman, age 19

I Corinthians 13:4: Love is patient, love is kind. It does not envy, it does not boast, it is not proud. Daughter of Katy and Shon, Madison Paige DeArman, age 17

John 11:35: Jesus wept. Our precious nephew, Ellis Paddack

Ruth 1:16-17, KJV: And Ruth said, Entreat me not to leave thee, or to return from following after thee: for whither thou goest, I will go; and where thou lodgest, I will lodge: thy people shall be my people, and thy God my God: Where thou diest, will I die, and there will I be buried: the Lord do so to me, and more also, if ought but death part thee and me. Caring physical therapist, DeWayne Kicklighter

Isaiah 40:31: But they that wait upon the Lord shall renew their strength; they shall mount up with wings as eagles; they shall run, and not be weary; and they shall walk, and not faint. My brother-in-law, George Edward (Bud) Gage

John 11:35: "Jesus wept." My sister, Marilyn Kay Gage, the most Bible literate person of our family. Marilyn said, "Why did Jesus weep? Was it because of his compassion for those who were weeping, or was it because he called Lazarus to come back from the glories of heaven to this earth?" Marilyn twice wrote a poem for every chapter of the Bible.

Hebrews 13: 1-2: Let brotherly love continue. Be not forgetful to entertain strangers, for thereby some have entertained angels unawares. My brother, Dr. Ronald Lloyd and wife, Hwa Yun Paddack, who love all people and who have entertained people from all over the world.

Jeremiah 33:3, KJV: Call unto me, and I will answer thee, and show thee great and mighty things that thou knowest not. My nephew & niece, Bryan and Marjorie Soon Mobley *The Lord has done great and mighty things in their lives!*

Luke 10:27, KJV: 'Love the Lord your God with all your heart and with all your soul and with all your strength and with all your mind'; and thy neighbor as thy self." Robert Grant Mobley, age 8.

Romans 8:38-39: Nothing can separate us from God's love. The twins, Meredith Amner and Juliette James Mobley, (On their third birthday). Their mother, Marjorie, said, "They memorized it at church! They have hand motions to go with it and it is precious!"

Isaiah 58:7: Is it not to share your food with the hungry and to provide the poor wanderer with shelter—when you see the naked, to clothe them, and not to turn away from your own flesh and blood? James Arlie and Stephanie Paddack did not give a favorite verse, but I have found this verse describes them. Mother always said "Arlie has such a good, kind heart."

All of Psalm 1: Blessed is the one who does not walk in step with the wicked or stand in the way that sinners take or sit in the company of mockers, but <u>whose delight is in the law of the LORD, and who meditates on his law day and night</u>. That person is like a tree planted by streams of water, which yields its fruit in season and whose leaf does not wither—whatever they do prospers. Not so the wicked! They are like chaff that the wind blows away. Therefore the wicked will not stand in the judgment, nor sinners in the assembly of the righteous. For the Lord watches over the way of the righteous, but the way of the wicked leads to destruction. Our special cousin, Jill Paddack Tarkoff

Favorite Scriptures of Our Church Family

These are the favorite scriptures that were given by friends from our church, the First Baptist Church of Wayne, OK.

Isaiah 26:3, KJV: Thou wilt keep him in perfect peace, whose mind is stayed on thee: because he trusteth in thee. Our Pastor, Dr. Rick McGee

Proverbs 2:5-6: Trust in the Lord with all your heart, and do not rely on your own understanding. In all your ways acknowledge him, and he will direct your path. Proverbs 3:5-6: Nancy McGee

John 10:10, KJV: The thief cometh not, but for to steal, and to kill, and to destroy: I am come that they might have life, and that they might have it more abundantly. Youth Director Daniel Duncan

John 10:27: My sheep hear my voice, and I know them, and they follow me. [28] And I give unto them eternal life; and they shall never perish; neither shall any man pluck them out of my hand. Lindy Beth Duncan

II Timothy 1:7, KJV: For God hath not given us the spirit of fear; but of power, and of love, and of a sound mind. Church Secretary, Jamie Cody, and husband, Adam.

Philippians 4:13: I can do all things through Christ who strengthens me. Brandon Cody, Karen Jennings, Linda Holden and Ryan Goodrich, Church pianist and ordained minister

II Timothy 2:15: Do your best to present yourself to God as one approved, a worker who does not need to be ashamed and who correctly handles the word of truth. Tag Goodrich, age 6, son of Ryan

I Cor. 13:4-8b: Love is patient, love is kind. It does not envy, it does not boast, it is not proud. [5] It does not dishonor others, it is not self-seeking, it is not easily angered, it keeps no record of wrongs. [6] Love does not delight in evil but rejoices with the truth. [7] It always protects, always trusts, always hopes, always perseveres. Love never fails. Don Holden, soloist and instrumentalist.

All of Psalm 23, KJV: The Lord is my shepherd; I shall not want. [2] He maketh me to lie down in green pastures: he leadeth me beside the still waters. [3] He restoreth my soul: he leadeth me in the paths of righteousness for his name's sake. [4] Yea, though I walk through the valley of the shadow of death, I will fear no evil: for thou art with me; thy rod and thy staff they comfort me. [5] Thou preparest a table before me in the presence of mine enemies: thou anointest my head with oil; my cup runneth over. [6] Surely goodness and mercy shall follow me all the days of my life: and I will dwell in the house of the Lord forever. June Murray, Mary Sue Penner, and Noreen Sharp

Romans 8:31-32: What, then, shall we say in response to these things? If God is for us, who can be against us? [32] He who did not spare his own Son, but gave him up for us all—how will he not also, along with him, graciously give us all things? Charles lack

Matthew 7:7-8: Ask and it will be given to you; seek and you will find; knock and the door will be opened to you. [8] For everyone who asks receives; the one who seeks finds; and to the one who knocks, the door will be opened. Robert Brown

Matthew 6:25-26: Therefore I say to you, do not worry about your life, what you will eat or what you will drink; nor about your body, what you will put on. Is not life more than food and the body more than clothing? [26] Look at the birds of the air, for they neither sow nor reap nor gather into barns; yet your heavenly Father feeds them. Kristi Smith and Teresa Brown

Romans 8:35-39: Who shall separate us from the love of Christ? Shall trouble or hardship or persecution or famine or nakedness or danger or sword. [37] No, in all these things we are more than conquerors through him who loved us. [38] For I am convinced that neither death nor life, neither angels nor demons, neither the present nor the future, nor any powers, [39] neither height nor depth, nor anything else in all creation, will be able to separate us from the love of God that is in Christ Jesus our Lord. Jeff Smith, Adult Sunday School Teacher

Matthew 6:33, KJV: But seek ye first the kingdom of God, and his righteousness; and all these things shall be added unto you. Hoot and Margie Keely This is their personal testimony.

Hebrews 11:1: KJV: Now faith is the substance of things hoped for and the evidence of things not seen. Rose and Norman Payne

Hebrews 13:3: I will never leave you nor forsake you. Deacon, Bob Hynds

Ecclesiastes 3:1-8: To everything there is a season, and a time to every purpose under the heaven: [2] A time to be born, and a time to die; a time to plant, and a time to pluck up that which is planted; [3] A time to kill, and a time to heal; a time to break down, and a time to build up; A time to weep, and a time to laugh; a time to mourn, and a time to dance; [5] A time to cast away stones, and a time to gather stones together; a time to embrace, and a time to refrain from embracing; [6] A time to get, and a time to lose; a time to keep, and a time to cast away; [7] A time to rend, and a time to sew; a time to keep silence, and a time to speak; [8] A time to love, and a time to hate; a time of war, and a time of peace. Dian Taylor

John 10:27-29: I give them eternal life, and they shall never perish; no one will snatch them out of my hand. [29] My Father, who has given them to me, is greater than all; no one can snatch them out of my Father's hand. Jim Paddack

Jeremiah 29:11: I know the plans that I have for you, declares the Lord. They are plans for peace and not disaster, plans to give you a future filled with hope. Janie Williams and Bruce Goodrich

Proverbs 17:22: To have a fool for a child brings grief; there is no joy for the parent of a godless fool. And Proverbs 22:3: The prudent see danger and take refuge, but the simple keep going and pay the penalty. Johnny Harris

Proverbs Isaiah 58:6-7: Is it not to share your food with the hungry and to provide the poor wanderer with shelter—when you see the naked, to clothe them, and not to turn away from your own flesh and blood? Gail & Vaughn Bryant

Psalm 46:01: God is our refuge and strength, a very present help in trouble. Glenna Salsman

John 3:16: For God so loved the world that he gave his only begotten Son that whosoever believeth in him should not perish, but have everlasting life. Caitlin Mantooth, Rena Mantooth, Connie Ellis, Dale Carson, &Linda Burton

Proverbs 31: 10-30: The Virtuous Woman. Verses 10-12: A wife of noble character who can find? She is worth far more than rubies.[1] Her husband has full confidence in her and lacks nothing of value. [12] She brings him good, not harm, all the days of her life. [28] Her children arise and call her blessed; her husband also, and he praises her. Tanya Mantooth

Ephesians 3:17-19: So that Christ may dwell in your hearts through faith. And I pray that you, being rooted and established in love, [18] may have power, together with all the Lord's holy people, to grasp how wide and long and high and deep is the love of Christ, [19] and to know this. Love that surpasses knowledge—that you may be filled to the measure of all the fullness of God. Judy Goodrich

FAVORITE SCRIPTURES OF
LONG-TIME DEAR FRIENDS

Psalm 139: KJV: [7] Whither shall I go from thy spirit? or whither shall I flee from thy presence? [8] If I ascend up into heaven, thou art there. . . . [9] If I take the wings of the morning, and dwell in the uttermost parts of the sea; [10] Even there shall thy hand lead me, and thy right hand shall hold me. 14. I am fearfully and wonderfully made: Marvelous are thy works; and that my soul knoweth right well. How precious also are thy thoughts unto me, O God! How great is the sum of them! [18] If I should count them, they are more in number than the sand: when I awake, I am still with thee. [23] Search me, O God, and know my heart: try me, and know my thoughts: [24] And see if there be any wicked way in me, and lead me in the way everlasting. Carol and Willie Williams, fishing and vacation friends for 53 years

John 10:10: [10] The thief comes only to steal and kill and destroy; I have come that they may have life, and have it to the full. Cherie and Bill Marcum, dear friends who have experienced what the thief can do and all that Jesus can do in their lives. How we all loved their precious Marcia Lynn, the best friend of our Lora Lynn.

Luke 8:48 NKJV And He said to her, "Daughter, be of good cheer; your faith has made you well. Go in peace." Bette and Leonard Fietz. Betty said her testimony is that Jesus healed her. Betty is one who constantly praises the Lord.

He replied, "If you have faith as small as a mustard seed, you can say to this mulberry tree, 'Be uprooted and planted in the sea,' and it will obey you." Goldie and Clayton Posey, local friends and foreign missionaries. Great will be their reward in heaven!

I Corinthians 13:13: And now these three remain: faith, hope and love. But the greatest of these is love. Mary Lloyd, lovely newer friend at painting class.

Philippians 4:6-7: Do not be anxious about anything, but in every situation, by prayer and petition, with thanksgiving, present your requests to God. [7] And the peace of God, which transcends all understanding, will guard your hearts and your minds in Christ Jesus. Linda Anderson, fellow retired teacher at Wayne, OK

Philippians 4:8: Finally, brethren, whatsoever things are true, whatsoever things are honest, whatsoever things are just, whatsoever things are pure, whatsoever things are lovely, whatsoever things are of good report; if there be any virtue, and if there be any praise, think on these things. Sandra Shepherd, fellow retired first grade teacher at Wayne, OK.

"Rather than a favorite verse, I have a beloved book of the Bible – the Book of James. It tells me everything I need to know about how to live the happy Christian life, in no uncertain terms!" Dori Salsman Bynum: My physical therapist and daughter of a great friend, Glenna

"I like the whole Book of Proverbs. It gives practical instruction for all of everyday life. And it is fun to read, too." Joelle Gray, fellow retired teacher at Wayne, OK

John 3:16: For God so loved the world that he gave his one and only Son, that whoever believes in him shall not perish but have eternal life. Margaret Maynard, fellow retired teacher at Wayne OK

Psalm 139:17-19: That Christ may dwell in your hearts through faith. And I pray that you, being rooted and established in love, [18] may have power, together with all the Lord's holy people, to grasp how wide and long and high and deep is the love of Christ, [19] and to know this love that surpasses knowledge—that you may be filled to the measure of all the fullness of God. Mary Ann and Frank Turner, dear friends at the lake.

Personal Favorite Scriptures to Memorize

I always memorize scripture in the *King James Version* of the Bible.

Because I believe the Christian world view is built upon the Biblical truth of Creationism, the following first four verses are among my favorites:

Genesis 1:1: In the beginning, God created the Heavens and the Earth.

Colossians 1:16-17: For by him were all things created, that are in heaven, and that are in Earth:. . .all things were created by Him, and for Him; and He is before all things, and by Him all things consist.

John 1:1-3: In the beginning was the Word, and the Word was with God, and the Word was God. 2 The same was in the beginning with God. 3 All things were made by Him; and without Him was not anything made that was made.

Psalm 19:1: The heavens declare the glory of God; and the firmament sheweth his handiwork.

John 14:6: Jesus said, "I am the Way, the Truth, and the Life. No man cometh unto the Father except by Me."

Joel 1:3: Tell ye your children of it, let your children tell their children, and their children another generation. *(Pass the Baton of Faith to the Next Generation.)*

Philippians 1:6: Being confident of this, that he who began a good work in you will carry it on to completion until the day of Christ Jesus. *(This is good for our grandchildren.)*

John 4:14: Whosoever drinks of the water that I give him shall never thirst; but the water that I shall give Him shall be in him a well of water springing up into everlasting life.

John 15:7: If ye abide in Me, and My words abide in you, ye shall ask what ye will, and it shall be done unto you. *(John 15:7 was my New Year's resolution for 2 years. My resolution was to remain in God's word, and everything else would be taken care of.)*

Matthew 19:14: And Jesus said, "Let the little children come unto Me, for of such is the kingdom of Heaven." *(This and John 14:6 (above) will be on our tombstone, which is already engraved. These are a witness that Jesus is the only way to Heaven and of my life working with children. Dale had our National Motto "In God We Trust" and our national emblem of the Eagle put on it.)*

Ephesians 2: 8-9: For by grace are ye saved through faith; and that not of yourselves, it is the gift of God, not of works, lest any man should boast.

Romans 12:1-2: I beseech you therefore, brethren, by the mercies of God, that ye present your bodies a living sacrifice, holy, acceptable unto God, which is your reasonable service. 2. And be not conformed to this world: but be ye transformed by the renewing of your mind, that ye may prove what is that good, and acceptable, and perfect, will of God.

I John 1:7: But if we walk in the light, as He is in the light, we have fellowship one with another. and the blood of Jesus Christ his Son cleanseth us from all sin.

Matthew 7:12: The Golden Rule: Therefore all things whatsoever ye would that men should do unto you, do ye even so to them; for this is the law and the prophets.

2 Chronicles 7:14: [14]If my people, which are called by my name, shall humble themselves, and pray, and seek my face, and turn from their wicked ways; then will I hear from heaven, and will forgive their sin, and will heal their land.

Matthew 22:37-40: Jesus said unto him, Thou shalt love the Lord thy God with all thy heart, and with all thy soul, and with all thy mind. [38] This is the first and great commandment. [39] And the second is like unto it, Thou shalt love thy neighbor as thyself. [40] On these two commandments hang all the law and the prophets.

Exodus 20:3-17: The Ten Commandments: They are in this book two times – in Exodus and in Deuteronomy.

Wonderful longer scriptures are The Armor of God in Ephesians 6:10-17; the Love Chapter of the Bible, I Corinthians chapter 13; and Psalms chapters 1; 23; and 100.

At age 9, I started seriously memorizing scriptures. While going to the Methodist church with Grandma Hubbard during Mother's extended illness, I had a wonderful Sunday School teacher who gave us large cards with much work on it. Of course, Mother encouraged and helped me constantly. I have other stories of memory work throughout this book.

Our granddaughter, Halle Grace Taylor, age 5 ½, is memorizing scripture and is learning the books of the Bible at her Christian School. Children at our Wayne First Baptist Church, under the leadership of Glenna Salsman, have just been declared winners in the State Memory Work and Bible Drill Contest for the Baptist General Convention of Oklahoma.

It is very important to learn the 66 books of the Bible in order so you can easily find scripture. Precious Ones, please start memorizing scriptures today.

PART 3: Scriptures for Special Occasions

Contents:

We Stand on God's Promises: With Each Comes a Command
Concern for Children and Grandchildren
Pray the Bible for Your Children
Marriage: Husbands and Wives
Love
Forgiveness, Salvation, Freedom, Eternal Life
Assurance of Salvation
Grace and Faith
Baptism and the Lord's Supper
The Church
Creation
Prayer
Persecution
In Times of Pain, Illness, Death, Trials
Victory, Courage, Perseverance, Hope
Temptation
Pornography
Sexual Sin
Beer, Wine, Drunkenness
When We Are Tested
Power, Guidance, Decisions
Praise and Thanksgiving
Heaven
The Resurrection
Concern for Our Nation, America
Finances

{Please look in the appendix for understanding of the Biblical Vocabulary as you read "Scriptures for Special Occasions."}

PART FOUR

Scriptures for Special Occasion

WE CAN STAND ON GOD'S PROMISES
With each promise comes a command.

Only be strong and very courageous, faithfully doing everything in the teachings that my servant Moses commanded you. Don't turn away from them. Then you will succeed wherever you go. Joshua 1:7

If you abide in Me, and My word abides in you, you shall ask what you will, and it will be done unto you. John 15:7

They that wait upon the Lord shall renew their strength; They shall mount up with wings as eagles; They shall run, and not be weary; And they shall walk and not faint. Isaiah 40:29, 31

All things work together for good to those who love God, to them who are called according to his purpose. Romans 8:28

But seek ye first the kingdom of God, and his righteousness; and all these things shall be added unto you. Matthew 6:33, KJV

Be not deceived; God is not mocked: for whatsoever a man soweth, that shall he also reap. For he that soweth to his flesh shall of the flesh reap corruption; but he that soweth to the Spirit shall of the Spirit reap life everlasting. Galatians 6:7-8, KJV

Concern for Children and Grand Children

He shall give his angels charge over thee, to keep thee in all ways. Psalm 91:11, KJV

Children are an inheritance from the Lord; they are a reward from Him. The children born to a man are like arrows in the hand of a warrior. Blessed is the man who has filled his quiver with them. Psalm 127:3-4

Train a child in the way he should go, and even when he is old he will not turn away from it. Proverbs 22:6

Jesus said, "Don't stop the children from coming to Me. Children like these are part of the kingdom of God. I can guarantee this truth; whoever doesn't receive the kingdom of God as a little child receives it will never enter it." Jesus put his arms around the children and blessed them. Mark 10:14-16

Children, obey your parents in the Lord, for this is right. Fathers, do not provoke your children to wrath, but bring them up in the training and admonition of the Lord. Ephesians 6:1, 4

And thou shalt love the Lord thy God with all thine heart, and with all thy soul, and with all thy might. [6] And these words, which I command thee this day, shall be in thine heart: [7] And thou shalt teach them diligently unto thy children, and shalt talk of them when thou sittest in thine house, and when thou walkest by the way, and when thou liest down, and when thou risest up. Deuteronomy 6:5-7, KJV

But if you don't want to serve the Lord, then choose today whom you will serve....My family and I will still serve the Lord. Joshua 24:15

Train a child in the way he should go, and even when he is old he will not turn away from it. Proverbs 22:6

Pray the Bible for your children:

Lord, I dedicate my son to you. As long as he lives, he is dedicated to you. Bless him indeed; may your hand be upon him and keep him from harm. I Samuel 1:28; I Chronicles 4:10

Dear Father, It is not your will that my little daughter should perish, but that she should come to repentance. Lord Jesus, I thank you that you came to save the lost, including my precious one. Matthew 18:11, 14 and II Peter 3:9

Thank you, dear Father, that You have given your angels charge over my little one. Thank You that everything that comes into her life is working together for good for her because she loves You. Psalm 91:11; Romans 8:28

Thank You, Lord, that You know the plans you have for my little one, for peace and not evil. I pray that You will give him a future of hope. I pray that he will delight in Your word and will meditate upon it and will be like a tree planted by the rivers of water. Jeremiah 29:11 and Psalm 1

Dear Heavenly Father, I stand today on Ephesians 6:11-12. In the powerful name of Jesus Christ, I come against principalities and powers and the rulers of darkness of this world. Help us to put on the whole armor of God so we can withstand the wile of the devil. I bind the forces of evil from interfering with Your perfect plan for my children. Ephesians 6:11-12 and Matthew 18:18

Dear Jesus, I pray that my child, like You, when You were a child on earth, will increase in wisdom and stature and in favor with God and people in his life. Please give him a listening ear to parental instruction that he may gain understanding. Luke 2:52; Proverbs 4:1

Thank You, Father, that you know how to rescue my son and daughter from temptation. I pray that they will flee from youthful lusts will follow after righteousness, faith, love, and peace. Help my children to hide your words in their hearts. II Peter 2:9; II Timothy 2:22, 23; Psalm 119:9-11. Read *Learning How to Pray for Your Children*, from Agape Ministries; also, *Praying God's Word* (2003,) *by* Beth Moore.

Marriage; Husbands and Wives:

[22] Wives, submit yourselves unto your own husbands, as unto the Lord. [23] For the husband is the head of the wife, even as Christ is the head of the church: and he is the savior of the body. [24] Therefore as the church is subject unto Christ, so let the wives be to their own husbands in everything. [25] Husbands, love your wives, even as Christ also loved the church, and gave Himself for it; [31] For this cause shall a man leave his father and mother, and shall be joined unto his wife, and they two shall be one flesh. [33] Nevertheless let every one of you in particular so love his wife even as himself; and the wife see that she reverence her husband. Ephesians 5:22-25; 31- 33

(God defined and instituted marriage as being between one woman and one man.) When the Lord God made a woman from the rib He had taken out of the man, and he brought her to the man. [23] The man said, "This is now bone of my bones and flesh of my flesh; she shall be called 'woman,' for she was taken out of man." [24] That is why a man leaves his father and mother and is united to his wife, and they become one flesh. [25] Adam and his wife were both naked, and they felt no shame. Genesis 2:22-25

Love

[7] Beloved, let us love one another, for love is of God; and everyone who loves is born of God and knows God. [8] He who does not love does not know God, for God is love. [9] In this the love of God was manifested toward us, that God has sent His only begotten Son into the world, that we might live through Him. [10] In this is love, not that we loved God, but that

He loved us and sent His Son *to be* the propitiation for our sins. [11] Beloved, if God so loved us, we also ought to love one another. I John 4:7-11, KJV

Greater love hath no man than this that a man lay down his life for his friends. John 15:13, KJV

But I say unto you, Love your enemies, bless them that curse you, do good to them that hate you, and pray for them which despitefully use you, and persecute you. Matthew 5:55

Forgiveness, Salvation, Freedom, Eternal Life

For all have sinned and come short of the glory of God. Romans 3:23: KJV

[6] For when we were yet without strength, in due time Christ died for the ungodly. But God commended his love toward us, in that, while we were yet sinners, Christ died for us. Romans 5:8, KJV

For the wages of sin is death, but the gift of God is eternal life, through Jesus Christ, our Lord. Romans 6:23, KJV

That if thou shalt confess with thy mouth the Lord Jesus, and shalt believe in thine heart that God hath raised him from the dead, thou shalt be saved. [10] For with the heart man believeth unto righteousness; and with the mouth confession is made unto salvation. Romans 10:9-10, KLV

For God so loved the world that He gave His only Begotten Son, that whosoever believes in Him should not perish, but have everlasting life. John 3:16, KJV

You will know the truth, and the truth will set you free. John 8:32

So if the Son sets you free, you are free indeed! John 8:36

"Behold, I stand at the door and knock; if any man hear My voice, and open the door, I will come in to him." Revelation 3:20

Assurance of Salvation

My sheep hear My voice, and I know them, and they follow Me. And I give them eternal life, and they shall never perish; neither shall anyone snatch them out of My hand. [29] My Father, which gave them me, is greater than all; and no man is able to pluck them out of my Father's hand. [30] I and my Father are one. John 10:27-30

I know whom I have believed, and am persuaded that he is able to keep that which I have committed unto Him against that day" II Timothy 1:12, KJV

Though I walk through the valley of the shadow of death, I will fear no evil: for Thou art with me. Psalm 12:4, KJV

For I am convinced that neither death nor life, neither angels nor demons, neither the present nor the future, nor any powers, [39] neither height nor depth, nor anything else in all creation, will be able to separate us from the love of God. Romans 8:38-39, KJV

We know that we live in Him and He in us, because He has given us of is Spirit. And we have seen and testify that the Father has sent his Son to be the Savior of the world. If anyone acknowledges that Jesus is the Son of God, God lives in him and him in God. And so we know and rely on the love God has for us. God is love. Whoever lives in love lives in God, and God in Him. I John 4:13-18

Grace and Faith

For by grace are ye saved through faith; and that not of yourselves: it is the gift of God: [9] Not of works, lest any man should boast. Ephesians 2:8-9, KJV

Therefore no one will be declared righteous in God's sight by the works of the law; rather, through the law we become conscious of our sins. Romans 3:20, KJV

I do not frustrate the grace of God: for if righteousness come by the law, then Christ is dead in vain. Galatians 2:21

Hebrews *11 is the Faith Chapter of the Bible.* 1. Now faith is the substance of things hoped for, the evidence of things not seen. [2] For by it the elders obtained a good report. [3] Through faith we understand that the worlds were framed by the Word of God, so that things which are seen were not made of things which do appear. [6] But without faith it is impossible to please him: for he that cometh to God must believe that He is, and that He is a rewarder of them that diligently seek Him. [7] By faith Noah. . . . [8] By faith Abraham, Isaac, Jacob, Joseph. . . . [17] By faith Abraham, when he was tried, offered up Isaac. . .By faith, Moses, Gideon, Barak, Samson, David, Samuel, and the prophets:

[33] Who through faith subdued kingdoms, wrought righteousness, obtained promises, stopped the mouths of lions.[34] Quenched the violence of fire, escaped the edge of the sword, out of weakness were made strong, waxed valiant in fight. . . .They were stoned, they were sawn asunder. . . .[39] And these all, having obtained a good report through faith, received not the promise: [40] God having provided some better thing for us, that they without us should not be made perfect. (The better thing for us is Jesus Christ!) Hebrews 11: 1-40

Baptism and the Lord's Supper

The two church ordinances instituted by Christ, taught by the apostles, and practiced by the early church. They help us remember what Jesus Christ accomplished for us in his redemptive work.

Matthew 28:19: [19] Go therefore and make disciples of all the nations, baptizing them in the name of the Father and of the Son and of the Holy Spirit.

Romans 6:3-4: [3] Do you not know that all of us who have been baptized into Christ Jesus were baptized into his death? [4] We were buried therefore with him by baptism into death, in order that, just as Christ was raised from the dead by the glory of the Father, we too might walk in newness of life.

Acts 2:38: Then Peter said unto them, "Repent, and be baptized every one of you in the name of Jesus Christ for the remission of sins

Acts 2:41: Then they that gladly received his word were baptized: and the same day there were added unto them about three thousand souls. (Order of events: people *heard* the message regarding Christ, *responded* in saving faith, were *baptized* and *united* with the local body of believers)

I Corinthians:23-26: The Lord Jesus, on the night he was betrayed, took bread, [24] and when he had given thanks, he broke it and said, "This is my body, which is for you; do this in remembrance of me." [25] In the same way, after supper he took the cup, saying, "This cup is the new covenant in my blood; do this, whenever you drink it, in remembrance of me." *(The Lord's Supper)*

The Church:

I was glad when they said unto me, Let us go into the house of the LORD. Psalm 122:1

Then those who gladly received his word were baptized; and that day about three thousand souls were added *to them*. And they continued steadfastly in the apostles' doctrine and fellowship, in the breaking of bread, and in prayers. . . .[46] So continuing daily with one accord in the temple, and breaking bread from house to house, they ate their food with gladness and simplicity of heart, [47] praising God and having favor with all the people. And the Lord added to the church daily those who were being saved. Acts 2:41-47

Not forsaking the assembling of ourselves together, as the manner of some is; but exhorting one another: and so much the more, as ye see the day approaching. Hebrews 10:25, KJV

Creation

In the beginning was the Word (Jesus), and the Word was with God, and the Word was God. [2] The same was in the beginning with God. [3] All things were made by Him; and without Him was not anything made that was made. (John 1:1-3:KJV)

In the beginning, God created the Heavens and the Earth. (Genesis 1:1)

Colossians 1:16-17: For by Him were all things created, that are in heaven, and that are in Earth:. . .all things were created by Him, and for Him; and He is before all things, and by Him all things consist.

Psalm 19:1: The heavens declare the glory of God; and the firmament shows His handiwork.

Prayer

In Him and through faith in Him we approach God with freedom and confidence. Ephesians 3:12

Call unto me, and I will answer thee, and show thee great and mighty things, which thou knowest not. Jeremiah 33:3: KJV

Let us therefore come boldly unto the throne of grace, that we may obtain mercy, and find grace to help in time of need. Hebrews 4:16

If you abide in me and my word abides in you, you shall ask anything in my name and I will do it. John 15:7

(Jesus said) After this manner therefore pray ye: Our Father which art in heaven, Hallowed be thy name.[10] Thy kingdom come, Thy will be done in earth, as it is in heaven. [11] Give us this day our daily bread. [12] And forgive us our debts, as we forgive our debtors. [13] And lead us not into temptation, but deliver us from evil: For thine is the kingdom, and the power, and the glory, forever. Amen. Matthew 6:9-13, KJV

Persecution

Blessed are ye, when men shall revile you, and persecute you, and shall say all manner of evil against you falsely, for my sake. Rejoice, and be exceeding glad: for great is your reward in heaven: for so persecuted they the prophets which were before you. Matthew 5:11-12, KJV

My goal is to know Him and the power of his resurrection and the fellowship of his sufferings. Philippians 3:10

In every way we're troubled, but we aren't crushed by our troubles. We're frustrated, but we don't give up. We are persecuted, but we're not abandoned. 2 Corinthians 4:8-9

Greater is He that is in you than he that is in the world. I John 4:4

In Times of Pain, Illness, Death, Trials, Loneliness

Who shall separate us from the love of Christ? Shall tribulation, or distress, or persecution, or famine, or nakedness, or peril, or sword? [38] For I am persuaded, that neither death, nor life, nor angels, nor principalities, nor powers, nor things present, nor things to come, [39] nor height, nor depth, nor any other creature, shall be able to separate us from the love of God, which is in Christ Jesus our Lord. Romans 8:35, 38-39

Even though I walk through the dark valley of death, because You are with me, I fear no harm. Your rod and Your staff give me courage. Psalm 23:4

Don't be afraid, because I am with you. Don't be intimidated; I am your God. I will strengthen you. I will help you. I will support you with my victorious right hand. Isaiah 41:10

The Lord says, I will instruct you. I will teach you the way that you should go. I will advise you as my eyes watch over you. Psalm 32:8

Let go of your concerns! Then you will know that I am God. I rule the nations. I rule the earth. Psalm 46:10

God is fair. He won't forget what you've done or the love you've shown for him. Hebrews 6:10

Come to Me, all who are tired from carrying heavy loads and I will give you rest. Matthew 11:28

Keep your mind clear, and be alert. Your opponent the devil is prowling around like a roaring lion as he looks for someone to devour. I Peter 5:8

For this reason, put on the whole armor of God. Then you will be able to stand against the wiles of the devil. Once you have overcome all obstacles, you will be able to stand your ground. Ephesians 6:12-13

God is our refuge and strength, an ever-present help in trouble. Psalm 40:2, KJV

Casting all your care upon him, for he careth for you. I Peter 4:7, KJV

Victory, Courage, Boldness, Perseverance, Strength, and Hope

For whosoever is born of God overcomes the world: and this is the victory that overcomes the world, even our faith. Who is he that overcomes the world, but he that believes that Jesus is the Son of God? I John 5:4-5

I know the plans that I have for you, declares the Lord. They are plans for peace and not disaster, plans to give you a future filled with hope. Jeremiah 29:11

Blessed is the person who does not follow the advice of wicked people, take the path of sinners, or join the company of mockers. Rather, he delights in the teachings of the LORD and reflects on his teachings day and night. He is like a tree planted beside streams—a tree that produces fruit in season and whose leaves do not wither. He succeeds in everything he does. Psalm 1:1-3

Only be strong and very courageous, faithfully doing everything in the teachings that my servant Moses commanded you. Don't turn away from them. Then you will succeed wherever you go. Joshua 1:7

For this reason, put on the whole armor of God. Then you will be able to stand against the wiles of the devil. Once you have overcome all obstacles, you will be able to stand your ground. Ephesians 6:13

I can do all things through Christ, who strengthens me. Philippians 4:13

If God be for us, who can be against us? Romans 8:31

In all these things we are more than conquerors through Him that loved us and gave Himself for us. Romans 8:37

But if we walk in the light, as He is in the light, we have fellowship one with another, and the blood of Jesus Christ his Son cleanseth us from all sin. I John 1:7, KJV

Temptation

Flee youthful lusts; but follow rightcousncss, faith, charity, pcacc. II Timothy 2:22

Because Jesus experienced temptation when he suffered, he is able to help others when they are tempted. Hebrews 2:18

Flee youthful lusts: but follow righteousness, faith, charity, peace. I Tim. 2:22

Submit yourselves therefore to God. Resist the devil, and he will flee from you. Draw near to God, and He will draw near to you. James 4:7-8

I find this law at work: Although I want to do good, evil is right there with me. [22] For in my inner being I delight in God's law; [23] but I see another law at work in me, waging war against the law of my mind and making me a prisoner of the law of sin at work within me. [24] What a wretched man I am! Who will rescue me from this body that is subject to death? [25] Thanks be to God, Who delivers me through Jesus Christ our Lord! So then, I myself in my mind am a slave to God's law, but in my sinful nature a slave to the law of sin. Romans 7:21-25

There hath no temptation taken you but such as is common to man: but God is faithful, who will not suffer you to be tempted above that ye are able; but will with the temptation also make a way to escape, that ye may be able to bear it. I Corinthians 10:13, KJV

Pornography

[8] Finally, brothers, whatever is true, whatever is honorable, whatever is just, whatever is pure, whatever is lovely, whatever is commendable, if there is any excellence, if there is anything worthy of praise, think about these things. Philippians 4:8

But I tell you that anyone who looks at a woman lustfully has already committed adultery with her in his heart. Matthew 5:28

Sexual Sin

Flee from sexual immorality. All other sins a person commits are outside the body, but whoever sins sexually, sins against their own body. Do you not know that your bodies are temples of the Holy Spirit, Who is in you, whom you have received from God? You are not your own; you were bought at a price. Therefore honor God with your bodies. I Corinthians 6:18-20

Follow God's example, therefore, as dearly loved children and walk in the way of love, just as Christ loved us and gave himself up for us as a fragrant offering and sacrifice to

God. [3] But among you there must not be even a hint of sexual immorality, or of any kind of impurity, or of greed, because these are improper for God's holy people. Ephesians 5:1-3

Thou shalt not commit adultery. Exodus 20:14, KJV

It is God's will that you should be sanctified: that you should avoid sexual immorality; [4] that each of you should learn to control your own body in a way that is holy and honorable, [5] not in passionate lust like the pagans, who do not know God; [6] and that in this matter no one should wrong or take advantage of a brother or sister. The Lord will punish all those who commit such sins, as we told you and warned you before. [7] For God did not call us to be impure, but to live a holy life. [8] I Thessalonians 4:3-7

For although they knew God, they neither glorified him as God nor gave thanks to him, but their thinking became futile and their foolish hearts were darkened. . .[24] Therefore God gave them over in the sinful desires of their hearts to sexual impurity for the degrading of their bodies with one another. [25] They exchanged the truth about God for a lie, and worshiped and served created things rather than the Creator—who is forever praised. Amen. [26] Because of this, God gave them over to shameful lusts. Even their women exchanged natural sexual relations for unnatural ones. [27] In the same way the men also abandoned natural relations with women and were inflamed with lust for one another. Men committed shameful acts with other men, and received in themselves the due penalty for their error. Romans 1:21, 24-27

[22] "'Do not have sexual relations with a man as one does with a woman; that is detestable. Leviticus 18:22

In a similar way, Sodom and Gomorrah and the surrounding towns gave themselves up to sexual immorality and perversion. They serve as an example of those who suffer the punishment of eternal fire. Jude 17

Beer, wine, drunkenness

Wine is a mocker. Strong drink is raging; and whoever is deceived by it is not wise. Proverbs 20:1

Who hath woe? Who hath sorrow? Who hath contentions? Who hath babbling? Who hath wounds without cause? Who hath redness of eyes? They that tarry long at the wine; they that go to seek mixed wine. [31] Look not thou upon the wine when it is red, when it gives his color in the cup, when it moves itself aright. [32] At the last it bites like a serpent, and stings like an adder. Proverbs 23:29-32, KJV

Don't get drunk on wine, which leads to wild living. Instead, be filled with the Spirit. Ephesians 5:18

When We Are Tested

Endure until your testing is over. Then you will be mature and complete, and you won't need anything. *James 1:4*

We can't allow ourselves to get tired of living the right way. Certainly, each of us will receive everlasting life at the proper time, if we don't give up. Galatians 6:9

Blessed are those who endure when they are tested. When they pass the test, they will receive the crown of life that God has promised to those who love him. James 1:12

Because Jesus experienced temptation when he suffered, he is able to help others when they are tempted. Hebrews 2:18

And Jesus withdrew himself into the wilderness and prayed. Luke 5:16

And I pray that you, being rooted and established in love, [18] may have power, together with all the Lord's holy people, to grasp how wide and long and high and deep is the love of Christ,[19] and to know this love that surpasses knowledge—that you may be filled to the measure of all the fullness of God. [20] Now to him who is able to do immeasurably more than all we ask or imagine, according to HIs power that is at work within us. Ephesians 3:17-20

Through him we have also obtained access by faith into this grace in which we stand, and we rejoice in hope of the glory of God. More than that, we rejoice in our sufferings, knowing that suffering produces endurance, and endurance produces character, and character produces hope, and hope does not put us to shame, because God's love has been poured into our hearts through the Holy Spirit who has been given to us. Romans 5:2-5

Likewise the Spirit also helpeth our infirmities: for we know not what we should pray for as we ought: but the Spirit itself maketh intercession for us with groanings which cannot be uttered. [27] And He that searcheth the hearts knoweth what is the mind of the Spirit, because He maketh intercession for the saints according to the will of God. [28] And we know that all things work together for good to them that love God, to them who are the called according to His purpose. Romans 8:26-28, KJV

Power, Guidance, Decisions

If you abide in Me, and My words abide in you, you shall ask what you will and it shall be done unto you. John 15:7, KJV

Trust in the Lord with all your heart, and do not rely on your own understanding. In all your ways acknowledge Him, and He will direct your path. Proverbs 3:5-6

Call unto me, and I will answer thee, and shew thee great and mighty things which thou knowest not. Jeremiah 33:3, KJV

The effectual fervent prayer of a righteous man availeth much. James 5:17, KJV

Whoever is a believer in Christ is a new creation. The old way of living has disappeared. A new way of living has come into existence. 2 Corinthians 5:17

If any of you lacks wisdom; let him ask of God, who gives to all men liberally and without reproach, and it will be given to him. James 1:5

Praise and Thanksgiving

I will praise You, O Lord, with all my heart, I will tell of Your wonders. I will be glad and rejoice in You. I will sing praise to Your name, O Most High. Psalm 9:1-2

O clap your hands, all ye people; shout unto God with the voice of triumph. Psalm 47:1:kjv

Praise the Lord! Praise God in his sanctuary; praise Him in His mighty heavens! ² Praise him for His mighty deeds; praise Him according to His excellent greatness! 6. Let everything that has breath praise the Lord! Praise the Lord! Psalm 150:1, 2, 6

"Stand up and praise the Lord your God, who is from everlasting to everlasting. "Blessed be Your glorious name, and may it be exalted above all blessing and praise. ⁶ You alone are the Lord. You made the heavens, even the highest heavens, and their entire starry host, the earth and all that is on it, the seas and all that is in them. You give life to everything, and the multitudes of heaven worship You. Nehemiah 9:5-6

² The Lord is my rock, and my fortress, and my deliverer; my God, my strength, in whom I will trust; my buckler, and the horn of my salvation, and my high tower.³ I will call upon the Lord, Who is worthy to be praised: so shall I be saved from mine enemies. Psalm 18:2-3

Heaven

In my Father's house are many mansions: if it were not so, I would have told you. I go to prepare a place for you. ³ And if I go and prepare a place for you, I will come again, and receive you unto Myself; that where I am, there ye may be also. John 14:2-3

¹⁴ For if we believe that Jesus died and rose again, even so them also which sleep in Jesus will God bring with Him. ¹⁵ For this we say unto you by the word of the Lord, that we which are alive and remain unto the coming of the Lord shall not prevent them which are asleep. ¹⁶ For the Lord himself shall descend from heaven with a shout, with the voice of the archangel, and with the trump of God: and the dead in Christ shall rise first: ¹⁷ Then we which are alive and remain shall be caught up together with them in the clouds, to meet the Lord in the air: and so shall we ever be with the Lord. I Thessalonians 4:14-17

Day and night they never stop saying: "'Holy, holy, holy is the Lord God Almighty,' who was, and is, and is to come." ⁹ Whenever the living creatures give glory, honor and thanks to Him who sits on the throne and Who lives for ever and ever, ¹⁰ the twenty-four elders fall down before Him who sits on the throne and worship Him who lives for ever and ever. They lay their crowns before the throne and say: ¹¹ "You are worthy, our Lord and

God, to receive glory and honor and power, for You created all things, and by Your will they were created and have their being." Revelation 4:8-11

For I am already being poured out as an offering, and the time for me to depart is at hand. I have competed well; I have finished the race; I have kept the faith! Finally the crown of righteousness is reserved for me. The Lord, the righteous Judge, will award it to me in that day – and not to me only, but also to all who have set their affection on His appearing. II Timothy 4:6-8

For this perishable must put on the imperishable, and this mortal must put on immortality. But when this perishable will have put on the imperishable, and this mortal will have put on immortality, then will come about the saying that is written, "Death is swallowed up in victory. I Corinthians 15:53-54

[20] But our citizenship is in heaven. And we eagerly await a Savior from there, the Lord Jesus Christ,[21] who, by the power that enables Him to bring everything under his control, will transform our lowly bodies so that they will be like His glorious body. Philippians 3:20-21

And I saw a new heaven and a new earth: for the first heaven and the first earth were passed away; and there was no more sea.[2] And I John saw the holy city, new Jerusalem, coming down from God out of heaven, prepared as a bride adorned for her husband.[3] And I heard a great voice out of heaven saying, Behold, the tabernacle of God is with men, and He will dwell with them, and they shall be his people, and God himself shall be with them, and be their God.[4] And God shall wipe away all tears from their eyes; and there shall be no more death, neither sorrow, nor crying, neither shall there be any more pain: for the former things are passed away.[5] And He that sat upon the throne said, Behold, I make all things new. Revelation 21:1-5

The Resurrection:

The angel answered and said to the women, "Do not be afraid, for I know that you seek Jesus who was crucified.[6] He is not here; for He is risen, as He said. Come, see the place where the Lord lay. Matthew 28:5-6

For the Lord himself will come down from heaven, with a loud command, with the voice of the archangel and with the trumpet call of God, and the dead in Christ will rise first.[17] After that, we who are still alive and are left will be caught up together with them in the clouds to meet the Lord in the air. And so we will be with the Lord forever.[18] Therefore encourage one another with these words. I Thessalonians 4:16-18

Concern for Our Nation,

Chronicles 7:14: [14] If My people, which are called by My name, shall humble themselves, and pray, and seek My face, and turn from their wicked ways; then will I hear from heaven, and will forgive their sin, and will heal their land.

Blessed is the nation whose God is the Lord, the people whom he has chosen as his heritage! Psalm 33:12

And Jesus came and said to them, "All authority in heaven and on earth has been given to Me. Go therefore and make disciples of all nations, baptizing them in the name of the Father and of the Son and of the Holy Spirit. . . .Matthew 28:18-19

He shall judge between many peoples, and shall decide for strong nations far away; and they shall beat their swords into plowshares, and their spears into pruning hooks; nation shall not lift up sword against nation, neither shall they learn war anymore. Micah 4:3

For the nation and kingdom that will not serve you shall perish; those nations shall be utterly laid waste. Isaiah 60:12.

Finances

Bring ye all the tithes into the storehouse, that there may be meat in Mine house, and prove Me now herewith, saith the Lord of hosts, if I will not open you the windows of heaven, and pour you out a blessing, that there shall not be room enough to receive it. Malachi 3:10, KJV

In the house of the wise are stores of choice food and oil, but a foolish man devours all he has. Proverbs 21:20

Lay not up for yourselves treasures upon earth, where moth and rust doth corrupt, and where thieves break through and steal: [20] But lay up for yourselves treasures in heaven, where neither moth nor rust doth corrupt, and where thieves do not break through nor steal: [21] For where your treasure is, there will your heart be also. Matthew 6:19-21, KJV

For the love of money is a root of all kinds of evil. Some people, eager for money, have wandered from the faith and pierced themselves with many griefs. I Timothy 6:10

[8] Let no debt remain outstanding, except the continuing debt to love one another, for whoever loves others has fulfilled the law. Romans 13:8

Go to the ant, you sluggard; consider its ways and be wise! It has no commander, no overseer or ruler, yet it stores its provisions in summer and gathers its food at harvest. Proverbs 6:6-8

[12] I know what it is to be in need, and I know what it is to have plenty. I have learned the secret of being content in any and every situation, whether well fed or hungry, whether living in plenty or in want. [13] I can do all this through him who gives me strength. [19] And my God will meet all your needs according to the riches of his glory in Christ Jesus. Philippians 4: 12-13, 19

Keep your lives free from the love of money and be content with what you have, because God has said, "Never will I leave you; neither will I forsake you. Hebrews 13:5

PART FIVE

God's Plan from Genesis to Revelation: Key Verses

The King James Version of the Bible

1. In the beginning, God created the Heavens and the Earth. (Genesis 1:1).
2. And God said, "Let Us make man in Our image, according to Our likeness; let them have dominion over. . .the earth and over every creeping thing. . .(Genesis 1:26)
3. Then God blessed them, and God said to them, "Be fruitful and multiply; fill the earth and subdue it; Have dominion over the fish of the sea, over the birds of the air, And over every living thing that moves on the earth." (Genesis 1:28)
4. And the Lord God commanded the man, saying, ". . .of the tree of the knowledge of good and evil you shall not eat, for in the day that you eat of it you shall surely die. (Genesis 2:16a-17).
5. So when the woman saw that the tree was good for food, that it was pleasant to the eyes, and a tree desirable to make one wise, she took of its fruit and ate. She also gave to her husband with her, and he ate. (Genesis 3:6)
6. Therefore, just as through one man sin entered the world, and death through sin, and thus death spread to all men, because all sinned. (Romans 5:12)
7. Then the Lord saw that the wickedness of man was great in the earth. . .So the Lord said, "I will destroy man whom I have created from the face of the earth. (Genesis 6:5a; 7a)
8. For since by man came death, by Man also came the resurrection of the dead. As in Adam all die, even so in Christ all shall be made alive. (I Corinthians 15:21, 22)

9. For unto us a Child is born, unto us a Son is given; and the government will be upon His shoulder. And His name will be called Wonderful, Counselor, Mighty God, Everlasting Father, Prince of Peace. (Isaiah 9:6)
10. "For there is born to you this day in the City of David a Savior, Who is Christ the Lord. (Luke 2:11).
11. In the beginning was the Word, and the Word (Jesus) was with God, and the Word was God. He was in the beginning with God. All things were made through Him, and without Him nothing was made that was made. In Him was life, and the life was the light of men. (John 1:1-4)
12. "He is not here, but is risen! Remember how He spoke to you when He was still in Galilee, saying, "The Son of Man must be delivered into the hands of sinful men, and be crucified, and the third day rise again." (Luke 24:6-7)
13. So then, after the Lord had spoken to them, He (Jesus) was received up into heaven, And sat down at the right hand of God. (Mark 16:19)
14. For the Lord Himself will descend from heaven with a shout, with the voice of an archangel, and with the trumpet of God. And the dead in Christ will rise first. Then we who are alive and remain shall be caught up together with them in the clouds to meet the Lord in the Air. And thus we shall always be with the Lord. (II Thessalonians 4:16-17)
15. He humbled Himself and became obedient to the point of death, even the death on the cross. Therefore God also has highly exalted Him and given Him the name which is above every name, that at the name of Jesus every knee should bow. . .and that every tongue should confess that Jesus Christ is Lord. (Philippians 2:8b-11a)

Following is my short explanation of the above 15 scriptures:

1. God created the heavens and the earth.
2. God created man to have dominion over the earth.
3. God blessed man and gave him the scientific mandate to understand God's creation and to take charge of and to govern it. Here is the birthplace of science.
4. God commanded man to obey Him (not to eat of forbidden fruit). If he disobeyed, he would die.
5. The Devil tempted Adam and Eve, and they chose to disobey God. They sinned when they disobeyed God.
6. After Adam sinned, death came to all men, because all have sinned.
7. God sent a worldwide flood to destroy the wickedness of the earth.
8. Through Adam all men are sinners and sentenced to death, but through Christ, all can live. This is the good news!
9. The Bible prophesies that God will send the Messiah, a Savior, a King.

10. Jesus was born on earth as the prophesied Messiah and Savior.
11. This same Jesus created the earth and became the light of the world.
12. Jesus was crucified for our sins and arose the third day from the grave.
13. Jesus ascended into Heaven and sits at the right hand of God.
14. Jesus will come to earth again, and we who believe in Jesus will be taken up with Him to be forever with Him.
15. Jesus humbled Himself and died on the cross, but He will be exalted when every person will bow and confess that Jesus Christ is Lord.

Aren't the last two scriptures wonderful promises that Christ will be victorious? When we've read the "back of the book" we know we who are in Christ will win! (Taken from my school curriculum book, *Putting the Pieces Together*, Carson, 2008.)

PLAN FOR READING THE BIBLE IN ONE MONTH

How wonderful that God has a wonderful plan for our lives – when we give our lives to Him. He tells us that plan. I pray that my precious readers will be able to put together God's wonderful plan as you consider Genesis to Revelation. I pray that you will find a *"Purpose Driven Life"* as proposed by Rick Warren. Then I especially pray that you will be drawn to the great blessing of memorizing and hiding God's Word of Truth in your hearts. It will change your life!

We can know the Bible is the Word of God and is all Truth because of the <u>unity of the Bible</u>. Though its 66 books were penned by 35 different people over a period of over 1500 years, all the 66 books have a central theme and there are no contradictions in the original manuscripts. Why? Because God is the author of the Bible. Authenticity has been proven by the prophecies in the Bible that have come true. The Bible is inerrant and infallible. The central theme is that of none other than Jesus Christ, the Son of God, who takes away the sin of the world.

The Words of the song, *"He Is,"* written by Aaron & Jeoffrey, show Jesus to be the theme of all the Bible books. In Genesis, "He's the breath of life," in Exodus, the Passover Lamb, etc. Each of these will be used at the beginning of the books of the Bible to show how Jesus is the theme for that book.

<u>Jesus is the central theme in each of the Books of the Bible</u>. Also, a careful examination of *the characters* of the Old Testament shows they are each a picture or a foreshadowing of the Coming Messiah, Jesus Christ. A Scarlet Thread of Redemption runs through the Bible.

Revelation 1:5: "Unto Him that loved us, and washed us from our sins in his own blood." Dr. W. A. Criswell of First Baptist Church of Dallas, Texas, said in his famed four-hour-New Year's Eve sermon, "This is <u>the scarlet thread of redemption</u> that began with the blood of covering in the Garden of Eden and finds its ultimate consummation in the blood-washed throng before the throne of God in glory." For each of the 66 books of the Bible, we will see the scarlet thread, and will see foreshadowing of Jesus Christ and what it means for our lives today.

In addition, a recurring theme that affects us today is this: When we as individuals and as a nation <u>follow God's commandments, He blesses.</u> When we turn from Him, He withdraws his hand of protection from us. But through it all, we will learn that God is longsuffering and is a God of compassion. God is a God of justice and of love!

Throughout, we will see the unity of the 66 books of the Bible, proving the authorship of the whole Bible. The Old Testament is a compilation of 39 books written before Jesus was born. The New Testament begins at the time Jesus is born, and is composed of 27 books. We will see God's plan for our lives as we review Genesis to Revelation!

My <u>PURPOSE</u> is to motivate you to hide God's Word in your heart. One way is to <u>memorize scriptures</u>. *Another is to read the Bible through.* You could use this writing *in two ways:*

1. You could first read a book of the Bible in summarized form from my book, and then read the entire book from the Bible. <u>Or</u> -
2. Following the guide in this book, you <u>could read the Bible through in short form in one month</u>. The King James Version of the Bible has a total of 823,156 words, many of them long words. I've attempted to make this reading 1/12 as long. People usually read through the Bible in one year. Follow this 3o day plan, if you like:

Day 1: The Book of Genesis
Day 2: The Book of Exodus
Day 3: The Books of Leviticus and Numbers
Day 4: The Book of Deuteronomy
Day 5: The Books of Joshua and Judges
Day 6: The Books Ruth and I Samuel
Day 7: The Book of II Samuel
Day 8: The Books of I and II Kings
Day 9: The Books of I and II Chronicles
Day 10: The Books of Ezra and Nehemiah
Day 11: The Books Esther and Job
Day 12: The Book of Psalms
Day 13: The Books of Proverbs and Ecclesiastes
Day 14: The Books of Song of Solomon and Isaiah
Day 15: The Books of Jeremiah and Lamentations
Day 16: The Books of Ezekiel and Daniel
Day 17: The Books of Hosea, Joel, and Amos
Day 18: The Books of Obadiah, Jonah, and Micah and Nahum
Day 19: The Books of Habakkuk, Zephaniah, Haggai, Zachariah, and Malachi
Day 20: The first half of the Four Gospels, Harmonized (Matthew, Mark, Luke and John)
Day 21: The second half of the Four Gospels, Harmonized.
Day 22: The first half of the Book of Acts
Day 23: The second half of Acts
Day 24: The Books of Romans and I and II Corinthians
Day 25: The Books of Galatians, Ephesians, Philippians, Colossians
Day 26: The Books of I and II Thessalonians, I and II Timothy
Day 27: The Books of Titus, Philemon, Hebrews
Day 28: The Books of James, and I and II Peter,

Day 29: The Books of I, II, III John and Jude
Day 30: The Book of Revelation
Day 31: Heaven (The New Heaven and the New Earth)

In 30 days, you will read all books of the Bible and on day 31, you will be blessed as you read about Heaven.

<u>To make for clarity of what is scripture and what is not:</u>

All words from the Bible will be in regular font.
My own words of narration will be printed in italics.
Preface to each book is in regular font.
Poetry by Marilyn Kay Gage is in regular font.

The Books of Law: The first five books of the Old Testament are inspired by God and penned by Moses, and are called the *Pentateuch*.

THE BOOK OF GENESIS

In Genesis, Jesus is the Breath of Life.

Theme: Everything begins with God, who elected a people of His own. (Most of the themes for the books of the Bible are used with permission and are from *God's Game Plan*, The Fellowship of Christian Athletes Bible, 2008.)

Message: The first three chapters of Genesis set the stage for all that happens in the rest of the Bible. Adam and Eve's sin separated men from God. But God promised that a descendant of Adam and Eve would restore harmony between God and His creation. Throughout the rest of the Bible, God is at work setting things right. All of history is moving to the point where God's plan of salvation for the universe will be complete when we read in Revelation that God will dwell with men and they will be his people. The time of the Patriarchs, Abraham, Isaac, Jacob, and Joseph is in the Book of Genesis. It was through the descendants of the Patriarchs that God promised to bless the whole world through Jesus Christ, His Son.

The word Genesis means origins, and the book is about the origins of humanity and of the Jewish people. The first 11 chapters are about mankind in general, from the creation of heaven and earth through the flood. Chapters twelve through fifty are about the Israelite patriarchs, Abraham, Isaac, Jacob, and Joseph.

Because Genesis is the seed-plot of the Bible, we will devote more time to this book than to others. In Genesis, we have in germ form, almost all of the great doctrines which are afterwards fully developed in the books of scripture which follow (Pink, *Gleanings in Genesis, 1922*).

1. In Genesis God is revealed as the Creator-God and as the Covenant-God; and we have the first hint of the Blessed Trinity. In Genesis man is exhibited. First as the creature of God's hands, then as a fallen and sinful being. (Also, in Genesis we see the Eden, the perfect Earth that God created, the same as will be The New Earth in which the Redeemed will live forever, as also seen in Revelation 22)

2. In Genesis the truth of salvation, of justification by faith, and of the believer's security are introduced.

3. In Genesis the wiles of Satan are exposed and first made known. In Genesis we see of the direful consequences of being unequally yoked with unbelievers, and of having fellowship with the unfruitful works of darkness. The truths of "You reap what you sow" are manifested. But in the end we are shown how Divine grace triumphs over human frailty.

4. In Genesis we are shown the importance and value of prayer.
5. In Genesis the divine incarnation is first declared. The Coming One was to be supernaturally begotten. He was to enter this world as none other ever did. He was to be the Son of Man, and yet have no human father. The One who should bruise the serpent's head was to be the woman's "Seed."
6. In Genesis the death and resurrection of the Savior are strikingly foreshadowed and we also learn of the Savior's coming exaltation. In Genesis the priesthood of Christ is anticipated and the coming Antichrist is announced. In Genesis we first read of God giving Palestine to Abraham and to his seed: In Genesis the wondrous future of Israel is made known.

What a marvelous proof is all this of the Divine Authorship! Only the one who knew the end from the beginning could have embodied, in germ form, what is afterwards amplified in the rest of the Bible! What proof that God directed the pens of all who wrote the later books of Holy Scripture! May God bless my Dear Ones, as we seek God's Plan from Genesis to Revelation!

IN THE BEGINNING: THE CREATION

Genesis 1:1-5, KJV: In the beginning God created the heavens and the earth.
[2] And the earth was without form, and void; and darkness was upon the face of the deep. And the Spirit of God moved upon the face of the waters. [3] And God said, Let there be light: and there was light. [4] And God saw the light, that it was good: and God divided the light from the darkness. [5] And God called the light Day, and the darkness he called Night. And the evening and the morning were the first day.
(Note in the first chapter of John, that Jesus was God and that all things were made by Him and without Him nothing was made that was made. Also, THE THIRD PERSON OF THE TRINITY, THE HOLY SPIRIT, WAS PRESENT AT THE CREATION. In verse 2, the spirit of God moved. So in the first chapter of the Bible we see THE FATHER, THE SON, and THE HOLY SPIRIT.)
Genesis 1:25, KJV: And God made the beasts of the earth according to their kinds and the livestock according to their kinds, and everything that creeps on the ground according to its kind. And God saw that it was good.
KJV: Genesis 1:26-28, KJV: And God said, Let Us make man in our image, after our likeness, and let them have dominion over the fish of the sea, and over the fowl of the air, and over all the earth, and over every creeping thing that creepeth upon the earth. So God created man in his own image, in the image of God created he him, male and female created he them. And God blessed them, and God said unto them, "Be fruitful and multiply, and replenish the earth and subdue it: and have dominion over the fish of the sea and over the

fowl of the air, and over every living thing that moves upon the earth." *Scientists call this the Scientific Mandate.*

Here we find God's purpose for Man. We are to take care of this earth and all that is in it. *He made man to have dominion over the earth. You are no accident. You are alive because God wanted to create you. He will fulfill his purpose for you. (Psalm 138:8) We are the focus of His love and the most valuable of His creation. God decided to give us life through the word of truth so we might be the most important of all the things he made. (James 1:18) Yes, we were created by God and for God. Everything was made for his glory. All of creation reveals God's glory.* Isaiah 26:3 says "They are my own people and I created them to bring me glory." *So our number one purpose should be to bring God glory. (R. Warren, 2004)*

And God saw everything that he had made, and behold, it was very good. And the evening and the morning were the sixth day. Genesis 2:1-3: Thus the heavens and the earth were finished, and all the host of them. And on the seventh day God ended his work which he had made; and he rested on the seventh day from all his work which he had made. And God blessed the seventh day, and sanctified it: because that in it he had rested from all his work which God created and made. Genesis 2:1-3:KJV

(Creationism is the foundation of the whole Christian Worldview. Evolution is the foundation of the Worldly Worldview. Creationism is the belief that God created everything just over 6,000 years ago, according to Genesis! Evolution says everything came about over billions of years without intelligent design! Read *Rising Millennials Face Worldview Conflict: Search for Truth and Foundation*, 2002, by Shirley A. Carson.)

Genesis 2:7: And the Lord God formed man of the dust of the ground, and breathed into his nostrils *the breath of life*, and man became a living soul.

ADAM AND EVE AND THE FIRST SIN

Genesis 2:15-18, KJV: And the Lord God took the man and put him into the Garden of Eden to dress it and to keep it. And the Lord God commanded the man, saying, of every tree of the garden thou mayest freely eat; But of the tree of the knowledge of good and evil, thou shalt not eat of it, for in the day that thou eatest thereof thou shalt surely die. And the Lord God said, it is not good that the man should be alone; I will make a helpmeet for him.

Genesis 2:23-24: And Adam said, "This is now bone of my bones, and flesh of my flesh: she shall be called Woman because she was taken out of Man."

(GOD INSTITUTED AND DEFINED MARRIAGE.)

Therefore shall a man leave his father and his mother, and shall cleave unto his wife; and they shall be one flesh.

Genesis 3:1-6, KJV: THE ORIGINAL SIN

Now the serpent was more subtle than any beast of the field which the Lord God had made. And he said unto the woman, "Yea, hath God said, Ye shall not eat of every tree of the garden?"

[2] And the woman said unto the serpent, "We may eat of the fruit of the trees of the garden: [3] But of the fruit of the tree which is in the midst of the garden, God hath said, Ye shall not eat of it, neither shall ye touch it, lest ye die."

[4] And the serpent said unto the woman, "Ye shall not surely die: 5. For God doth know that in the day ye eat thereof, then your eyes shall be opened, and ye shall be as gods, knowing good and evil."

[6] And when the woman saw that the tree was good for food, and that it was pleasant to the eyes, and a tree to be desired to make one wise, she took of the fruit thereof, and did eat, and gave also unto her husband with her; and he did eat. (*Here, we see the wiles of Satan exposed. He calls into question the integrity of the word of God.*)

Genesis, the first book of the Bible, gives us the earliest picture of the Blood. God Himself killed an animal and clothed Adam and Eve with skin. Blood had to be spilled for our first parents to have the nakedness of their sins covered. (Hymers, 2002). "Unto Adam also and to his wife did the Lord God make coats of skins, and clothed them" (Genesis 3:21: KJV). Their sins were covered up and forgotten, but "not without blood." (Hebrews 9:7: KJV)

FIRST PROPHECY OF THE MESSIAH BEING SENT:

Genesis 3:15, KJV: God said to the serpent, "And I will put enmity between thee and the woman, and between thy seed and her seed; it shall bruise thy head, and thou shalt bruise his heel."

The Gospel in a Nutshell: I wrote the following in *The Women's Ministry Handbook:*

Genesis Chapters 1-3: *God created the heavens and the earth in 6 days. His most important creation was man, whom He created in the image of God with a living soul. Man was the only creation who was given the gift of* choice. *Man could choose to be obedient to God or could choose his own way. Adam and Eve, the first man and woman chose to disobey God. They sinned. God had told them, "The penalty of sin is death."*

But right there after they sinned, God gave them hope. He killed an animal, which died in their place and shed its blood for them, and God covered their nakedness and their sin with the skin of the animal. Because sin is so bad in the eyes of a just God, throughout the Old Testament, animals had to shed their blood over and over and died in the place of people so they could be forgiven of sin when they repented of their sins.

Throughout the Old Testament, God also promised to send a Messiah, a Savior, who would live without sin and would redeem His people. That Promise was fulfilled through Jesus Christ, God's Son, whom he sent to earth to be born as a baby and to live 33 years among us. Jesus died once, for all. He shed His blood for our sins so we would not have to die but could live forever in eternity with Him. His blood becomes a covering for our sins. When we accept Christ, God gives to us His Righteousness, and he takes upon Himself our sins. He took our sins to the cross with Him. So we are seen as righteous in the eyes of a just God. Our good deeds are not good enough. Only the covering of Jesus' blood and God's righteousness can fulfill God's requirement for us to be saved and go to heaven. So God loved us and sent His son to die for our sins.

Thus, <u>A scarlet thread</u> *is woven from Genesis to Revelation. The scarlet thread running through the Bible is a picture of the Blood of Jesus Christ, shed on the Cross to wash away sin. The Old Testament Book of Genesis gives us the earliest picture of the Blood. The scarlet thread running through the Bible is a picture of the Blood of Jesus Christ, shed on the Cross to wash away sin. God, Himself killed an animal and clothed Adam and Eve with skin. Blood had to be spilled for our first parents to have the nakedness of their sins covered,* "Unto Adam also and to his wife did the Lord God make coats of skins, and clothed them" (Genesis 3:21:KJV). Their sins were covered up and forgotten, but "not without blood" (Hebrews 9:7). *One man's sin brought death. One man's death brought redemption (Romans 5:12-19).*

The Effect of Sin on Nature: God created a perfect earth. Man had perfect fellowship with God until sin entered. With sin, death entered the picture. The Earth is now under the curse of sin. But the time will come when we will have a New Earth, when the Earth will be restored to its original state (Revelation, chapters 21-22), The New Earth will be God's dwelling place, and it will be fashioned for resurrected people to live there (Alcorn, 2004).

Our first parents had two sons, Cain and Abel. "And Abel was a keeper of sheep, but Cain was a tiller of the ground. And in process of time it came to pass, that Cain brought of the fruit of the ground an offering unto the Lord. And Abel, he also brought of the firstlings of his flock and of the fat thereof. And the Lord had respect unto Abel and to his offering: But unto Cain and to his offering he had not respect" (Genesis 4:2-5). *No blood - no respect. - End of argument! Abel's offering was accepted, but* "not without blood" (Hebrews 9:7).

After the Great Flood, the first thing Noah did was to offer a blood sacrifice.

"Noah built an altar unto the Lord; and took of every clean beast, and of every clean fowl, and offered burnt-offerings on the altar. And the Lord smelled a sweet savor; and the Lord said in his heart, I will not again curse the ground any more for man's sake. . ." (Genesis 8:20-21).

Just as Abel brought a blood sacrifice, so did Noah. The scarlet line of blood, pointing to the Blood of Christ, continued.

NOAH AND THE ARK: The ark, itself, is a picture of Jesus. The ark was the only place people could come to be safe and to be saved. Jesus is our Ark of Safety. The believer's security is illustrated in Noah, who found grace in the eyes of the Lord and was safely preserved.

Genesis 6: 6-8: And it repented the Lord that he made man on the earth and it grieved him at his heart. And the Lord said, I will destroy man whom I have created from the face of the earth, both man and beast, and the creeping thing, and the fowls of the air, for it repented me that I have made them. But Noah found grace in the eyes of the Lord.

Genesis 6:13a and 14a: KJV: And God said unto Noah. . .make thee an ark of gopher wood.

Genesis 6:17a, 18, and 19a: KJV: I do bring a flood of water upon the earth to destroy all flesh. . . .But with thee will I establish my covenant; and thou shalt come into the ark, thou, and thy sons, and thy wife, and thy sons' wives with thee. And of every living thing of all flesh, two of every sort shalt thou bring into the ark.

Genesis 7:5, KJV: And Noah did according unto all that the Lord commanded him.

Genesis 7:1-12, KJV: They went in two and two unto Noah into the ark, the male and the female, as God had commanded Noah. [10] And it came to pass after seven days, that the waters of the flood were upon the earth. [11] In the six hundredth year of Noah's life, in the second month, the seventeenth day of the month, the same day were all the fountains of the great deep broken up, and the windows of heaven were opened. [12] And the rain was upon the earth forty days and forty nights

Note that the fountains of the deep were broken up. The catastrophic world-wide flood is a foundation for creationism. Evidence is found in the rock strata filled with billions of dead things that were laid down quickly. Rapid burial and fossilization were necessary for their state of preservation. Physical evidence fits what the Bible says. The most compelling of recent scientific evidence for the catastrophic flood and for water's erupting from inside the earth came with the eruption of Mt. St. Helens. The power of the eruption was water. (Parker, 1994; Carson, 2002; Ham, Sarfati, & Wieland, 2000)

Genesis 7:17, 23, KJV: And the flood was forty days upon the earth; and the waters increased, and bare up the ark, and it was lifted up above the earth. And every living substance was destroyed which was upon the face of the ground, both man, and cattle, and the creeping things, and the fowl of the heaven; and they were destroyed from the earth, and Noah only remained alive, and they that were in the ark with him.

Genesis 8:2: KJV: The fountains also of the deep and the windows of heaven were stopped, and the rain from heaven was restrained.

God made a covenant with Noah in Genesis 9:11-13 that there would be no more flood to destroy all flesh and set <u>the rainbow</u> as a token of His covenant.

<u>The Scarlet Thread</u>: Genesis 8:20: And Noah built an altar unto the Lord; and took of every clean beast and every clean fowl, and offered burnt offerings on the altar.

I will interrupt the scarlet thread thought for a moment as we go to see the world when it was all of one language:

Genesis 11:1: Now the whole world had one language and a common speech. [2] As people moved eastward, they found a plain in Shinar and settled there. [3] They said to each other, "Come, let's make bricks and bake them thoroughly." Then they said, "Come, let us build ourselves a city, with a tower that reaches to the heavens, so that we may make a name for ourselves; otherwise we will be scattered over the face of the whole earth."

⁵ But the Lord came down to see the city and the tower the people were building. ⁶ The Lord said, "If as one people speaking the same language they have begun to do this, then nothing they plan to do will be impossible for them. ⁷ Come, let us go down and confuse their language so they will not understand each other."

⁸ So the Lord scattered them from there over all the earth, and they stopped building the city. ⁹ That is why it was called Babel¯because there the Lord confused the language of the whole world. From there the Lord scattered them over the face of the whole earth.

The shedding of blood for sin continues through Abraham. God is seen as the Covenant God.

ABRAHAM and the Patriarchs: Redemption Begins.

Genesis 12:1-3: KJV: Now the Lord had said unto Abram, Get thee out of thy country, and from thy kindred, and from thy father's house, unto a land that I will shew thee: ² And I will make of thee a great nation, and I will bless thee, and make thy name great; and thou shalt be a blessing: (*The world would be blessed through Jesus, the descendent of Abraham.*)

But Abraham was 100 years of age and had nearly lost faith that he would have any descendants because he and Sarah had no children, but the Covenant God kept his promise:

Genesis 21:1: Now the Lord was gracious to Sarah as he had said, and the Lord did for Sarah what he had promised. ² Sarah became pregnant and bore a son to Abraham in his old age, at the very time God had promised him. ³ Abraham gave the name Isaac to the son Sarah bore him. ⁴ When his son Isaac was eight days old, Abraham circumcised him, as God commanded him. ⁵ Abraham was a hundred years old when his son Isaac was born to him. How they loved their son!

The Scarlet Thread: *In Genesis chapter 22, KJV, God said to Abraham*, "Take thy son, thine only son, Isaac, whom thou lovest, and get thee into the land of Mariah, and offer him there for a burnt offering. (Verse 2)

Genesis 22: 7, KJV: And Isaac spake unto Abraham his father, and said, My father. . .Behold the fire and the wood: but where is the lamb for a burnt offering? 8 And Abraham said, "My son, God will provide himself a lamb for a burnt offering." 9 And they came to the place which God had told him of; and Abraham built an altar there, and laid the wood in order, and bound Isaac his son, and laid him on the altar upon the wood. 10 And Abraham stretched forth his hand, and took the knife to slay his son. 11 And the angel of the Lord said, Lay not thine hand upon the lad, neither do thou anything unto him: for now I know that thou fearest God, seeing thou hast not withheld thy son, thine only son from me.

13 And Abraham lifted up his eyes, and looked, and behold behind him a ram caught in a thicket by his horns: and Abraham went and took the ram, and offered him up for a burnt

offering in the stead of his son. 15 And the angel of the LORD called unto Abraham out of heaven the second time, 16 And said, By myself have I sworn, saith the LORD, for because thou hast done this thing, and hast not withheld thy son, thine only son:

17 That in blessing I will bless thee, and in multiplying I will multiply thy seed as the stars of the heaven, and as the sand which is upon the sea shore; and thy seed shall possess the gate of his enemies; 18 And in thy seed shall all the nations of the earth be blessed; because thou hast obeyed my voice. Genesis 22:2-18, KJV

So Isaac is a picture of Jesus, who would become the lamb who would willingly die for us. It was on the same mountain that Jesus would die for our sins. Jesus is the one who would be the seed of Abraham.

Throughout the Old Testament, God's people had to kill an animal, preferably a lamb without blemish, and let it die in their place for their sins. All blood sacrifices pointed to the ultimate sacrifice of The Lamb of God, Jesus Christ, who would die to take away the sin of the world!

THE PATRIARCHS CONTINUED: *In Genesis 24, Abraham sent his trusted servant to find a wife among his kindred for his son, Isaac. The story of God's leadership in the finding of Rebekah for Isaac is intriguing. Rebekah's family gave her the similar blessing that Isaac and Abraham had been given:* Genesis 24:60, KJV: Thou art our sister, be thou the mother of thousands of millions, and let thy seed possess the gate of those that hate them.

Isaac and Rebekah had twin sons, one of which was Jacob. The story of Jacob is found in Genesis chapters 27-36. God changed Jacob's name to Israel. He will become the Father of all the Tribes of Israel. As God dealt with Jacob, we see God's disciplinary chastisements of his child and how Jacob reaped what he sowed. In chapter 27, Jacob deceived his blind father, Isaac and received the birthright that belonged to his twin brother, Esau. Jacob had to flee from home to get away from the wrath of Esau. He went to his Uncle Laban's home. Here, Jacob reaped what he sowed because Laban deceived Jacob and he married Leah, not his beloved Rachel. This deceit by Laban brought many problems on Jacob's family. He had 12 sons; the two who were born later to Rachel, (Joseph and Benjamin) were Jacob's favorites.

God continued his covenant with Jacob that he would be the father of a great nation. Jacob's 12 sons became the heads of the 12 tribes of Israel.

Jesus, the promised Messiah and Savior, would come from the tribe of Judah. However, Joseph is the son through which Jacob's family would be saved from famine here on earth.

In chapters 37 to 50, we read the whole story of Joseph.

Pass the Baton of Faith to your children: *Often, while driving to see my mama and daddy at Lindsay, Oklahoma, with our granddaughters, Brooke and Jordan Taylor, they would want me to tell the whole story of Joseph. I loved to tell it! From Joseph, we learn all about how God has us in His hand and plans what is best for us, even when so much seems to be going wrong. You see, Joseph is also said to be a picture of Jesus Christ in 100 ways!*
(Pink, Gleanings in Genesis, 1922)

In chapter 37, we find that Jacob loved Joseph more than the other sons. Joseph, like Jesus, was a shepherd. Like Jesus, he was hated by his brethren and was envied because of his words. When a youth, Joseph, like Jesus, foretold of his future sovereignty.

In what ways did Joseph foreshadow Jesus? First, Joseph is sent forth to seek his brethren. When we turn to the Gospels we find the correspondence is perfect. When the Beloved of the Father visited this world, His earthly mission was restricted to His brethren according to the flesh. As we read in John 1:11, "He came unto His own, and His own received Him not." His "own" here refers to His own people, the Jews.

In the second place, observe the character of Joseph's mission: Jacob said," Go, I pray thee, see whether it be well with thy brethren." He was sent not to censure them, but to inquire after their welfare. *So, again, it was as with the Lord Jesus Christ. As we read in John 3:17,* KJV, "For God sent not His Son into the world to condemn the world; but that the world through Him might be saved."

I love this story of Joseph for adults and children because we see that Joseph suffered much, but he was always faithful, and God used all of his experiences to make of him an amazing person and influence on the world. What a lesson for us! Read Genesis Chapters 37 to 50. Remember the coat of many colors that Jacob, his father made for him and how his brothers were jealous? Also, he dreamed dreams that were interpreted that his brothers would in the future bow down to him. Then they hated him.

Joseph's father, Jacob, sent Joseph to check on his brothers in the fields. They first conspired to kill him, but instead, they sold him as a slave. The brothers took his coat of many colors to their father, soaked in the blood of an animal, and deceived Jacob into thinking Joseph was dead. (Jacob has been a deceiver all of his life and was now "reaping what he had sowed.") Jacob cried for many days, but no one could comfort him.

Now Joseph started out as a slave, but the Lord was with Joseph and He helped him do everything right. So Potiphar made him his helper, and put him in charge of everything that he owned. The problem came when Potiphar's wife lied about Joseph to her husband, and Potiphar had Joseph put into jail. The Lord was still with Joseph in jail, and the warden put Joseph in charge of all the prisoners. While in jail, Joseph told Pharaoh's cupbearer and baker the meaning of their dreams.

After Joseph had been in prison for seven years, Pharaoh had a troubling dream. Joseph said "God will help me explain the meaning of your dream."

Gen. 41:28-31: This *is* the thing which I have spoken to Pharaoh. God has shown Pharaoh what He *is* about to do. [29] Indeed seven years of great plenty will come throughout all the land of Egypt; [30] but after them seven years of famine will arise, and all the plenty will be forgotten in the land of Egypt; and the famine will deplete the land. [31] So the plenty will not be known in the land because of the famine following, for it *will be* very severe.

In Gen. 41:32-36, Joseph advised that grain be saved during the good years for the seven years of famine. Pharaoh put Joseph in charge of all the land of Egypt

[33] "Now therefore, let Pharaoh select a discerning and wise man, and set him over the land of Egypt. [34] Let Pharaoh do *this,* and let him appoint officers over the land, to collect one-fifth *of the produce* of the land of Egypt in the seven plentiful years. [35] And let them gather all the food of those good years that are coming, and store up grain under the authority of Pharaoh, and let them keep food in the cities. [36] Then so food shall be as a reserve for the land for the seven years of famine which shall be in the land of Egypt, that the land may not perish during the famine."

Joseph's Rise to Power

[37] So the advice was good in the eyes of Pharaoh and in the eyes of all his servants. [38] And Pharaoh said to his servants, "Can we find *such a one* as this, a man in whom *is* the Spirit of God?"

[39] Then Pharaoh said to Joseph, "Inasmuch as God has shown you all this, there is no one as discerning and wise as you. [40] You shall be over my house, and all my people shall be ruled according to your word; only in regard to the throne will I be greater than you." [41] And Pharaoh said to Joseph, "See, I have set you over all the land of Egypt."

Pharaoh believed all that Joseph told him, and put him in charge of all the land of Egypt. People came from all countries to buy grain from Joseph, because the whole world was in need of food. Some of those people were Joseph's brothers*. When his brothers came, Joseph recognized them, but they did not know who he was. The brothers all bowed to him because he was an important person. Just as he dreamed they would bow at the beginning of the story! Just as Jesus will be exalted and every knee shall bow before him in Philippians 2:9-11!*

The story of how Joseph learned whether his brothers had changed, whether they were good to the younger brother, Benjamin, and how he learned about his father Jacob is quite exciting. After a few meetings with his brothers he could not keep it in any longer and Joseph said to his brothers, "I am Joseph! Is my father alive?" *But his brothers couldn't answer him because they were afraid. Then Joseph wept aloud and said,*" I am your brother Joseph, the one you sold into Egypt! And now, do not be distressed and do not be angry with yourselves for selling me here, because it was to save lives that God sent me ahead of you." Genesis 45:4-5

"Now hurry back to my father and tell him, 'This is what your son Joseph says: God has made me master over all the land of Egypt. So come down to me immediately! [10] You can live in the region of Goshen, where you can be near me with all your children and grandchildren, your flocks and herds, and everything you own. [11] I will take care of you there. . ." Genesis 45:9-11

Unity of the Bible: *God's promise continued from Abraham to Isaac to Jacob*: Genesis 46:2-5: And God spoke to Israel in visions of the night and said, "Jacob, Jacob." And he said, "Here I am." [3] Then he said, "I am God, the God of your father. Do not be afraid to go down to Egypt, for <u>there I will make you into a great nation</u>. [4] I myself will go down with you to Egypt, and I will also bring you up again, and Joseph's hand shall close your eyes." [5] Then Jacob set out from Beersheba. The sons of Israel carried Jacob their father, their little ones, and their wives, in the wagons that Pharaoh had sent to carry him. Genesis 46:2-5

Throughout the lives of Jacob and of Joseph, the Israelite people were special guests in Egypt.

Jacob, in chapter 49, blessed each of the 12 sons, who would become the heads of the 12 tribes of Israel. When Jacob died and the sons carried him back to Canaan to bury him, the brothers were again afraid of Joseph. But Joseph said to them, "Fear not: for am I in the place of God? But as for you, you thought evil against me; but God meant it unto good, to bring to pass, as it is this day, to save much people alive." Genesis 46:19-21, KJV. *Joseph lived to be 110 years old and his bones would also be taken back to Canaan 400 years later!*

The stories of the patriarchs are bound together by a single theme: God would bring them to a homeland and would make of them a great nation, through which all the world would be blessed. Also, we see how Genesis is the seed-plot of the whole Bible because in it the great themes of the Bible are introduced.

THE BOOK OF EXODUS
In Exodus, Jesus is the Passover Lamb

Theme: Deliverance of Israel from Egyptian slavery; giving of the law; building the Tabernacle; God's Redemptive Plan for Man.

Exodus focuses upon Moses, the deliverer and picture of Jesus Christ.

The Message: In the Book of Exodus, we find that a new King Pharaoh, who did not know Joseph, arose; and the Israelites became slaves in Egypt for 400 years. But Baby Moses was protected by God and was prepared to become deliverer of God's people from bondage. *The scarlet thread continued* as Moses was commanded by the Lord to tell all Israelites to put the *blood of a lamb* over their door posts so they could be saved. Moses delivered them. God made a covenant with the people of Israel on Mount Sinai. God gave them a body of laws, including the Ten Commandments to govern them when they reached the Promise Land. God's covenant included the warning the disobedience would bring disaster and obedience would bring blessing. They learned this truth when their disobedience led to a 40-year period of wandering in the wilderness before they were allowed to enter the Promised Land. The Tabernacle was built as the place of sacrifice of animals for sins. Sin must be covered with blood.

The following are <u>Key Verses, Passages, and Ideas in Exodus:</u>

At the time of Joseph, the Hebrew people went down into Egypt during a famine, because there was food in Egypt. They grew into a great nation there, but a new Pharaoh enslaved them.

Exodus 1:6 Now Joseph and all his brothers and all that generation died, [7] but the Israelites were exceedingly fruitful; they multiplied greatly, increased in numbers. . . .*The new king feared they would become so strong that they would fight against them.*

[11] So they put slave masters over them to oppress them with forced labor, and they built Python and Rameses as store cities for Pharaoh. [12] But the more they were oppressed, the more they multiplied and spread; so the Egyptians came to dread the Israelites [13] and worked them ruthlessly. Exodus 1:22: Then Pharaoh gave this order to all his people: "Every Hebrew boy that is born you must throw into the Nile, but let every girl live."

Pass the baton of faith to the next generation: *The story of Baby Moses being saved in a basket floating on the Nile River from the wrath of King Pharaoh is a favorite for children. Exodus 2:1:* Now a man of the tribe of Levi married a Levite woman, [2] and she became pregnant and gave birth to a son. When she saw that he was a fine child, she hid him for three months.[3] But when she could hide him no longer, she got a papyrus basket for him and coated it with tar and pitch. Then she placed the child in it and put it among the reeds along the bank of the Nile. [4] His sister stood at a distance to see what would happen to him.

[5] Then Pharaoh's daughter went down to the Nile to bathe, and her attendants were walking along the riverbank. She saw the basket among the reeds and sent her female slave

to get it. [6] She opened it and saw the baby. He was crying, and she felt sorry for him. "This is one of the Hebrew babies," she said.

Then in verses 7 to 8, we find that Pharaoh's daughter allowed Moses' own mother to nurse the baby. Then in verse 10, when the child grew older, she took him to Pharaoh's daughter and he became her son. She named him Moses, saying, "I drew him out of the water."

So Moses became the prince of Egypt for 40 years. He received the best of education in all ways. Then in Exodus 2:11, we find that Moses couldn't bear the terrible way the Israelites were treated. [11] One day, after Moses had grown up, he went out to where his own people were and watched them at their hard labor. He saw an Egyptian beating a Hebrew, one of his own people. [12] Looking this way and that and seeing no one, he killed the Egyptian and hid him in the sand. *When Pharaoh heard this, he sought to kill Moses and Moses fled to the land of Midian. So Moses began life as an outcast, become a prince, and then he became a fugitive from Egypt.*

Moses is the one whom God chose to become a new leader. God called Moses to lead his chosen people out of Egyptian slavery, back into the Promised Land: While Moses was a shepherd in Midian, God called him from a burning bush.

Exodus Chapter 3: From a burning bush, God said, "Moses, Moses. . .The ground on which you stand is holy. I have heard the cries of my people by reason of their taskmasters. I am come down to deliver them and to take them to that land of milk and honey. . .I will send you to Pharaoh." Exodus 3: 4-10

[13] Moses said to God, "Suppose I go to the Israelites and say to them, 'The God of your fathers has sent me to you,' and they ask me, 'What is his name?' Then what shall I tell them?" This is what you are to say to the Israelites: 'I am has sent me to you.'

The Great "I Am."! What does this mean? I am What? Complete the sentence. I am _____, Yes, God is complete. Mosees would learn that when he was incomplete and inadequate, God could be totally sufficient. The Great "I Am" is from the beginning, self-existent. "I am" holy; I am "comfort: I am "eternal." Oh, the depths and yet the simplicity of the Gospel!

Aaron, the brother of Moses was chosen by God to be the spokesman for Moses, because Moses said he was "Slow of Speech." Aaron, of the tribe of Levi will later become the High Priest who will offer sacrifices for the sin of the people.

Among the most dramatic scenes in the Old Testament is Moses' confrontation with Pharaoh. Moses demanded that Pharaoh let the people go. But God hardened Pharaoh's heart. Why? So God's divine power can be demonstrated to His own people and to future generations. Also, so the Passover can be initiated. When Pharaoh would not relent, God ordered Moses to initiate a series of ten horrible plagues. The last was the death of the firstborn of all of Egypt!

After God had performed 9 miracles or plagues, (chapters 5 through 10) to entice Pharaoh to let God's people go, God said He would send And God said, "I will be with you. And this will be the sign to you that it is I who have sent you: When you have brought the people out of Egypt, you^{ll} will worship God on this mountain."

¹³ *Moses said to God, "Suppose I go to the Israelites and say to them, 'The God of your fathers has sent me to you,' and they ask me, 'What is his name?' Then what shall I tell them?"*

¹⁴ *God said to Moses, "I am who I am.¹ This is what you are to say to the Israelites: 'I am has sent me to you.'"*

¹⁵ *God also said to Moses, "Say to the Israelites, 'The Lord, the God of your fathers— the God of Abraham, the God of Isaac and the God of Jacob—has sent me to you.'*

"This is my name forever,

the name you shall call me

from generation to generation.

¹⁶ *"Go, assemble the elders of Israel and say to them, 'The Lord, the God of your fathers—the God of Abraham, Isaac and Jacob—appeared to me and said: I have watched over you and have seen what has been done to you in Egypt. ¹⁷ And I have promised to bring you up out of your misery in Egypt into the land of the Canaanites, Hittites, Amorites, Perizzites, Hivites and Jebusites—a land flowing with milk and honey*

one more plague. It is what is now referred to as The Passover. Moses instructed the Israelite families to prepare by killing a lamb. Moses called the elders together and said, "This day shall be the beginning to you, for the Lord hath spoken".

Take of the blood and strike it on the two doorposts of your house. Exodus 12:2

For I will pass through the land of Egypt this night and will smite all the firstborn in the land of Egypt. Exodus 12:12a

The Scarlet Thread: And the blood shall be to you for a token upon the houses where ye are and *when I see the blood, I will pass over you*, and the plague shall not be upon you to destroy you, when I smite the land of Egypt. Exodus 12:13

After the Children of Israel had been in Egypt for 450 years, the Exodus {the going out} of Egypt began. Moses said, "We will go, with our young and our old, our sons and daughters, our flocks, and our herds. We have seen this day that God lives!"

Exodus 13:9, KJV: And it shall be for a sign unto thee upon thine hand, and for a memorial between thine eyes, that the Lord's law may be in thy mouth: for with a strong hand hath the Lord brought thee out of Egypt.

¹⁸ But God led the people about, through the way of the wilderness of the Red sea: and the children of Israel went up harnessed out of the land of Egypt.

²¹ And the Lord went before them by day in a pillar of a cloud, to lead them the way; and by night in a pillar of fire, to give them light; to go by day and night:

(The wonderful account of the <u>parting of the Red Sea</u> so the Israelites could get away from the Egyptian Army is in Exodus, Chapter 14. Moses stretched out his hand over the Red Sea, and the waters parted and the children of Israel went across on dry land. When the Egyptians pursued after them, through the sea, Moses said, "Fear not, Stand still, and see the salvation of the Lord." And the waters returned and drowned all of Pharaoh's army.)

The story of Pharaoh Remises' fall is fascinating. He had great riches and power, but was brought down by his own wickedness. The victory of the Israelites is a powerful expression of hope and faith.

It seemed that after the Israelites had seen all God's wonderful miracles and provisions for them that they would have been grateful and would have praised God. But they didn't. Though God sent quail each evening and manna for them to eat each morning, they complained and had no faith. Even while Moses was on Mount Sinai receiving God's Ten Commandments, they made an idol as another god. They asked Aaron to make a Golden Calf for them to worship:

Exodus 32:1; When the people saw that Moses was so long in coming down from the mountain, they gathered around Aaron and said, "Come, make us gods who will go before us. As for this fellow Moses who brought us up out of Egypt, we don't know what has happened to him."

[2] Aaron answered them, "Take off the gold earrings that your wives, your sons and your daughters are wearing, and bring them to me." [3] So all the people took off their earrings and brought them to Aaron. [4] He took what they handed him and made it into an idol cast in the shape of a calf, fashioning it with a tool. Then they said, "These are your gods, Israel, who brought you up out of Egypt." [5] When Aaron saw this, he built an altar in front of the calf and announced, "Tomorrow there will be a festival to the Lord." [6] So the next day the people rose early and sacrificed burnt offerings and presented fellowship offerings. Afterward they sat down to eat and drink and got up to indulge in revelry.

[7] Then the Lord said to Moses, "Go down, because your people, whom you brought up out of Egypt, have become corrupt. [8] They have been quick to turn away from what I commanded them. . .They are a stiff-necked people.

[15] Moses turned and went down the mountain with the two tablets of the covenant law in his hands. They were inscribed on both sides, front and back. [16] The tablets were the work of God; the writing was the writing of God, engraved on the tablets. [19] When Moses approached the camp and saw the calf and the dancing, his anger burned and he threw the tablets out of his hands, breaking them to pieces at the foot of the mountain. [20] And he took the calf the people had made and burned it in the fire; then he ground it to powder, scattered it on the water and made the Israelites drink it.

[30] The next day Moses said to the people, "You have committed a great sin. . . ."[35] And the Lord struck the people with a plague because of what they did with the calf Aaron had made.

The Hebrew people left Egypt and went out into the wilderness. They came to Mount Sinai. Moses went up the mountain and God gave him the Ten Commandments, written "with the finger of God" on two tablets of stone.

The Ten Commandments are found in Exodus 20: 1-17, KJV. In short form, they are:

[3] Thou shalt have no other gods before me.
[4] Thou shalt not make unto thee any graven image.
[7] Thou shalt not take the name of the Lord thy God in vain.
[8] Remember the Sabbath day, to keep it holy.
[12] Honour thy father and thy mother.
[13] Thou shalt not kill.
[14] Thou shalt not commit adultery.
[15] Thou shalt not steal.
[16] Thou shalt not bear false witness against thy neighbor.
[17] Thou shalt not covet.

Yes, these are carved in stone. They are for everyone. Keeping them brings happiness. Breaking the Ten Commandments brings unhappiness and even destruction! The Ten Commandments have endured and have become the cornerstone of ethical philosophy of Western civilization.

The covenant of the Law was established with a blood sacrifice:

(Moses was instructed by the Lord to teach the people the awfulness of sin and that the penalty of sin is death. Exodus accounts the ceremonial law.)

Exodus 24:3: And Moses came and told the people all the words of the Lord, and all the judgments: and all the people answered with one voice, and said, "All the words which the Lord hath said will we do." [4] And Moses wrote all the words of the Lord, and rose up early in the morning, and built an altar under the hill, and twelve pillars, according to the twelve tribes of Israel.

All poetry is written by Marilyn Kay Paddack Gage:

Exodus 24
In the days of Moses, the Book of the Covenant was read.
All worshiped at a twelve-pillared altar where young men were led,
With blood to show the covenant sealed.
Moses spent forty days at Mt. Sinai, where the Lord, His plans revealed.

Exodus 24:5: And he sent young men of the children of Israel, which offered *burnt offerings,* and sacrificed peace offerings of oxen unto the Lord. [6] And Moses took half of *the blood,* and put it in basins; and half of the blood he sprinkled on the altar. [8] And Moses said, Behold the blood of the covenant, which the Lord hath made with you concerning all these words. *Moses took the blood, and sprinkled it on the people.*

God gave instructions how to sacrifice
Each and every animal fit to pay the price,
Whether it be a bullock or ram,
A burnt offering continually of unblemished lamb.

(Plans for building The Tabernacle are given in chapters 25-28.) Laws for the Priesthood and laws for sacrifices and atonement are given in Chapters 29-30. The tabernacle was a tent that could be moved with them as they wandered for 40 years. In some way, everything in the tabernacle foreshadowed Jesus Christ, the ultimate sacrifice.)
God said, "Let them make me a sanctuary; that I may dwell among them." Exodus 25:8 (*God has always had a dwelling place in the midst of His people. It was first in the tabernacle, and later in the Old Testament period it was in the temple. In the gospels, God dwelt among His people in the person of His Son, the Lord Jesus Christ. Now, in the church age, God dwells in the church, or in the hearts of people who are the church.) Tabernacle means "tent," "place of dwelling" or "sanctuary." And so God dwelled among His people in the tabernacle in the wilderness. He appeared as a pillar of cloud over the tabernacle by day and a pillar of fire by night in the sight of all Israel. The people would not set out on their journey unless the cloud lifted. It was an unmistakably powerful visual statement indicating God's presence among them.*

Exodus 25
God will meet you at the mercy seat,
The bread of life from the table eat.
To show God's presence is the ark.
Shekinah's glory lights up the dark.

The tribe of Levi, with Aaron as leader, was to be the priesthood. The priests had to first make an offering for their sins, and then offer up a sacrifice for the sins of the people. Only the priests could go into the Holy of Holies behind the curtain.
Ten curtains, intertwined, and enormous were placed in the tabernacle.

Exodu 26
In the tabernacle a veil divided the most holy from the holy place,
But at Christ's death we can now meet God face to face.
No longer can just the high priest

Enter to offer sacrifices of a slain lowly beast.

Unity of the Bible: Matthew 27:51: At that moment the curtain of the temple was torn in two from top to bottom. The earth shook and the rocks split. *(When Jesus died, the veil was ripped showing that we now need no priest or blood sacrifice. Jesus is our high priest and the sacrifice. We are all priests and can come boldly to God, ourselves.)*

When we read the Book of Hebrews, we will see in Hebrews 1 and Hebrews 5 the meaning of the curtain and the fact that we no longer have to have a priest to intercede for us because Jesus is our high priest.

Laws for the Priesthood and laws for sacrifices and atonement are given in Exodus Chapters 29-30. The tabernacle was a tent that could be moved with them as they wandered for 40 years. Inside it was the Ark of the Covenant, which was carried by priests wherever they went. In some

Exodus 29
God gave instructions how to sacrifice
Each and every animal fit to pay the price.
Whether it be a bullock or ram,
A burnt offering continually of unblemished lamb.

Exodus 30:6: Put the altar in front of the curtain that shields the Ark of the Covenant law—before the atonement cover that is over the tablets of the covenant law—where I will meet with you.

[7] "Aaron must burn fragrant incense on the altar every morning when he tends the lamps. [8] He must burn incense again when he lights the lamps at twilight so incense will burn regularly before the LORD for the generations to come. . . .[10] Once a year Aaron shall make atonement on its horns. This annual atonement must be made with the blood of the atoning sin offering for the generations

(Praise be to God, we no longer have to laboriously observe all these ceremonies to get our sins forgiven! If we believe upon Jesus, his blood covers our sins.)

Unity of the Bible: Hebrews 9:19, KJV: For when Moses had spoken every precept to all the people according to the law, he took the blood of calves and of goats, with water, and scarlet wool, and hyssop, and sprinkled both the book, and all the people, [20] Saying, This is the blood of the testament which God hath enjoined unto you.

Hebrews 10:19-23: [19] Therefore, brothers and sisters, since we have confidence to enter the Most Holy Place by the blood of Jesus, [20] by a new and living way opened for us through the curtain, that is, his body, [21] and since we have a great priest over the house of God, [22] let us draw near to God with a sincere heart and with the full assurance that faith brings, having our hearts sprinkled to cleanse us from a guilty conscience.

Exodus 27
God commanded Israel to bring pure oil olive beaten for the light,
To cause the lamp of the tabernacle to burn always bright.
Now the light of the world is Christ, the Son.
The oil is the Holy Spirit, the Comforter, come.

Exodus 30
Cleanliness is next to Godliness—
Before Aaron and his sons enter to confess,
They wash hands and feet in a brass laver.
A confection of perfume enhances a holy savor.

Exodus 31
"Verily my Sabbaths ye shall keep."
Six days only may work be done,
Fields planted and crops to reap.
The finger of God wrote on two tables of stone.

While Moses was on the mountain talking with God, the people became impatient:

Exodus 32
People cannot wait.
They proceed and never hesitate.
Demanded a god without delay.
Aaron hastily was forced to say,
"Break off your gold earrings and bring them to me."
A moltened calf was fashioned for their gods to be.
"Let me alone, that my wrath may wax hot.
Whosoever hath sinned against me, him out of my book will I blot."

Exodus 33:1-4: Then the Lord said to Moses, "Leave this place, you and the people you brought up out of Egypt, and go up to the land I promised on oath to Abraham, Isaac and Jacob, saying, 'I will give it to your descendants.' [2] I will send an angel before you and drive out the Canaanites, Amorites, Hittites, Perizzites, Hivites and Jebusites. [3] Go up to the land flowing with milk and honey. But I will not go with you, because you are a stiff-necked people and I might destroy you on the way." [4] When the people heard these distressing words, they began to mourn.

Moses and the Glory of the Lord

[12] Moses said to the Lord, "You have been telling me, 'Lead these people,' but you have not let me know whom you will send with me. You have said, 'I know you by name and you have found favor with me.' [13] If you are pleased with me, teach me your ways so I may know you and continue to find favor with you. Remember that this nation is your people."

[14] The Lord replied, "My Presence will go with you, and I will give you rest."

[15] Then Moses said to him, "If your Presence does not go with us, do not send us up from here. [16] How will anyone know that you are pleased with me and with your people unless you go with us? What else will distinguish me and your people from all the other people on the face of the earth?"

[17] And the Lord said to Moses, "I will do the very thing you have asked, because I am pleased with you and I know you by name."

[18] Then Moses said, "Now show me your glory."

[19] And the Lord said, "I will cause all my goodness to pass in front of you, and I will proclaim my name, the Lord, in your presence. I will have mercy on whom I will have mercy, and I will have compassion on whom I will have compassion. [20] But," He said, "You cannot see my face, for no one may see me and live."

[21] Then the Lord said, "There is a place near Me where you may stand on a rock. [22] When My glory passes by, I will put you in a cleft in the rock and cover you with My hand until I have passed by. [23] Then I will remove my hand and you will see my back; but My face must not be seen."

Exodus 34
Moses stayed with the Lord 40 nights and 40 days
When he wrote the words of the covenant.
He learned right from wrong in all ways
Abbreviated in the 10 Commandments.

After God had written the 10 Commandments again, the Children of Israel repented and brought offerings and worked on building the tabernacle. Each gave and worked, according to his ability. In fact, they brought too much!

Exodus 35
The children of Israel a willing offering brought
To furnish the tabernacle as Moses was taught.
The wise hearted women did spin,
And metal and stone cutting work were devised by the men.

Exodus 36
How many more missionaries, preachers, and evangelists would be trained,
If in our offering, we had to be restrained.
What churches today can brag as such?
That the members had brought sufficient—in fact, too much.

Exodus 37
Cherubims spread their wings over the mercy seat.
They hear the high priest's confession repeat.
Beaten out of a piece of gold
A work of art, precious to behold.

Exodus 38
God invented color-like a vivid rainbow.
The tabernacle hangings radiated a sparkling glow.
Heaven represented by blue.
Royal purple—not just a few.
Scarlet red points to Christ's shed blood-the cure.
Linen white—sinless and pure.

Much is said about the altar upon which sacrifice will be made in the tabernacle.
Chapter 38 and 39 detail the work. Exodus 39:43: Moses inspected the work and saw that they had done it just as the Lord had commanded. So Moses blessed them.
Chapter 40 tells us more about the importance of the tabernacle.
The Glory of the Lord
[34] Then the cloud covered the tent of meeting, and the glory of the Lord filled the tabernacle. [35] Moses could not enter the tent of meeting because the cloud had settled on it, and the glory of the Lord filled the tabernacle. [36] In all the travels of the Israelites, whenever the cloud lifted from above the tabernacle, they would set out; [37] but if the cloud did not lift, they did not set out—until the day it lifted. [38] So the cloud of the Lord was over the tabernacle by day, and fire was in the cloud by night, in the sight of all the Israelites during all their travels.
Why would the children of Israel ever forget such miraculous experiences? But they did!
So we see the Book of Exodus was arranged around two great redemptive acts: The Exodus from bondage in Egypt and the establishment of God's covenant (The Ten Commandments) at Mount Sinai. Much of the Bible explains the redemptive plan of God as it is revealed in Exodus.
Exodus presented Jesus as The Passover Lamb. The Scarlet Thread continues.

THE BOOK OF LEVITICUS
In Leviticus, Jesus is Our High Priest

THEME: God's Reconciliation and Sanctification of His People
The Message: These questions are answered. How do we remain reconciled to God? How are we sanctified and set apart for His service? How are we to worship God and treat each other? (FCA, God's Game Plan: An athlete's Study Bible. 2008)

The events in Leviticus take place after the Exodus from Egypt and the giving of the Law at Sinai. Regulations are given for how to worship in the tabernacle. The word, Leviticus, comes from its emphasis on the Levitical Priesthood. (The tribe of Levi) Emphasis is put upon the work of Aaron's sons, the priests. Punishment for disobedience is again empha-sized. It is in Leviticus that most of the laws under which the Hebrew Nation lived – the laws administered by the Levitical Priesthood.

In chapters one through seven, the priests were instructed of how to offer the burnt offering, the fellowship sacrifice, the restitution offering, and the sin offering. How detailed and burdensome were the rules for offering sacrifices for their sins!

Leviticus 1:1-12: The Lord called to Moses and spoke to him from the tent of meeting. He said, [2] "Speak to the Israelites and say to them: 'When anyone among you brings an offering to the Lord, bring as your offering an animal from either the herd or the flock.

[3] "If the offering is a burnt offering from the herd, you are to offer a male without defect. You must present it at the entrance to the tent of meeting so that it will be acceptable to the Lord. [4] You are to lay your hand on the head of the burnt offering, and it will be accepted on your behalf to make atonement for you. [5] You are to slaughter the young bull before the Lord, and then Aaron's sons the priests shall bring the blood and splash it against the sides of the altar at the entrance to the tent of meeting[10]

The smell of blood must have been terrible. God wanted people to know how much he hated sin. (Well, he must have hated sin to have given his own precious Son to redeem us from our sins.)

Leviticus 4:5: Then the anointed priest shall take some of the bull's blood and carry it into the tent of meeting. [6] He is to dip his finger into the blood and sprinkle some of it seven times before the Lord, in front of the curtain of the sanctuary.

Leviticus 7:37-38: This is the law of the burnt offering, of the meat offering, and of the sin offering, and of the trespass offering, and of the consecrations, and of the sacrifice of the peace offerings; which the Lord commanded Moses in Mount Sinai.

In chapters eight through ten, God ordained Aaron and his sons as priests and gave regulations for the priests.

[8] Then the Lord said to Aaron, [9] "You and your sons are not to drink wine or other fermented drink whenever you go into the tent of meeting, or you will die. This is a lasting ordinance for the generations to come, [10] so that you can distinguish between the holy and

the common, between the unclean and the clean, [11] and so you can teach the Israelites all the decrees the Lord has given them through Moses."

Leviticus chapters 11-15: God *gave many laws concerning healthful and unhealthful animals, skin diseases, purification after childbirth, and health rules concerning body discharges.*

Leviticus Chapter 16: The Day of Atonement. Aaron, the High Priest, was instructed how he should enter into the Holy Place to the Mercy Seat. He must first come with the blood of a young bull for a sin offering for himself, before the high priest could make atonement for the nation, he had to make atonement for himself. And in the New Testament, we see the scarlet thread and the unity of the scriptures:

Hebrews 7:26-28, When Jesus offered a perfect atonement for sin, He did not need to make a sin offering for Himself: For such a High Priest was fitting for us, who is holy, harmless, undefiled, separate from sinners, and has become higher than the heavens; who does not need daily, as those high priests, to offer up sacrifices, first for His own sins and then for the people's, for this He did once for all when He offered up Himself. For the law appoints as high priests men who have weakness, but the word of the oath, which came after the law, appoints the Son who has been perfected forever..

Aaron could not come into the Holy Place any time he pleased, but only at God's invitation and at the appointed time and place. The same is true today: We can only come into God's Holy Place at His invitation. Romans 5:1-2 specifically says that because of Jesus' work on our behalf, we have standing access to God.

There was extensive preparation for an important day. To the ancient Jews the Day of Atonement was called "the great day" or sometimes even just "the day." It was and remains the only day of commanded fasting on the Jewish calendar. Modern Jews still regard Yom Kippur an important day of fasting and, soul searching,

"And Aaron shall bring the bull of the sin offering, which is for himself, and make atonement for himself and for his house, and shall kill the bull as the sin offering which is for himself" Before the high priest could make atonement for the nation, he had to make atonement for himself.

He shall take some of the blood of the bull and sprinkle it with his finger on the mercy seat: The blood of this sin offering had to be sprinkled on the mercy seat, which was the lid to the Ark of the Covenant, which sat in the Holy Place. When he came into the Holy Place, he had to come with a smoking censer that gave off a cloud of incense.

Before the mercy seat he shall sprinkle some of the blood: The idea was that God was above the mercy seat (I will appear in the cloud above the mercy seat, Leviticus 16:2), and as He looked down upon the Ark of the Covenant, He saw the sin of man. Man's sin was represented by the items in the Ark of the Covenant: Manna, which Israel complained about, tablets of law Israel broke, and a budding almond rod given as a response to Israel's rebellion. Then, the high priest sprinkled atoning blood seven times on the mercy seat

- *covering over the emblems of Israel's sin. God saw the blood cover over the sin, and atonement was made.*

a. This captures the thought behind the Hebrew word for atonement: Kipper, which means, "to cover." Sin was not removed, but covered over by sacrificial blood. The New Testament idea of atonement is that our sin is not merely covered, but <u>removed</u> *- taken away by the blood of Jesus, so there is no barrier between God and man any longer.*

b. So he shall make atonement for the Holy Place, because of the uncleanness of the children of Israel: This blood was applied to the mercy seat, but also the tabernacle and altar itself. This blood cleansed the house of God itself, which was made ceremonially unclean by man's constant touch.

Punishment for Disobedience

Leviticus 16:14: But if you will not listen to me and carry out all these commands, [15] and if you reject my decrees and abhor my laws and fail to carry out all my commands and so violate my covenant, [16] then I will do this to you: I will bring on you sudden terror, wasting diseases and fever that will destroy your sight and sap your strength. You will plant seed in vain, because your enemies will eat it. [17] I will set my face against you so that you will be defeated by your enemies; those who hate you will rule over you, and you will flee even when no one is pursuing you.

[40] But if they will confess their sins and the sins of their ancestors—their unfaithfulness and their hostility toward me,. . .[42] I will remember my covenant with Jacob and my covenant with Isaac and my covenant with Abraham, and I will remember the land. I am the Lord their God. [46] These are the decrees, the laws and the regulations that the Lord established at Mount Sinai between himself and the Israelites through Moses.

God does promise material blessings for obedience and holiness, but his promise of His presence is the greatest blessing of all. However, we live a holy life out of gratitude and love for God who has given us eternal life.

Leviticus 26:3: If you walk in My statutes and keep My commandments, and perform them,

[4] then I will give you rain in its season, the land shall yield its produce, and the trees of the field shall yield their fruit. [5] Your threshing shall last till the time of vintage, and the vintage shall last till the time of sowing; you shall eat your bread to the full, and dwell in your land safely.

[6] I will give peace in the land, and you shall lie down, and none will make *you* afraid;
I will rid the land of evil beasts, and the sword will not go through your land.

Also, if we wander from him, he promises the blessing of restoration when we repent and turn to him.

Leviticus 26:40: If they confess their iniquity and the iniquity of their fathers, with their unfaithfulness in which they were unfaithful to Me, and that they also have walked contrary to Me, [41] and *that* I also have walked contrary to them and have brought them into the land of their enemies. *He concluded with the promise that if they would confess their sins and unfaithfulness that He would remember His covenant with Abraham and Isaac and would bless them.*

(God gave this promise in II Chronicles 7:14. This promise is for America, today. If we will humble ourselves and pray and turn from our wicked ways, God will bless and will heal our land."

Chapter 26: There were always signs of hope. God promised blessings upon Israel when they kept his statutes and commands. Verses 3-4: 'If you follow my decrees and are careful to obey my commands, [4] I will send you rain in its season, and the ground will yield its crops and the trees their fruit. [6] "'I will grant peace in the land, and you will lie down and no one will make you afraid. I will remove wild beasts from the land, and the sword will not pass through your country.[7] You will pursue your enemies, and they will fall by the sword before [9] "'I will look on you with favor and make you fruitful and increase your numbers, and I will keep my covenant with you. [11] I will put my dwelling place among you, and I will not abhor you. [12] I will walk among you and be your God, and you will be my people.[13] I am the Lord your God, who brought you out of Egypt so that you would no longer be slaves to the Egyptians; I broke the bars of your yoke and enabled you to walk with heads held high.

Leviticus 27 *tells how the Sanctuary is to be funded – how exact calculations and valuations will be made. The tithe, (a tenth) is stressed in this chapter, just as it is throughout the Bible.*

The greatest hope is that one day, a savior would be born. The sacrifices made in the tabernacle in Leviticus pointed to the sacrifice of the Lamb of God.

THE BOOK OF NUMBERS
In Numbers, Jesus is the Fire by Night

Theme: Despite Israel's rebellion against God, which resulted in the wandering in the wilderness for forty years, God was faithful and merciful.

Summary: Because the people disobeyed God, they must wander for 40 years in the wilderness before going to the Promised Land of Canaan. Numbers relates the story of the 40 years during which Israel journeyed from Mount Sinai to the edge of Canaan. God's actions during this time show God's faithfulness in spite of rebellion of the Israelites. The central human figure is Moses, who acts as mediator between God and His people.

Key Verses: Numbers 6:24-26: The Lord bless you and keep you; [25] the Lord make his face shine on you and be gracious to you; [26] the Lord turn his face toward you and give you peace.'"

Numbers 32:13: The Lord's anger burned against Israel and he made them wander in the wilderness forty years, until the whole generation of those who had done evil in his sight was gone.

The first four chapters *number* the Israelites (take a census) as they muster an Israelite army in preparation for invading the Promised Land. Chapter One is a very important chapter.

1. The Lord spoke to Moses in the tent of meeting in the Desert of Sinai on the first day of the second month of the second year after the Israelites came out of Egypt. He said: "Take a census of the whole Israelite community by their clans and families, listing every man by name, one by one. [3] You and Aaron are to count according to their divisions all the men in Israel who are twenty years old or more and able to serve in the army.

[44] These were the men counted by Moses and Aaron and the twelve leaders of Israel, each one representing his family. [45] All the Israelites twenty years old or more who were able to serve in Israel's army were counted according to their families. [46] The total number was 603,550. *Can we imagine that this is the number of men over 20 who made the Exodus from Egypt? Also, the men of the Tribe of Levi were not counted*

What a wonderful job Cecil B. De Mille did with the Exodus in the 1956 Film, "The Ten Commandments." The exodus was possibly the greatest single movie scene, using the most people, in history. A good assignment you could give yourself is to watch "The Ten Commandments" or "The Prince of Egypt" and at the same time read the books of Exodus and Deuteronomy and determine - 1. What is Biblical; 2.What could have happened; and 3. What actually contradicts the Bible? I did this with 5th through 7th graders when we watched "The Prince of Egypt" together. It really makes one "dig" in the Bible, and lots of exciting debate takes place among middle school kids!

Numbers 6:48: The Lord had said to Moses: [49] "You must not count the tribe of Levi or include them in the census of the other Israelites. [50] Instead, appoint the Levites to be in charge of the tabernacle of the covenant law. . .

The twelve tribes are all numbered, except for the Tribe of Levi. They do not fight. Chapters 7 and 8 again give the laborious cleansing of priests and the sacrifice of blood offerings for sin. Chapter 9 tells of the celebration of the Passover, when the death angel passed over the homes in which the blood of the lamb was put over the doors.

Excitement builds in Numbers 13 when God commanded Moses to send the head of each tribe as spies into the Promised Land of Canaan. Numbers 13 17: When Moses sent them to explore Canaan, he said, "Go up through the Negev and on into the hill country. [18] See what the land is like and whether the people who live there are strong or weak, few or many. [19] What kind of land do they live in? Is it good or bad? What kind of towns do they live in? Are they unwalled or fortified? [20] How is the soil? Is it fertile or poor? Are there trees in it or not? Do your best to bring back some of the fruit of the land." (It was the season for the first ripe grapes.)

[21] So they went up and explored the land. . .They cut off a branch bearing a single cluster of grapes. Two of them carried it on a pole between them, along with some pomegranates and figs. [25] At the end of forty days they returned from exploring the land.

[26] They came back to Moses and Aaron and the whole Israelite community at Kadesh in the Desert of Paran. There they reported to them and to the whole assembly and showed them the fruit of the land. [27] They gave Moses this account: "We went into the land to which you sent us, and it does flow with milk and honey! Here is its fruit. [28] But the people who live there are powerful and the cities are fortified and very large"

[30] Then Caleb silenced the people before Moses and said, "We should go up and take possession of the land, for we can certainly do it." [31] But the men who had gone up with him said, "We can't attack those people; they are stronger than we are." [32] And they spread among the Israelites a bad report about the land they had explored. They said, "The land we explored devours those living in it. All the people we saw there are of great size. . . .We seemed like grasshoppers in our own eyes, and we looked the same to them."

(Again, the people rebelled and showed no faith, though they had seen so many miracles from God.)

14 That night all the members of the community raised their voices and wept aloud. [2] All the Israelites grumbled against Moses and Aaron, and the whole assembly said to them, "If only we had died in Egypt! Or in this wilderness! [3] Why is the Lord bringing us to this land only to let us fall by the sword? Our wives and children will be taken as plunder. Wouldn't it be better for us to go back to Egypt?" [4] And they said to each other, "We should choose a leader and go back to Egypt."

[5] Then Moses and Aaron fell face down in front of the whole Israelite assembly gathered there. [6] Joshua son of Nun and Caleb son of Jephunneh, who were among those who had explored the land, tore their clothes [7] and said to the entire Israelite assembly, "The land we passed through and explored is exceedingly good. [8] If the Lord is pleased with us, he will lead us into that land, a land flowing with milk and honey, and will give it to us. [9] Only do

not rebel against the Lord. And do not be afraid of the people of the land, because we will devour them. Their protection is gone, but the Lord is with us. Do not be afraid of them."

[10] But the whole assembly talked about stoning them. Then the glory of the Lord appeared at the tent of meeting to all the Israelites. [11] The Lord said to Moses, "How long will these people treat me with contempt? How long will they refuse to believe in me, in spite of all the signs I have performed among them? [12] I will strike them down with a plague and destroy them, but I will make you into a nation greater and stronger than they."

(Moses prayed for forgiveness for the people.) Then. . . .[20] The Lord replied, "I have forgiven them, as you asked. [21] Nevertheless, as surely as I live and as surely as the glory of the Lord fills the whole earth, [22] not one of those who saw my glory and the signs I performed in Egypt and in the wilderness but who disobeyed me and tested me ten times—[23] not one of them will ever see the land I promised on oath to their ancestors.

[29] In this wilderness your bodies will fall—every one of you twenty years old or more who was counted in the census and who has grumbled against me. [30] Not one of you will enter the land I swore with uplifted hand to make your home, except Caleb son of Jephunneh and Joshua son of Nun. [31] As for your children that you said would be taken as plunder, I will bring them in to enjoy the land you have rejected. [32] But as for you, your bodies will fall in this wilderness. [33] Your children will be shepherds here for forty years, suffering for your unfaithfulness, until the last of your bodies lies in the wilderness. [34] For forty years—one year for each of the forty days you explored the land—you will suffer for your sins and know what it is like to have me against you.' [35] I, the Lord, have spoken, and I will surely do these things to this whole wicked community, which has banded together against me. They will meet their end in this wilderness; here they will die."

[36] So the men Moses had sent to explore the land, who returned and made the whole community grumble against him by spreading a bad report about it—[37] these men who were responsible for spreading the bad report about the land were struck down and died of a plague before the Lord. [38] Of the men who went to explore the land, only Joshua son of Nun and Caleb son of Jephunneh survived.

(Blood offerings were made for the sin of disbelief in God. The rest of Numbers describes the wonderings in the wilderness for 40 years. Chapter 18 tells of the Levites' being in charge of the tabernacle and instructs the children of Israel to give tithes to the Levites.)

Numbers Chapter 20
Moses in disobedience struck the rock.
The Holy One's instructions he did mock.
So often a kind word will do the task,
But in a fit of temper we will not wait to ask.

Flowing rivers of water from the rock gushed,
As Jesus' blood at Calvary rushed.
The Rock need only be struck once, if Moses had heeded;
A one-time only crucified Christ is needed.

21."We have no water, and we are so tired of this manna we hate."
God dealt punishment with a fiery snake.
The people to Moses cried,
"Pray to the Lord before we all have died."

Moses lifted a serpent of brass
As a sign of judgment on the bitten mass.
A snake on a pole could not make well,
Unless the victim looked to it from his miserable fiery hell.
Later Christ was raised upon a wooden pole.
If we look to Him in faith, He will heal our wounded soul.
The whole human family felt the Serpent's sting of sin.
The sacrificed Lord makes us whole again!

23. God is not a man that He should lie.
Since He knows all things from beginning to the end,
Could I, a mortal, question, "Why?
How come, where, and since when?"

24. Out of Jacob came a Star.
To a dark sin covered Earth.
What Eastern Wise Men observed from afar
Were fireworks celebrating the Savior's birth.

Yes, in Numbers 24, <u>we see the prophecy of Jesus being born to the seed of Jacob</u>. Then we again see a numbering of the families of all the tribes and the giving of land for an inheritance for the children of those who died in the wilderness. In chapter 27, verses 16-23, God told Moses to lay hands upon Joshua and gave him charge over Israel after Moses would die. God then gave many laws to Moses, and Moses told them to the people. In Chapter 33, Moses told the Israelites what they must do when they go in to possess Canaan:

Genesis 33:51: 1 Speak unto the children of <u>Israel</u>, and say unto them, When ye are passed over <u>Jordan</u> into the land of <u>Canaan</u>; 52 Then ye shall drive out all the inhabitants of the land from before you, and destroy all their pictures, and destroy all their molten images, and quite pluck down all their high places: 53 And ye shall dispossess the inhabitants of the land, and dwell therein: for I have given you the land to possess it.

55 But if ye will not drive out the inhabitants of the land from before you, then it shall come to pass, that those which ye let remain of them shall be pricks in your eyes, and thorns in your sides, and shall vex you in the land wherein ye dwell. 56 Moreover it shall come to pass, that I shall do unto you, as I thought to do unto them.

Numbers 32: [20] Then Moses said to them, "If you will do this—if you will arm yourselves before the Lord for battle [21] and if all of you who are armed cross over the Jordan before the Lord until he has driven his enemies out before him—[22] then when the land is subdued before the Lord, you may return and be free from your obligation to the Lord and to Israel. And this land will be your possession before the Lord. [23] But if you fail to do this, you will be sinning against the Lord; and *you may be sure that your sin will find you out*."

Of course, the Children of Israel did not do as God instructed. They chose to settle down with idol worshippers, and their children intermarried with them. The Lord blessed when they obeyed; he punished when they did not obey His commandments. <u>A lesson for America?</u>

THE BOOK OF DEUTERONOMY
In Deuteronomy, Jesus is Moses' Voice

Theme: God's covenant with Israel and Moses' personal plea with Israel to return to God.

Summary: The events take place on the plains of Moab as the Israelites prepare to enter the Promised Land. Moses would not get to go into the Promised Land; therefore, he transferred his leadership to Joshua. Moses gave his final instructions to the people, emphasizing the most important laws and renewing Israel's covenant with the Lord. We learn the responsibilities, rewards, and punishments involved in the covenant.

According to FCA, God's Game Plan (2008). The great theological themes of Judaism are introduced:

A God who acts in history for the redemption of His people.
The Israelite concept of punishment and rewards for their behavior,
And the creed of Judaism, "Hear, O Israel: The Lord our God, the Lord is one."

Deuteronomy is quoted much in the rest of the scripture because of its spiritual emphasis and its call to total commitment to the Lord. It is concluded with the death of Moses.

Deuteronomy Chapter 1
Moses at the end of his life gave instructions;
He encouraged the people to learn from God's lessons.
Having kept a diary he enumerated their wanderings,
Reminding the people that God, alone, is king.

These are the words which Moses spoke unto all Israel on this side of Jordan in the wilderness Deuteronomy 1: 8: I have set the land before you: go in and possess the land which the Lord:swore unto your fathers, Abraham, Isaac, and Jacob, and to give to their seed after them. . .Behold, you are as the stars of heaven for multitude.

Then Moses told about the problems that resulted when they multiplied and how God had told him that he could no longer be the only judge over them. God told Moses to find wise men of understanding from among the tribes to make them rulers, chiefs, captains, and officers.

Verse 16: And I charged your judges saying, Hear the causes between your brethren, and judge righteously between every man and his brother. . .17. Ye shall not respect persons in judgment, but ye shall hear the small as well as the great.

Chapter 2

While preparing the Israellies for entry into the Promised Land, Moses reviewed the times the people had obeyed God and when they had rebelled *and the blessings and judgments they had received. In fact chapters 2 and 3 revue Numbers 1 to 33. He also reviewed allotments made to different peoples: Go*d did not neglect Jacob's brother, Esau.

He gave his children Mount Seir.
Neither was Lot abandoned after his fall,
For to the Moabites was given Ar,
And the Ammonites had land their own to call.

Deuteronomy 3:22: Ye shall not fear them, for the Lord your God will fight for you.

So often like giants our problems arise;
We think God can't hear our pitiful cries.
Just remember Og, the king,
True fear to the children of Ammon he did bring.
He was no competition for God, regardless of his size.
His land and cattle became property of the men of Israel and their wives.

Deuteronomy 4:1: Israel, hear the decrees and laws I am about to teach you. Follow them so that you may live and may go in and take possession of the land the Lord, the God of your ancestors, is giving you. [2] Do not add to what I command you and do not subtract from it, but keep the commands of the Lord your God that I give you.

[5] See, I have taught you decrees and laws as the Lord my God commanded me, so that you may follow them in the land you are entering to take possession of it. [6] Observe them carefully, for this will show your wisdom and understanding to the nations, who will hear about all these decrees and say, "Surely this great nation is a wise and understanding people." [7] What other nation is so great as to have their gods near them the way the Lord our God is near us whenever we pray to him? [8] And what other nation is so great as to have such righteous decrees and laws as this body of laws I am setting before you today?

[9] Only be careful, and watch yourselves closely so that you do not forget the things your eyes have seen or let them fade from your heart as long as you live. Teach them to your children and to their children after them. [10] Remember the day you stood before the Lord your God at Horeb, when he said to me, "Assemble the people before me to hear my words so that they may learn to revere me as long as they live in the land and may teach them to their children. [13] He declared to you his covenant, the Ten Commandments, which he commanded you to follow and then wrote them on two stone tablets. [14] And the Lord

directed me at that time to teach you the decrees and laws you are to follow in the land that you are crossing the Jordan to possess.

Idolatry was forbidden. They were told not to make any kind of image to worship and not to worship God's beautiful creation. [19] And when you look up to the sky and see the sun, the moon and the stars—all the heavenly array—do not be enticed into bowing down to them and worshiping things the Lord your God has apportioned to all the nations under heaven.

[21] The Lord was angry with me because of you, and he solemnly swore that I would not cross the Jordan and enter the good land the Lord your God is giving you as your inheritance. [22] I will die in this land; I will not cross the Jordan; but you are about to cross over and take possession of that good land. [23] Be careful not to forget the covenant of the Lord your God that he made with you; do not make for yourselves an idol in the form of anything the Lord your God has forbidden. [24] For the Lord your God is a consuming fire, a jealous God.

[25] After you have had children and grandchildren and have lived in the land a long time—if you then become corrupt and make any kind of idol, doing evil in the eyes of the Lord your God and arousing his anger, [26] I call the heavens and the earth as witnesses against you this day that you will quickly perish from the land that you are crossing the Jordan to possess. You will not live there long but will certainly be destroyed. [29] But if from there you seek the Lord your God, you will find him if you seek him with all your heart and with all your soul. [30] When you are in distress and all these things have happened to you, then in later days you will return to your God and obey him. [31] For the Lord your God is a merciful God; he will not abandon or destroy you or forget the covenant with your ancestors, which he confirmed to them by oath.

The Lord Is God.

[32] Ask now about the former days, long before your time, from the day God created human beings on the earth; ask from one end of the heavens to the other. Has anything so great as this ever happened, or has anything like it ever been heard of? [35] You were shown these things so that you might know that the Lord is God; besides him there is no other. [36] From heaven he made you hear his voice to discipline you. On earth he showed you his great fire, and you heard his words from out of the fire. [37] Because he loved your ancestors and chose their descendants after them, he brought you out of Egypt by his Presence and his great strength, [38] to drive out before you nations greater and stronger than you and to bring you into their land to give it to you for your inheritance, as it is today.

[39] Acknowledge and take to heart this day that the Lord is God in heaven above and on the earth below. There is no other. [40] Keep his decrees and commands, which I am giving you today, so that it may go well with you and your children after you and that you may live long in the land the Lord your God gives you for all time.

In Deuteronomy 5, we find the <u>Ten Commandments</u> again, like in Exodus 20.

Moses summoned all Israel and said: Hear, Israel, the decrees and laws I declare in your hearing today. Learn them and be sure to follow them. [2] The Lord our God made a covenant with us at Horeb. [3] It was not with our ancestors that the Lord made this covenant, but with us, with all of us who are alive here today. [4] The Lord spoke to you face to face out of the fire on the mountain. [5] (At that time I stood between the Lord and you to declare to you the word of the Lord, because you were afraid of the fire and did not go up the mountain.) And he said:

[6] "I am the Lord your God, who brought you out of Egypt, out of the land of slavery.

[7] "You shall have no other gods before me.

[8] "You shall not make for yourself an image. in the form of anything in heaven above or on the earth beneath or in the waters below. [9] You shall not bow down to them or worship them; for I, the Lord your God, am a jealous God, punishing the children for the sin of the parents to the third and fourth generation of those who hate me, [10] but showing love to a thousand generations of those who love me and keep my commandments.

[11] "You shall not misuse the name of the Lord your God, for the Lord will not hold anyone guiltless who misuses his name.

[12] "Observe the Sabbath day by keeping it holy, as the Lord your God has commanded you. [13] Six days you shall labor and do all your work, [14] but the seventh day is a Sabbath to the Lord your God. On it you shall not do any work, neither you, nor your son or daughter, nor your male or female servant, nor your ox, your donkey or any of your animals, nor any foreigner residing in your towns, so that your male and female servants may rest, as you do. [15] Remember that you were slaves in Egypt and that the Lord your God brought you out of there with a mighty hand and an outstretched arm. Therefore the Lord your God has commanded you to observe the Sabbath day.

[16] "Honor your father and your mother, as the Lord your God has commanded you, so that you may live long and that it may go well with you in the land the Lord your God is giving you.

[17] You shall not murder.

[18] You shall not commit adultery.

[19] You shall not steal.

[20] You shall not give false testimony against your neighbor.

[21] You shall not covet your neighbor's wife. You shall not set your desire on your neighbor's house or land, his male or female servant, his ox or donkey, or anything that belongs to your neighbor."

[22] These are the commandments the Lord proclaimed in a loud voice to your whole assembly there on the mountain from out of the fire, the cloud and the deep darkness; and He added nothing more. Then He wrote them on two stone tablets and gave them to me.

[32] So be careful to do what the Lord your God has commanded you; do not turn aside to the right or to the left. [33] Walk in obedience to all that the Lord your God has commanded you, so that you may live and prosper and prolong your days in the land that you will possess.

Deuteronomy 6 is a favorite of mine because Moses said to <u>teach our children the commandments of God. Pass the Baton of Faith to the next generation.</u>

Deuteronomy 6:1: These are the commands, decrees and laws the Lord your God directed me to teach you to observe in the land that you are crossing the Jordan to possess, [2] so that you, your children and their children after them may fear the Lord your God as long as you live by keeping all His decrees and commands that I give you, and so that you may enjoy long life. [3] Hear, Israel, and be careful to obey so that it may go well with you and that you may increase greatly in a land flowing with milk and honey, just as the Lord, the God of your ancestors, promised you.

[4] Hear, O Israel: The Lord our God, the Lord is one. Talk about them when you sit at home and when you walk along the road, when you lie down. 5. Love the Lord your God with all your heart and with all your soul and with all your strength. [6] These commandments that I give you today are to be on your hearts. [7] Impress them on your children when you lie down and when you get up. [8] Tie them as symbols on your hands and bind them on your foreheads. [9] Write them on the doorframes of your houses and on your gates. *(Pass the baton of faith to the next generation.)*

[10] When the Lord your God brings you into the land he swore to your fathers, to Abraham, Isaac and Jacob, to give you—a land with large, flourishing cities you did not build, [11] houses filled with all kinds of good things you did not provide, wells you did not dig, and vineyards and olive groves you did not plant—then when you eat and are satisfied, [12] be careful that you do not forget the Lord, who brought you out of Egypt, out of the land of slavery.

[13] Fear the Lord your God, serve him only. . . . [20] In the future, when your son asks you, "What is the meaning of the stipulations, decrees and laws the Lord our God has commanded you?" [21] tell him: "We were slaves of Pharaoh in Egypt, but the Lord brought us out of Egypt with a mighty hand. [22] Before our eyes the Lord sent signs and wonders—great and terrible—on Egypt and Pharaoh and his whole household. [23] But He brought us out from there to bring us in and give us the land he promised on oath to our ancestors. [24] The Lord commanded us to obey all these decrees and to fear the Lord our God, so that we might always prosper and be kept alive, as is the case today. [25] And if we are careful to obey all this law before the Lord our God, as He has commanded us, that will be our righteousness."

(We Christians of America must do exactly what God told the Israelites to do. Remember that it was God who made our country great and teach our children what was great about it. America was founded upon the Bible. The founding fathers were Christians. David Barton, founder of WallBuilders and collector of 70,000 documents written before 1812

says historical documents show our founding fathers go be Christians. We should also teach our children to obey all of the Commandments of the Lord, and He will be our righteousness.)

In Deuteronomy 7, God told the people that they <u>were not to make marriages with unbelievers.</u> *In Moses' address, he recalled the sins of the people of the past and told of God's faithfulness, regardless of their rebellion.*

Deuteronomy 10:12-13:: [12] And now, Israel, what does the Lord your God ask of you but to fear the Lord your God, to walk in obedience to Him, to love Him, to serve the Lord your God with all your heart and with all your soul, 13 and to observe the Lord's commands and decrees that I am giving you today for your own good?

God kept His promise to Abraham and the Israelites

Deuteronomy 10:22: Our ancestors who went down into Egypt were seventy in all, and now the Lord your God has made you as numerous as the stars in the sky.

Chapter 10
The tribe of Levi was separated the ark to bear.
For the tabernacle of the Lord, they are to care.
No inheritance was theirs to be,
For the Lord gave Himself abundantly.

God, through Moses, again and again told His people to teach the commandments to their children when they cross on the other side of Jordan. He told them to continue offering blood sacrifices for their sins.

Deuteronomy 12
God does not require our daughters or sons to burn.
Merely, to him with contrite heart, turn.
Christ has already paid in full the price. . .
Our bodies are to be a LIVING SACRIFICE.

13. When a brother says, "Other gods let us serve,"
God commands me to keep my nerve,
I must not consent or Him conceal.
The first stone I must cast, the idolater to kill.

Chapter 14 tells laws for food, what they should and should not eat.

Deut. 16:17: Every man shall give as he is able, according to the blessing of the Lord thy God which he hath given thee.

17. Better to be out of fashion than out of God's favor,
God's requirements of a king do not waver.
Every day of his life, he was to read the law,
Four things forbidden to kings, and Solomon did them all.
He was not to return to Egypt to multiply horses, money or wives
So he could prolong his and his children's lives.

18. From among your brethren a Prophet shall rise.
Those who hearken to him are wise.
The test of a prophet of which there are few,
What he speaks, that thing will come true.

19. One witness is not enough to establish the guilt of a man,
He was sentenced to death by the religious abuser,
Yet Christ had no one true accuser
Against Him to take a stand.

21. To be hung on a tree
Is the ultimate shame
Christ died there for all to see,
Accursed of God, although in Him is no blame.

Chapter 22 has laws for punishment of sexual sins. God hates sexual sin so much! Why? Because he loves us so much!
Verse 22: If a man is found sleeping with another man's wife, both the man who slept with her and the woman must die. You must purge the evil from Israel. *There are many laws about divorce in chapter 24. Why? Because God instituted the family and knows what is best for us.*

Deuteronomy 25
Thou shalt not muzzle the oxen when the corn they tread,
As one works, he is entitled to eat,
Pay those who labor amply for bread
And enough their obligations to meet.

26. God brought us out of Egypt with a mighty hand,
Flowing with milk and honey was the land.
The first fruits for my tithes I bring,
To God I now worship, praise, and sing.

27. Israel, thou art become the people of God this day,
His statues and commandments are etched in stone to stay.
On two mounts the people were to stand,
Curses and blessings were proclaimed throughout the land.

I have written in my Bible to put not only my country, but also my own family's names into the promises in Deuteronomy 38, which tells of God's protection for us and his promises of blessings.

Deut. 38:1: If you fully obey the L ORD your God and carefully follow all his commands I give you today, the L ORD your God will set you high above all the nations on earth. [2] All these blessings will come on you and accompany you if you obey the L ORD your God:

[3] You will be blessed in the city and blessed in the country. [4] The fruit of your womb will be blessed, and the crops of your land and the young of your livestock—the calves of your herds and the lambs of your flocks. [5] Your basket and your kneading trough will be blessed. [6] You will be blessed when you come in and blessed when you go out. . . . [9] The L ORD will establish you as his holy people, as he promised you on oath, if you keep the commands of the L ORD your God and walk in obedience to him. [10] Then all the peoples on earth will see that you are called by the name of the L ORD, and they will fear you. [11] The L ORD will grant you abundant prosperity—in the fruit of your womb, the young of your livestock and the crops of your ground—in the land He swore to your ancestors to give you.

What wonderful promises for us when we follow His commandments. This describes America during our first over 200 years The United States was birthed by God for the purpose of advancing the gospel of Jesus Christ unlike any other country in history. We never had to borrow from other countries. God blessed the work of our hands, just as he did Israel.

[12] The L ORD will open the heavens, the storehouse of his bounty, to send rain on your land in season and to bless all the work of your hands. You will lend to many nations but will borrow from none. [13] The L ORD will make you the head, not the tail. If you pay attention to the commands of the L ORD your God that I give you this day and carefully follow them, you will always be at the top, never at the bottom. [14] Do not turn aside from any of the commands I give you today, to the right or to the left, following other gods and serving them.

Curses for Disobedience:

Deuteronomy 28:15: However, if you do not obey the L ORD your God and do not carefully follow all his commands and decrees I am giving you today, all these curses will come on you and overtake you: [16] You will be cursed in the city and cursed in the country. [17] Your basket and your kneading trough will be cursed. [18] The fruit of your womb will be cursed, and the crops of your land, and the calves of your herds and the lambs of your flocks.

[20] The LORD will send on you curses, confusion and rebuke in everything you put your hand to, until you are destroyed and come to sudden ruin because of the evil you have done in forsaking him.[a] [21] The LORD will plague you with diseases. . . .[25] The LORD will cause you to be defeated before your enemies. You will be unsuccessful in everything you do, day after day you will be oppressed and robbed, with no one to rescue you.

[36] The LORD will drive you and the king you set over you to a nation unknown to you or your ancestors. There you will worship other gods, gods of wood and stone. [38] You will sow much seed in the field but you will harvest little, because locusts will devour it. . . .[41] You will have sons and daughters but you will not keep them, because they will go into captivity.

[43] The foreigners who reside among you will rise above you higher and higher, but you will sink lower and lower. [45] All these curses will come on you. They will pursue you and overtake you until you are destroyed, because you did not obey the LORD your God and observe the commands and decrees he gave you. [46] They will be a sign and a wonder to you and your descendants forever. [47] Because you did not serve the LORD your God joyfully and gladly in the time of prosperity,[48] therefore in hunger and thirst, in nakedness and dire poverty, you will serve the enemies the LORD sends against you.

What can we do to prevent the wrath of God? We can go to church; only 43% of Americans go to church. We can pray to God that he will send revival to America. We can build Christian Families. We can be active in the political arena, electing those who reflect the Christian Values. Hold high the standard of righteousness. Hide God's Word in your Heart!

[49] The LORD will bring a nation against you from far away, from the ends of the earth, like an eagle swooping down, a nation whose language you will not understand,. . .52 They will lay siege to all the cities throughout your land until the high fortified walls in which you trust fall [58] If you do not carefully follow all the words of this law, which are written in this book, and do not revere this glorious and awesome name—the LORD your God—[59] the LORD will send fearful plagues on you and your descendants, harsh and prolonged disasters, and severe and lingering illnesses. [61] The LORD will also bring on you every kind of sickness and disaster not recorded in this Book of the Law, until you are destroyed. [62] You who were as numerous as the stars in the sky will be left but few in number, because you did not obey the LORD your God. . . .You will be uprooted from the land you are entering to possess.

[64] Then the LORD will scatter you among all nations, from one end of the earth to the other. There you will worship other gods—gods of wood and stone, which neither you nor your ancestors have known. [65] Among those nations you will find no repose, no resting place for the sole of your foot.

Yes, God did scatter the Jews because of their disbelief.

Deuteronomy 28
Obey the law of God? What does it matter?
Among all people the Jew In disbelief, God did scatter.
Restless and sorrowful even until now,
I hope to Christ Jesus their knee will yet bow.

America, we must bow before the Lord!
In Chapter 31, Moses prepares to die. He commissioned Joshua in verses 6-8 and also in verse 23. *And he gave Joshua a charge and said, be strong and of good courage, for thou shalt bring the children of Israel into the land which I swore unto them: and I will be with thee.*

In Chapter 32, Moses sings a song of praise to God, as he recalls his life. In chapter 33, Moses blesses Israel.

Deuteronomy 33
My refuge is God eternal,
Underneath is his everlasting arm.
The Lord's shield and sword are my arsenal.
He thrusts out my enemies so they can do me no harm.

The Death of Moses: Chapter 34, KJV: *At 120 years, Moses went to the top of Mount Pisgah, and the Lord showed him all the land that He had sworn to Abraham and to their seed. Moses died and the Lord buried him in the land of Moab.* [10] And there arose not a prophet since in Israel like unto Moses, whom the LORD knew face to face, [11] In all the signs and the wonders, which the LORD sent him to do in the land of Egypt to Pharaoh, and to all his servants, and to all his land, [12] And in all that mighty hand, and in all the great terror which Moses shewed in the sight of all Israel. *Moses had written the Pentateuch, the first five books of the Bible. Moses put all of this together in a book and gave them to Joshua. This is the Book of Law.*

In Heaven, other than Jesus, Moses is the person with whom I want most to talk!

"The constant reading of God's written Word to the people is the safest and most effective way to guard against the corruption of their religion. . .The Reformation began when Luther read the Word of God. God's Word is the power of the Human heart. . .Oh, that the present day pulpit would somehow learn to keep itself in the background while putting God's Word in the foreground" (Halley, 2007, page 173)

The Books of History are Joshua, Judges, Ruth, I and II Samuel, I and II Kings, I and II Chronicles, Ezra, Nehemiah, Esther, and Job.

THE BOOK OF JOSHUA
In Joshua, Jesus is Salvation's Choice

Theme: Obedience brings long awaited victory in the Promised Land.

Savior, Joshua, Jehovah, Jesus:
They are all the same.
From different languages so numerous
Deliverer is the name.

Summary: In Joshua, we begin to see the conquest and settlement of Canaan. Joshua recorded the Israelite conquest of the land of Canaan under the leadership of Joshua, the successor of Moses. God had promised to Abraham that his descendants would possess the land of Canaan. God fought for the Israelites and blessed them when they were obedient. God had a moral purpose in allowing the wicked Canaanites to be destroyed. The book opens when the Israelites are camped on the east side of the Jordan River. God commanded the people to pass through the Jordan on dry land. A series of military victories, including the miraculous fall of Jericho, for the 12 tribes is recorded. The book ends with Joshua's charge to the people before his death. (Halley, 2007; FCA, 2005)

Joshua Chapter 1: After the death of Moses the servant of the Lord, the Lord said to Joshua son of Nun, Moses' aide: [2] "Moses My servant is dead. Now then, you and all these people, get ready to cross the Jordan River into the land I am about to give to them—to the Israelites. [3] I will give you every place where you set your foot, as I promised Moses. . .I will never leave you nor forsake you. [6] Be strong and courageous, because you will lead these people to inherit the land I swore to their ancestors to give them. How does Joshua foreshadow Jesus? Joshua was the leader who led the people to the Promised Land. Jesus will lead us to The Promised Land of Heaven.

[7] "Be strong and very courageous. Be careful to obey all the law My servant Moses gave you; do not turn from it to the right or to the left, that you may be successful wherever you go. [8] Keep this Book of the Law always on your lips; meditate on it day and night, so that you may be careful to do everything written in it. Then you will be prosperous and successful.

(*This is God's plan for us today. If we obey the laws of God and meditate upon his word, we are promised that we will be successful.*)

The Scarlet Thread: The origin of this term, the scarlet thread, is found in Joshua 2:18. In chapter 2, Joshua sent 2 spies to Jericho before they were planning to invade the land. A prostitute, named Rahab, saved the lives of the 2 spies. She had heard of how the Lord had dried up the Red Sea for them and had heard of the Plagues of Egypt, and she knew they served God above. They, in turn, promised to protect her and her family when the Israelites returned to conquer them. She let them down out of her window over the wall with a scarlet cord. They told her to place a line of scarlet thread in that same window and promised that her whole family would be saved.

*Rahab professed faith in the Israelites' God. Her faith is recalled twice in the New Testament (*Hebrews 11:31; James 2:25*) Faith in God has always been a criterion for salvation, just as the scarlet thread has become the symbol for the blood of Christ, through which we obtain salvation.*

In WA Criswell's famous 4 ½ hour New Years' Eve sermon, The Scarlet Thread of Redemption, he used Joshua 2:18 as his beginning text.

Dr. W. A. Criswell said, "Rahab the harlot is an example of the grace of God at work. Her salvation was not based on her character or merit. She acted upon faith and was spared the judgment of God which was executed at the hands of the Israelites. In addition to her deliverance, Rahab was rewarded beyond measure. . . .Rahab became the mother of Boaz and ancestress of David in the Messianic line of those who were the ancestors of Jesus. Throughout the Bible 'scarlet' speaks of sacrifice made on the behalf of the believer, and it is seen in the vestments of the tabernacle and in the priestly garments in Exodus." Rahab was saved from destruction because she had enough faith in God to hang a red rope out of her window. This blood-red rope is a type (or picture) of the blood-red scarlet thread that runs through the Bible, from Genesis to Revelation."

When preparing to finally cross the Jordan River into the Promised Land, Joshua told the people:

Joshua 3: When you see the ark of the covenant of the Lord your God, and the Levitical priests carrying it, you are to move out from your positions and follow it. [6] Joshua said to the priests, "Take up the ark of the covenant and pass on ahead of the people." So they took it up and went ahead of them.

[7] And the Lord said to Joshua, "Today I will begin to exalt you in the eyes of all Israel, so they may know that I am with you as I was with Moses. [8] Tell the priests who carry the Ark of the Covenant: 'When you reach the edge of the Jordan's waters, go and stand in the river.'"

[9] Joshua said to the Israelites, "Come here and listen to the words of the Lord your God. [10] This is how you will know that the living God is among you and that He will certainly drive out before you the Canaanites, Hittites, Hivites, Perizzites, Girgashites, Amorites and Jebusites. [11] See, the Ark of the Covenant of the Lord of all the earth will go into the Jordan ahead of you. [12] Now then, choose twelve men from the tribes of Israel, one from each tribe. [13] And as soon as the priests who carry the ark of the Lord—the Lord of all the earth—set foot in the Jordan, its waters flowing downstream will be cut off and stand up in a heap."

[14] So when the people broke camp to cross the Jordan, the priests carrying the Ark of the Covenant went ahead of them. [15] Now the Jordan is at flood stage all during harvest. Yet as soon as the priests who carried the ark reached the Jordan and their feet touched the water's edge, [16] the water from upstream stopped flowing. It piled up in a heap a great distance away, at a town called Adam in the vicinity of Zarethan, while the water flowing down to the Sea of the Arabah (that is, the Dead Sea) was completely cut off. So the people crossed over opposite Jericho. [17] The priests who carried the ark of the covenant of the Lord stopped in the middle of the Jordan and stood on dry ground, while all Israel passed by until the whole nation had completed the crossing on dry ground.

Joshua Chapter 4:1. When the whole nation had finished crossing the Jordan, the Lord said to Joshua, [2] "Choose twelve men from among the people, one from each tribe, [3] and tell them to take up twelve stones from the middle of the Jordan, from right where the priests are standing, and carry them over with you and put them down at the place where you stay tonight."

[4] So Joshua called together the twelve men he had appointed from the Israelites, one from each tribe, [5] and said to them, "Go over before the ark of the Lord your God into the middle of the Jordan. Each of you is to take up a stone on his shoulder, according to the number of the tribes of the Israelites, [6] to serve as a sign among you. In the future, when your children ask you, 'What do these stones mean?' [7] tell them that the flow of the Jordan was cut off before the ark of the covenant of the Lord. When it crossed the Jordan, the waters of the Jordan were cut off. These stones are to be a memorial to the people of Israel forever."

[8] So the Israelites did as Joshua commanded them. They took twelve stones from the middle of the Jordan, according to the number of the tribes of the Israelites, as the Lord had told Joshua; and they carried them over with them to their camp, where they put them down. [9] Joshua set up the twelve stones that had been in the middle of the Jordan at the spot where the priests who carried the Ark of the Covenant had stood. And they are there to this day.

[10] Now the priests who carried the ark remained standing in the middle of the Jordan until everything the Lord had commanded Joshua was done by the people, just as Moses had directed Joshua. The people hurried over, [11] and as soon as all of them had crossed, the ark of the Lord and the priests came to the other side while the people watched. [12] The men of Reuben, Gad and the half-tribe of Manasseh crossed over, ready for battle, in front of the Israelites, as Moses had directed them. [13] About forty thousand armed for battle crossed over before the Lord to the plains of Jericho for war.

[14] That day the Lord exalted Joshua in the sight of all Israel; and they stood in awe of him all the days of his life, just as they had stood in awe of Moses. [15] Then the Lord said to Joshua, [16] "Command the priests carrying the Ark of the Covenant law to come up out of the Jordan." [17] So Joshua commanded the priests, "Come up out of the Jordan." [18] And the

priests came up out of the river carrying the ark of the covenant of the Lord. No sooner had they set their feet on the dry ground than the waters of the Jordan returned to their place and ran at flood stage as before.

[20] And Joshua set up at Gilgal the twelve stones they had taken out of the Jordan. [21] He said to the Israelites, "In the future when your descendants ask their parents, 'What do these stones mean?' [22] tell them, 'Israel crossed the Jordan on dry ground.' [23] For the Lord your God dried up the Jordan before you until you had crossed over. The Lord your God did to the Jordan what He had done to the Red Sea when he dried it up before us until we had crossed over. [24] He did this so that all the peoples of the earth might know that the hand of the Lord is powerful and so that you might always fear the Lord your God."

The Walls of Jericho Came Tumbling Down! *How many times I've told this story to children! We've dramatized it and have built the walls in many ways. No fiction story can be as exciting as a real history story, especially one with eternals significance! Also, in the character of Joshua, we see a foreshadowing of Jesus Christ. The children's book, "Jesus Story Book Bible," by S. L. Jones, tells us that Joshua is a picture of Jesus Christ. Joshua took the people to the Promised Land. Jesus will take us to the Promised Land of Heaven.* I highly recommend this book to you because it shows how most of the characters of the Bible are pictures of Jesus!

Joshua was going to lead the Children of Israel to a new and beautiful land. The children were excited! But there was one barrier: The City of Jericho had enormous walls around it. God said, "I'll always be with you." It wasn't with their army or by fighting that they took the city. It was by doing what God said.

Joshua, Chapter 6:1: Now the gates of Jericho were securely barred because of the Israelites. No one went out and no one came in.[2] Then the Lord said to Joshua, "See, I have delivered Jericho into your hands, along with its king and its fighting men. [3] March around the city once with all the armed men. Do this for six days. [4] Have seven priests carry trumpets of rams' horns in front of the ark. On the seventh day, march around the city seven times, with the priests blowing the trumpets.[5] When you hear them sound a long blast on the trumpets, have the whole army give a loud shout; then the wall of the city will collapse and the army will go up, everyone straight in."

[6] So Joshua son of Nun called the priests and said to them, "Take up the ark of the covenant of the Lord and have seven priests carry trumpets in front of it." [7] And he ordered the army, "Advance! March around the city, with an armed guard going ahead of the ark of the Lord."

[8] When Joshua had spoken to the people, the seven priests carrying the seven trumpets before the Lord went forward, blowing their trumpets, and the ark of the Lord's covenant followed them. [9] The armed guard marched ahead of the priests who blew the trumpets, and the rear guard followed the ark. All this time the trumpets were sounding. [10] But Joshua had commanded the army, "Do not give a war cry, do not raise your voices and do not say a

word until the day I tell you to shout. Then shout!" [11] So he had the ark of the Lord carried around the city, circling it once. Then the army returned to camp and spent the night there. [12] Joshua got up early the next morning and the priests took up the ark of the Lord. [13] The seven priests carrying the seven trumpets went forward, marching before the ark of the Lord and blowing the trumpets. The armed men went ahead of them and the rear guard followed the ark of the Lord, while the trumpets kept sounding. [14] So on the second day they marched around the city once and returned to the camp. They did this for six days.

[15] On the seventh day, they got up at daybreak and marched around the city seven times in the same manner, except that on that day they circled the city seven times. [16] The seventh time around, when the priests sounded the trumpet blast, Joshua commanded the army, "Shout! For the Lord has given you the city! [17] The city and all that is in it are to be devoted to the Lord. Only Rahab the prostitute and all who are with her in her house shall be spared, because she hid the spies we sent. [18] But keep away from the devoted things, so that you will not bring about your own destruction by taking any of them. Otherwise you will make the camp of Israel liable to destruction and bring trouble on it. [19] All the silver and gold and the articles of bronze and iron are sacred to the Lord and must go into his treasury."

[20] When the trumpets sounded, the army shouted, and at the sound of the trumpet, when the men gave a loud shout, the wall collapsed; so everyone charged straight in, and they took the city. [21] They devoted the city to the Lord and destroyed with the sword every living thing in it—except for Rahab and her family. When they saw the Scarlet Cord in the window, her family was carried to safety in Joshua 6:23.

[27] So the Lord was with Joshua, and his fame spread throughout the land.

But we find in chapters 7 and 8 that Israel did not trust in God, nor did they obey His commandments. Against the commandments of God, they took stuff from those they had conquered. Then in Chapter 8, Joshua read all of the laws from Moses to the Children of Israel. Then as natives of Canaan heard of the fame of Joshua, they wanted an alliance with Joshua, and Joshua signed peace treaties with wicked people, though God had instructed that they should not do this.

But when Joshua and the Israelites obeyed God, again and again, God showed His might. He even caused the sun to stand still until Israel could defeat its enemy.

Moses had told the Israelites that everywhere their feet had trodden would be their inheritance, and in Joshua 11:23: So Joshua took the whole land, according to all that the Lord had spoken to Moses. And Joshua gave it for an inheritance to Israel according to their tribal allotments. And the land had rest from war.

Remember that not only Joshua, but also Caleb, was a faithful spy who believed God. Chapter 14 tells of all the ways God blessed Caleb for his faithfulness.

Other key passages of significance to Joshua and to our lives today include: Joshua 22:5: But be very careful to keep the commandment and the law that Moses the servant of the Lord gave you: to love the Lord your God, to walk in obedience to Him, to keep His commands, to hold fast to Him and to serve Him with all your heart and with all your soul."

Joshua 23:6-8: "Be very strong; be careful to obey all that is written in the Book of the Law of Moses, without turning aside to the right or to the left. [7] Do not associate with these nations that remain among you; do not invoke the names of their gods or swear by them. You must not serve them or bow down to them. [8] But you are to hold fast to the LORD your God, as you have until now.

After Joshua gathered the people together and reviewed all the Lord had done for them from the time of Abraham through the conquering of Canaan, God said in Joshua 24:13-31 [13] So I gave you a land on which you did not toil and cities you did not build; and you live in them and eat from vineyards and olive groves that you did not plant.' [14] "Now fear the LORD and serve him with all faithfulness. Throw away the gods your ancestors worshiped beyond the Euphrates River and in Egypt, and serve the LORD. [15] But if serving the LORD seems undesirable to you, then choose for yourselves this day whom you will serve, whether the gods your ancestors served beyond the Euphrates, or the gods of the Amorites, in whose land you are living. But as for me and my household, we will serve the LORD." *Please, men, fathers, mothers, make this proclamation today!*

[16] Then the people answered, "Far be it from us to forsake the LORD to serve other gods! [17] It was the LORD our God Himself who brought us and our parents up out of Egypt, from that land of slavery, and performed those great signs before our eyes. He protected us on our entire journey and among all the nations through which we traveled. [18] And the LORD drove out before us all the nations, including the Amorites, who lived in the land. We too will serve the LORD, because He is our God."

[19] Joshua said to the people, "You are not able to serve the LORD. He is a holy God; he is a jealous God. He will not forgive your rebellion and your sins. [20] If you forsake the LORD and serve foreign gods, he will turn and bring disaster on you and make an end of you, after he has been good to you." [21] But the people said to Joshua, "No! We will serve the LORD."

[23] "Now then," said Joshua, "throw away the foreign gods that are among you and yield your hearts to the LORD, the God of Israel."

[24] And the people said to Joshua, "We will serve the LORD our God and obey Him."

31 And Israel served the Lord all the days of Joshua. . . .

Could not this same story be rewritten for America? Look at the wonderful and great things the Lord has done for us! Greater miracles have we not seen? We have hind sight and should know that if we serve God, he will bless us. If we forsake God, He will forsake us. But He will be faithful to us, if only we who believe on him will turn from our wicked ways!

THE BOOK OF JUDGES
In Judges, Jesus is the Lawgiver.

The Israelites had the law of God to govern them, and they had the gospel of the promised Savior to give them hope.

Theme: God is merciful and longsuffering despite the sin of his people.

When God's people, the Israelites, came to the Promised Land of Canaan, they only needed to obey God. They had everything they needed to be happy. While Joshua lived, they lived victorious lives. Although surrounded by enemies, they had constant victory because they remained true to God.

But soon they followed the sinful example of the Canaanites. Their sin led to the following cycle that we see throughout the book of Judges: 1. They rebelled against God. 2. God raised up foreign oppressors to chasten his people. 3. A prayer goes up to God from the Israelites. 4. God raised up a deliverer, or judge, who took up arms to defend the homeland and rescue the repentant people. The book shows that even in dark times, God is in control. (Shepperson, 1986)

Judges 2: 10B – 11, 16, KJV: There arose another generation after them, which knew not the Lord nor the works which He had done for Israel. *(Remember, God had said that they must always teach the next generation.)* 11. And the Children of Israel did evil in the sight of the Lord and served Baalim. 16. Nevertheless the Lord raised up judges that delivered them out of the hand of those that oppressed them. The first judge was Othniel. God used him for forty years.

But God's people took wives from among the evil Canaanites. They did evil over and over.

Judges 3:9: And when the children of Israel cried unto the Lord, the Lord raised up a deliverer to the children of Israel. *The period of the Judges could be described in 5 words: Idolatry, bondage, repentance, delivery, rest.*

In Judges 4 and 5, God allowed the Canaanites to oppress Israel, and God raised up a woman judge, Deborah, a prophetess. Read the exciting story of this brave and wise woman who worshipped God. She reminded the people of God's commands, and the people respected her.

She marched with 10,000 volunteers and defeated the Canaanites. And the land rested for 40 years.

Gideon! Children love to dramatize the story of Gideon.

Read the story of Gideon in Joshua chapters 6, 7, and 8. Again Israel began to build altars and worship gods of wood, stone, and metal. God allowed the Midianites to destroy the crops of Israel.

Judges 6:6: Israel was greatly impoverished because of the Midianites, and the children of Israel cried unto the Lord. *(God called Gideon, the youngest of the lowest of families. Gideon could not believe God, and when you hear the term, "throwing out the fleece," you will know it comes from Judges 6:36-40, when Gideon had to have proof that God would really call and use him.) Yes, Gideon is to be a picture of Jesus Christ, as he is the deliverer of his people. The spirit of the Lord came upon Gideon and filled him with courage. He blew a trumpet and sent messengers throughout the land and 32,000 came to fight against 135, 000 Midianites.*

Judges 7:2, KJV: And the LORD said unto Gideon, The people that are with thee are too many for me to give the Midianites into their hands, lest Israel vaunt themselves against Me, saying, Mine own hand hath saved me.

3: Now therefore go to, proclaim in the ears of the people, saying, whosoever is fearful and afraid, let him return and depart early from mount Gilead. And there returned of the people twenty and two thousand; and there remained ten thousand.

4: And the LORD said unto Gideon, The people are yet too many; bring them down unto the water, and I will try them for thee there: and it shall be, that of whom I say unto thee, This shall go with thee, the same shall go with thee; and of whomsoever I say unto thee, This shall not go with thee, the same shall not go.

(This past year, a group of 20 children dramatized Gideon, and a large group of them lined up at our pond; some of them bowed down on their knees, and some sat up to watch with their water in their hands. This was videoed and was shown to the church. They were so cute.)

5: So he brought down the people unto the water: and the LORD said unto Gideon, Every one that lappeth of the water with his tongue, as a dog lappeth, him shalt thou set by himself; likewise every one that boweth down upon his knees to drink.

6: And the number of them that lapped, putting their hand to their mouth, was three hundred men: but all the rest of the people bowed down upon their knees to drink water.

7: And the LORD said unto Gideon, "By the three hundred men that lapped will I save you, and deliver the Midianites into thine hand: and let all the other people go every man unto his place."

God devised a plan that is so exciting for children to dramatize.

Judges 7:15: (Gideon said) Arise; for the LORD hath delivered into your hand the host of Median. *16:* And he divided the three hundred men into three companies, and he put a trumpet in every man's hand, with empty pitchers, and lamps within the pitchers.

17: And he said unto them, Look on me, and do likewise: and, behold, when I come to the outside of the camp, it shall be that, as I do, so shall ye do.

18: When I blow with a trumpet, I and all that are with me, then blow ye the trumpets also on every side of all the camp, and say, "The sword of the LORD, and of Gideon."

19: So Gideon, and the hundred men that were with him, came unto the outside of the camp in the beginning of the middle watch; and they had but newly set the watch: and they blew the trumpets, and brake the pitchers that were in their hands.

20: And the three companies blew the trumpets, and broke the pitchers, and held the lamps in their left hands, and the trumpets in their right hands to blow withal: and they cried, "The sword of the LORD, and of Gideon!"

21: And they stood every man in his place round about the camp: and all the host ran, and cried, and fled.

22: And the three hundred blew the trumpets, and the LORD set every man's sword against his fellow, even throughout all the host: and the host fled. . . .

For 40 years the people served the Lord, but when Gideon died, the people turned from God to idolatry. God raised up another exciting judge:

Samson, the strongest man who ever lived.

Judges 13:1-24: And the children of Israel did evil again in the sight of the LORD; and the LORD delivered them into the hand of the Philistines forty years.

2: And there was a certain man of Zorah, of the family of the Danites, whose name was Manoah; and his wife was barren, and bare not.

3: And the angel of the LORD appeared unto the woman, and said unto her, Behold now, thou art barren, and bearest not: but thou shalt conceive, and bear a son.

4: Now therefore beware, I pray thee, and drink not wine nor strong drink, and eat not any unclean thing:

5: For, lo, thou shalt conceive, and bear a son; and no razor shall come on his head: for the child shall be a Nazarite unto God from the womb: and He shall begin to deliver Israel out of the hand of the Philistines.

6: Then the woman came and told her husband, saying, A man of God came unto me, and his countenance was like the countenance of an angel of God, very terrible: but I asked him not whence he was, neither told he me his name:

7: But he said unto me, Behold, thou shalt conceive, and bear a son; and now drink no wine nor strong drink, neither eat any unclean thing: for the child shall be a Nazarite to God from the womb to the day of his death. *14:* She may not eat of any thing that cometh of the vine, neither let her drink wine or strong drink, nor eat any unclean thing: all that I commanded her let her observe. (*Also, to carry out the Nazarite vow, 3 things were necessary: Samson was not to drink wine, not touch any dead body, and not cut his hair.*)

24: And the woman bare a son, and called his name Samson: and the child grew, and the LORD blessed him.

(God blessed Samson with supernatural strength. And two natures began to work, the divine nature and his own selfish nature, just like every child of God. His parents taught him, but he saw a woman of the Philistines:)

Judges 14:2: 1: And Samson went down to Timnath, and saw a woman in Timnath of the daughters of the Philistines.

2: And he came up, and told his father and his mother, and said, I have seen a woman in Timnath of the daughters of the Philistines: now therefore get her for me to wife.

3: Then his father and his mother said unto him, is there never a woman among the daughters of thy brethren, or among all my people, that thou goest to take a wife of the uncircumcised Philistines? And Samson said unto his father; Get her for me; for she pleaseth me well.

(Then we read in verses 5-8 that Samson encountered a lion while on the way to Timnath and he killed the lion with his bare hands. Then when he returned the carcass of the lion had bees and honey in it, and they ate it. His parents didn't know where the honey came from.)

5: Then went Samson down, and his father and his mother, to Timnath, and came to the vineyards of Timnath: and, behold, a young lion roared against him.

6: And the Spirit of the LORD came mightily upon him, and he rent him as he would have rent a kid, and he had nothing in his hand: but he told not his father or his mother what he had done.

7: And he went down, and talked with the woman; and she pleased Samson well.

8: And after a time he returned to take her, and he turned aside to see the carcass of the lion: and, behold, there was a swarm of bees and honey in the carcass of the lion.

9: And he took thereof in his hands, and went on eating, and came to his father and mother, and he gave them, and they did eat: but he told not them that he had taken the honey out *the lion and the honey for the young men of the enemy. His pride led to his downfall. His* of the carcass of the lion.

He married the woman, and at the wedding feast, in verses 11-20, *Samson made a riddle about wife told them the answer to the riddle, and he got even by killing 30 Philistine men. But disobedience brought sorrow. God had chosen Samson to the highest place in the land. He went everywhere he should not go. His wife got him into much trouble.*

10: So his father went down unto the woman: and Samson made there a feast; for so used the young men to do. 11: And it came to pass, when they saw him, that they brought thirty companions to be with him. 12: And Samson said unto them, I will now put forth a riddle unto you: if ye can certainly declare it me within the seven days of the feast, and find it out, then I will give you thirty sheets and thirty change of garments: 13: But if ye cannot declare it me, then shall ye give me thirty sheets and thirty changes of garments. And they said unto him, Put forth thy riddle, that we may hear it.

14: And he said unto them, Out of the eater came forth meat, and out of the strong came forth sweetness. And they could not in three days expound the riddle. 15: And it came to pass on the seventh day, that they said unto Samson's wife, Entice thy husband, that he may declare unto us the riddle. . .

When the wife told the answer of the riddle to them, Samson was angry:

19: And the Spirit of the LORD came upon him, and he went down to Ashkelon, and slew thirty men of them, and took their spoil, and gave change of garments unto them which expounded the riddle. And his anger was kindled, and he went up to his father's house.

20: But Samson's wife was given to his companion, whom he had used as his friend.

Samson never used his strength wisely:

Judges 15:4: And Samson went and caught three hundred foxes, and took firebrands, and turned tail to tail, and put a firebrand in the midst between two tails.

5: And when he had set the brands on fire, he let them go into the standing corn of the Philistines, and burnt up both the shocks, and also the standing corn, with the vineyards and olives.

6: Then the Philistines said, Who hath done this? And they answered, Samson.

(Then they came to capture Samson and bound him with new ropes)

13. And they bound him with two new cords, and brought him up from the rock. *14:* And when he came unto Lehi, the Philistines shouted against him: and the Spirit of the LORD came mightily upon him, and the cords that were upon his arms became as flax that was burnt with fire, and his bands loosed from off his hands. *15:* And he found a new jawbone of an ass, and put forth his hand, and took it, and slew a thousand men therewith. *16:* And Samson said, "With the jawbone of an ass, heaps upon heaps, with the jaw of an ass have I slain a thousand men.

For 20 years, Samson had conflicts with the Philistines and overpowered them on many occasions. As long as Samson was alive, they could not oppress Israel.

The best-known is the story of Samson and Delilah. The Philistines wanted to know where Samson's strength lay. They enticed Delilah to find out from Samson. Again, he showed weakness. After much enticement from Delilah –

Judges 16: *15:* And she said unto him, "How canst thou say, I love thee, when thine heart is not with me? Thou hast mocked me these three times, and hast not told me wherein thy great strength lieth." *16:* And it came to pass, when she pressed him daily with her words, and urged him, so that his soul was vexed unto death; *17:* That he told her all his heart, and said unto her. There hath not come a razor upon mine head; for I have been a Nazarite unto God from my mother's womb: if I be shaven, then my strength will go from me, and I shall become weak, and be like any other man.

18: And when Delilah saw that he had told her all his heart, she sent and called for the lords of the Philistines, saying, Come up this once, for he hath shown me all his heart. Then the lords of the Philistines came up unto her, and brought money in their hand. *19:* And she made him sleep upon her knees; and she called for a man, and she caused him to shave off the seven locks of his head; and she began to afflict him, and his strength went from him. *20:* And she said, The Philistines be upon thee, Samson. And he awoke out of his sleep, and said, I will go out as at other times before, and shake myself. And he wist not that the LORD was departed from him.

21: But the Philistines took him, and put out his eyes, and brought him down to Gaza, and bound him with fetters of brass; and he did grind in the prison house. *22:* Howbeit the hair of his head began to grow again after he was shaven.

(When the worshippers of Dagon gathered in their temple, they called Samson from the prison house to make sport of him and set him between two pillars.)

Judges 16:27, KJV: Now the house was full of men and women; and all the lords of the Philistines were there; and there were upon the roof about three thousand men and women that beheld while Samson made sport.

Samson killed more wicked Philistines in his death than in his life.

28: And Samson called unto the LORD, and said, O Lord GOD, remember me, I pray thee, and strengthen me, I pray thee, only this once, O God, that I may be at once avenged of the Philistines for my two eyes. *29:* And Samson took hold of the two middle pillars upon which the house stood, and on which it was borne up, of the one with his right hand, and of the other with his left. *30:* And Samson said, Let me die with the Philistines. And he bowed himself with all his might; and the house fell upon the lords, and upon all the people that were therein. So the dead which he slew at his death were more than they which he slew in his life. He judged Israel twenty years.

What wasted talent! Samson could have been the greatest man in history had he not obeyed his own desires rather than obeying God. Judges 21:25: In those days there was no king in Israel: every man did that which was right in his own eyes. *God had been king of Israel! Very soon, in I Samuel, the people will demand an earthly king.*

THE BOOK OF RUTH

In Ruth, Jesus is the Kinsman Redeemer.

Theme: Divine providence and human loyalty in one family and the legal procedure of kinsman-redeemer illustrate the **Biblical theme of redemption.**

Message: The Hebrew word for redemption occurs 23 times in the book of Ruth. What a contrast between the turbulent storms of Judges and the calm, lovely story of a lovely woman! In this dramatic love story, we see an illustration of God's self-giving love. Ruth, who is not a Jew, is a person that God loves. In fact, the lineage of David and then of Jesus will come from Ruth. (Halley, 2007)

Ruth 1:1, KJV: Now it came to pass, in the days when the judges ruled, that there was a famine in the land. And a certain man of Bethlehem, Judah, went to dwell in the country of Moab, he and his wife and his two sons. [2] The name of the man *was* Elimelech; the name of his wife *was* Naomi. *(They had 2 sons; Elimelech died. The two sons took wives in Moab. One was Ruth. Then both sons died.)*

Naomi Returns to Judah with Ruth: *Naomi told her two daughters-in-law that she would return to Judah but that they must return to their mothers' homes.*

Ruth 1:9, KJV: So she kissed them, and they lifted up their voices and wept.

[16] But Ruth said: "Entreat me not to leave you, *Or to* turn back from following after you; For wherever you go, I will go; And wherever you lodge, I will lodge; Your people *shall be* my people, And your God, my God.

[17] Where you die, I will die, and there will I be buried. The Lord do so to me, and more also, If *anything but* death parts you and me."

(These words, "Wheresoever thou goest, I will go" are now words to a favorite song for weddings.)

[22] So Naomi returned, and Ruth the Moabitess her daughter-in-law with her. . . .Now they came to Bethlehem at the beginning of barley harvest.

Ruth 2:1, KJV: And Naomi had a kinsman of her husband's, a mighty man of wealth, of the family of Elimelech; and his name was Boaz. 2 And Ruth the Moabitess said unto Naomi, Let me now go to the field, and glean ears of corn after him in whose sight I shall find grace.3 And she went, and came, and gleaned in the field after the reapers on a part of the field belonging unto Boaz, who was of the kindred of Elimelech. 4 And, behold, Boaz came from Bethlehem, and said unto the reapers. . ."Whose damsel is this?" *(Boaz was told that she was the daughter-in-law of Naomi.)*

2:8 Then said Boaz unto Ruth, Hearest thou not, my daughter? Go not to glean in another field, neither go from hence, but abide here fast by my maidens: 9 Let thine eyes be on the field that they do reap, and go thou after them: have I not charged the young men that they shall not touch thee? and when thou art athirst, go unto the vessels, and drink of that which the young men have drawn.

2:10 Then she fell on her face, and bowed herself to the ground, and said unto him, Why have I found grace in thine eyes, that thou shouldest take knowledge of me, seeing I am a stranger? 2:11 And Boaz answered and said unto her, It hath fully been shewed me, all that thou hast done unto thy mother in law since the death of thine husband: and how thou hast left thy father and thy mother, and the land of thy nativity, and art come unto a people which thou knowest not heretofore. 2:12 The LORD recompense thy work, and a full reward be given thee of the LORD God of Israel, under whose wings thou art come to trust.

According to Halley (2007), Boaz becomes the kinsman-redeemer for Ruth and Naomi. Boaz declares the redemption before 10 witnesses so there would be no question of the integrity of his actions.

In Boaz' kindness we see an illustration of God's self-giving love. Later, Ruth and Boaz marry.

Ruth 4:13: [13] So Boaz took Ruth and she became his wife; and when he went in to her, the Lord gave her conception, and she bore a son. And they called his name Obed. He *is* the father of Jesse, the father of David. Note the genealogy of David in Ruth 4:17-32.

The Scarlet Thread: *God had told Abraham he would be the father of a great nation and that through his descendants, the entire world would be blessed. Jesus was born of the lineage of Abraham,. Isaac, and Jacob, but also, through the bloodline of Ruth and Boaz, would come the Messiah for all nations. Boaz was a descendant of Rahab, the prostitute. Remember, Rahab is the one who put the scarlet cord up, which saved the Israelite spies. Rahab and Ruth, neither of them Israelites, became part of God's promise just like we do—through faith and commitment to God.*

Ruth Chapters 1 – 4:
Ruth's sacrificial love
Was the king Christ portrayed.
Leaving family and home, He came from above
Journeying as a stranger in a foreign land unafraid.

Boaz allowed Ruth to glean in his field
Of the barley grain held in its yield.
He protected her from unruly men.
To this loving kinsman it mattered not her origin.

Go as Ruth to the redeemer's feet
As your elders tell you to.
You'll find love and food to eat,
Plus a life that is blessed and new.

Boaz purchased Ruth for a wife
Giving Naomi a new lease on life.
Unto him was born a son, Obed,
Whose seed would relieve the world of sin and dread.

Note that the field belonging to Boaz, in which Ruth gleaned, was near Bethlehem. It was here that hundreds of years later, angels announced to shepherds the birth of Ruth's descendant, Jesus! (Halley, 2007)

THE BOOK OF FIRST SAMUEL

In Samuel, Jesus is our trusted prophet.

<u>Theme:</u> The prophet, Samuel, and the first king, Saul.

<u>Message:</u> A major transition occurred for Israel. Israel had been a theocracy, ruled by God and by judges. Israel now demanded an earthly king. Around 1050 BC, Samuel, the last judge, anointed Saul as Israel's first king. Then he anointed David to succeed Saul. We see that the Bible tells both the good and the bad of all its characters. Samuel, David, and Saul are highlighted. Saul self-destructs. Samuel stood firm and godly as the prophet of God. David, the man after God's own heart, is youthful, courageous, and popular, always abounding in faith in the almighty God in the context of constant warfare. God is seen as the rejected king, revealer of the unknown and the deliverer of His people. (FCA: God's Game Plan, 2008)

I Samuel begins with the birth of Samuel. Hannah longed for a baby boy so much that she promised God to give him forever to his service if God would answer her prayer.

I Samuel 1, KJV: And she made a vow, saying, "Lord Almighty, if you will only look on your servant's misery and remember me, and not forget your servant but give her a son, then I will give him to the Lord for all the days of his life. . . ." [20] So in the course of time Hannah became pregnant and gave birth to a son. She named him Samuel, saying, "Because I asked the Lord for him."

[24] After he was weaned, she took Samuel with her, young as he was, along with a three-year-old bull, an epha of flour and a skin of wine, and brought him to the house of the Lord at Shiloh. [25] When the bull had been sacrificed, they brought the boy to Eli, [26] and she said to him, "Pardon me, my lord. As surely as you live, I am the woman who stood here beside you praying to the Lord. [27] I prayed for this child, and the Lord has granted me what I asked of Him. [28] So now I give him to the Lord. For his whole life he will be given over to the Lord."

I Samuel 2:18: But Samuel ministered before the Lord, being a child, girded with a linen ephod. 19: His mother made him a little coat and brought it to him from year to year, when she came up with her husband to offer the yearly sacrifice.

Samuel chapter 2 reveals the sins of the sons of Eli, the priest. They did not know the Lord. It seems that Eli was too permissive a father. Young Samuel is the person God used to set the matter straight. (Again, I will choose stories that children love for emphasis for this book. Not only am I picturing my grandchildren, but also their future children.)

I Samuel 3:1: Now the boy Samuel ministered to the Lord before Eli. . . .And it came to pass at that time, while Eli *was* lying down in his place, and when his eyes had begun to grow so dim that he could not see,. . .and while Samuel was lying down, [4] that the Lord called Samuel. And he answered, "Here I am!" [5] So he ran to Eli and said, "Here I am, for you called me."

And he said, "I did not call; lie down again." And he went and lay down. [6] Then the Lord called yet again, "Samuel!" So Samuel arose and went to Eli, and said, "Here I am, for you called me." He answered, "I did not call, my son; lie down again." [7] (Now Samuel did not yet know the Lord, nor was the word of the Lord yet revealed to him.)

[8] And the Lord called Samuel again the third time. So he arose and went to Eli, and said, "Here I am, for you did call me." Then Eli perceived that the Lord had called the boy. [9] Therefore Eli said to Samuel, "Go, lie down; and it shall be, if He calls you, that you must say, 'Speak, Lord, for Your servant hears.'" So Samuel went and lay down in his place.

[10] Now the Lord came and stood and called as at other times, "Samuel! Samuel!" And Samuel answered, "Speak, for Your servant hears." [11] Then the Lord said to Samuel: "Behold, I will do something in Israel at which both ears of everyone who hears it will tingle. [12] In that day I will perform against Eli all that I have spoken concerning his house, from beginning to end. [13] For I have told him that I will judge his house forever for the iniquity which he knows, because his sons made themselves vile, and he did not restrain them. [14] And therefore I have sworn to the house of Eli that the iniquity of Eli's house shall not be atoned for by sacrifice or offering forever."

And Samuel was afraid to tell Eli the vision. [16] Then Eli called Samuel and said, "Samuel, my son!" 17 And he said, "What *is* the word that *the Lord* spoke to you? Please do not hide *it* from me. God do so to you, and more also, if you hide anything from me of all the things that He said to you." [18] Then Samuel told him everything, and hid nothing from him. And he said, "It *is* the Lord. Let Him do what seems good to Him."

[19] So Samuel grew, and the Lord was with him and let none of his words fall to the ground.[20] And all Israel from Dan to Beersheba knew that Samuel *had been* established as a prophet of the Lord.

This is a sad time in the history of Israel. Because of decay from within, God allowed the Ark of the Covenant, which represented the presence of the Lord, to be taken by the Philistines.

I Samuel 7:15: And Samuel judged Israel all the days of his life. 8:1: When Samuel was old, he made his sons judges over Israel.

When the elders of Israel came to Samuel at Ramah, they said, I Samuel 8:6: Give us a king to judge us. And Samuel prayed unto the Lord. [6] But the thing displeased Samuel, when they said; Give us a king to judge us. And Samuel prayed unto the Lord.

[7] And the Lord said unto Samuel, Hearken unto the voice of the people in all that they say unto thee: for they have not rejected thee, but they have rejected me, that I should not reign over them. [8] According to all the works which they have done since the day that I brought them up out of Egypt even unto this day, wherewith they have forsaken me, and served other gods, so do they also unto thee. [9] Now therefore hearken unto their voice:

howbeit yet protest solemnly unto them, and show them the manner of the king that shall reign over them.

[10] And Samuel told all the words of the Lord unto the people that asked of him a king. [1] And he said," This will be the manner of the king that shall reign over you: He will take your sons, and appoint them for himself, for his chariots, and to be his horsemen; and some shall run before his chariots. . . .to make his instruments of war, and instruments of his chariots. [13] And He will take your daughters. . . .[14] And He will take your fields, and your vineyards, and your olive yards, even the best of them, and give them to his servants. . . .[17] He will take the tenth of your sheep: and ye shall be his servants.

[18] And ye shall cry out in that day because of your king which ye shall have chosen you; and the Lord will not hear you in that day. [19] Nevertheless the people refused to obey the voice of Samuel; and they said, Nay; but we will have a king over us; [20] That we also may be like all the nations; and that our king may judge us, and go out before us, and fight our battles. [22] And the Lord said to Samuel, Hearken unto their voice, and make them a king.

(If only we would pray that God's will be done, we could learn from the mistakes of others and not have to pay the consequences of our own mistakes. God has given us all the guidance we need in His Word.)

The son of Kish, a mighty man of power from the Tribe of Benjamin was chosen to be king.

I Samuel 9:2: And he had a son, whose name was Saul, a choice young man, and a goodly: and there was not among the children of Israel a goodlier person than he: from his shoulders and upward he was higher than any of the people. *(At first, Saul was an humble man.)*

I Samuel 10:1:Then Samuel took a vial of oil, and poured it upon his head, and kissed him, and said, is it not because the Lord hath anointed thee to be captain over his inheritance?

I Samuel 11:17:And Samuel called the people together unto the Lord to Mizpeh; [18] And said unto the children of Israel, Thus saith the Lord God of Israel," I brought up Israel out of Egypt, and delivered you out of the hand of the Egyptians, and out of the hand of all kingdoms, and of them that oppressed you: [19] And ye have this day rejected your God, who himself saved you out of all your adversities and your tribulations; and ye have said unto him, Nay, but set a king over us. . . .' 23. . . .when Saul stood among the people, he was higher than any of the people from his shoulders and upward. [24] And Samuel said to all the people, "See ye him whom the Lord hath chosen, that there is none like him among all the people?" And all the people shouted, and said, "God save the king."

Samuel than addressed Israel in chapter 12, reviewing the history of Israel when they rebelled against the Lord, and then giving them a warning:

[14] If you fear the Lord and serve and obey him and do not rebel against His commands, and if both you and the king who reigns over you follow the Lord your God—good! [15] But

if you do not obey the Lord, and if you rebel against His commandments, then the hand of the Lord will be against you. . . .

King Saul became a successful king of war. His successes made him very arrogant, rather than humble. In chapter 13 Saul offered sacrifices, which was the exclusive function of priests. Then in chapter 14, he ordered his army to sustain from food and ordered the death sentence for his son, Jonathan. When Saul deliberately disobeyed God, Samuel said to Saul:

I Samuel 13:14: But now thy kingdom shall not continue: the Lord hath sought him a man after his own heart, and the Lord hath commanded him to be captain over his people, because thou hast not kept that which the Lord commanded thee. *Samuel mourned for Saul.*

I Samuel 16:1: And the Lord said unto Samuel, "How long wilt thou mourn for Saul, seeing I have rejected him from reigning over Israel? I will send thee to Jesse the Bethlehemite: for I have provided me a king among his sons."

Pass the Baton of Faith to the Next Generation: The drama of David begins! The grand children and Sunday School kids enjoyed the telling of the whole story of David, which began with David as a shepherd boy. Connect it to Psalm 23 and tell what the life of a shepherd was. Tell how David protected his sheep.

⁷ But the Lord said unto Samuel, "Look not on his countenance or on the height of his stature; because I have refused him: for the Lord seeth not as man seeth; for man looketh on the outward appearance, but the Lord looketh on the heart."

⁸ Then Jesse called Abinadab, and made him pass before Samuel. And he said, "Neither hath the Lord chosen this." ¹⁰ Again, Jesse made seven of his sons to pass before Samuel. And Samuel said unto Jesse, The Lord hath not chosen these. ¹¹ And Samuel said unto Jesse, "Are here all thy children?" And he said, "There remained yet the youngest, and, behold, he keepeth the sheep. And Samuel said unto Jesse, Send and fetch him: ¹² And he sent, and brought him in. Now he was ruddy, and withal of a beautiful countenance, and goodly to look to. And the Lord said, "Arise, anoint him: for this is he."

¹³ Then Samuel took the horn of oil, and anointed him in the midst of his brethren: and the Spirit of the Lord came upon David from that day forward.

Now, the "coincidence" begins. <u>God had a plan.</u>

I Samuel 16:14, KJV: But the Spirit of the Lord departed from Saul, and an evil spirit from the Lord troubled him. ¹⁵ And Saul's servants said unto him, "Behold now, an evil spirit from God troubleth thee. ¹⁶ Let our lord now command thy servants, which are before thee, to seek out a man, who is a cunning player on an harp: and it shall come to pass, when the evil spirit from God is upon thee, that he shall play with his hand, and thou shalt be well."

¹⁷ And Saul said unto his servants, Provide me now a man that can play well, and bring him to me. ¹⁸ Then answered one of the servants, and said, Behold, I have seen a son of Jesse the Bethlehemite, that is cunning in playing, and a mighty valiant man, and a man of war, and prudent in matters, and a comely person, and the Lord is with him.

[19] Wherefore Saul sent messengers unto Jesse, and said, "Send me David thy son, which is with the sheep." And David came to Saul, and stood before him: and he loved him greatly; and he became his armor bearer. 22 And Saul sent to Jesse, saying, Let David, I pray thee, stand before me; for he hath found favor in my sight. 23 And it came to pass, when the evil spirit from God was upon Saul, that David took an harp, and played with his hand: so Saul was refreshed, and was well, and the evil spirit departed from him.

David and Goliath: Chapter 17

The Philistines gathered together on a mountain on one side, and Israel stood on a mountain on the other side; there was a valley between them. Goliath, the champion of the Philistines was a giant, who was heavily armed. He stood and cried, "If he be able to fight with me, and to kill me, then will we be your servants: but if I prevail against him, and kill him, then shall ye be our servants, and serve us." [10] And the Philistine said, I defy the armies of Israel this day; give me a man, that we may fight together. [11] When Saul and all Israel heard those words of the Philistine, they were dismayed, and greatly afraid.

Jesse's three oldest sons followed Saul to battle. After the Philistine had presented himself every morning and evening for 40 days, Jesse sent David to the camp to check on his brothers. When David arrived, he heard the Philistine speak.

I Samuel 17:26: And David spake to the men that stood by him, saying, What shall be done to the man that killeth this Philistine, and taketh away the reproach from Israel? for who is this uncircumcised Philistine, that he should defy the armies of the living God? [31] And when the words were heard which David spake, they rehearsed them before Saul: and he sent for him.

David said he would fight the Philistine. He told of the times he had killed a lion and a bear while caring for his sheep. Verse 36: Thy servant slew both the lion and the bear: and this uncircumcised Philistine shall be as one of them, seeing he hath defied the armies of the living God. *Saul put his own armor on David, but David refused to wear it.*

[40] And he took his staff in his hand, and chose him five smooth stones out of the brook, and put them in a shepherd's bag which he had, even in a scrip; and his sling was in his hand: and he drew near to the Philistine.

[42] And when the Philistine looked about, and saw David, he disdained him: for he was but a youth, and ruddy, and of a fair countenance. [43] And the Philistine said unto David, Am I a dog, that thou comest to me with staves? And the Philistine cursed David by his gods. [44] And the Philistine said to David, Come to me, and I will give thy flesh unto the fowls of the air, and to the beasts of the field.

[45] Then said David to the Philistine, Thou comest to me with a sword, and with a spear, and with a shield: but I come to thee in the name of the Lord of hosts, the God of the armies of Israel, whom thou hast defied. [46] This day will the Lord deliver thee into mine hand; and

I will smite thee, and take thine head from thee; and I will give the carcasses of the host of the Philistines this day unto the fowls of the air, and to the wild beasts of the earth; that all the earth may know that there is a God in Israel. [47] And all this assembly shall know that the Lord saveth not with sword and spear: for the battle is the Lord's, and he will give you into our hands.

[48] And it came to pass, when the Philistine arose, and came, and drew nigh to meet David, that David hastened, and ran toward the army to meet the Philistine. [49] And David put his hand in his bag, and took thence a stone, and slang it, and smote the Philistine in his forehead, that the stone sunk into his forehead; and he fell upon his face to the earth. [50] So David prevailed over the Philistine with a sling and with a stone, and smote the Philistine, and slew him; but there was no sword in the hand of David.

[51] Therefore David ran, and stood upon the Philistine, and took his sword, and drew it out of the sheath thereof, and slew him, and cut off his head therewith. And when the Philistines saw their champion was dead, they fled

In Chapter 18, Jonathan, the son of Saul, and David become great friends.

I Samuel 18:1b: The soul of Jonathan was knit with the soul of David, and Jonathan loved him as his own soul. [2] And Saul took him that day, and would let him go no more home to his father's house. [3] Then Jonathan and David made a covenant, because he loved him as his own soul. [4] And Jonathan stripped himself of the robe that was upon him, and gave it to David, and his garments, even to his sword, and to his bow, and to his girdle.

[5] And David went out whithersoever Saul sent him, and behaved himself wisely: and Saul set him over the men of war, and he was accepted in the sight of all the people, and also in the sight of Saul's servants. [6] And it came to pass as they came, when David was returned from the slaughter of the Philistine, that the women came out of all cities of Israel, singing and dancing. . .and saying, " Saul hath slain his thousands, and David his ten thousands."

[8] And Saul was very wroth, and the saying displeased him; and he said, They have ascribed unto David ten thousands, and to me they have ascribed but thousands: and what can he have more but the kingdom? [9] And Saul eyed David from that day *and forward.*

Chapter 19 shows Jonathan's love for David and King Saul's evil spirit toward David. Jonathan, who was heir to the throne, himself, stayed true to David when he could have hated his rival. The story of Jonathan and David is one of the noblest accounts of friendship of history.

I Samuel 20:16-17: So Jonathan made a covenant with the house of David, saying, Let the Lord even require it at the hand of David's enemies. Jonathan caused David to swear again, because he loved him: for he loved him as he loved his own soul.

I Samuel 20:18- 42 tells the beloved story of how Jonathan arranged to let David know whether he could stay or whether his life was in danger. It is the story of the shooting of three arrows which signaled whether Saul had again threatened David. The result was that David had to flee again. He escaped to the Philistines, to the cave of Adullam, to Moab, and to many other places. *(David composed five of the Psalms while he was a fugitive.) David had opportunity to kill Saul but did not.*

The Philistines invaded the land of Israel again. The Philistines slew Jonathan and 2 other of Saul's sons. During a battle, Saul committed suicide, after reigning for 40 years. (Later, we will see that David always showed extreme kindness to the family of Jonathan.) The drama of David continues through II Samuel and I Kings. All stories are in the Bible for a purpose. What can we learn from the lives of Samuel, Saul, and David that will bless our own lives? What Bible Points could go with this story? What a contrast of characters!

THE BOOK OF SECOND SAMUEL
Theme: The Life and Times of King David

Message: David has been a fugitive, running from King Saul. Now that Saul is dead, David takes his rightful place as King of Israel. He must now heal the war-torn country. Surrounding countries still pose the threat of war, however, Israel is militarily strong under David's victorious reign. In this book, God is seen as the One who establishes David upon the throne of Israel and gives him victory over his enemies. Chapters 1 – 10 tell of the prosperous reign of David over Judah. Then in chapters 11 – 12, David's adultery with Bathsheba marks a turning point; the sword will never leave David's house. David had to suffer the consequences. But David was a man after God's own heart. He was devoted to the ways of God and was always repentant. His two greatest accomplishments were the kingdom and the Psalms. (FCA Press: 2008)

II Samuel chapters 1 to 6 cover the period from the death of Saul up to God's promise to David. They describe the war between the house of Saul and the house of David.

When David heard of the death of Saul and of Jonathan, he was wroth.

II Samuel 1:11, KJV: Then David took hold on his clothes, and rent them; and likewise all the men that were with him: [12] And they mourned, and wept, and fasted until even, for Saul, and for Jonathan his son, and for the people of the Lord, and for the house of Israel; because they were fallen by the sword. [17] And David lamented with this lamentation over Saul and over Jonathan his son: mighty. . . .[25] How are the mighty fallen in the midst of the battle! O Jonathan, thou wast slain in thine high places.[26] I am distressed for thee, my brother Jonathan: very pleasant hast thou been unto me: thy love to me was wonderful, passing the love of women

After the lamenting ended:

II Samuel 3:1, KJV: Now there was long war between the house of Saul and the house of David; but David waxed stronger and stronger, and the house of Saul waxed weaker and weaker.

II Samuel 5:3b, KJV: David was thirty years old when he began to reign, and he reigned forty years.

[5] In Hebron he reigned over Judah seven years and six months: and in Jerusalem he reigned thirty and three years over all Israel and Judah. (This is a total of 40 years that David reigned

In Chapter 6, we see a great celebration when the Ark of the Covenant is returned to The City of David. Verse 15: So David and all the house of Israel brought up the ark of the Lord with shouting, and with the sound of the trumpet.

In Chapter 7, David felt guilty that he dwelt in a house of cedar, and they still had only the tabernacle made of curtains. However, God did not allow David to build the great temple because he was a man of war.

The Crimson Thread and the Unity of the Bible: *The Old Testament is the story of God's dealing with the Hebrew nation for the purpose of someday blessing all nations. The Hebrew Nation will be blessed through the family of David. The promise of an eternal king who will come from the seed of David is repeated over and over in the Psalms and by the prophets over a period of 500 years. Then in Luke 1:31-33,* [30] Then the angel said to Mary, "Do not be afraid, Mary, for you have found favor with God.[31] And behold, you will conceive in your womb and bring forth a Son, and shall call His name Jesus. [32] He will be great, and will be called the Son of the Highest; and the Lord God will give Him the throne of His father David. [33] And He will reign over the house of Jacob forever, and of His kingdom there will be no end."

II Samuel 7:11, KJV: Now therefore, thus shall you say to My servant David[12] "When your days are fulfilled and you rest with your fathers, I will set up your seed after you, who will come from your body, and I will establish his kingdom. [13] He shall build a house for My name, and I will establish the throne of his kingdom forever. [14] I will be his Father, and he shall be My son. If he commits iniquity, I will chasten him with the rod of men and with the blows of the sons of men. [15] But My mercy shall not depart from him, as I took *it* from Saul, whom I removed from before you. [16] And your house and your kingdom shall be established forever before you. Your throne shall be established forever." *David's son, Solomon, will build the house for God, and Jesus will be the seed of David.*

David's Thanksgiving to God

[18] Then King David went in and sat before the Lord; and he said: "Who *am* I, O Lord God? And what is my house, that You have brought me this far? [19] And yet this was a small thing in Your sight, O Lord God. . . .22 You are great, O Lord God. For *there is* none like You, nor *is there any* God besides You,. . .[24] For You have made Your people Israel Your very own people forever; and You, Lord, have become their God. . .You have revealed *this* to Your servant, saying, 'I will build you a house.' Therefore, Your servant has found it in his heart to pray this prayer to You.. [29] Now therefore, let it please You to bless the house of Your servant, that it may continue before You forever; for You, O Lord God, have spoken *it*, and with Your blessing let the house of Your servant be blessed forever."

In Chapters 8 to 10, we found that God gave victory to David in war wherever he went. David took an insignificant nation and built it into a mighty kingdom, perhaps the single most powerful kingdom on earth at that time.

In Chapter 9, David wanted to show kindness to anyone of Saul's household for the sake of Jonathan. He learned that Jonathan had a son, Mephibosheth, which was lame. Continuing this historical friendship, David showed great kindness to him:

II Samuel 9:6: Now when Mephibosheth the son of Jonathan, the son of Saul, had come to David, he fell on his face and prostrated himself. Then David said, "Mephibosheth?"

And he answered, "Here is your servant!"

⁷ So David said to him, "Do not fear, for I will surely show you kindness for Jonathan your father's sake, and will restore to you all the land of Saul your grandfather; and you shall eat bread at my table continually."

"As for Mephibosheth," *said the king,* "he shall eat at my table like one of the king's sons." ¹² Mephibosheth had a young son whose name *was* Micha. And all who dwelt in the house of Ziba *were* servants of Mephibosheth. ¹³ So Mephibosheth dwelt in Jerusalem, for he ate continually at the king's table. And he was lame in both his feet.

The Lord continued to bless Israel and David, until. . .II Samuel 11:2:

² Then it happened one evening that David arose from his bed and walked on the roof of the king's house. And from the roof he saw a woman bathing, and the woman *was* very beautiful to behold. ³ So David sent and inquired about the woman. And *someone said, "Is this not Bathsheba, the daughter of Eliam, the wife of Uriah the Hittite?"* ⁴ *Then David sent messengers, and* took her; and she came to him, and he lay with her, for she was cleansed from her impurity; and she returned to her house. ⁵ And the woman conceived; so she sent and told David, and said, "I *am* with child."

What a web we weave! Now David must cover up what he has done. He arranged for Bathsheba's husband, Uriah, to be killed in battle. He wrote a letter to Joab saying:

II Samuel 11:15: 'Set Uriah in the forefront of the hottest battle, and retreat from him, that he may be struck down and die." When Uriah was killed, Bathsheba mourned for her husband.

II Samuel 11:27: Then when mourning was past, David fetched her to his house, and she became his wife, and bare him a son. But the thing that David had done displeased the Lord. *David, like us, must suffer the consequences of sin, for we "reap what we sow." Through Nathan, the prophet, God reminded David of all he had done for him. Then the judgment of the just God: II Samuel 12:10:* Now, therefore, the sword shall never depart from thine house; because thou hast despised me and hast taken the wife of Uriah to be thy wife. 14. The child also that is born unto thee shall die.

David loved the child very much. All the time he was sick, David fasted and wept. But when the child died, David said, II Samuel 12:23 "Now he is dead, why should I fast? Can I bring him back again? I shall go to him, but he shall not return to me." 24. And Then David comforted Bathsheba his wife, and went in to her and lay with her. So she bore a son, and he called his name Solomon. How the Lord loved him,

David did reap a harvest of what he had sown. His daughter, Tamar, was raped by her brother, Amnon, who was murdered by their brother, Absalom (chapter 13). Absalom led in rebellion against David and was killed in the struggle. Through it all, David wept

and repented. What a lesson for those who feel they can sin and sin and get by without consequences!

Absalom probably knew Solomon was to be David's successor as king because he constantly tried to steal the throne. Absalom was one of the king's greatest sorrows. He was constantly in battle against him. In II Samuel 18, we see that David told his men to deal gently with Absalom. But this is what happened: Verse 9: Absalom rode on a mule. The mule went under the thick boughs of a great terebinth tree, and his head caught in the terebinth; so he was left hanging between heaven and earth. And the mule which *was* under him went on. *(The consequences of sin. Whom the Lord loveth, he chastens!)*

David was a man after God's own heart and his reactions showed him to be just that. Look at Psalm 32 and 51 to see his reaction to this bitter experience.

After David's many victories in war, as well as turbulence at home, David sang a song of praise, which exhibited his total trust in God and his gratitude to God. This is a familiar and loved Psalm of David, found in II Samuel 22. Here are only parts of it.

God is my rock, in whom I take refuge, my shield and the horn of my salvation.

He is my stronghold, my refuge and my savior—from violent people you save me.

[4] "I called to the Lord, who is worthy of praise, and have been saved from my enemies.

"He reached down from on high and took hold of me; he drew me out of deep waters.

[18] He rescued me from my powerful enemy, from my foes, who were too strong for me.

[19] They confronted me in the day of my disaster, but the Lord was my support.

[21] "The Lord has dealt with me according to my righteousness;

according to the cleanness of my hands he has rewarded me.

47 "The Lord lives! Praise be to my Rock! Exalted be my God, the Rock, my Savior!

In II Samuel 23, David's last words focused on his troubled, but glorious life, the justice of his reign as king, his creation of the Psalms, his devotion to God's Word, and God's covenant with him that promised an eternal dynasty.

David stood like a rock in a nation that continually fell away into idolatry. David was a grand character. Tell his story to your children—especially David, the Shepherd, the Psalmist, the Harpist, the slayer of the Giant, the friend of Jonathan and of Mephibosheth, the one who planned the temple, the king who led his people to follow God, and the king from whom Jesus would be born.

THE BOOK OF I KINGS
In Kings and Chronicles, Jesus is sovereign
Theme: Israel's Golden Age: Its coronation and corrosion.

Message: Solomon reaped the reward of David's military success. Solomon asked God for wisdom when he inherited the throne. The early chapters of I Kings display Solomon's wisdom, wealth, and fame. Solomon got to build the Temple, for which David had drawn the plans. But when Solomon turned to foreign women and false gods, his end was pitiful. Following Solomon's death, the country divided into two separate nations: Israel and Judah, bringing an end to the Golden Age of Israel. None of Israel's kings were faithful to God, and only half of Judah's rulers followed God. (FCA Press: 2008)

First and Second Kings are long books of history and also of interesting personalities, including David, Solomon, the Queen of Sheba, the prophets, Elijah, Elisha, and evil King Ahab, and the most hated of women, Jezebel. We are introduced briefly to many kings of Judah and of Israel. David is dying at the beginning of I Kings:

I Kings 1:1: When King David was very old; he could not keep warm even when they put covers over him. *While David was about to die, his fourth son, Adonijah declared himself king. However, David chose Solomon, the son of Bathsheba, to be his successor.*

I Kings 2:1-4: When the time drew near for David to die, he gave a charge to Solomon his son. [2]"I am about to go the way of all the earth," he said. "So be strong, act like a man, [3] and observe what the Lord your God requires: Walk in obedience to him, and keep his decrees and commands, his laws and regulations, as written in the Law of Moses. Do this so that you may prosper in all you do and wherever you go [4] and that the Lord may keep his promise to me: 'If your descendants watch how they live, and if they walk faithfully before me with all their heart and soul, you will never fail to have a successor on the throne of Israel.'

Solomon loved the Lord and felt humble before him. He talked to God:

I Kings 3:7: [7]Now, O Lord my God, You have made Your servant king instead of my father David, but I *am* a little child; I do not know *how* to go out or come in. [8]And Your servant *is* in the midst of Your people whom You have chosen, a great people, too numerous to be numbered or counted. [9]Therefore give to Your servant an understanding heart to judge Your people, that I may discern between good and evil. For who is able to judge this great people of Yours?"

[10]The speech pleased the Lord, that Solomon had asked this thing. [11]Then God said to him: "Because you have asked this thing, and have not asked long life for yourself, nor have asked riches for yourself, nor have asked the life of your enemies, but have asked for yourself understanding to discern justice, [12]behold, I have done according to your words;

see, I have given you a wise and understanding heart, so that there has not been anyone like you before you, nor shall any like you arise after you. [13] And I have also given you what you have not asked: both riches and honor, so that there shall not be anyone like you among the kings all your days. [14] So if you walk in My ways, to keep My statutes and My commandments, as your father David walked, then I will lengthen your days."

I Kings 4:30, 32: And Solomon's wisdom excelled the wisdom of all the children of the east country, and all the wisdom of Egypt. And he spoke three thousand proverbs and his songs were a thousand five.

In chapters five and six, 480 years after the Children of Israel had made their Exodus from Egypt, Solomon led in the building of the great Temple of Jerusalem He built it according to specific design instructions that God had given to David. It took seven years to build the temple. More specifications are given in II Chronicles 2-7.

I Kings 6:2: The temple that King Solomon built for the Lord was sixty cubits long, twenty wide and thirty high. [3] The portico at the front of the main hall of the temple extended the width of [7] In building the temple, only blocks dressed at the quarry were used, and no hammer, chisel or any other iron tool was heard at the temple site while it was being built.

He covered the whole house with pure gold and the altar of the holy of holies was covered with pure gold. The greatest of craftsmen were used, and all was very ornate.

[11] The word of the Lord came to Solomon: [12] "As for this temple you are building, if you follow my decrees, observe my laws and keep all my commands and obey them, I will fulfill through you the promise I gave to David your father. [13] And I will live among the Israelites and will not abandon my people Israel."

The Temple Is Built.

[14] So Solomon built the temple and completed it. [15] He lined its interior walls with cedar boards, paneling them from the floor of the temple to the ceiling, and covered the floor of the temple with planks of juniper. [16] He partitioned off twenty cubits at the rear of the temple with cedar boards from floor to ceiling to form within the temple an inner sanctuary, the Most Holy Place.,.. All was cedar; no stone was to be seen.

[19] He prepared the inner sanctuary within the temple to set the ark of the covenant of the Lord there,,,. He overlaid the inside with pure gold, and he also overlaid the altar of cedar. [21] Solomon covered the inside of the temple with pure gold, and he extended gold chains across the front of the inner sanctuary, which was overlaid with gold. [22] So he overlaid the whole interior with gold.

[37] The foundation of the temple of the Lord was laid in the fourth year, in the month of Ziv. [38] In the eleventh year in the month of Bul, the eighth month, the temple was finished in all its details according to its specifications. He had spent seven years building it.

I Kings 8: Poetry by Kay Gage
The Lord filled the temple with his glory, as He settled there to dwell.
His cloud was declaratory, that God is here; all is well.

When the temple was completed, Solomon brought the people together for a solemn dedication and reminded the people of the covenant relationship signified by the temple. They were now to remain faithful to God,

I Kings 8:6:[6] The priests then brought the ark of the Lord's covenant to its place in the inner sanctuary of the temple, the Most Holy Place. . . .[9] There was nothing in the ark except the two stone tablets that Moses had placed in it at Horeb, where the Lord made a covenant with the Israelites after they came out of Egypt. [10] When the priests withdrew from the Holy Place, the cloud filled the temple of the Lord.[11] And the priests could not perform their service because of the cloud, for the glory of the Lord filled his temple.

(Solomon said that his father David had wanted to build the temple, but Solomon, his own flesh and blood, would build the temple. He said the Lord had kept his promise because the temple was built for the Lord God of Israel. Verse 21 says: I have provided a place there for the ark, in which is the covenant of the Lord that he made with our ancestors when he brought them out of Egypt."

Solomon's Prayer of Dedication: [22] Then Solomon stood before the altar of the Lord in front of the whole assembly of Israel, spread out his hands toward heaven [23] and said: "Lord, the God of Israel, there is no God like you in heaven above or on earth below You who keep your covenant of love with your servants who continue wholeheartedly in your way. [24] You have kept your promise to your servant David my father; with your mouth you have promised and with your hand you have fulfilled it—as it is today.

[25] "Now Lord, the God of Israel, keep for your servant David my father the promises you made to him when you said, 'You shall never fail to have a successor to sit before me on the throne of Israel, if only your descendants are careful in all they do to walk before me faithfully as you have done.'

[27] "But will God really dwell on earth? The heavens, even the highest heaven, cannot contain you. How much less this temple I have built! [28] Yet give attention to your servant's prayer and his plea for mercy, Lord my God. *Solomon prayed that God would bless and bring his people back to him when they have sinned against him and have been defeated by the enemy and when they have sinned and famine has come and when they have sinned and been taken as exiles from their country.*

[54] When Solomon had finished all these prayers and supplications to the Lord, he rose from before the altar of the Lord, where he had been kneeling with his hands spread out toward heaven. [55] He stood and blessed the whole assembly of Israel in a loud voice, saying:

[56] "Praise be to the Lord, who has given rest to his people Israel just as he promised. Not one word has failed of all the good promises he gave through his servant Moses. [57] May the

Lord our God be with us as he was with our ancestors; may he never leave us nor forsake us. [58] May he turn our hearts to him, to walk in obedience to him and keep the commands, decrees and laws he gave our ancestors. [59] And may these words of mine, which I have prayed before the Lord, be near to the Lord our God day and night, that he may uphold the cause of his servant and the cause of his people Israel according to each day's need, [60] so that all the peoples of the earth may know that the Lord is God and that there is no other. [61] And may your hearts be fully committed to the Lord our God, to live by his decrees and obey his commands, as at this time."

The Scarlet Thread: [62] Then the king and all Israel with him offered sacrifices before the Lord. [63] Solomon offered a sacrifice of fellowship offerings to the Lord: twenty-two thousand cattle and a hundred and twenty thousand sheep and goats. So the king and all the Israelites dedicated the temple of the Lord.

Chapters 9 and 10 tell of all the great achievements of King Solomon. The era of David and Solomon was the golden era of Hebrew History. They ruled over all of Israel during the time that Israel was the most powerful kingdom in the entire ancient near East. King David had been a warrior, and King Solomon was a builder. People came from the ends of the earth to hear Solomon's wisdom. Solomon's annual; income and supply of gold was enormous. As long as Solomon and Israel followed God, he blessed as promised. But. . .

I Kings 9:6 "But if you or your descendants turn away from me and do not observe the commands and decrees I have given you and go off to serve other gods and worship them, [7] then I will cut off Israel from the land I have given them and will reject this temple.

I Kings 11 tells of Solomon's apostasy and his many wives. For political reasons, Solomon married many women from other nations, who brought their idols with them. David had been careful to suppress idol worship, but Solomon re-established idolatry. Solomon's story of his old age is one of the most pitiful in the Bible. Why does God want this included in his word? Perhaps it shows us what ceaseless pleasure and luxury can do to the best of men.

I Kings 9, 10 and 11:
If you walk before me as David thy father in integrity,
I will establish your throne, forever for the children of my own.

Depending on horses and wives his kingdom to save, Solomon failed and did not obey.
The commandment of God concerning the way a king should behave.

Solomon did evil in God's sight, by turning his heart away.
Wicked women, black as the night, have led many Godly men astray.

I Kings 12 tells of the division of the kingdom. The kingdom has lasted 120 years, 40 years under Saul, 40 under David, and 40 under Solomon. When divided, ten tribes took the name of Israel and formed the Northern Kingdom. Judah and Benjamin formed the Southern Kingdom and were called Judah. After the division, continuous war between the two kingdoms existed.

Close reading of I Kings and of I Chronicles will show the reign of kings from 931 BC to 852 BC. Each reign is usually prefaced with "And he did that which was evil in the sight of the Lord" *or* " he was more evil than his father". Jeroboam institut*ed calf worship, Rehoboam made slaves of the people in chapter 12. Ahab, the most wicked of all the kings, married Jezebel, who killed God's prophets and abolished the worship of the Lord. But God had an answer for Jezebel:*

In I Kings, we have Elijah and Elisha, prophets of God. A breath of fresh air! Some of the most wonderful of stories for children are found in I Kings. Elijah is in I Kings 17 to II Kings 2. Elijah is one of the grandest characters Israel ever produced! He even appeared on the Mount of Transfiguration with Jesus Christ in Matthew 17:3-4. His departure from the earth in a chariot of fire, his fiery zeal on Mount Carmel, and his encounters with Ahab and Jezebel make Elijah a character to make exciting stories for children.

Elijah Fed by Ravens: I Kings 17:1: Now Elijah. . .said to Ahab, "As the Lord, the God of Israel, lives, whom I serve, there will be neither dew nor rain in the next few years except at my word."[2] Then the word of the Lord came to Elijah: [3] "Leave here, turn eastward and hide in the Kerith Ravine, east of the Jordan. [4] You will drink from the brook, and I have directed the ravens to supply you with food there." [5] So he did what the Lord had told him. He went to the Kerith Ravine, east of the Jordan, and stayed there. [6] The ravens brought him bread and meat in the morning and bread and meat in the evening, and he drank from the brook.

The Widow at Zarephath

I Kings 17: 7: Some time later the brook dried up because there had been no rain in the land. [8] Then the word of the Lord came to him: [9] "Go at once to Zarephath in the region of Sidon and stay there. I have directed a widow there to supply you with food." [10] So he went to Zarephath. When he came to the town gate, a widow was there gathering sticks. He called to her and asked, "Would you bring me a little water in a jar so I may have a drink?" [11] As she was going to get it, he called, "And bring me, please, a piece of bread."

[12] "As surely as the Lord your God lives," she replied, "I don't have any bread—only a handful of flour in a jar and a little olive oil in a jug. I am gathering a few sticks to take home and make a meal for myself and my son, that we may eat it—and die."

[13] Elijah said to her, "Don't be afraid. Go home and do as you have said. But first make a small loaf of bread for me from what you have and bring it to me, and then make something

for yourself and your son. [14] For this is what the Lord, the God of Israel, says: 'The jar of flour will not be used up and the jug of oil will not run dry until the day the Lord sends rain on the land.'"

[15] She went away and did as Elijah had told her. So there was food every day for Elijah and for the woman and her family. [16] For the jar of flour was not used up and the jug of oil did not run dry, in keeping with the word of the Lord spoken by Elijah.

Elijah raised the widow's son from the dead. [17] Sometime later the son of the woman who owned the house became ill. He grew worse and worse, and finally stopped breathing. . . . [19] "Give me your son," Elijah replied. He took him from her arms, carried him to the upper room where he was staying, and laid him on his bed. [20] Then he cried out to the Lord, "Lord my God, have you brought tragedy even on this widow I am staying with, by causing her son to die?" [21] Then he stretched himself out on the boy three times and cried out to the Lord, "Lord my God, let this boy's life return to him!"

[22] The Lord heard Elijah's cry, and the boy's life returned to him, and he lived. [23] Elijah picked up the child and carried him down from the room into the house. He gave him to his mother and said, "Look, your son is alive!" [24] Then the woman said to Elijah, "Now I know that you are a man of God and that the word of the Lord from your mouth is the truth."

Children love to dramatize the history story of Elijah and the 450 prophets of Baal on Mount Carmel.

I Kings 17-18: *The Drought: God gave Elijah power to shut the heavens for 3 ½ years so it did not rain. I Kings 17:1:* 17 Now Elijah the Tishbite, from Tishbe in Gilead, said to Ahab, "As the Lord, the God of Israel, lives, whom I serve, there will be neither dew nor rain in the next few years except at my word."

I Kings 18:1: After a long time, in the third year, the word of the Lord came to Elijah: "Go and present yourself to Ahab, and I will send rain on the land." [2] So Elijah went to present himself to Ahab. [15] Elijah said, "As the Lord Almighty lives, whom I serve, I will surely present myself to Ahab today."

Elijah on Mount Carmel: Ahab went to meet Elijah. [17] When he saw Elijah, he said to him, "Is that you, you troubler of Israel?"

[18] "I have not made trouble for Israel," Elijah replied. "But you and your father's family have. You have abandoned the Lord's commands and have followed the Baals. [19] Now summon the people from all over Israel to meet me on Mount Carmel. And bring the four hundred and fifty prophets of Baal and the four hundred prophets of Asherah, who eat at Jezebel's table."

[20] So Ahab sent word throughout all Israel and assembled the prophets on Mount Carmel. [21] Elijah went before the people and said, "How long will you waver between two opinions? If the Lord is God, follow him; but if Baal is God, follow him."

But the people said nothing.

²² Then Elijah said to them, "I am the only one of the Lord's prophets left, but Baal has four hundred and fifty prophets. ²³ Get two bulls for us. Let Baal's prophets choose one for themselves, and let them cut it into pieces and put it on the wood but not set fire to it. I will prepare the other bull and put it on the wood but not set fire to it. ²⁴ Then you call on the name of your god, and I will call on the name of the Lord. The god who answers by fire—he is God."

Then all the people said, "What you say is good."

²⁵ Elijah said to the prophets of Baal, "Choose one of the bulls and prepare it first, since there are so many of you. Call on the name of your god, but do not light the fire." ²⁶ So they took the bull given them and prepared it. Then they called on the name of Baal from morning till noon. "Baal, answer us!" they shouted. But there was no response; no one answered. And they danced around the altar they had made.

²⁷ At noon Elijah began to taunt them. "Shout louder!" he said. "Surely he is a god! Perhaps he is deep in thought, or busy, or traveling. Maybe he is sleeping and must be awakened."²⁸ So they shouted louder and slashed themselves with swords and spears, as was their custom, until their blood flowed. ²⁹ Midday passed, and they continued their frantic prophesying until the time for the evening sacrifice. But there was no response, no one answered, and no one paid attention.

³⁰ Then Elijah said to all the people, "Come here to me." They came to him, and he repaired the altar of the Lord, which had been torn down. ³¹ Elijah took twelve stones, one for each of the tribes descended from Jacob, to whom the word of the Lord had come, saying, "Your name shall be Israel." ³² With the stones he built an altar in the name of the Lord, and he dug a trench around it large enough to hold two seahs of seed. ³³ He arranged the wood, cut the bull into pieces and laid it on the wood. Then he said to them, "Fill four large jars with water and pour it on the offering and on the wood."

³⁴ "Do it again," he said, and they did it again. "Do it a third time," he ordered, and they did it the third time. ³⁵ The water ran down around the altar and even filled the trench.

³⁶ At the time of sacrifice, the prophet Elijah stepped forward and prayed: "Lord, the God of Abraham, Isaac and Israel, let it be known today that you are God in Israel and that I am your servant and have done all these things at your command. ³⁷ Answer me, Lord, answer me, so these people will know that you, Lord, are God, and that you are turning their hearts back again."

³⁸ Then the fire of the Lord fell and burned up the sacrifice, the wood, the stones and the soil, and also licked up the water in the trench. ³⁹ When all the people saw this, they fell prostrate and cried, "The Lord—he is God! The Lord—he is God!"

⁴⁰ Then Elijah commanded them, "Seize the prophets of Baal. Don't let anyone get away!" They seized them, and Elijah had them brought down to the Kishon Valley and slaughtered there.

[41] And Elijah said to Ahab, "Go, eat and drink, for there is the sound of a heavy rain." [42] So Ahab went off to eat and drink, but Elijah climbed to the top of Carmel, bent down to the ground and put his face between his knees.

So Elijah said, "Go and tell Ahab, 'Hitch up your chariot and go down before the rain stops you.'" [45] Meanwhile, the sky grew black with clouds, the wind rose, a heavy rain started falling and Ahab rode off to Jezreel. [46] The power of the Lord came on Elijah and, tucking his cloak into his belt, he ran ahead of Ahab all the way to Jezreel

What a lesson we can learn from the story of Elijah and "The Still, Small Voice." In it, we learn that while spectacular demonstrations of power are sometimes necessary, God's real work is achieved with a still, small voice. In Chapter 19, Ahab told Jezebel all that Elijah had done, how he had slain all of her prophets. Jezebel swore to Elijah that he would take his life by tomorrow. After Elijah's mountain-top experience, he was low. He wanted to die. He prayed that the Lord would take his life away. But the Lord fed him, and he ate and went in the strength of that meat 40 days into Horeb, the Mount of God, where Moses was given the Ten Commandments. He went into a cave and in Verse 10, Elijah complained that he was the only prophet of God left and that they were going to take his life, also.

[11] The Lord said, "Go out and stand on the mountain in the presence of the Lord, for the Lord is about to pass by." Then a great and powerful wind tore the mountains apart and shattered the rocks before the Lord, but the Lord was not in the wind. After the wind there was an earthquake, but the Lord was not in the earthquake. [12] After the earthquake came a fire, but the Lord was not in the fire. And after the fire came a gentle whisper. [13] When Elijah heard it, he pulled his cloak over his face and went out and stood at the mouth of the cave. Then a voice said to him, "What are you doing here, Elijah?"

[14] He replied, "I have been very zealous for the Lord God Almighty. The Israelites have rejected your covenant, torn down your altars, and put your prophets to death with the sword. I am the only one left, and now they are trying to kill me too."

[15] The Lord said to him, "Go back the way you came, and go to the Desert of Damascus. When you get there, anoint Hazael king over Aram. [16] Also, anoint Jehu son of Nimshi king over Israel, and anoint Elisha son of Shaphat from Abel Meholah to succeed you as prophet. [17] Jehu will put to death any who escape the sword of Hazael, and Elisha will put to death any who escape the sword of Jehu. [18] Yet I reserve seven thousand in Israel—all whose knees have not bowed down to Baal and whose mouths have not kissed him."

Then in verses 19-21, God called Elisha to minister to Elijah.

In I Kings 20-22, we see the death of Ahab and also of Jezebel. Ahab wanted a vineyard belonging the Naboth, which was close to his palace. But Naboth wanted to keep it because it was an inheritance. Ahab was sullen and wouldn't eat. So Jezebel intervened and wrote letters in Ahab's name and sent them to the elders.

Jezebel arranged in I Kings 21:9-14 for Naboth to be stoned to death.

15. As soon as Jezebel heard that Naboth had been stoned to death, she said to Ahab, "Get up and take possession of the vineyard of Naboth the Jezreelite that he refused to sell you. He is no longer alive, but dead." [16] When Ahab heard that Naboth was dead, he got up and went down to take possession of Naboth's vineyard.

[17] Then the word of the Lord came to Elijah the Tishbite: [18] "Go down to meet Ahab king of Israel, who rules in Samaria. He is now in Naboth's vineyard, where he has gone to take possession of it. [19] Say to him, 'This is what the Lord says: Have you not murdered a man and seized his property?' Then say to him, 'This is what the Lord says: In the place where dogs licked up Naboth's blood, dogs will lick up your blood—yes, yours!'"

"And also concerning Jezebel the Lord says: 'Dogs will devour Jezebel by the wall of Jezreel."

[25] (There was never anyone like Ahab, who sold himself to do evil in the eyes of the Lord, urged on by Jezebel his wife. [26] He behaved in the vilest manner by going after idols, like the Amorites the Lord drove out before Israel.)

I Kings ends with Jehoshephat's reign in Judah in which he walked in the ways of the Lord. The Saga continues in II Kings.

The BOOK OF II KINGS

In Kings, Jesus is Sovereign
Theme: The spiral of destruction of Judah and of Israel

Message: According to Halley (2007), the entire history of the kingdom of Israel is told in the two books of Samuel and the two books of Kings. A continuation of the historical narrative of I Kings, we see the kingdom divided, then the end of both kingdoms. Also an account is given of the succession of kings of the Kingdom of Israel and of Judah. The last twelve kings of the Northern Kingdom are covered and the last 16 kings of the Southern kingdom are included. Most of the kings did that which was evil in the eyes of the Lord. But God keeps speaking through Elijah and Elisha, who are blessed with the Lord's Spirit. Parallel stories can be read in II Kings and II Chronicles.

II Kings chapter 1 *tells of the continued reign of Ahab's son, Ahaziah, of Israel, who like his father, did that which was evil in the sight of the Lord.*

Another story exciting to children is Elijah being taken up to Heaven in a Chariot of Fire. Elijah had thought he failed. He had done very rough and disagreeable work for 15 years during the reigns of wicked Ahab and Ahaziah. But God didn't think he had failed. God sent angelic chariots to take Elijah away in triumph to heaven. He had recently been at Mount Nebo, and knowing he was soon to die, he went to Moses' death place to be near Moses. He had called down fire from heaven to destroy the false prophets, and now God would take him to heaven in a chariot of fire. Only Elijah and Enoch were transported to heaven without dying. Perhaps this is a foreshadowing of the Rapture of the church, when angel chariots will swing low to gather us to welcome the returning savior! (Halley, 2007)

II Kings 2: Elisha Stays with Elijah.

2 When the Lord was about to take Elijah up to heaven in a whirlwind, Elijah and Elisha were on their way from Gilgal. ² Elijah said to Elisha, "Stay here; the Lord has sent me to Bethel." But Elisha said, "As surely as the Lord lives and as you live, I will not leave you." So they went down to Bethel.

(Everywhere they went, Elisha was reminded that Elijah was going to be taken away today, but Elisha stayed with him. Finally, in II Kings 2:7:

Fifty men from the company of the prophets went and stood at a distance, facing the place where Elijah and Elisha had stopped at the Jordan. ⁸ Elijah took his cloak, rolled it up and struck the water with it. The water divided to the right and to the left, and the two of them crossed over on dry ground.

⁹ When they had crossed, Elijah said to Elisha, "Tell me, what can I do for you before I am taken from you?"

"Let me inherit a double portion of your spirit," Elisha replied.

[10] "You have asked a difficult thing," Elijah said, "yet if you see me when I am taken from you, it will be yours—otherwise, it will not."

[11] As they were walking along and talking together, suddenly a chariot of fire and horses of fire appeared and separated the two of them, and Elijah went up to heaven in a whirlwind.[12] Elisha saw this and cried out, "My father! My father! The chariots and horsemen of Israel!" And Elisha saw him no more. Then he took hold of his garment and tore it in two.

[13] Elisha then picked up Elijah's cloak that had fallen from him and went back and stood on the bank of the Jordan. [14] He took the cloak that had fallen from Elijah and struck the water with it. "Where now is the Lord, the God of Elijah?" he asked. When he struck the water, it divided to the right and to the left, and he crossed over.

[15] The company of the prophets from Jericho, who were watching, said, "The spirit of Elijah is resting on Elisha." And they went to meet him and bowed to the ground before him.

Indeed, Elisha did receive a double portion of Elijah's spirit. In II Kings chapters 2-6, Elisha's Miracles included:

The Jordan River divided; Jericho's spring water purified; the widow's oil multiplied, the widow's son resuscitated, poisonous stew multiplied; Naaman healed of leprosy; the floating ax head; horses and chariots surrounded the city of Dothan; Syrian soldiers blinded. (MacArthur: 2005). Elisha also conducted schools for prophets. The account of Elisha's multiplying the food for the widow and bringing her son back to life is especially intriguing for children.

One evil king after another reigned over Israel. Ahab was perhaps the most wicked. He and his wife, Jezebel, would often threaten God's prophets when they prophesied what would happen because of their sins. Elijah had told Jezebel that the dogs would eat her.

II Kings 9:33: "Throw her down!" Jehu said. So they threw her down, and some of her blood spattered the wall and the horses as they trampled her underfoot.

[34] Jehu went in and ate and drank. "Take care of that cursed woman," he said, "and bury her, for she was a king's daughter." [35] But when they went out to bury her, they found nothing except her skull, her feet and her hands. [36] They went back and told Jehu, who said, "This is the word of the Lord that he spoke through his servant Elijah the Tishbite: On the plot of ground at Jezreel dogs will devour Jezebel's flesh.[37] Jezebel's body will be like dung on the ground in the plot at Jezreel, so that no one will be able to say, 'This is Jezebel.'"

The consequences of sin are found throughout II Kings: Famine in the land caused people to eat their children. Elisha appointed a foreign king, Ben-Hadadf to be king of Syria so he could punish the prophet's own nation. In 2 Kins 14, Jeroboam II, King of Israel brought war for 41 years. The prophets, Amos and Hosea, challenged the idolatry and abominable social conditions of Jeroboam's reign. (Halley, 2007) In 2 Kings 15, Zechariah became king of Israel and was assassinated after reigning for only six months. In this chapter many kings reigned; most were cold-blooded and brutal kings. II Kings 17: The Assyrians defeated the northern kingdom of Judah. Though God had sent the prophets

Hosea, Isaiah, and Micah, the kings and people wouldn't listen and walked in the sins of Jereboam, the king who was the founder of Judah.

<u>*Israel is Exiled Because of Sin: II Kings 17:7*</u> All this took place because the Israelites had sinned against the Lord their God, who had brought them up out of Egypt from under the power of Pharaoh king of Egypt. They worshiped other gods [8] and followed the practices of the nations the Lord had driven out before them, as well as the practices that the kings of Israel had introduced. [9] The Israelites secretly did things against the Lord their God that were not right. From watchtower to fortified city they built themselves high places in all their towns. [10] They set up sacred stones and Asherah poles on every high hill and under every spreading tree. [11] At every high place they burned incense, as the nations whom the Lord had driven out before them had done. They did wicked things that aroused the Lord's anger. [12] They worshiped idols, though the Lord had said, "You shall not do this.

[13] The Lord warned Israel and Judah through all his prophets and seers: "Turn from your evil ways. Observe my commands and decrees, in accordance with the entire Law that I commanded your ancestors to obey and that I delivered to you through my servants the prophets."

[14] But they would not listen and were as stiff-necked as their ancestors, who did not trust in the Lord their God. [15] They rejected his decrees and the covenant he had made with their ancestors and the statutes he had warned them to keep. They followed worthless idols and themselves became worthless. They imitated the nations around them although the Lord had ordered them, "Do not do as they do."

[16] They forsook all the commands of the Lord their God and made for themselves two idols cast in the shape of calves, and an Asherah pole. They bowed down to all the starry hosts, and they worshiped Baal. [17] They sacrificed their sons and daughters in the fire. They practiced divination and sought omens and sold themselves to do evil in the eyes of the Lord, arousing His anger.

[18] So the Lord was very angry with Israel and removed them from his presence. Only the tribe of Judah was left, [19] and even Judah did not keep the commands of the Lord their God. They followed the practices Israel had introduced. [20] Therefore the Lord rejected all the people of Israel; He afflicted them and gave them into the hands of plunderers, until he thrust them from his presence.

II Kings chapters 18-25: *We see the last 8 kings of Judah. Ahaz did that which was right in the sight of the Lord. He removed idols and clave to the Lord. And the Lord blessed Ahaz and his reign. But most did that which was evil in the sight of the Lord. Judah was deported to Babylon in the year 605 BC.*

Ii Kings Chapter 20
Set your affairs in order
And prepare to die,

Don't wait until you're at Jordan's border
To make excuses for your life to justify.

25. Judah was exiled from its land,
Having refused to obey God's command.
Subjected to death, capture, and humiliation—
No home, no temple, no nation.

As we look at all the scriptures and history, we can find that Nebuchadnezzar, though he could have done it sooner, was 20 years in the process of destroying Jerusalem. Because Daniel was a captive and was a friend of Nebuchadnezzar and because of an influence of Esther, it took him longer to subdue it. The fall of Jerusalem was accompanied by the ministry of three great prophets, Jeremiah, Ezekiel, and Daniel. This captivity had been prophesied 100 years before. Jeremiah predicted the captivity would last 70 years, which did come to pass.

"This ended the earthly kingdom of David. But it revived in a spiritual sense, with the arrival of Christ, and will be consummated in glory at His return." (Halley: 2007, page 245)

THE BOOK OF I CHRONICLES
In Chronicles, Jesus is sovereign.

Theme: A family record to remind exiled and returning Israelites of God's chosen king and of their place in the restored Jerusalem

[15] Do your best to present yourself to God as one approved, a worker who does not need to be ashamed and who correctly handles the word of truth.

Message: The preservation of the national archives was very important to the nation of Israel. The author recounts the history of Israel, which was taken from the books of Samuel, Kings, the Pentateuch, Judges, and Ruth. The reign of David was the Golden Age of Israel when all kingdoms were united. Several of the events and genealogies lists are found in other books of the Bible. Special attention is given to the royal tribe of Judah, from which Jesus was to be born, and the priestly line of Levi. The first chapter begins with Adam and takes us to Noah and his sons, then later to Abraham and Isaac. Also, the twelve tribes descending from Jacob, with the exception of Dan and Zebulun are counted. (FCA Press: God's Game Plan. 2008)

I Chronicles 1:3-4: *(Genealogy from Adam to Noah)* Adam, Seth, Enoch, Kenan, Mahalalel, Jared, Enoch, Methuselah, Lamech, Noah. The sons of Noah are Shem, Ham, and Japheth.

I Chronicles 3:1-9: *The sons of David are listed.* These were the sons of David born to him in Hebron. . . .4.David reigned in Jerusalem thirty-three years, [5] and these were the children born to him there:. . .

The Kings of Judah beginning with the death of Solomon to the time of the exile are listed in verses 10-16. Then following a long list of genealogies, God tells about Jabez and his prayer:

I Chronicles 4:9-10: Now Jabez was more honorable than his brothers, and his mother called his name Jabez, saying, "Because I bore him in pain." 10 And Jabez called on the God of Israel saying, "Oh, that You would bless me indeed, and enlarge my territory, that Your hand would be with me, and that You would keep me from evil, that I may not cause pain!" So God granted him what he requested.

The Book, The Prayer of Jabez (2000), by Bruce Wilkinson, made this scripture famous and changed the lives of many. I prayed this prayer daily after reading the book—especially the part that says, "Bless me and enlarge my territory. Let your hand be on me, and keep me from the evil one." It is difficult to sincerely pray "Enlarge my territory of influence" because it brings more responsibility. For many, prayer became a treasured, life-long habit and significant changes were seen in lives.

I Chronicles 6:1-19: *The Tribe of Levi, beginning with Rohath and going to the exile are listed. Then Levi's sons and grandsons are listed.*

I Chronicles 6:31-47: *The temple musicians are accounted: 31:* These are the men David put in charge of the music in the house of the Lord after the ark came to rest there. [32] They ministered with music before the tabernacle, the tent of meeting, until Solomon built the temple of the Lord in Jerusalem.

The Tribe of Levi and the High Priests are elaborated upon in I Chronicles 6:48-61.

The Scarlet Thread: Their fellow Levites were assigned to all the other duties of the tabernacle, the house of God. [49] But Aaron and his descendants were the ones who presented offerings on the altar of burnt offering and on the altar of incense in connection with all that was done in the Most Holy Place, making atonement for Israel, in accordance with all that Moses the servant

[64] So the Israelites gave the Levites these towns and their pasturelands. [65] From the tribes of Judah, Simeon and Benjamin they allotted the previously named towns. (*Then a listing of the lands given by each of the 11 other tribes to the Levites is given.*)

The Genealogy of some of Jacob's sons, or of some of the 12 tribes is given in I Chronicles 7.

We are told that all Israel was listed in the genealogies recorded in the book of Kings of Israel.

In I Chronicles 9 the inhabitants of Jerusalem after Judah returned from captivity in Babylon are given. Also, duties of the Levite Families in the temple are listed.

The Bible is not in chronological order. Especially, Chronicles are not in the order of the calendar. *I Chronicles 12 tells of the tribes all volunteering in David's army and wanting him to be King instead of Saul.* These were the men who came to David at Ziklag, while he was banished from the presence of Saul son of Kish.

I Chron. 12:38: All these were fighting men who volunteered to serve in the ranks. They came to Hebron fully determined to make David king over all Israel. All the rest of the Israelites were also of one mind to make David king. (*We know that David had all 12 tribes under him in the United Kingdom.*)

In I Chron. 13 David wants to bring the Ark of the Covenant Lord to the Temple in Jerusalem.

[2] He then said to the whole assembly of Israel, "If it seems good to you and if it is the will of the Lord our God, let us send word far and wide to the rest of our people throughout the territories of Israel, and also to the priests and Levites who are with them in their towns and pasturelands, to come and join us. [3] Let us bring the ark of our God back to us, for we did not inquire of it during the reign of Saul." [4] The whole assembly agreed to do this, because it seemed right to all the people.

[7] They moved the ark of God from Abinadab's house on a new cart, with Uzzah and Ahio guiding it. [8] David and all the Israelites were celebrating with all their might before God, with songs and with harps, lyres, timbrels, cymbals and trumpets.

But Uzzah died while carrying the ark. Only those of the tribe of Levi are to carry the ark.

5 After David had constructed buildings for himself in the City of David, he prepared a place for the ark of God and pitched a tent for it. [2] Then David said, "No one but the Levites may carry the ark of God, because the Lord chose them to carry the ark of the Lord and to minister before Him forever." *When God makes a covenant with man, it is very serious*

The Ark Brought to Jerusalem

I Chronicles 15:1: After David had constructed buildings for himself in the City of David, he prepared a place for the ark of God and pitched a tent for it. [2] Then David said, "No one but the Levites may carry the ark of God, because the Lord chose them to carry the ark of the Lord and to minister before him forever."

[3] David assembled all Israel in Jerusalem to bring up the ark of the Lord to the place he had prepared for it. [4] He called together the descendants of Aaron and the Levites: *Next, the descendants of Levi are counted.*

Then David told the Priests and Levites that only they are to consecrate themselves to bring the Ark of the Lord to the place he had prepared, as Moses had commanded.

.[16] *David told the leaders of the Levites to appoint their fellow Levites as musicians to make a joyful sound with musical instruments: lyres, harps and cymbals.*

So the Levites appointed relatives as musicians. Their names are listed.

They also appointed doorkeepers for the Ark. Their names are listed. Priests were to blow trumpets before the ark of God.

So David and the elders of Israel and the commanders of units of a thousand went to bring up the ark of the covenant of the Lord from the house of Obed-Edom, with rejoicing.

David wanted to build a house for the Lord, but he didn't get to because he is a king of war.

David told Nathan that his own house is better than that of the Lord. Nathan is the prophet of the Lord who advised David. The word of the Lord came to Nathan saying:

I Chronicles 17:4: Go and tell David, Thus saith the Lord, Thou shalt not build Me an house to dwell in. *Then God tells of all the ways He has blessed David and He makes a promise to him.*

I Chronicles 17: 11-14: [11] When your days are over and you go to be with your ancestors, I will raise up your offspring to succeed you, one of your own sons, and I will establish his kingdom. [12] He is the one who will build a house for Me, and I will establish his throne forever. [13] I will be his father, and he will be My son. I will never take my love away from him, as I took it away from your predecessor. [14] I will set him over my house and My kingdom forever; his throne will be established forever.'"

We know that David's son, Solomon, built the temple after David had drawn up the plans. What a wonderful blessing it was for David that his throne would be established forever. Jesus will be a descendant of David.

Remaining chapters show that God did bless David in war, as he had promised to do when kings and nations honored him. Chapter 18:14: So David reigned over all Israel and executed judgment and justice among all his people.

Preparations for the Temple

I Chronicles 22:1: Then David said, "The house of the Lord God is to be here, and also the altar of burnt offering for Israel." [2] So David gave orders to assemble the foreigners residing in Israel, and from among them he appointed stonecutters to prepare dressed stone for building the house of God. [3] He provided a large amount of iron to make nails for the doors of the gateways and for the fittings, and more bronze than could be weighed. [4] He also provided more cedar logs than could be counted, for the Sardinians and Tyrians had brought large numbers of them to David.

[5] David said, "My son Solomon is young and inexperienced, and the house to be built for the Lord should be of great magnificence and fame and splendor in the sight of all the nations. Therefore I will make preparations for it." So David made extensive preparations before his death.

[6] Then he called for his son Solomon and charged him to build a house for the Lord, the God of Israel [9] But you will have a son who will be a man of peace and rest, and I will give him rest from all his enemies on every side. His name will be Solomon, and I will grant Israel peace and quiet during his reign. [10] He is the one who will build a house for My Name. He will be My son, and I will be his father. And I will establish the throne of his kingdom over Israel forever.'

[11] "Now, my son, the Lord be with you, and may you have success and build the house of the Lord your God, as he said you would. [12] May the Lord give you discretion and understanding when he puts you in command over Israel, so that you may keep the law of the Lord your God. [13] Then you will have success if you are careful to observe the decrees and laws that the Lord gave Moses for Israel. Be strong and courageous. Do not be afraid

[19] Now devote your heart and soul to seeking the Lord your God. Begin to build the sanctuary of the Lord God, so that you may bring the ark of the covenant of the Lord and the sacred articles belonging to God into the temple that will be built for the Name of the Lord."

David's Last Words: Then King David said to the whole assembly: "My son Solomon, the one whom God has chosen, is young and inexperienced. The task is great, because this palatial structure is not for man but for the Lord God. [2] With all my resources I have provided for the temple of my God—Now, who is willing to consecrate themselves to the Lord today?"

[6] Then the leaders of families, the officers of the tribes of Israel, the commanders of thousands and commanders of hundreds, and the officials in charge of the king's work gave willingly. . . .[9] The people rejoiced at the willing response of their leaders, for they had given freely and wholeheartedly to the Lord. David the king also rejoiced greatly.

David's Prayer

[10] David praised the Lord in the presence of the whole assembly, saying,

"Praise be to You, Lord, the God of our father Israel, from everlasting to everlasting.

[11] Yours, Lord, is the greatness and the power and the glory and the majesty and the splendor, for everything in heaven and earth is Yours.

Yours, Lord, is the kingdom; You are exalted as head over all.

[12] Wealth and honor come from you; you are the ruler of all things.

In your hands are strength and power to exalt and give strength to all.

[13] Now, our God, we give you thanks, and praise your glorious name.

[14] "But who am I, and who are my people, that we should be able to give as generously as this? Everything comes from you, and we have given you only what comes from your hand.[15] We are foreigners and strangers in your sight, as were all our ancestors. Our days on earth are like a shadow, without hope. [16] Lord our God, all this abundance that we have provided for [20] Then David said to the whole assembly, "Praise the Lord your God." So they all praised the Lord, the God of their fathers; they bowed down, prostrating themselves before the Lord and the king. Then they acknowledged Solomon son of David as king a second time, anointing him before the Lord to be ruler and Zadok to be priest. [23] So Solomon sat on the throne of the Lord as king in place of his father David. He prospered and all Israel obeyed him.

[25] The Lord highly exalted Solomon in the sight of all Israel and bestowed on him royal splendor such as no king over Israel ever had before.

The Death of David: [26] David son of Jesse was king over all Israel. [27] He ruled over Israel forty years—seven in Hebron and thirty-three in Jerusalem. [28] He died at a good old age, having enjoyed long life, wealth and honor. His son Solomon succeeded him as king.

David, the man after God's own heart had served God nobly. How blessed he must have felt when he later met Him who bore his name, "Son of David."

THE BOOK OF II CHRONICLES

In II Chronicles, Jesus is sovereign.
Theme: The kingship and worship in Judah from Solomon to the Exile.

Message: The events narrated span a period from 970 to 538 B.C. After the glory days of Solomon, the people forsook temple worship and worshipped idols. They lost their national identity when Jerusalem was destroyed in 586 B. C. There were periods of time when they would decline when led by evil kings and periods of spiritual reformation and restored national pride when led by good kings. Chronicles ends with the exile into Babylon, but we do get a brief glimpse into the future restoration of Israel.

Details included in II Chronicles that are not in Samuel and Kings are the plans for the building of the temple and the tabernacle, the facts that the spoils of war were used for the building of them and the people gave generously for the building. Also, the glory cloud appeared at the dedication of both buildings. In chapters 1 through 9, the great wealth, worldwide acclaim, political stability, and the magnificent temple are emphasized. Each king is evaluated upon his worship of God and obedience to the law. (FCA Press, 2008)

II Chron. 1:2 Then Solomon spoke to all Israel—to the commanders of thousands and commanders of hundreds, to the judges and to all the leaders in Israel, the heads of families—³ and Solomon and the whole assembly went to the high place at Gibeon, for God's tent of meeting was there, which Moses the Lord's servant had made in the wilderness. ⁶ Solomon went up to the bronze altar before the Lord in the tent of meeting and offered a thousand burnt offerings on it.⁷ That night God appeared to Solomon and said to him, "Ask for whatever You want me to give You."

⁸ Solomon answered God, "You have shown great kindness to David my father and have made me king in his place. ⁹ Now, Lord God, let your promise to my father David be confirmed, for You have made me king over a people who are as numerous as the dust of the earth. ¹⁰ Give me wisdom and knowledge, that I may lead this people, for who is able to govern this great people of Yours?"

¹¹ God said to Solomon, "Since this is your heart's desire and You have not asked for wealth, possessions or honor, nor for the death of your enemies, and since You have not asked for a long life but for wisdom and knowledge to govern my people over whom I have made You king, ¹² therefore wisdom and knowledge will be given You. And I will also give you wealth, possessions and honor, such as no king who was before you ever had and none after you will have."

¹³ Then Solomon went to Jerusalem from the high place at Gibeon, from before the tent of meeting. And he reigned over Israel.

¹⁴ Solomon accumulated chariots and horses; he had fourteen hundred chariots and twelve thousand horses,[a] which he kept in the chariot cities and also with him in Jerusalem.¹⁵ The king made silver and gold as common in Jerusalem as stones, and cedar

as plentiful as sycamore-fig trees in the foothills. [16] Solomon's horses were imported from Egypt and from Kue. . .

II Chronicles, Chapter 1
Solomon of himself accomplished naught.
Only when to God for wisdom he sought,
He was granted riches unknown.
As Solomon planted in luxury, with tears he reaped what he had sown.

2. In all ways so unskilled
Who am I, chosen to build
A house for our God so great?
Not even the heavens his vastness can equate.

3. The sight where Abraham offered His precious son
Was built the temple of the Lord on Moriah's Mount.
My temple is my heart where I can count
On Christ living after His sacrifice was done.

II Chron 2:1: Then Solomon determined to build a temple for the name of the Lord, and a royal house for himself. *This temple would replace the tabernacle, the house in which sacrifices were made while the Israelites were camped at the foot of Mount Sinai.*

Verse 2 *tells us that Solomon had 70,000 men to bear burdens, 80,000 men to hew the mountain and 3600 men to oversee them.*

II Chron. 3:1:Then Solomon began to build the temple of the Lord in Jerusalem on Mount Moriah, where the Lord had appeared to his father David. It was on the threshing floor of Araunah[a] the Jebusite, the place provided by David. [2] He began building on the second day of the second month in the fourth year of his reign.

He overlaid the inside with pure gold. (*It appears that nearly everything was overlaid with gold*) [9] The gold nails weighed fifty shekels. [0] He also overlaid the upper parts with gold. *The furnishings were also made of pure gold.*

The extravaganza of the building is found throughout chapters 2, 3, 4 and 5.

4. In the temple only gold was used.
The purest and costliest is not abused
When dedicated to Almighty's glory
To help foretell the Gospel's story.

5. The trumpeters and singers praised God with one sound aloud.
The glory of the Lord filled the house as a cloud.
The priests could not even stand
To minister or perform their duties on command.

6. For months there has been no rain.
The earth is barren. The livestock's in thirsty pain.
If I confess thy name and turn from my sin.
God will hear from heaven and send blessings again.
God, in this place I seek You and pray.
Clothed in Your saving grace, I am strengthened every day.

The Ark of the Covenant of the Lord is placed in the temple in II Chronicles 5: 2-13.
Then Solomon said, "The Lord has said that He would dwell in a dark cloud; I have built a magnificent temple for You, a place for you to dwell forever."

[3] While the whole assembly of Israel was standing there, the king turned around and blessed them. [4] Then he said: "Praise be to the Lord, the God of Israel, who with His hands has fulfilled what he promised with His mouth to my father David. For He said, [5] 'Since the day I brought My people out of Egypt, I have not chosen a city in any tribe of Israel to have a temple built so that My Name might be there, nor have I chosen anyone to be ruler over My people Israel. [6] But now I have chosen Jerusalem for My Name to be there, and I have chosen David to rule My people Israel.'

[7] "My father David had it in his heart to build a temple for the Name of the Lord, the God of Israel. [8] But the Lord said to my father David, 'You did well to have it in your heart to build a temple for my Name. [9] Nevertheless, you are not the one to build the temple, but your son, your own flesh and blood—he is the one who will build the temple for My Name.'

[10] "The Lord has kept the promise he made. I have succeeded David my father and now I sit on the throne of Israel, just as the Lord promised, and I have built the temple for the Name of the Lord, the God of Israel. [11] There I have placed the ark, in which is the covenant of the Lord that He made with the people of Israel."

Solomon's Prayer of Dedication: II Chron 6:12: Then Solomon stood before the altar of the Lord in front of the whole assembly of Israel and spread out his hands. [14] He said:

"Lord, the God of Israel, there is no God like You in heaven or on earth—You who keep your covenant of love with Your servants who continue wholeheartedly in Your way. [15] You have kept your promise to your servant David my father; with Your mouth you have promised and with Your hand you have fulfilled it—as it is today. . . . [17] And now, Lord, the God of Israel, let Your word that you promised Your servant David come true.

[18] "But will God really dwell on earth with humans? The heavens, even the highest heavens, cannot contain You. How much less this temple I have built! [19] Yet, Lord my God,

give attention to Your servant's prayer and his plea for mercy. Hear from heaven, Your dwelling place; and when You hear, forgive.

[24] "When Your people Israel have been defeated by an enemy because they have sinned against You and when they turn back and give praise to Your name, praying and making supplication before You in this temple, [25] then hear from heaven and forgive the sin of Your people Israel and bring them back to the land You gave to them and their ancestors.

[26] "When the heavens are shut up and there is no rain because Your people have sinned against You, and when they pray toward this place and give praise to Your name and turn from their sin because You have afflicted them, [27] then hear from heaven and forgive the sin of Your servants, Your people Israel. Teach them the right way to live, and send rain on the land You gave Your people for an inheritance.,,,30. Forgive, and deal with everyone according to all they do, since You know their hearts (for You alone know the human heart), [31] so that they will fear You and

[36] "When they sin against You—for there is no one who does not sin—and You become angry with them and give them over to the enemy, who takes them captive to a land far away or near; [37] and if they have a change of heart in the land where they are held captive, and repent and plead with You in the land of their captivity and say, 'We have sinned, we have done wrong and acted wickedly'; [38] and if they turn back to You with all their heart and soul in the land of their captivity where they were taken, and pray toward the land you gave their ancestors, toward the city you have chosen and toward the temple I have built for your Name; [39] then from heaven, your dwelling place, hear their prayer and their pleas, and uphold their cause. And forgive your people, who have sinned against you.

A beloved scripture and promise for America today is II Chronicles 7:14: If my people, which are called by My name, shall humble themselves, and pray, and seek My face, and turn from their wicked ways; then will I hear from heaven, and will forgive their sin, and will heal their land. *As long as Israel obeyed God, they were blessed. We have hindsight. We should know what to expect because the same thing has happened to all nations in history.*

How people long for freedom! Today I listened to the Gaither Homecoming Songs of Freedom, and the Gaither Vocal Band had sung "Let Freedom Ring" at Carnegie Hall after the 911 Bombing. All we have to do is to turn to God to be blessed with Freedom.

II Chronicles 7. If my people who are called by my name
Shall humble themselves and pray,
I will heal their land of its blame.
No mention is made of the unbelievers who are astray.

142

Solomon completed what he planned to do.
With honor he was treated as King of the Hebrew.

8: Solomon conscripted slaves of the foreigners of the land.
Much expense he saved by forcing work from innocent man.

9: Silver was too cheap to count in Solomon's day;
Ore of gold by the heap was paid by kings far away.

II Chron. 9:22: And King Solomon passed all the kings of the earth in riches and wisdom. And all the kings of the earth sought the presence of Solomon to hear the wisdom that God had given him. Verse 30: And Solomon reigned in Jerusalem over all Israel forty years.

Chapters 10-12: Rehoboam, Solomon's son, reigned for 18 years. The magnificent kingdom plunged into sin and the kingdom split. Ten of the twelve tribes seceded and formed the northern kingdom. Judah is made up of the tribes of Judah and of Benjamin. Constant war developed between Judah and Israel! .In Chapter 12: 12, however, we find that because Rehoboam humbled himself before the Lord, God's anger was turned away from him.

10 "What do you want as a king," Rehoboam asked the young men,
"Deal harshly in everything. Make them endure a worse burden."
The word of the Lord spoken by Ahijah the Shilonite
Fast proved to be absolutely right.
Because of Rehoboam's cruel treatment,
Ten tribes of Israel to Jeroboam set up their tent.

(Here, we see the division of Israel into two Kingdoms. Ten tribes left Israel and went with Jeroboam to form Judah.)

11. What will Israel do without any holy priests?
All will bow down to carved idols of unholy beasts.
Jeroboam in himself grew wise.
False priests, idols, and temples he subsidizes,
To keep Israel from going to Jerusalem to worship,
The Levites had already from this evil hand slipped.

12 Rehoboam forsook God's law,
In the hand of Egyptians King Shishak, God was to destroy all.
When humbled were the princes and king,
God decided not to allow Shishak everything.

He took the temple's treasures and golden shields;
Rehoboam to brass armaments had to yield.

After the division of Israel into two kingdoms, a great contrast between Judah and Israel developed. Judah had 2 great kings, Asa, and his son, Jehoshaphat. In chapters 12-14, Asa reformed and fortified Judah. Israel, on the other hand, had seven kings that did evil in God's sight, including King Ahab! Jehosephat reigned in Judah while Ahab reigned in Israel. Though Ahab, king of Israel, had the great prophet, Elijah, to advise him he didn't heed him.

II Chronicles 15
For a long season Israel had been without a priest to teach;
The evil nation had not one to reach.
Without a hand to aid in adversity,
Asa, King of Judah, hearkened to Obed's prophecy;
"Be strong, let not your hands be weak,
When in time of trouble, the true God seek.

In II Chronicles, chapters 17-20, Jehoshaphat sent the priests and Levites to the Book of the Law and he established a system of justice throughout the land. (Going to the Book of the Law is always the answer, as we were told in Leviticus.)

17 Jehoshaphat's heart was lifted up in the Lord's ways.
Garrisons and fenced cities against Israel naves
The kingdom as established in his hand.
Levites taught the book of the law throughout all the land.

18. As Micaiah declared, "What the Lord says I will speak."
False prophets even in these days, upt the spiritually weak.

19 "Upon thee is the Lord's wrath."
Jehoshaphat misused the witness he hath,
He loved those to whom the Lord showed hate;
However, as a courageous king, he was great.

In chapter 20, many nations were threatening Judah, and Jehoshaphat's prayer to God is recorded. In fact, all of Judah prayed. In the remaining chapters, many kings reigned in Judah and in Israel. Many "did that which was evil in the sight of the Lord."

20. Moab and Ammon,
A battle against Judah had begun.
Jehoshaphat bowed his head with his face to the ground;
Judah's victory in the wilderness was profound.

The poetry by Marilyn Kay Gage shows a tiny portion <u>of the horror that came upon Israel when they sinned against God.</u>

21 Jehoram had Ahab's evil daughter as wife.
She undermined her husband and national life.
Jerusalem and Judah to fornicate were compelled.
He died of a sore sickness when his bowels fell.

22. Athaliah was an unholy mother,
Known by all as the one who did murder.
All the royal seed of Judah
Except Joash, son of Ahaziah.

24. When seven years old, Joash began to reign,
The temple was in ill repair.
Throughout Judah he began to proclaim,
"Into a chest a collection will be made for all to have a share."

29. Hezekiah cleansed the temple.
That had been corrupt so long.
An undertaking not so simple,
Since Judah, for generations, had worshipped wrong.

30 Hezekiah sent letters by post
To Israel and Judah, and most
Laughed and mocked them to scorn.
Be not stiff-necked as your fathers, you new-born.
Yield yourselves to the Lord and enter into His sanctuary.
Serve the Lord, don't be so contrary!

31. Israel brought its first fruits in abundance
To present their portions to the priests.
The Lord blessed His people for this extravagance
From the fields and increase.

32. From the hand of Sennacherib God saved
Judah because Hezekiah and Isaiah the prophet prayed.
The Lord sent an angel who forced the king of Assyria home with the battle unwon.

33. Manasseh made Judah to err.
In thorns and fetters he was carried to Babylon.
He humbled himself before God. The Lord did hear
And answer his supplication.

In II Chronicles 14 and 25, *Josiah, the child of eight years old was king. He returned to the Law of the Lord. If only he had taught his sons, so they would have ruled as his father did! "Pass your faith to the next generation!"*

34. Can I ever at the altar say, "No, you are too young."
Josiah was only eight when on him a whole kingdom hung.
He searched the Book of the Law for the Lord's will.
If his sons had followed Josiah's example, Judah would be in freedom still.

35. Josiah kept the Passover feast.
There had not been one to compare since Samuel's day.
All the inhabitants of Judah and Israel including Levites and priests
Were present for the holy stay.

36. Judah transgresses willingly,
The Law of Moses no one remembers.
God sent messengers,
Who were misused. Against God's wrath there is now no remedy.

The King of the Chaldeans
Slew everyone, regardless of age.
Those who from the sword fled
Were carried to Babylon as captive from their heritage.

The people of Israel were taken to Babylonia, in what is known as the Babylonian Exile. But Judah survived the captivity. About 50 years later, they would initiate the rebuilding of Jerusalem and the Temple. And to Judah, he gives hope of the Messiah

The books of Ezra. Nehemiah. and Esther tell of the Babylonian Exile and the return from exile. Because the Israelites had not fulfilled their obligations to God under the covenants with Abraham, his people, and with David, God allowed evil people to defeat and to carry them away from their homeland.

THE BOOK OF EZRA

In Ezra, Jesus is the true and faithful scribe.
Theme: Beginning again by rebuilding the temple

Message: The principal character is Ezra. Ezra is often seen as the "father of Judaism" because he promoted a way of life centering on total allegiance to the Torah (God's Law.) His policies saved Judaism from oblivion at a critical period in their history. According to Halley (2007), the events from this book last from 538-458 B. C. Chapters 1 to 7 weave together various lists of official documents and memoirs of Ezra. God used both Persian leaders and Jewish leaders to discipline and to bless His people.

Key Verses: Ezra 7:21-23a: Now I, King Artaxerxes, decree that all the treasurers of Trans-Euphrates are to provide with diligence whatever Ezra the priest, the teacher of the Law of the God of heaven, may ask of you—[22] up to a hundred talents of silver, a hundred measures of wheat, a hundred baths of wine, a hundred baths of olive oil, and salt without limit. [23] Whatever the God of heaven has prescribed. let it be done with diligence for the temple of the God of heaven.

Ezra 1: The Proclamation of Cyrus: *King Cyrus made the proclamation permitting the Jews to return to Jerusalem from Babylonian captivity shortly after Daniel had read "the handwriting on the wall."* Ezra 2 gives a register of those who returned to Jerusalem.

Ezra 3 tells of the laying of the foundation of the temple. *When completed, the people made the "heavens ring" with their praise and thanksgiving. In Ezra 4, the work was stopped until the reign of King Darius I. When we read the book of Daniel, we will find that Daniel, a young Jew who was in captivity in Babylon, was greatly admired by King Darius. In chapters 5 and 6, King Darius gave an order that funds needed for completion would be drawn from his royal treasury of Babylon, and the temple was completed!*

Chapters 7 and 8 *reveal how Ezra journeyed to Jerusalem to teach Judah the Law of God and to restore the temple service.* Ezra 7:10: For Ezra had prepared his heart to seek the law of the Lord and to do it, and to teach in Israel statutes and judgments.

But when Ezra arrived in Jerusalem, he was heartsick because the people, the priests, Levites, and leaders had again married idolatrous neighbors. This was exactly what they had been warned against from the beginning. Ezra told them what they must do to rid them of non-Jewish wives. Ezra's prayer for the *Jews is recorded in Ezra 9.*

5. . .I fell on my knees with my hands spread out to the Lord my God [6] and prayed: "I am too ashamed and disgraced, my God, to lift up my face to you, because our sins are higher than our heads and our guilt has reached to the heavens. [7] From the days of our ancestors until now, our guilt has been great. Because of our sins, we and our kings and our priests have been subjected to the sword and captivity. . . . [8] "But now, for a brief moment, the Lord our God has been gracious in leaving us a remnant and giving us a firm place in his sanctuary, and so our God gives light to our eyes and a little relief in our bondage. [9] Though

we are slaves, our God has not forsaken us in our bondage. He has shown us kindness in the sight of the kings of Persia: He has granted us new life to rebuild the house of our God and repair its ruins, and he has given us a wall of protection in Judah and Jerusalem. *(America, God has done much more than this for us. Can we not learn from history?)*

[10] "But now, our God, what can we say after this? For we have forsaken the commands [11] you gave through your servants the prophets when you said: 'The land you are entering to possess is a land polluted by the corruption of its peoples. By their detestable practices they have filled it with their impurity from one end to the other. [12] Therefore, do not give Your daughters in marriage to their sons or take their daughters for your sons. Do not seek a treaty of friendship with them at any time, that you may be strong and eat the good things of the land and leave it to your children as an everlasting inheritance. [13] "What has happened to us is a result of our evil deeds and our great guilt, and yet, our God, You have punished us less than our sins deserved and have given us a remnant like this. [14] Shall we then break your commands again and intermarry with the peoples who commit such detestable practices? Would You not be angry enough with us to destroy us, leaving us no remnant or survivor? [15] Lord, the God of Israel, You are righteous! We are left this day as a remnant. Here we are before You in our guilt, though because of it not one of us can stand in Your presence."

The People's Confession of Sin

Then in Ezra 10, all the men of Judah and Benjamin gathered, trembling because of this matter, and Ezra spoke and said, "You have been unfaithful; you have married foreign women, adding to Israel's guilt. [11] Now honor the Lord, the God of your ancestors, and do His will. Separate yourselves from the peoples around you and from your foreign wives."

[12] The whole assembly responded with a loud voice: "You are right! We must do as you say."

(God initiated marriage, and who we marry is very important, not only because we must obey God, but because following his commandments will bring happiness.)

Further reforms are noted in the book of Nehemiah. Nehemiah returned from captivity to rebuild the walls of Jerusalem.

THE BOOK OF NEHEMIAH
In Nehemiah, Jesus is the rebuilder of broken walls and lives.

Theme: Restoration of the walls of Jerusalem and revival of the people, providing a legacy of God-given leadership principles.

Message: Events cover a cycle from 445-432 B.C. The principle character is Nehemiah, as he describes the rebuilding of the walls of Jerusalem. We see that as Nehemiah follows God, he models invaluable, God-given leadership principles for all types of situations. This book complements Ezra in reporting the restoration of Israel after 70 years of captivity in Babylon. Ezra had revived spiritual and nationalistic fervor, which caused Nehemiah to be distressed over the broken-down walls of Jerusalem. The physical condition of the walls parallels the spiritual condition of the people. As the walls are restored the people are rehabilitated. (FCA, God's Game Plan 2008)

Key Verses: When all our enemies heard about this, all the surrounding nations were afraid and lost their self-confidence, because they realized that this work had been done with the help of our God. Nehemiah 6:16

In Nehemiah 1, *Nehemiah enquired concerning the Jews that were left of the captivity and concerning Jerusalem.*

[3] They said to me, "Those who survived the exile and are back in the province are in great trouble and disgrace. The wall of Jerusalem is broken down, and its gates have been burned with fire." [4] When I heard these things, I sat down and wept. For some days I mourned and fasted and prayed before the God of heaven. [5] Then I said:

"Lord, the God of heaven, the great and awesome God, who keeps His covenant of love with those who love him and keep his commandments, [6] let Your ear be attentive and your eyes open to hear the prayer your servant is praying before You day and night for your servants, the people of Israel. I confess the sins we Israelites, including myself and my father's family, have committed against You. [7] We have acted very wickedly toward You. We have not obeyed the commands, decrees and laws You gave your servant Moses.

[8] "Remember the instruction you gave your servant Moses, saying, 'If you are unfaithful, I will scatter you among the nations, [9] but if you return to me and obey my commands, then even if your exiled people are at the farthest horizon, I will gather them from there and bring them to the place I have chosen as a dwelling for my Name.'

[10] "They are your servants and your people, whom you redeemed by Your great strength and your mighty hand. [11] Lord, let Your ear be attentive to the prayer of this Your servant and to the prayer of your servants who delight in revering Your name. Give your servant success today by granting him favor in the presence of this man." (*We can pray the Bible. This is an example of how we should pray.*)

Nehemiah 2:5 *tells how Nehemiah went to King Artaxerxrs and made the following request:*

"If it pleases the king and if Your servant has found favor in His sight, let Him send me to the city in Judah where my ancestors are buried so that I can rebuild it." *His request was granted. We probably have Queen Esther to thank for this*

In Nehemiah 3, the gates of the city are rebuilt; in chapters 4 and 5, the wall is miraculously built. Though many enemies of the Jews bitterly opposed the building of the wall, Nehemiah, with faith in God, armed and arranged his men and finished in 52 days.

[17] Then I said to them, "You see the trouble we are in: Jerusalem lies in ruins, and its gates have been burned with fire. Come, let us rebuild the wall of Jerusalem, and we will no longer be in disgrace." [18] I also told them about the gracious hand of my God on me and what the king had said to me.

They replied, "Let us start rebuilding." So they began this good work.

[19] But when Sanballat the Horonite, Tobiah the Ammonite official and Geshem the Arab heard about it, they mocked and ridiculed us. "What is this you are doing?" they asked. "Are you rebelling against the king?"

[20] I answered them by saying, "The God of heaven will give us success. We His servants will start rebuilding, but as for you, you have no share in Jerusalem or any claim or historic right to it."

(This is what the Jews of today reiterate to the many surrounding enemies. They gallantly defend Israel against innumerable odds.)

Jerusalem again became a fortified city in 586 BC. In Nehemiah 7 and 8: *Nehemiah and Ezra gathered the people together, and Ezra read every day for seven days from the Book of the Law and explained it so the people understood. A great revival and a solemn covenant to keep the law resulted.*

Nehemiah 8:8: They read from the Book of the Law of God, making it clear[a] and giving the meaning so that the people understood what was being read. [9] Then Nehemiah the governor, Ezra the priest and teacher of the Law, and the Levites who were instructing the people said to them all, "This day is holy to the Lord your God. Do not mourn or weep." For all the people had been weeping as they listened to the words of the Law. Nehemiah said, "Go and enjoy choice food and sweet drinks, and send some to those who have nothing prepared. This day is holy to our Lord. Do not grieve, for the joy of the Lord is your strength."

The finding of the book of Law also brought about Josiah's great reformation in 2 Kings 22. When Martin Luther found a Bible, it led to the great reformation and brought religious liberty to our modern world. Today, when the Bible is really read and explained, we may also have revival.

In Nehemiah 9, Ezra and Nehemiah reviewed the history of the Israelites, which resulted in their confession of sin, and they made a covenant with God. Nehemiah 9-12 *tells of the covenant and dedication of the wall. They bound themselves to walk in God's law:*

Nehemiah 9:38: In view of all this, we are making a binding agreement, putting it in writing, and our leaders, our Levites and our priests are affixing their seals to it.

We citizens of America have also been blessed more than any other country of history. Should this not make us want to return to God with praise and thanksgiving!

Nehemiah 13 gives reforms concerning tithes, the Sabbath, and marriage. Nehemiah lived to a great age and governed Judah for the rest of his life. He was a man of prayer, patriotism, action, courage, and perseverance. (Halley. 2006)

THE BOOK OF ESTHER
In Esther, Jesus is Mordecai's courage.

Theme: A Profile of Human Courage and the providence of God in the free decisions of people, especially in using Esther to deliver the Jews.

Background. According to Halley (2007), more than a generation after the Jews were allowed to return to Israel from Babylonian captivity, Esther and some of the Jews remained scattered throughout the known world. Esther's family was in Persia. Esther reads like a modern day suspense novel with a plot and counterplot, danger, and unexpected twists of fate, but it is really a significant historical event, telling of how the Jews were delivered from annihilation. Esther's marriage to the King made possible the rebuilding of the walls of Jerusalem. Except for her, the story of the Jews and of the world might be quite different. No Hebrew Nation, no Messiah. No Messiah, a lost world.

The books of the Bible are not in chronological order. The book of Esther is one of the last books of the Old Testament and takes place in 483 B, C. God's sovereign and providential care of His people is emphasized. In the year 2006 the epic film, *One Night with the King*, was released, telling the Biblical story of Esther, who risked her life by approaching the king to request that he save the Jewish people.

I first became interested in Esther when my mother underlined in my Bible and wrote in the margins of the book of Esther, showing me the intrigue of it all. My mother presented to me this story, making Haman the villain, Esther the heroine, and Mordecai, her Father-figure, the hero. She showed me how God was in the background all the time, though God's name is never used in the book of Esther. I will share verses and thoughts she shared with me.

The first chapter tells of King Ahasuerus, who reigned over 127 provinces. He gave feasts showing the riches of his glorious kingdom. His queen, Vashti, who was very beautiful, refused to come to a banquet at which he planned to show her beauty. He banished Vashti.

Esther 2:2: Then the king's personal attendants proposed, "Let a search be made for beautiful young virgins for the king. . . .bring all these beautiful young women into the harem at the citadel of Susa. . . .[4]Then let the young woman who pleases the king be queen instead of Vashti." This advice appealed to the king, and he followed it.

[5]Now there was, a Jew of the tribe of Benjamin, named Mordecai, who had been carried into exile from Jerusalem by Nebuchadnezzar king of Babylon. [7]Mordecai had a cousin, Esther, whom he had brought up because she had neither father nor mother. . . .[8]When the king's order and edict had been proclaimed, many young women were brought. . . .Esther also was taken to the king's palace. . .[9]She pleased him and won his favor. [10]Esther had not revealed her nationality and family background, because Mordecai had forbidden her to do so. [11]Every day he walked back and forth near the courtyard of the harem to find out how Esther was.

15b. And Esther won the favor of everyone who saw her. [16] She was taken to King Xerxes (Ahasaurus) in the royal residence. . . .[17] Now the king was attracted to Esther more than to any of the other virgins. . . .So he set a royal crown on her head and made her queen instead of Vashti. [18] And the king gave a great banquet, Esther's banquet, for all his nobles and officials.

Haman's Plot to Destroy the Jews

Esther 3:1: After these events, King Ahasuerus honored Haman, giving him a seat of honor higher than that of all the other nobles. [2] All the royal officials at the king's gate knelt down and paid honor to Haman, for the king had commanded this concerning him. But Mordecai would not kneel down or pay him honor. [3] Then the royal officials at the king's gate asked Mordecai, "Why do you disobey the king's command?" [4] Day after day they spoke to him but he refused to comply. Therefore they told Haman about it to see whether Mordecai's behavior would be tolerated, for he had told them he was a Jew. [5] When Haman saw that Mordecai would not kneel down or pay him honor, he was enraged.[6] Yet having learned who Mordecai's people were, he scorned the idea of killing only Mordecai. Instead Haman looked for a way to destroy all Mordecai's people, the Jews, throughout the whole kingdom.

[8] Then Haman said to the King, "There is a certain people dispersed among the peoples in all the provinces of your kingdom who keep themselves separate. Their customs are different from those of all other people, and they do not obey the king's laws; it is not in the king's best interest to tolerate them. [9] If it pleases the king, let a decree be issued to destroy them. . . .

So the king gladly made the decree, sealed with his own ring. Letters were sent out to all the provinces to destroy all Jews, young and old.

Esther 4:1: When Mordecai learned of all that had been done, he tore his clothes, put on sackcloth and ashes, and went out into the city, wailing loudly and bitterly. *Mordecai sent a text of the edict for the annihilation of the Jews to Esther and asked her to go to the king and beg for mercy for her people. Esther then sent these words to Mordecai:*

Esther 4:11b: any man or woman who approaches the king in the inner court without being summoned the king has but one law: that they be put to death unless the king extends the gold scepter to them and spares their lives. But thirty days have passed since I was called to go to the king." *In the Girls' Auxiliary in the Southern Baptists, the highest honor a young lady could achieve by doing much Bible Memory Work was "The Queen with the Scepter? My niece, Marjorie Soon Paddack Mobley, achieved this honor!*

[12] When Esther's words were reported to Mordecai, [13] he sent back this answer: "Do not think that because you are in the king's house you alone of all the Jews will escape. [14] For if you remain silent at this time, relief and deliverance for the Jews will arise from another

place, but you and your father's family will perish. And who knows but that you have come to your royal position for such a time as this?" (God is working in the background!)

[15] Then Esther sent this reply to Mordecai: [16] "Go, gather together all the Jews who are in Susa, and fast for me. Do not eat or drink for three days, night or day. I and my attendants will fast as you do. When this is done, I will go to the king, even though it is against the law. And if I perish, I perish." [17] So Mordecai went away and carried out all of Esther's instructions.

As my mother said, "Esther was not just beautiful; she was wise and had favor with God."

Esther's Request to the King

Esther 5:1: On the third day Esther put on her royal robes and stood in the inner court of the palace. . . .The king was sitting on his royal throne in the hall, facing the entrance. [2] When the king saw Queen Esther standing in the court, he was pleased with her and held out to her the gold scepter that was in his hand. So Esther approached and touched the tip of the scepter.

[3] Then the king asked, "What is it, Queen Esther? What is your request? Even up to half the kingdom, it will be given you."

[4] "If it pleases the king," replied Esther, "let the king, together with Haman, come today to a banquet I have prepared for him." *The king and Haman went to the banquet, and Esther's request was for Haman and the king to come to a banquet tomorrow that she would prepare for them, and then she would tell her request.*

[9] Haman went out that day happy and in high spirits. But when he saw Mordecai at the king's gate and observed that he neither rose nor showed fear in his presence, he was filled with rage against Mordecai. *Then Haman boasted to his friends that the king honored him and elevated him above all officials.* Esther 5:12: "I am the only person Queen Esther invited to accompany the king to the banquet. . . . .But all this gives me no satisfaction as long as I see that Jew Mordecai sitting at the king's gate. [14] His wife Zeresh and all his friends said to him, "Have a pole set up, reaching to a height of fifty cubits, and ask the king in the morning to have Mordecai hanged on it. This suggestion delighted Haman, and he had the pole set up.

Now, back to the tidbit I mentioned from the end of chapter 2: In Chapter 6, the king looked at the records in the Chronicles and was reminded that Mordecai was the one who had saved him. He found that no honor had ever been done for Mordecai. It so happened that Haman was in his court for the purpose of asking the king to hang Mordecai on the gallows he had prepared for him. The king asked Haman to come in.

Esther 6:6: When Haman entered, the king asked him, "What should be done for the man the king delights to honor?" Now Haman thought to himself, "Who is there that the king would rather honor than me?"[7] So he answered the king, "For the man the king delights to honor, [8] have them bring a royal robe the king has worn and a horse the king has ridden, one with a royal crest placed on its head. [9] Then let the robe and horse be entrusted to one of the king's most noble princes. Let them robe the man the king delights to honor, and lead him on the horse through the city streets, proclaiming before him, 'This is what is done for the man the king delights to honor!'" [10] "Go at once," the king commanded Haman. "Get the robe and the horse and do just as you have suggested for Mordecai the Jew, who sits at the king's gate. Do not neglect anything you have recommended."

[11] So Haman got the robe and the horse. He robed <u>Mordecai,</u> and led him on horseback through the city streets, proclaiming before him, "<u>This is what is done for the man the king delights to honor!</u>"

Esther 7:1 So the king and Haman went to Queen Esther's banquet. . .and the king again asked, "Queen Esther, what is your petition? It will be given you. [3] Then Queen Esther answered, "If I have found favor with you, Your Majesty, and if it pleases you, grant me my life—this is my petition. And spare my people—this is my request. [4] For I and my people have been sold to be destroyed, killed and annihilated. . . .[5] King Ahasuerus asked Queen Esther, "Who is he? Where is he—the man who has dared to do such a thing?"

[6] Esther said, "An adversary and enemy! <u>This vile Haman</u>!"

Then Haman was terrified before the king and queen. [7] The king got up in a rage, left his wine and went out into the palace garden. But Haman, realizing that the king had already decided his fate, stayed behind to beg Queen Esther for his life.

[8] Just as the king returned from the palace garden to the banquet hall, Haman was falling on the couch where Esther was reclining. The king exclaimed, "Will he even molest the queen while she is with me in the house?"

As soon as the word left the king's mouth, they covered Haman's face. [9] Then Harbona, one of the eunuchs attending the king, said, "A pole reaching to a height of fifty cubits stands by Haman's house. He had it set up for Mordecai, who spoke up to help the king."

The king said, "Hang him on it!" [10] So they hanged Haman on the pole he had set up for Mordecai. Then the king's fury subsided.

Esther 8:1: The King's Edict: That same day King Xerxes gave Queen Esther the estate of Haman, the enemy of the Jews. And Mordecai came into the presence of the king, for Esther had told how he was related to her. [2] The king took off his signet ring, which he had reclaimed from Haman, and presented it to Mordecai. And Esther appointed him over Haman's estate.

[3] Esther again pleaded with the king, falling at his feet and weeping. She begged him to put an end to the evil plan of Haman the Agagite, which he had devised against the Jews.[4] Then the king extended the gold scepter to Esther and she arose and stood before him. [5] "If it pleases the king," she said, "and if he regards me with favor,. . .let an order be written overruling the dispatches that Haman devised to destroy the Jews in all the king's

provinces. . . .[7] King Ahaszaras replied to Queen Esther and to Mordecai the Jew, "Because Haman attacked the Jews, I have given his estate to Esther, and they have hanged him on the pole he set up. [8] Now write another decree in the king's name in behalf of the Jews and seal it with the king's signet ring. . . .

The remainder of chapter 8 recounts the history of Mordecai's orders to the Jews and to all in the 127 provinces in their own languages.

Esther 9:11: The king's edict granted the Jews in every city the right to assemble and protect themselves; to destroy, kill and annihilate the armed men of any nationality or province who might attack them and their women and children, and to plunder the property of their enemies,

An important point to make is that though the king gave to the Jews the right to take the plunder of their enemies, that they chose not to take anything when they defeated the enemy. See Esther 9:10: "But on the spoil laid they not their hand." And in Esther 9:16, "they laid not their hands on the prey." This is very significant! America seems to be the only great world power in recent history who has not conquered for itself. When we win a war or battle, we build up the country and leave them better off than before. England, Napoleon, Rome, Hitler, Germany, all other rulers and countries of power conquered for themselves. America was richly blessed each time we did not conquer and keep for ourselves.

[15] When Mordecai left the king's presence, he was wearing. . .a large crown of gold and a purple robe of fine linen. And the city of Susa held a joyous celebration. [16] For the Jews it was a time of happiness and joy, gladness and honor. [17] In every province and in every city to which the edict of the king came, there was joy and gladness among the Jews, with feasting and celebrating. And many people of other nationalities became Jews because fear of the Jews had seized them.

The Jews struck down all their enemies: 75,000 of the enemies of the Jews were killed.

[20] Mordecai recorded these events, and he sent letters to all the Jews throughout the provinces of King Xerxes, near and far, [21] to have them celebrate the time when the Jews got relief from their enemies, when. . .their mourning was tuned into a day of celebration. . . .[28] These days should be remembered and observed in every generation by every family, and in every province and in every city. And these days of Purim should never fail to be celebrated by the Jews—nor should the memory of these days die out among their descendants. [32] Esther's decree confirmed these regulations about Purim, and it was written down in the records.

This historical account of Esther must surely be an inspiration to Jews whose ancestors have suffered continual persecution. It is a patriotic story. We see that those who have favor with God can intervene in civil law. Also, what a story to inspire young ladies!

THE BOOK OF JOB
In Job, Jesus is the timeless redeemer

Theme: The justice of God in the light of human suffering.

Summary: (This book is very applicable today because good people suffer and wonder why.) After the first deportation from Judah, God's chosen nation was still a dispersed people. They had suffered much. How could they believe in God who would allow such suffering? Where is the justice of God? In this setting, the historical poem about the Patriarch, Job, was written. First, we see the enviable prosperity of Job, which turns to a conversation between God and Satan. Satan said that Job worshipped God only because all was well with him. God allowed Satan to take away everything he had so Satan could prove that Job would curse God if he were deprived of all his blessings.

When Job is alienated from God, we see Satan, as accuser, is actively driving a wedge between God and his beloved. While Job is suffering, his friends' counsel does not comfort him. They say that Job's suffering is because of sin he has committed. All is finally silenced when God breaks in and blesses Job even more greatly than before and points to his glory and power. For the most awesome insight, we look ahead to the time that God takes on Himself human suffering by the death of His Son on the Cross. Jesus, our redeemer, defeated suffering forever, a solution only hinted at in the Book of Job.

Job chapter 1: In the land of Uz there lived a man whose name was Job. This man was blameless and upright; he feared God and shunned evil. [2] He had seven sons and three daughters, [3] and he owned seven thousand sheep, three thousand camels, five hundred yoke of oxen and five hundred donkeys, and had a large number of servants. He was the greatest man among all the people of the East.

[4] His sons used to hold feasts in their homes on their birthdays, and they would invite their three sisters to eat and drink with them. [5] When a period of feasting had run its course, Job would make arrangements for them to be purified. Early in the morning he would sacrifice a burnt offering for each of them, thinking, "Perhaps my children have sinned and cursed God in their hearts." This was Job's regular custom.

[6] One day the angels came to present themselves before the Lord, and Satan also came with them. [7] The Lord said to Satan, "Where have you come from?"

Satan answered the Lord, "From roaming throughout the earth, going back and forth on it."

[8] Then the Lord said to Satan, "Have you considered My servant Job? There is no one on earth like him; he is blameless and upright, a man who fears God and shuns evil."

[9] "Does Job fear God for nothing?" Satan replied. [10] "Have you not put a hedge around him and his household and everything he has? You have blessed the work of his hands, so that his flocks and herds are spread throughout the land. [11] But now stretch out Your hand and strike everything he has, and he will surely curse you to your face."

[12] The Lord said to Satan, "Very well, then, everything he has is in your power, but on the man himself do not lay a finger." Then Satan went out from the presence of the Lord.

[13] One day when Job's sons and daughters were feasting and drinking wine at the oldest brother's house, [14] a messenger came to Job and said, "The oxen were plowing and the donkeys were grazing nearby, [15] and the Sabeans attacked and made off with them. They put the servants to the sword, and I am the only one who has escaped to tell you!"

[16] While he was still speaking, another messenger came and said, "The fire of God fell from the heavens and burned up the sheep and the servants, and I am the only one who has escaped to tell you!"

[17] While he was still speaking, another messenger came and said, "The Chaldeans formed three raiding parties and swept down on your camels and made off with them. They put the servants to the sword, and I am the only one who has escaped to tell you!"

[18] While he was still speaking, yet another messenger came and said, "Your sons and daughters were feasting and drinking wine at the oldest brother's house, [19] when suddenly a mighty wind swept in from the desert and struck the four corners of the house. It collapsed on them and they are dead, and I am the only one who has escaped to tell you!"

[20] At this, Job got up and tore his robe and shaved his head. Then he fell to the ground in worship [21] and said: "Naked I came from my mother's womb, and naked I will depart.

The Lord gave and the Lord has taken away; may the name of the Lord be praised." [22] In all this, Job did not sin by charging God with wrongdoing.

Job 2: *The Lord and Satan conversed again, and the Lord points out that Job still is a man of integrity even after he has lost everything. Satan tells him in verse 5*: Put forth thine hand now, and touch his bone and his flesh and he will curse thee to thy face. 7. So Satan. . .smote Job with sore boils from the sole of his foot unto his crown. 9. Then his wife said unto him,.. Curse God and die." 10. He replied, "You are talking like a foolish[b] woman. Shall we accept good from God, and not trouble?"

In all this, Job did not sin in what he said.

[11] When Job's three friends, Eliphaz the Temanite, Bildad the Shuhite and Zophar the Naamathite, heard about all the troubles that had come upon him, they set out from their homes and met together by agreement to go and sympathize with him and comfort him.[12] When they saw him from a distance, they could hardly recognize him; they began to weep aloud, and they tore their robes and sprinkled dust on their heads. [13] Then they sat on the ground with him for seven days and seven nights. No one said a word to him, because they saw how great his suffering was.

Note that Job never knew why he was suffering or what the final outcome would be.

In chapter 3, *Job curses his birth, but does not curse God. He wishes he had died in the womb. Then, throughout much of Job, the three friends focus on three arguments:*

God is almighty. God is just. No human is entirely innocent in God's eye. Therefore, say his friends, "Your punishment is because of some sin you have committed." But as we read, we find that the punishment was not because of his sins but is a test of Job's faith.

Blessings Follow God's Discipline: Job 5:17:"Blessed is the one whom God corrects; do not despise the discipline of the Almighty. [18] For he wounds, but he also binds up; he injures, but his hands also heal. [19] From six calamities he will rescue you; in seven no harm will touch you.

[20] In famine he will deliver you from death, and in battle from the stroke of the sword.

[21] You will be protected from the lash of the tongue, and need not fear when destruction comes.

A verse for us today: Job 7:17: What is mankind that you make so much of them, that You give them so much attention, [18] that You examine them every morning and test them every moment?

After the accusations by his friends in chapter 8, Job replied:

Job 9:2: But how can mere mortals prove their innocence before God?

[3] Though they wished to dispute with Him, they could not answer Him onece out of a thousand.

[4] His wisdom is profound, His power is vast. Who has resisted Him and come out unscathed?

[5] He moves mountains without their knowing it and overturns them in his anger.

[6] He shakes the earth from its place and makes its pillars tremble.

Promises: Troubles will pass. There is hope for the righteous.

Job 11:13: "Yet if you devote your heart to Him and stretch out your hands to Him,
[14] if you put away the sin that is in your hand and allow no evil to dwell in your tent,
[15] then, free of fault, you will lift up your face; you will stand firm and without fear.
[16] You will surely forget your trouble, recalling it only as waters gone by.
[17] Life will be brighter than noonday, and darkness will become like morning.
[18] You will be secure, because there is hope; you will take your rest in safety.
[19] You will lie down, with no one to make you afraid, and many will court your favor.
[20] But the eyes of the wicked will fail, and escape will elude them;
their hope will become a dying gasp."

Only those who have suffered can truly enter into the suffering of others. Christ, who suffered, can understand our suffering: Hebrews 2:18: Because Jesus experienced temptation, he is able to help those who are tempted.

In Job, chapters 16-17, Job tells his friends that if he were in their place, he would encourage them. In Job 18, the friend, Bildad, assumed the wickedness of Job, and tells him the doom of the wicked. Then in Job's reply is one of the most sublime expressions of faith ever uttered:

Job 19: 25: I know that my redeemer lives, and that in the end He will stand on the earth

[26] And after my skin has been destroyed, yet in my flesh I will see God;

[27] I myself will see Him with my own eyes,

Job 21.15. What is the almighty that we serve Him? And what profit should we have if we pray unto Him? In chapters 22-24, *the friends continue a third cycle of speeches, accusing him more of wickedness and assuming he has misrelated the poor. Chapter 28 is like the book of Proverbs and is an interlude on wisdom.*

GOD SPEAKS! *Please read all the poem in Job 38 to learn good apologetics for humanists and evolutionists.* Job 38:1: Then the Lord spoke to Job out of the storm. He said: "Who is this that obscures My plans with words without knowledge? [4]"Where were you when I laid the earth's foundation? Tell me, if you understand.

[8] "Who shut up the sea behind doors when it burst forth from the womb,

[9] when I made the clouds its garment and wrapped it in thick darkness,

[10] when I fixed limits for it and set its doors and bars in place,

[11] when I said, 'This far you may come and no farther; here is where your proud waves halt'?

[12] "Have you ever given orders to the morning, or shown the dawn its place,

[16] "Have you journeyed to the springs of the sea or walked in the recesses of the deep?

[17] Have the gates of death been shown to you? Have you seen the gates of the deepest darkness?

[18] Have you comprehended the vast expanses of the earth? Tell me, if you know all this. . . .

[24] What is the way to the place where the lightning is dispersed,

or the place where the east winds are scattered over the earth?

[34] "Can you raise your voice to the clouds and cover yourself with a flood of water?

[35] Do you send the lightning bolts on their way?

(Job had become very wroth with his friends, who appeared to turn against him. But while reading Charles Spurgeon's sermons about prayer, I was amazed to learn what changed the situation with Job. It was intercessory prayer. The key to answered prayer is Intercessory prayer. The verse given is Job 41:10. After Job had prayed for his friends, the Lord restored his fortunes and gave him twice as much as he had before.

[11] All his brothers and sisters and everyone who had known him before came and ate with him in his house. They comforted and consoled him over all the trouble the Lord had brought on him, and each one gave him a piece of silver and a gold ring.

[12]The Lord blessed the latter part of Job's life more than the former part. He had fourteen thousand sheep, six thousand camels, a thousand yoke of oxen and a thousand donkeys.[13] And he also had seven sons and three daughters[15] Nowhere in all the land were there found

women as beautiful as Job's daughters, and their father granted them an inheritance along with their brothers. (*Does not Job's experience call us to pray for those who cause us to suffer?*)

Job 41:16: After this, Job lived a hundred and forty years; he saw his children and their children to the fourth generation. [17] And so Job died, an old man and full of years.

Job was a blessing to his family and he was blessed by living to see the fourth generation of the second set of children! (I pray the promise in Psalm 128 for my husband and children.)

What a blessing the book of Job is!

The Books of Poetry are Psalms, Proverbs, Ecclesiastes, & Song of Solomon

THE BOOK OF PSALMS
In Psalms, Jesus is the morning song.

Theme: The range of human response to God and His world.

The Psalms help us express and pray with all our emotions. They also move us steadily along the path of knowing God. When I am feeling a great need to be closer to the Lord, to praise him, and to find his promises, I look through Psalms and read the scriptures I have highlighted. That is exactly what I am doing now, at 3:50 AM August 19, 2013, as I attempt to hold our daughter, Dayla and husband, Steve's, family up in prayer. Their precious, humble son, Toby Ray, is at the side of his beloved wife Sarah, who is critical in the hospital. Their children are Landry Kate, age 3 years, and Henry Ray, age 3 months. How dependent we are upon God, and how precious His Word is to us right now. There is power in praise! I will now praise God as I pray for them in the name of Jesus.

Message: The Book of Psalms is a collection of prayers, poems, and hymns that focus the worshiper's thoughts on God in praise and adoration. Parts of this book were used as a hymnal in the worship services of ancient Israel.

The most meaningful scriptures that I have memorized are included in this section. I pray they will be a blessing to you. The book of Psalms is in the King James Version of the Bible because that is the version in which I memorized.

Psalm 46:1: God is our refuge and strength, a very present help in trouble.

Psalm 119:28: My soul melts from heaviness; strengthen me according to your word.

Psalm 18:2: The Lord is my rock, and my fortress, and my deliverer; my God, my strength, in whom I will trust; my buckler, and the horn of my salvation, and my high tower.

I memorized Psalm Chapter 1 when I represented Oklahoma teachers at Portland Oregon at the National Education Association Convention. It contains the promise that if we meditate upon the word of God that we will be blessed. (Our Toby Ray has always meditated on your Word, oh Lord. Now bless him and make him like a "tree planted by the water.")

Psalm 1:1-6 Blessed is the man that walketh not in the counsel of the ungodly, nor standeth in the way of sinners, nor sitteth in the seat of the scornful. 2 But his delight is in the law of the Lord; and in his law doth he meditate day and night. 3 And he shall be like a tree planted by the rivers of water, that bringeth forth his fruit in his season; his leaf also shall not wither; and whatsoever he doeth shall prosper. 4 The ungodly are not so: but are like the chaff which the wind driveth away. 5 Therefore the ungodly shall not stand in the judgment, nor sinners in the congregation of the righteous.6 For the Lord knoweth the way of the righteous: but the way of the ungodly shall perish.

Psalm 4:8: I will lay me down in peace and sleep; for thou, Lord, only makest me dwell in safety

Psalm 8:1a, 3-4: KJV: O Lord, our Lord, how excellent is thy name in all the earth! [3] When I consider thy heavens, the work of thy fingers, the moon and the stars, which thou hast ordained; [4] what is man, that thou art mindful of him? And the son of man, that thou visitest him?

[5] For thou hast made him a little lower than the angels, and hast crowned him with glory and honour. [6] Thou madest him to have dominion over the works of thy hands; thou hast put all things under his feet: [7] All sheep and oxen, yea, and the beasts of the field; [8] the fowl of the air, and the fish of the sea. . . [9] O Lord our Lord, how excellent is thy name in all the earth!

Psalm 8:9: O Lord, our Lord, how excellent is thy name in all the earth!

Psalm 14:1: The fool hath said in his heart, "There is no God."

Psalm 18:16: The Lord liveth; and blessed be the rock; and let the God of my salvation be exalted.

Psalm 19: 1: The heavens declare the glory of God; and the firmament sheweth his handiwork.

Psalm 19:7-10: The law of the Lord is perfect, converting the soul; the testimony of the Lord is sure, making wise the simple. The statutes of the Lord are right, rejoicing the heart; the commandment of the Lord is pure, enlightening the eyes. The fear of the Lord is clean, enduring forever; the judgments of the Lord are true and righteous altogether. More are they to be desired than gold, yea, than much fine gold; sweeter also than honey and the honeycomb.

Psalm 19:14: Let the words of my mouth, and the meditation of my heart, be acceptable in thy sight, O Lord, my strength, and my redeemer.

Psalm 23: Memorized when I was 9 years old. MAMA SAID A PERSON WHO IS GOING THROUGH DEPRESSION SHOULD SAY THIS CHAPTER SEVEN TIMES A DAY.

1 The Lord is my shepherd; I shall not want. He maketh me to lie down in green pastures: he leadeth me beside the still waters. [3] He restoreth my soul: He leadeth me in the paths of righteousness for his name's sake. [4] Yea, though I walk through the valley of the shadow of death, I will fear no evil: for Thou art with me; Thy rod and Thy staff they comfort me.

[5] Thou preparest a table before me in the presence of mine enemies: Thou anointest my head with oil; my cup runneth over. [6] Surely goodness and mercy shall follow me all the days of my life: and I will dwell in the house of the Lord forever.

Psalm 24:1-10

24 The earth is the Lord's, and the fullness thereof; the world, and they that dwell therein. [2] For he hath founded it upon the seas, and established it upon the floods. [3] Who

shall ascend into the hill of the Lord? or who shall stand in his holy place?[4] He that hath clean hands, and a pure heart; who hath not lifted up his soul unto vanity, nor sworn deceitfully. [5] He shall receive the blessing from the Lord, and righteousness from the God of his salvation.

[6] This is the generation of them that seek Him, that seek thy face, O Jacob. Selah.

[7] Lift up your heads, O ye gates; and be ye lift up, ye everlasting doors; and the King of glory shall come in. [8] Who is this King of glory? The Lord strong and mighty, the Lord mighty in battle. 10. Who is this King of glory? The Lord of hosts, He is the King of glory. Selah.

Psalm 25: 1-5: Unto thee, O Lord, do I lift up my soul. [2] O my God, I trust in thee: let me not be ashamed, let not mine enemies triumph over me. [3] Yea, let none that wait on thee be ashamed: let them be ashamed which transgress without cause.

[4] Shew me thy ways, O Lord; teach me thy paths. [5] Lead me in thy truth, and teach me: for thou art the God of my salvation; on thee do I wait all the day.

Psalm 25: 21-22: Let integrity and uprightness preserve me, for I wait on thee. Redeem Israel, O God, out of all his troubles. *(Redeem America, O God.)*

Psalm 27:1: The Lord is my light and my salvation; whom shall I fear? The Lord is the strength of my life; of whom shall I be afraid. 4 One thing have I desired of the Lord, that will I seek after; that I may dwell in the house of the Lord all the days of my life, to behold the beauty of the Lord, and to enquire in his temple. 5 For in the time of trouble He shall hide me in His pavilion: in the secret of his tabernacle shall he hide me; He shall set me up upon a rock. 10 When my father and my mother forsake me, then the Lord will take me up. 13 I had fainted, unless I had believed to see the goodness of the Lord in the land of the living. 14 Wait on the Lord: be of good courage, and He shall strengthen thine heart: wait, I say, on the Lord.

Psalm 33:11: But the plans of the LORD stand firm forever, the purposes of his heart through all generations. *(God has plans for you as an individual, when you give your heart to Him.)*

In my King James Study bible, most of Psalm 37 is starred or high-lighted. It is full of promises for those who delight in the Lord.

Psalm 37:1; Fret not thyself because of evildoers, neither be thou envious against the workers of iniquity. [2] For they shall soon be cut down like the grass, and wither as the green herb.

[3] Trust in the Lord, and do good; so shalt thou dwell in the land, and verily thou shalt be fed. [4] Delight thyself also in the Lord: and He shall give thee the desires of thine heart. Commit thy way unto the Lord; trust also in Him; and He shall bring it to pass.

[6] And He shall bring forth thy righteousness as the light, and thy judgment as the noonday.

[7] Rest in the Lord, and wait patiently for him: fret not thyself because of him who prospereth in his way, because of the man who bringeth wicked devices to pass. [8] Cease from anger, and forsake wrath: fret not thyself in any wise to do evil.

(*Who will inherit the earth and rule on the New Earth? The Meek! Also, Jesus said in the Beatitudes in the Sermon on the Mount, "Blessed are the meek, for they shall inherit the Earth."*

[11] But the meek shall inherit the earth; and shall delight themselves in the abundance of peace.

[16] A little that a righteous man hath is better than the riches of many wicked.

[23] The steps of a good man are ordered by the Lord: and he delighteth in his way. [24] Though he fall, he shall not be utterly cast down: for the Lord upholdeth him with his hand.

[25] I have been young, and now am old; yet have I not seen the righteous forsaken, nor his seed begging bread. [26] He is ever merciful, and lendeth; and his seed is blessed.

[27] Depart from evil, and do good; and dwell for evermore.

[28] For the Lord loveth judgment, and forsaketh not his saints; they are preserved for ever: but the seed of the wicked shall be cut off. [29] The righteous shall inherit the land, and dwell therein forever. [30] The mouth of the righteous speaketh wisdom, and his tongue talketh of judgment.

Psalm 46 *is good for when we need calming and need to stop and think about God.* Psalm 46: God is our refuge and strength, a very present help in trouble. [2] Therefore will not we fear, though the earth be removed, and though the mountains be carried into the midst of the sea; [3] Though the waters thereof roar and be troubled, though the mountains shake with the swelling thereof. Selah. [4] There is a river, the streams whereof shall make glad the city of God, the holy place of the tabernacles of the most High.

[8] Come, behold the works of the Lord. . . . [10] Be still, and know that I am God: I will be exalted among the heathen; I will be exalted in the earth. [11] The Lord of hosts is with us; the God of Jacob is our refuge.

Psalm 51 *was written by David after his sin with Bathsheba. In it, he cries to God for him to cleanse from sin and begs God to create in him a clean heart and to restore unto him the joy of his salvation.*

Psalm 51: l Have mercy upon me, O God, according to thy loving kindness: according unto the multitude of thy tender mercies blot out my transgressions. [2] Wash me thoroughly from mine iniquity, and cleanse me from my sin. [3] For I acknowledge my transgressions: and my sin is ever before me. [4] Against thee, thee only, have I sinned, and done this evil in thy sight: that thou mightest be justified when thou speakest, and be clear when thou judgest. [9] Hide thy face from my sins, and blot out all mine iniquities.

[10] Create in me a clean heart, O God; and renew a right spirit within me. [11] Cast me not away from thy presence; and take not thy holy spirit from me. [12] Restore unto me the joy

of thy salvation; and uphold me with thy free spirit. [13] Then will I teach transgressors thy ways; and sinners shall be converted unto thee.

Psalm 91: A favorite of mine. It is full of promises, if we dwell in the secret place of the most high. Verse 1: He that dwelleth in the secret place of the most High shall abide under the shadow of the Almighty. [2] I will say of the Lord, He is my refuge and my fortress: my God; in him will I trust.

[5] Thou shalt not be afraid for the terror by night; nor for the arrow that flieth by day; [6] Nor for the pestilence that walketh in darkness; nor for the destruction that wasteth at noonday. [7] A thousand shall fall at thy side, and ten thousand at thy right hand; but it shall not come nigh thee.

[9] Because thou hast made the Lord, which is my refuge, even the most High, thy habitation; [10] There shall no evil befall thee, neither shall any plague come nigh thy dwelling. [11] For He shall give his angels charge over thee, to keep thee in all thy ways. [12] They shall bear thee up in their hands, lest thou dash thy foot against a stone.

[14] Because He hath set his love upon me, therefore will I deliver him: I will set him on high, because he hath known my name. [15] He shall call upon me, and I will answer him: I will be with him in trouble; I will deliver him, and honour him. [16] With long life will I satisfy him, and shew him my salvation.

Psalm 100: *I have often recited this wonderful praise Psalm at Thanksgiving programs at nursing homes and at family reunions. Now, our granddaughter, Halle Grace, can say all of it at age 5 1/2 years.*

1. Make a joyful noise unto the Lord, all ye lands. [2] Serve the Lord with gladness: come before his presence with singing. [3] Know ye that the Lord he is God: it is he that hath made us, and not we ourselves; we are his people, and the sheep of his pasture. [4] Enter into his gates with thanksgiving, and into his courts with praise: be thankful unto him, and bless his name. [5] For the Lord is good; his mercy is everlasting; and his truth endures to all generations. (*God's purpose for us is that we should give him praise for all good things.*)

It is God's purpose that we come to Him and have our sins forgiven. His love is great:

Psalm 103:11-12: So great is His love for those who fear Him; [12] as far as the east is from the west,

so far has He removed our transgressions from us. [13] As a father has compassion on his children,

so the LORD has compassion on those who fear Him.

Psalm 119, the longest chapter in the Bible, includes the verse from which I obtained "I Have Hidden Your Word in My Heart," the title of this book. We are reminded by David of the importance of hiding God's word in our hearts. This is the clue to living a purpose filled life because His Word is where we go to find God's plan for our lives.

Verses 10 and 11: Wherewithal shall a young man cleanse his way? By taking heed thereto according to thy word. [10] With my whole heart have I sought thee: O let me not wander from thy commandments. [11] Thy word have I hid in mine heart, that I might not sin against thee.

105: Thy word is a lamp unto my feet, and a light unto my path.

129: Thy testimonies are wonderful: therefore doth my soul keep them.140: Thy word is very pure: therefore thy servant loveth it. 150: They draw nigh that follow after mischief: they are far from thy law. 151 Thou art near, O Lord; and all thy commandments are truth. ``150: "Thy word is true from the beginning: and every one of thy righteous judgments endureth forever."

Psalm 121:1-2: I will lift up mine eyes unto the hills, from whence cometh my strength. My help cometh from the Lord, which made heaven and earth.

Psalm 122: 1: I was glad when they said unto me; Let us go into the house of the Lord.

Psalm 125:1: They that trust in the Lord shall be as mount Zion, which cannot be removed, but abideth forever.

Psalm 126:5: They that sow in tears shall reap in joy. He that goeth forth and weepeth, bearing precious seed, shall doubtless come again with rejoicing, bringing in the sheaves. *MY MOTHER TAUGHT ME THIS WHEN SHE TAUGHT ME TO PLAY ON THE PIANO MY FIRST HYMN, "BRINGING IN THE SHEAVES."*

Psalm 127: 1: Except the Lord build the house, they labor in vain that build it; except the Lord keep the city, the watchman waketh but in vain. 3. Children are an heritage of the Lord and the fruit of the womb is his reward. 4. As arrows are in the hand of a mighty man, so are children of the youth. 5. Happy is the man that hath a quiver full of them.

Psalm 128:1, 6: Blessed is everyone what feareth the Lord, that walketh in His ways. 6. Yes, thou shalt see thy children's children, and peace upon Israel.

Psalm 139: [23] Search me, O God, and know my heart: try me, and know my thoughts: [24] And see if there be any wicked way in me, and lead me in the way everlasting.

Psalm 150:1, 6: Praise ye the Lord. Praise God in his sanctuary; praise him in the firmament of His power. Let everything that hath breath praise the Lord.

The Scarlet Thread: Foreshadowings: *God's provision of a Savior for His people is a recurring theme in the Psalms. Prophetic pictures of the Messiah are seen in numerous Psalms. Psalm 2:1-12 portrays the Messiah's triumph and kingdom. Psalm 16:8-11 foreshadows His death and resurrection. Psalm 22 shows us the suffering Savior on the cross and presents detailed prophecies of the crucifixion, all of which were fulfilled perfectly. The glories of the Messiah and His bride are on exhibit in Psalm 45:6-7, while Psalms 72:6-17, 89:3-37,110:1-7 and 132:12-18 present the glory and universality of His reign.*

What a marvelous God we worship, the psalmist declares: One who is high and lifted up beyond our human experiences but also one who is close enough to touch and who walks beside us along life's way. The psalmist teaches us that the most profound prayer of all is a cry for help as we find ourselves overwhelmed by the problems of life. And that is exactly what I have been doing.

As I complete the book of Psalms, I can now say," Praise the Lord! He answered prayers. Sarah, Toby's wife, was diagnosed as having a parasite, which she got on a mission trip. After diagnosis, treatment was effective. Their precious family is now together at home as Sarah heals. " Oh Lord, David only cried to God, the Father, but I cry to the Holy Trinity: God, the Father, God, the Son, and God, the Holy Spirit! I praise you for what you did for Toby and Sarah. It was when we were weak that you listened and answered our prayer.

THE BOOK OF PROVERBS OF SOLOMON
In Proverbs, Jesus is Wisdom's Cry.

Theme: To impart moral wisdom and uncommon sense for right living.

Message: Historical record shows that King Solomon wrote thousands of Proverbs. Proverbs speaks much to his son, showing him what true wisdom is. I have chosen to divide Proverbs into categories, following the example in Smith's (1984) *Daily Bible in Chronological Order*.

WISDOM

Proverbs 1:2-3 To know wisdom and instruction, to perceive the words of understanding; To receive the instruction of wisdom, justice, and judgment, and equity.

Proverbs 1:5: A wise man will hear, and will increase learning; and a man of understanding shall attain unto wise counsels:

Proverbs 1:7; 8: The fear of the Lord is the beginning of knowledge: but fools despise wisdom and instruction. My son, hear the instruction of thy father, and forsake not the law of thy mother.

Proverbs 1:10: My son, if sinners entice thee, consent thou not.

Proverbs 2:10-11: When wisdom entereth into thine heart, and knowledge is pleasant unto the soul; Discretion shall preserve thee, understanding shall keep thee.

Note that Proverbs 3 begins with "My son." When Solomon speaks to his son, he is giving valuable instruction and discipline to his own son. These verses tell us exactly how to instruct and discipline our own children!

Proverbs 3:1-9: My son, forget not my law; but let thine heart keep my commandments:[2] For length of days, and long life, and peace, shall they add to thee.[3] Let not mercy and truth forsake thee: bind them about thy neck; write them upon the table of thine heart:[4] So shalt thou find favour and good understanding in the sight of God and man. [5] Trust in the Lord with all thine heart; and lean not unto thine own understanding.[6] In all thy ways acknowledge him, and he shall direct thy paths.[7] Be not wise in thine own eyes: fear the Lord, and depart from evil. [8] It shall be health to thy navel, and marrow to thy bones. [9] Honour the Lord with thy substance, and with the firstfruits of all thine increase:

[13] Happy *is* the man *who* finds wisdom, And the man *who* gains understanding;

[14] For her proceeds *are* better than the profits of silver,

And her gain than fine gold. Proverbs 3:13-14

[19] The Lord by wisdom founded the earth; By understanding He established the heavens. Proverbs 3:19

DISCIPLINE

[11] My son, despise not the chastening of the Lord; neither be weary of his correction:[12] For whom the Lord loveth he correcteth; even as a father the son in whom he delighteth. Proverbs 3:11-12

Train a child in the way he should go, and when he is old he will not turn from it. Proverbs 22:6

The rod of correction imparts wisdom, but a child left to himself disgraces his mother. Proverbs 29:15

RIGHTEOUSNESS AND WICKEDNESS

Misfortune pursues the sinner, but prosperity is the reward of the righteous. Proverbs 13:21

Righteousness exalts a nation, but sin is a disgrace to any people. Proverbs 14:34

Do not fret because of evil men or be envious of the wicked, for the evil man has no future hope, and the lamp of the wicked will be snuffed out. Proverbs 24:19-20

When the righteous thrive, the people rejoice. When the wicked rule, the people groan. Proverbs 29:2

PRIDE AND HUMILITY

When pride comes, then comes disgrace, but with humility comes wisdom. Proverbs 11:2
Pride goes before destruction; a haughty spirit before a fall. Proverbs 16:18
Humility and the fear of the Lord bring wealth and honor and life. Proverbs 22:4

KINDNESS AND MERCY

A kind man benefits himself; but a cruel man brings trouble on himself. Proverbs 11;17
A righteous man cares for the needs of his animal, but the kindest acts of the wicked are cruel. Proverbs 12:10

DRUNKENNESS

Wine is a mocker, and beer is a brawler; whoever is deceived by them is not wise. Proverbs 20:1

Who has won? Who has sorrow? Who has strife? Who has complaints?
Who has needless bruises? Who has bloodshot eyes?
[30] Those who linger over wine, who go to sample bowls of mixed wine.

[31] Do not gaze at wine when it is red, when it sparkles in the cup,
when it goes down smoothly!
[32] In the end it bites like a snake and poisons like a viper,
and your mind will imagine confusing things.
[34] You will be like one sleeping on the high seas, lying on top of the rigging.
[35] "They hit me," you will say, "but I'm not hurt! They beat me, but I don't feel it!
When will I wake up so I can find another drink?" Proverbs 23: 29-35

ADULTERY

My son, keep your father's command, And do not forsake the law of your mother.
[21] Bind them continually upon your heart; Reproofs of instruction *are* the way of life:
[24] To keep you from the evil woman, From the flattering tongue of a seductress.
[25] Do not lust after her beauty in your heart, Nor let her allure you with her eyelids.
[26] For by means of a harlot *A man is reduced* to a crust of bread;
And an adulteress will prey upon his precious life. [27] Can a man take fire to his bosom,
And his clothes not be burned? [28] Can one walk on hot coals, And his feet not be seared?
[29] So *is* he who goes in to his neighbor's wife; Whoever touches her shall not be innocent. Proverbs 6:20-21, 24-29
[3] For the lips of an immoral woman drip honey, And her mouth *is* smoother than oil;
[4] But in the end she is bitter as wormwood, Sharp as a two-edged sword.
[5] Her feet go down to death, Her steps lay hold of hell.
[6] Lest you ponder *her* path of life—Her ways are unstable;
You do not know *them*. [7] Therefore hear me now, *my* children,
And do not depart from the words of my mouth. [8] Remove your way far from her,
And do not go near the door of her house, [20] For why should you, my son,
Be enraptured by an immoral woman, aAnd be embraced in the arms of a seductress?
Proverbs 5:3-8, 20
A prostitute is a deep pit and a wayward wife is a narrow well. Proverbs 23:27

TEMPER AND PATIENCE:

A hot-tempered man stirs up dissension, but a patient man calms a quarrel. Proverbs 15:18
Do not make friends with a hot-tempered man. . . .or you may learn his ways and get yourself ensnared. Proverbs 22:24,25
A fool gives full vent to his anger, but a wise man keeps himself under control. Proverbs 29:11

KEEPING THE LAW:

Those who forsake the law praise the wicked, but those who keep the law resist them. Proverbs 28:4

Where there is no revelation, the people cast off restraint, but blessed is he who keeps the law. Proverbs 29.18

LOVE AND FAITHFULNESS:

Let love and faithfulness never leave you; bind them around your neck, write them on the tablet of your heart. [4]Then you will win favor and a good name in the sight of the Lord. Proverbs 3:3-4

Like a bad tooth or a lame foot is reliance on the unfaithful in times of trouble. Proverbs 25:29

REPENTENCE:

Fools mock at making amends for sin, but goodwill is found among the upright. Proverbs 14:9

He who conceals his sins does not prosper, but whoever confesses and renounces them finds mercy. Proverbs 28:13

Unlike other proverbs of the time of Solomon, or of today, this wisdom flows from the one true God, rather than the wisdom of man. Therefore, I urge the reader to read all of the Proverbs, doing so at least once a year. In doing this, one will gain discernment and understanding, will see the value of advisers, will discern the difference in integrity and perversion, and will learn the consequences of sin.

THE BOOK OF ECCLESIASTES
In Ecclesiastes, Jesus is the Time and the Seasons.

Theme: Life not focused on God is purposeless and meaningless. Without Him, nothing can satisfy. With God, all of life is to be enjoyed to the fullest.

The author desperately searches for meaning. The conclusion challenges the reader, especially youth, to remember our creator and to obey God.

Ecclesiastes 1:1a-3: Absolute futility. . . .What does a man gain for all his efforts he labors at under the sun? A generation goes and a generation comes, but the earth remains forever.

Then I saw that wisdom excelleth folly, as far as light excelleth darkness. Ecclesiastes 2:13, KJV

To the person who pleases him, God gives wisdom, knowledge and happiness, but to the sinner he gives the task of gathering and storing up wealth to hand it over to the one who pleases God. This too is meaningless, a chasing after the wind. Ecclesiastes 2:26

Ecclesiastes 2, KJV, is a most quoted chapter. To everything there is a season, and a time to every purpose under the heaven: [2] A time to be born, and a time to die; a time to plant, and a time to pluck up that which is planted; [3] A time to kill, and a time to heal; a time to break down, and a time to build up; [4] A time to weep, and a time to laugh; a time to mourn, and a time to dance; [5] A time to cast away stones, and a time to gather stones together; a time to embrace, and a time to refrain from embracing;

[6] A time to get, and a time to lose; a time to keep, and a time to cast away; [7] A time to rend, and a time to sew; a time to keep silence, and a time to speak; [8] A time to love, and a time to hate; a time of war, and a time of peace. [11] He hath made everything beautiful in his time: also he hath set the world in their heart, so that no man can find out the work that God maketh from the beginning to the end. [14] I know that, whatsoever God doeth, it shall be forever: nothing can be put to it, nor any thing taken from it: and God doeth it, that men should fear before him.

A good name is better than precious ointment. Ecclesiastes 7:1a

[17] Then I saw all that God has done. No one can comprehend what goes on under the sun. Despite all their efforts to search it out, no one can discover its meaning. Even if the wise claim they know, they cannot really comprehend it. Ecc: 8:17

Solomon speaks to youth.

Remember now thy Creator in the days of thy youth. Ecclesiastes 12:1a, KJV

Let us hear the conclusion of the whole matter: Fear God, and keep His commandments; for this is the whole duty of man. For God will bring every good work into judgment, with every secret thing, whether it be good, or whether it be evil. Ecclesiastes 12:13-14, KJV

BOOK OF SONG OF SOLOMON

In Solomon, Jesus is the Lover's Dream

Theme: A celebration of love between a man and a woman, which is about God's love for His people.

Author: Solomon wrote Song of Solomon, according to the first verse. This song is one of 1,005 that Solomon wrote (1 Kings 4:32). The title "Song of Songs" is a superlative, meaning this is the best one.

Purpose of Writing: The Song of Solomon is a lyric poem written to extol the virtues of love between a husband and his wife. The poem clearly presents marriage as God's design. A man and woman are to live together within the context of marriage, loving each other spiritually, emotionally, and physically.

This book combats two extremes: asceticism (the denial of all pleasure) and hedonism (the pursuit of only pleasure). The marriage profiled in Song of Solomon is a model of care, commitment, and delight.

Key Verses:

Solomon 2:1-4 I am the rose of Sharon, and the lily of the valleys. [2] As the lily among thorns, so is my love among the daughters. [3] As the apple tree among the trees of the wood, so is my beloved among the sons. I sat down under his shadow with great delight, and his fruit was sweet to my taste. [4] He brought me to the banqueting house, and his banner over me was love.

Song of Solomon 8:6-7 - "Place me like a seal over your heart, like a seal on your arm; for love is as strong as death, its jealousy unyielding as the grave. It burns like blazing fire, like a mighty flame. Many waters cannot quench love; rivers cannot wash it away. If one were to give all the wealth of his house for love, it would be utterly scorned."

Summary: The poetry takes the form of a dialogue between a husband (the king) and his wife (the Shulamite). We can divide the book into three sections: the courtship (1:1 - 3:5); the wedding (3:6 - 5:1); and the maturing marriage (5:2 - 8:14).

The song begins before the wedding, as the bride-to-be longs to be with her betrothed, and she looks forward to his intimate caresses. However, she advises letting love develop naturally, in its own time. The king praises the Shulamite's beauty, overcoming her feelings of insecurity about her appearance. On the wedding night, the husband again praises the beauty of his wife, and in highly symbolic language, the wife invites her spouse to partake of all she has to offer. They make love, and God blesses their union.

As the marriage matures, the husband and wife go through a difficult time, Things end happily as the lovers reunite and are reconciled. As the song ends, both the husband and wife are confident and secure in their love; they sing of the lasting nature of true love, and they yearn to be in each other's presence.

Practical Application: Our world is confused about marriage. Marriage is being redefined. Divorce is prevalent. Solomon says marriage is to be celebrated and revered. The Song of Solomon provides some practical guidelines for strengthening our marriages.

1) Give your spouse the attention he or she needs. Take the time to truly know your spouse.
2) Encouragement and praise, not criticism, are vital to a successful relationship.
3) Enjoy each other. Delight in God's gift of married love.
4) Do whatever is necessary to reassure your commitment to your spouse. Renew your vows; work through problems and do not consider divorce as a solution. God intends for you both to live in a deeply peaceful, secure love. (Got Questions.org)

The Books of Prophecy: The Major Prophets are: Isaiah, Jeremiah, Lamentations, Ezekiel, and Daniel,

THE BOOK OF ISAIAH
In Isaiah, Jesus is Prince of Peace

Theme: The sovereign Lord, judging and redeeming the whole earth.

Message: According to Halley (2007), Isaiah is called the Messianic prophet. Because he thoroughly records the fact that the wonderful blessing of the promised Messiah would come through his nation. Isaiah is quoted more in the New Testament than any other prophet. John 12:41: "Isaiah saw the glory of Christ and spoke of him." Isaiah was written when Assyria was threatening Jerusalem with conquest. Isaiah said this was the judgment of God, and the only hope for escape was with God's intervention. He encouraged Judah to come to its senses and to turn to God. His prophecies also include details about the New Heavens and the New Earth.

Isaiah 1:1: The vision concerning Judah and Jerusalem that Isaiah son of Amozn.

"I reared children and brought them up, but they have rebelled against me. [3] The ox knows its master, the donkey its owner's manger, but Israel does not know; my people do not understand."

[4] Woe to the sinful nation, a people whose guilt is great. . . .They have forsaken the Lord; they have spurned the Holy One of Israel and turned their backs on him.

The Scarlet Thread: God does not delight in the blood of bullocks or lambs. Then God calls the people to reason together.

Isaiah 1:18; "Come now, let us reason together," says the Lord.

"Though your sins are like scarlet, they shall be as white as snow; though they are red as crimson, they shall be like wool."

Chapter 2 shows the sin of pride, and shows that men cannot save themselves. Chapter 3 reveals the sin of the leaders and of women. Chapter 5 declares the sins of greed, of arrogance, of rationalization, of drunkenness, and of injustice. But each time after Isaiah says the Lord will judge for the sins of the people we see the hope given by Isaiah: God first calls Isaiah.

Chapter 6 gives God's call upon Isaiah's life: 1. I saw the Lord, high and exalted, seated on a throne. *Then Isaiah saw angels worshipping God and becomes very humble before the Lord, has his sins forgiven, and then God calls him:*

[Isaiah 6:8] Then I heard the voice of the Lord saying, "Whom shall I send? And who will go for us?" And I said, "Here am I. Send me!" *If only we would all become humble, ask for forgiveness, and volunteer to be the one whom God sends!*

Isaiah 7:14 is a prophecy of Jesus Christ's birth: Therefore the Lord himself shall give you a sign; Behold, a virgin shall conceive, and bear a Son and shall call his name Immanuel.

And the prophecy that reminds us of words sung so much at Christmas, when we honor the birth of the Savior, Jesus Christ: Isaiah 9:6: For unto us a child is born, unto us a son is given: and the government shall be upon His shoulder: and His name shall be called Wonderful, Counselor, The mighty God, The everlasting Father, The Prince of Peace.

Unity of the Scriptures: See Luke 1:16-31. Also, another prophecy of Jesus's birth: Isaiah 11:1:-2: And there shall come forth a rod out of the stem of Jesse, and a Branch shall grow out of his roots: [2]And the spirit of the Lord shall rest upon Him, the spirit of wisdom and understanding, the spirit of counsel and might, the spirit of knowledge and of the fear of the Lord;

[3]And shall make him of quick understanding in the fear of the Lord: and He shall not judge after the sight of his eyes, neither reprove after the hearing of His ears: [4]But with righteousness shall He judge the poor, and reprove with equity for the meek of the earth: and He shall smite the earth: with the rod of his mouth, and with the breath of his lips shall He slay the wicked. [5]And righteousness shall be the girdle of his loins, and faithfulness the girdle of his reins. *The following is a prophecy of the wonderful New Earth* (Alcorn, Heaven, 2004).

[6]The wolf will live with the lamb, the leopard will lie down with the goat,

the calf and the lion and the yearling together; and a little child will lead them.

[7]The cow will feed with the bear, their young will lie down together,

and the lion will eat straw like the ox. The infant will play near the cobra's den, and the young child will put its hand into the viper's nest.

[9]They will neither harm nor destroy on all my holy mountain,

for the earth will be filled with the knowledge of the Lord as the waters cover the sea.

[10]In that day the Root of Jesse will stand as a banner for the peoples; the nations will rally to him, and his resting place will be glorious. [11]In that day the Lord will reach out his hand a second time to reclaim the surviving remnant of his people from Assyria, from Lower Egypt, from Upper Egypt, from Cush, from Elam, from Babylonia,[c] from Hamath and from the islands of the Mediterranean.

[12]He will raise a banner for the nations and gather the exiles of Israel;

he will assemble the scattered people of Judah from the four quarters of the earth.

Isaiah 13 and 14 prophesies the Fall of Babylon.

Chapters 15 and 16 tell of the Moabites, who were descendants of Lot (the nephew of Abraham). Isaiah tells the Moabites it would be to their advantage to renew their relationship with Israel, the House of David, because the Messiah would come from it (Halley, 2000)

Song of Praise: Isaiah 26

In that day this song will be sung in the land of Judah:

We have a strong city; God makes salvation its walls and ramparts.

[2]Open the gates that the righteous nation may enter, the nation that keeps faith.

[3]You will keep in perfect peace those whose minds are steadfast,

because they trust in You.

[4] Trust in the Lord forever, for the Lord, the Lord Himself, is the Rock eternal.

[5] He humbles those who dwell on high,

He lays the lofty city low; He levels it to the ground

and casts it down to the dust [6] Feet trample it down—

the feet of the oppressed, the footsteps of the poor.

[7] The path of the righteous is level;

You, the Upright One, make the way of the righteous smooth.

[8] Yes, Lord, walking in the way of your laws, we wait for You;

Your name and renown are the desire of our hearts.

[9] My soul yearns for You in the night; in the morning my spirit longs for You.

[19] But Your dead will live, Lord; their bodies will rise—

let those who dwell in the dust wake up and shout for joy—

your dew is like the dew of the morning; the earth will give birth to her dead.

The prophecy of John the Baptist, the forerunner of Jesus:

Isaiah 40:3-5: [3] The voice of him that crieth in the wilderness, Prepare ye the way of the Lord, make straight in the desert a highway for our God. [4] Every valley shall be exalted, and every mountain and hill shall be made low: and the crooked shall be made straight, and the rough places plain: [5] And the glory of the Lord shall be revealed, and all flesh shall see it together: for the mouth of the Lord hath spoken it.

Here are some of my favorite scriptures to memorize:

Isaiah 41:31: They that wait upon the Lord shall renew their strength; they shall mount up with wings as eagles; they shall run, and not be weary; and they shall walk, and not faint.

Isaiah 11:6: The wolf will live with the lamb; the leopard will lie down with the goat,

the calf and the lion and the yearling together; and a little child will lead them. *(Yes, we shouldn't be surprised to realize the New Earth will have animals. They, too, will glorify God.)*

Isaiah 53, KJV: *tells of our suffering savior, Jesus Christ. I memorized the chapter when a young boy about 6 years old said it, and I felt ashamed of myself. From the King James Version, it is:*

Who hath believed our report? And to whom is the arm of the Lord revealed? [2] For he shall grow up before him as a tender plant, and as a root out of a dry ground: He hath no form nor comeliness; and when we shall see Him, there is no beauty that we should desire Him. [3] He is despised and rejected of men; a man of sorrows, and acquainted with grief: and we hid as it were our faces from Him; He was despised, and we esteemed Him not.

[4] Surely he hath borne our griefs, and carried our sorrows: yet we did esteem him stricken, smitten of God, and afflicted. [5] But He was wounded for our transgressions, He was bruised for our iniquities: the chastisement of our peace was upon Him; and with His

stripes we are healed. [6] All we like sheep have gone astray; we have turned everyone to His own way; and the Lord hath laid on Him the iniquity of us all.

[7] He was oppressed, and he was afflicted, yet he opened not His mouth: He is brought as a lamb to the slaughter, and as a sheep before her shearers is dumb, so He openeth not his mouth. [8] He was taken from prison and from judgment: and who shall declare His generation? for He was cut off out of the land of the living: for the transgression of my people was He stricken.

[9] And He made his grave with the wicked, and with the rich in His death; because He had done no violence, neither was any deceit in His mouth. [10] Yet it pleased the Lord to bruise him; He hath put him to grief: when thou shalt make His soul an offering for sin, He shall see his seed, He shall prolong his days, and the pleasure of the Lord shall prosper in his hand. [11] He shall see of the travail of his soul, and shall be satisfied: by His knowledge shall my righteous servant justify many; for He shall bear their iniquities.

[12] Therefore will I divide Him a portion with the great, and He shall divide the spoil with the strong; because He hath poured out his soul unto death: and He was numbered with the transgressors.; and He bare the sins of many, and made intercession for transgressors. *What a wonderful picture Isaiah 53 is our suffering Savior!*

Now, in chapter 55, notice all the wonderful one-liners that we have heard quoted!

Isaiah 55, KJV: Ho, every one that thirsteth, come ye to the waters, and he that hath no money; come ye, buy, and eat; yea, come, buy wine and milk without money and without price. [2] Wherefore do ye spend money for that which is not bread? and your labour for that which satisfieth not? hearken diligently unto me, and eat ye that which is good, and let your soul delight itself in fatness.

[3] Incline your ear, and come unto me: hear, and your soul shall live; and I will make an everlasting covenant with you, even the sure mercies of David. [6] Seek ye the Lord while he may be found, call ye upon him while he is near: [7] Let the wicked forsake his way, and the unrighteous man his thoughts: and let him return unto the Lord, and He will have mercy upon him; and to our God, for he will abundantly pardon.

[8] For my thoughts are not your thoughts, neither are your ways my ways, saith the Lord. [9] For as the heavens are higher than the earth, so are my ways higher than your ways, and my thoughts than your thoughts. [11] So shall my word be that goeth forth out of my mouth: it shall not return unto me void, but it shall accomplish that which I please, and it shall prosper in the thing whereto I sent it.

Isaiah 60: 1: Arise; shine; for your light has come, and the glory of the Lord is risen upon you.

[2] For behold, the darkness shall cover the earth, and deep darkness the people;
But the Lord will arise over you, and His glory will be seen upon you.
[3] The Gentiles shall come to Your light

The Good News of Salvation:

Isaiah 61:1-3 "The Spirit of the Lord God *is* upon Me, Because Lord has anointed Me to preach good tidings to the poor; He has sent Me to heal the brokenhearted, To proclaim liberty to the captives, And the opening of the prison to *those who are* bound;

To comfort all who mourn, [3] To console those who mourn in Zion,

To give them beauty for ashes, The oil of joy for mourning,

The garment of praise for the spirit of heaviness;

That they may be called trees of righteousness,

The planting of the Lord, that He may be glorified."

In chapters 63 and 64, the exiles prayed to God, and God will answer their prayers in chapters 65 and 66.

Great promises from the Lord are found in chapters 65 and 66: Chapter 65 is used by Alcorn in his book, Heaven, *to show us what Heaven will be like and that we will be very busy on the New Earth.*

New Heavens and a New Earth: Isaiah 65:17: [17] For, behold, I create new heavens and a new earth: and the former shall not be remembered, nor come into mind. [18] But be ye glad and rejoice forever in that which I create: for, behold, I create Jerusalem a rejoicing, and her people a joy.

[21] They will build houses and dwell in them; they will plant vineyards and eat their fruit.

[22] No longer will they build houses and others live in them, or plant and others eat.

For as the days of a tree, so will be the days of My people;

My chosen ones will long enjoy the work of their hands.

[23] They will not labor in vain, nor will they bear children doomed to misfortune;

for they will be a people blessed by the Lord, they and their descendants with them.

[24] Before they call I will answer; while they are still speaking I will hear.

[25] The wolf and the lamb will feed together, and the lion will eat straw like the ox.

They will neither harm nor destroy on all my holy mountain," says the Lord.

[23] They shall not labor in vain, nor bring forth for trouble; for they are the seed of the blessed of the Lord, and their offspring with them. [24] And it shall come to pass, that before they call, I will answer; and while they are yet speaking, I will hear.

Isaiah 66:18 and 22: For I *know* their works and their thoughts. It shall be that I will gather all nations and tongues; and they shall come and see My glory.

Unity of the Scriptures about Heaven: Philippians 2:9-11: Wherefore God also hath highly exalted Him, and given Him a name which is above every name: [10] That at the name of Jesus every knee should bow, of things in heaven, and things in earth, and things under the earth; [11] And that every tongue should confess that Jesus Christ is Lord, to the glory of God the Father.

Yes, on the new earth, we will all glorify God. Isaiah prophesies this, along with a prophecy for the Jews, his people:

Isaiah 66:22 "For as the new heavens and the new earth

Which I will make shall remain before Me," says the Lord,

"So shall your descendants and your name remain.

These were and are wonderful promises for God's people, the Jews. Also, now, we who are believers in Jesus receive the same blessings!

Also, Isaiah 9:7: Of <u>the increase</u> of *His* government and peace t*here will be* no end, upon the throne of David and over His kingdom, to order it and establish it with judgment and justice, from that time forward, even forever. *(Christ's government on the New Earth and the new universe will be ever-expanding. We know a little about how big our universe is. If God creates new worlds, who will he send to govern?.* <u>*His redeemed people!*</u> *Alcorn (2004) said this is not far-fetched to those who understand science and the Bible. God is glorified by what He creates, and He delights in delegating to His children to rule in His behalf.*

A careful reading of Isaiah will show that he prophesied many things. Some were fulfilled in his lifetime and some have been fulfilled since. A complete list of all the prophecies fulfilled in Isaiah's lifetime and those fulfilled after his lifetime are given by Halley (2000) on pages 358 and 359. The 19 predictions about the Messiah show that Jesus is the Messiah! And in the future, we shall reign with him forever when all things are made new.

THE BOOK OF JEREMIAH
In Jeremiah, Jesus is the weeping prophet.

Theme: God is just and must punish sin.. But in His grace, God promises Israel restoration and covenant renewal.

The book of Jeremiah, written over the course of half a century, is the longest book in the Bible (in terms of words and verses), and it is certainly one of the most complex. It was probably completed sometime during the Babylonian exile (587-538 B.C.E.).

Message: The book is a prophetic book concerned with the ministry of the prophet Jeremiah before and after the fall of Jerusalem to the Babylonians (587 B.C.E). The preaching of Jeremiah speaks sharp words of indictment and judgment. Initially Jeremiah speaks in the hope that they will turn from their wicked ways, but because of their lack of repentance the prophet portrays an inevitable judgment. Jeremiah also speaks words of hope, but recognizes that such a hopeful future will be realized only after the fall of Jerusalem. (Halley, 2007)

Following are some memorable verses as well as a summary of the book of Jeremiah:

Jeremiah 1:5, KJV: Before I formed thee in the belly, I knew thee, and before thou camest forth out of the womb, I sanctified thee, and I ordained thee a prophet unto the nations.

God called Jeremiah when he was "only a child." The first message Jeremiah had to deliver was that Jerusalem would be destroyed by Babylonia: Jer. 1:14: Out of the north an evil shall break forth upon all the inhabitants of the land.

In Chapter 2, Jeremiah rebuked Israel for its idolatry and compared Israel to an unfaithful wife. The word of the Lord came to me: 2 "Go and proclaim in the hearing of Jerusalem: "This is what the Lord says:" I remember the devotion of your youth, how as a bride you loved me and followed me through the wilderness, through a land not sown. Hear the word of the Lord, you descendants of Jacob. . .7 I brought you into a fertile land to eat its fruit, but you came and defiled My land and made My inheritance detestable.

19 Your wickedness will punish you; your backsliding will rebuke you. Consider then and realize how evil and bitter it is for you when you forsake the Lord your God and have no awe of me," declares the Lord, the Lord Almighty. . . .35 You say, 'I am innocent; He is not angry with me.' But I will pass judgment on you because you say, 'I have not sinned. . ." (*America, listen!*)

In Chapter 3, when God speaks of Israel, he is speaking of the northern kingdom, because Judah and Israel are split. Chapter three says that Judah is even worse than Israel. But God also said, "Return ye backsliding children and I will heal your backslidings." Jer. 3:22

Chapter 4 tells of the approaching desolation of Judah: Jeremiah 4: This is what the Lord says to the people of Judah and to Jerusalem: "Break up your unplowed ground and do not sow among thorns. ⁴Circumcise yourselves to the Lord, circumcise your hearts, you people of Judah and inhabitants of Jerusalem, or My wrath will flare up and burn like fire because of the evil you have done—

Disaster from the North:

[5]"Announce in Judah and proclaim in Jerusalem and say: 'Sound the trumpet throughout the land!' Cry aloud and say: 'Gather together! Let us flee to the fortified cities!'

[6]Raise the signal to go to Zion! Flee for safety without delay!

For I am bringing disaster from the north, even terrible destruction."

[18]"Your own conduct and actions have brought this on you.

This is your punishment. How bitter it is! How it pierces to the heart!"

[21]How long must I see the battle standard and hear the sound of the trumpet?

[22]"My people are fools; they do not know me. They are senseless children; they have no understanding. They are skilled in doing evil; they know not how to do good."

Jeremiah 5 shows the house of Israel and Judah to be deaf to Evangelism.

Jeremiah 5:7-9: Why should I forgive you? Your children have forsaken me and sworn by gods that are not gods. I supplied all their needs, yet they committed adultery and thronged to the houses of prostitutes. [8]They are well-fed, lusty stallions, each neighing for another man's wife.

[9]Should I not punish them for this?" declares the Lord. Should I not avenge Myself on such a nation as this?

Chapter 6 tells of destruction that will come from the North (the Babylonians). In Jeremiah 7, we read that repentance is their only hope.

Jer. 7:3-7: This is what the Lord Almighty, the God of Israel, says: Reform your ways and your actions, and I will let you live in this place. [4]Do not trust in deceptive words and say, "This is the temple of the Lord, the temple of the Lord, the temple of the Lord!" [5]If you really change your ways and your actions and deal with each other justly, [6]if you do not oppress the foreigner, the fatherless or the widow and do not shed innocent blood in this place, and if you do not follow other gods to your own harm, [7]then I will let you live in this place, in the land I gave your ancestors for ever and ever.[8]But look, you are trusting in deceptive words that are worthless.

Jeremiah endured many trials. The first was trial by death threats in Chapter 11:18-23.

The people believed the false prophets who said Jerusalem is in no danger. The greater the danger, the more Judah manufactured idols. When Jeremiah rebuked them, they began to plot Jeremiah's death. But though they ridiculed and hated him, Jeremiah prayed for them; his intercession before God approaches the spirit of Jesus Christ when he prayed for those who hated him. (Jer. 14-15)

In Chapter 15:15-21, *Jeremiah is tried by Isolation.*

Jeremiah 17: [5]This is what the Lord says: "Cursed is the one who trusts in man, who draws strength from mere flesh and whose heart turns away from the Lord. "But blessed is the one who trusts in the Lord, whose confidence is in Him. [8]They will be like a tree planted by the water that sends out its roots by the stream. "I the Lord search the heart and examine the mind, to reward each person according to His conduct, according to what their deeds deserve."

In Chapters 18 and 19, illustrations of the potter's clay and the clay jar are used to show God's power to alter the destiny of a nation, but this was in vain. In chapter 20, Jeremiah is imprisoned and suffers trial by stocks.. Jeremiah complained against God.

Jeremiah chapter 20. Pashur smote Jeremiah and bound him in stocks.
All that saw him made fun and mocked.
The man whom God himself sent.
The stubborn people would not repent.
Jeremiah claimed he would no longer say
Even the name of God! I cannot the sword stay. By Marilyn Kay Gage

Jeremiah 21:8: Behold, I set before you the way of life, and the way of death.

In Jeremiah 22, God said Jehoiachin's children would never be on the throne. He and Zedekiah were the last earthly kings to sit on the throne of David. Out of the line of Zedekiah would come Christ, the Messiah.

Prophecy of the Messiah: Jeremiah 23:5, 6b: I will raise unto David a righteous Branch and a King shall reign and prosper, and shall execute judgment and justice in the Earth. He shall be called THE LORD OUR RIGHTEOUSNESS.

Jeremiah 24:
Two baskets of figs—one good, the other bad.
The good are those who are sent to the Chaldean land.
There they will learn of their God first hand.
Those who remain will be driven away as a wandering nomad.

Unity of the scriptures: In Jeremiah 25, Jeremiah predicts 70 years of captivity. In II Chronicles 36:21, Ezra 1:1, Daniel 9:2, and Zechariah 7:5, the exact duration is prophesied. Jeremiah could not have known this except by revelation from God.

In Chapter 26, Jeremiah suffers trial by arrest. Friends saved him. In Jer. 27-28, Jeremiah put a yoke on his neck and walked among the people and said, "Thus shall Babylon put a yoke on the necks of this people."

In Jeremiah 29, Jeremiah wrote a letter to the cream of the people who had been taken to Babylon and advised them to be peaceful and obedient captives. Jeremiah 29:4-7: This is what the Lord Almighty, the God of Israel, says to all those I carried into exile from Jerusalem to Babylon: [5] "Build houses and settle down; plant gardens and eat what they produce. [6] Marry and have sons and daughters; find wives for your sons and give your daughters in marriage, so that they too may have sons and daughters. Increase in number there; do not decrease. [7] Also, seek the peace and prosperity of the city to which I have carried you into exile. Pray to the Lord for it, because if it prospers, you too will prosper.

How comforting the following verses must have been to them! Jeremiah 29:11-13: [11] For I know the thoughts that I think toward you, saith the Lord, thoughts of peace, and not of evil, to give you an expected end. [12] Then shall ye call upon me, and ye shall go and pray unto me, and I will hearken unto you. [13] And ye shall seek me, and find me, when ye shall search for me with all your heart. *Then he promises that they will return after 70 years to their homeland.*

Chapters 30 and 31 include prophecy of the Savior. *In verses 1-3 of chapter 30, God commanded that it be written so that later, Israel and Judah could compare this prophecy to those made earlier.*

Jeremiah 31:31: The days are coming," declares the LORD, "when I will make a new covenant with the people of Israel and with the people of Judah. [32] It will not be like the covenant I made with their ancestors when I took them by the hand to lead them out of Egypt, because they broke my covenant. . . .declares the LORD. [33] "This is the covenant I will make with the people of Israel after that time," declares the LORD. "I will put my law in their minds and write it on their hearts. I will be their God, and they will be my people. For I will forgive their wickedness and will remember their sins no more." *Here, we see that the new covenant in Christ will displace the Mosaic covenant of the Old Testament.*

How I love all of Jeremiah 33! First we have the promise that is the key to the power of prayer. I know that my precious mother believed this for when she prayed, he answered with bigger answers than she ever dreamed.

Jeremiah 33:3: Call unto me, and I will answer thee, and show thee great and mighty things, which thou knowest not.

Also in chapter 33, God included the prophecy of the branch, the one great King, who would reign. Jeremiah 33:14-15: 'The days are coming,' declares the Lord, 'when I will fulfill the good promise I made to the people of Israel and Judah. [15] "in those days and at that time I will make a righteous Branch sprout from David's line; he will do what is just and right in the land.

Also, as a Creationist who believes in the Young Earth as taught by the Bible, I like that God tied his covenant with the day and the night to the sacred covenant that he had made with Abraham, Isaac, and Jacob and with David.

[0] "This is what the LORD says: 'If you can break My covenant with the day and My covenant with the night, so that day and night no longer come at their appointed time, [21] then My covenant with David My servant—and My covenant with the Levites who are priests ministering before me—can be broken and David will no longer have a descendant to reign on his throne. . . . . [25] This is what the LORD says: 'If I have not made my covenant with day and night and established the laws of heaven and earth, [26] then I will reject the descendants of Jacob and David my servant and will not choose one of his sons to rule over

the descendants of Abraham, Isaac and Jacob. For I will restore their fortunes and have compassion on them.'"

In chapter 34, Zedekiah made a proclamation of liberty, but he failed to enforce his own law.

Jeremiah 35
God said, Early I rise
To teach you and to speak.
It does not matter how hard my servant tries,
Never do you hearken nor my face seek.

In Jeremiah 36, 1-32, Jeremiah suffered trial by destruction. Jeremiah was commanded to gather all of his prophecies of the last 23 years into a book so it could be read to the people. Baruch, Jeremiah's scribe, read it to them, and it made an impression upon some, but the King destroyed the book. Jeremiah then wrote it again.

In Jeremiah 37:15*, Jeremiah suffered trial by violence and imprisonment.*

Jeremiah 39 *As was prophesied by Jeremiah and also in 2 Kings 25 and 2 Chronicles 36, Jerusalem was burned by Babylon. Because Nebuchadnezzar knew Jeremiah had admonished Jerusalem to submit to him, he offered to give a place of honor to Jeremiah. But Jeremiah's trials were not over. He would still be tried by chains and tried by rejection. In Jeremiah 42, God told the remnant to stay and not to go to Egypt. They didn't obey.*

Jeremiah 42: To the remnant of the land,
The Lord said, "If you here remain,
I will give you my helping hand.
If you go to Egypt, never will you return, I do ordain."

Jeremiah 44: Judah is not humbled unto this day,
Neither has she any fear.
Never walking in my law and way,
She travels to Egypt for protection by its spear.

Chapters 46-51 includes the judgment on the Nations of Egypt, Philistia, Moab, Ammon, Edom, Damascus, Kadar and Hazard, Elam, and Babylon. In the midst of the Lord's judgment against Babylon, the Lord promises a redeemer for Israel and Judah:

Jeremiah 50: [33] This is what the LORD Almighty says: The people of Israel are oppressed, and the people of Judah as well. All their captors hold them fast, refusing to let them go. [34] Yet their Redeemer is strong;

the L<small>ORD</small> Almighty is His name. He will vigorously defend their cause
so that He may bring rest to their land, but unrest to those who live in Babylon.

In chapter 51, the fall and permanent destruction of Babylon are predicted. Jeremiah 52 tells of the fall of Jerusalem and the captivity of Judah. Verses 1-23 show how accurate Jeremiah was in his predictions of the fall. Verses 24-30 report the deportation of the Jews to Babylon.

According to MacArthur. 2005, the main themes of Jeremiah were judgment upon Judah with future restoration in the Kingdom of the Messiah and God's willingness to spare and bless the nation only if people repented. Other themes included God's longing for Israel to be tender toward Him as in the day of first Love, the suffering of Jeremiah and God's sufficiency in all troubles, the vital role God's Word can play in life; and the place of faith in expecting restoration from the God for whom nothing is too difficult.

We each have our own individual responsibility for the restoration of our nation. We can apply these themes to our own personal lives as well as to our nation. This is the way we can experience restoration, instead of punishment for America.

THE BOOK OF LAMENTATIONS
In Lamentations, Jesus is the cry for Israel.

Theme: Grief over Judah's fall and Jerusalem's destruction.

Jeremiah, the author, was an eyewitness to the fall of Jerusalem and Judah's forced exile to Babylon. The lamentations, or the tears of God and the prophet, Jeremiah, show the closeness of the relationship between God and people. Lamentations is an example of poetry that was read aloud at funerals in the Near East. It is used by Jews praying at the Wailing Wall, even to this day.

Jerusalem had been under siege by Babylon for 28 months. Many of Judah were killed or captured. Disease and famine claimed many lives. Lamentations depicts the amazing loss felt by the author over the destruction of Jerusalem, including the temple.

In the book of Lamentations, as well as Job, no easy answers are found. While Job lamented over his personal calamity, Jeremiah lamented over his City, Jerusalem. While Job had done nothing to deserve his calamity, the author of Lamentations confesses that Judah is guilty and God is just.

Lamentations 1:1: 1. How deserted lies the city, once so full of people! How like a widow is she, who once was great among the nations! She who was queen among the provinces has now become a slave. 2 Bitterly she weeps at night, tears are upon her cheeks. Among all her lovers there is none to comfort her. All her friends have betrayed her; they have become her enemies. 3 After affliction and harsh labor, Judah has gone into exile. She dwells among the nations; she finds no resting place. All who pursue her have overtaken her in the midst of her distress.

5 Her foes have become her masters; her enemies are at ease. The LORD has brought her grief because of her many sins. Her children have gone into exile, captive before the foe.

6 All the splendor has departed from the Daughter of Zion. . . .8 Jerusalem has sinned greatly and so has become unclean. . . .17 Zion stretches out her hands, but there is no one to comfort her. The LORD has decreed for Jacob that his neighbors become his foes; Jerusalem has become an unclean thing among them. . . .20 "O LORD, how distressed I am! I am in torment within, and in my heart I am disturbed, for I have been most rebellious. Outside, the sword bereaves; inside, there is only death.

After the author confesses the sins of the people, he trusts God to renew hope and to be merciful. What a lesson for us!

Lamentations 3:21-33: Let this I call to mind and therefore I have hope:
[22] Because of the Lord's great love we are not consumed, for his compassions never fail.
[23] They are new every morning; great is your faithfulness.
[24] I say to myself, "The Lord is my portion; therefore I will wait for him."

²⁵ The Lord is good to those whose hope is in him, to the one who seeks him;

²⁶ It is good to wait quietly for the salvation of the Lord.

²⁷ It is good for a man to bear the yoke while he is young.

²⁸ Let him sit alone in silence, for the Lord has laid it on him.

²⁹ Let him bury his face in the dust—there may yet be hope.

³⁰ Let him offer his cheek to one who would strike him, and let him be filled with disgrace.

³¹ For no one is cast off by the Lord forever.

³² Though he brings grief, he will show compassion, so great is his unfailing love.

³³ For he does not willingly bring affliction or grief to anyone.

Lamentations 3:
It is for God's mercy we are not consumed.
His compassions are new every morning and do not fail.
My soul to misery of wormwood and gall is not doomed.
Great is His faithfulness to life's every detail.

Lamentations 5:15

¹⁵ Joy is gone from our hearts; our dancing has turned to mourning.

¹⁶ The crown has fallen from our head. Woe to us, for we have sinned!

¹⁷ Because of this our hearts are faint, because of these things our eyes grow dim

¹⁸ for Mount Zion, which lies desolate, with jackals prowling over it.

¹⁹ You, Lord, reign forever; your throne endures from generation to generation.

²⁰ Why do you always forget us? Why do you forsake us so long?

²¹ Restore us to yourself, Lord, that we may return; renew our days as of old

²² unless you have utterly rejected us.

The contents of Lamentations (to trust God's mercy) have inspired Christian devotion and hymn writing. I think everyone, at some time in life, laments as this author did, and can be comforted with Lamentations, with the Psalms, and with the Book of Job.

THE BOOK OF EZEKIEL
In Ezekiel, Jesus is the call from sin.

Theme: God acts in the events of human history so that everyone will come to know Him and find new life.

Message. The prophet, Ezekiel, a Jewish Priest and exile in Babylon, addresses the people who are exiled in Babylon, who continue to listen to false prophets and practice idolatry. He emphasizes God's sovereignty which will bring judgment and restoration. His purpose is to stress the need for individual responsibility and national accountability before God. Ezekiel used vivid imagery throughout. (Halley, 2007)

Chapters 1—24 speak of judgment since the fall of Jerusalem is coming. Chapters 25—32 emphasize judgment upon the nations after the fall of Jerusalem for being participants in the day of Jacob's trouble Chapters 33-48 speak of the hope of restoration for the people held in captivity after the fall of Jerusalem. (Halley, 2007)

Ezekiel's Call to Be a Prophet: Ezekiel 2:1: He said to me, "Son of man, stand up on your feet and I will speak to you." [2] As he spoke, the Spirit came into me and raised me to my feet, and I heard him speaking to me.

[3] He said: "Son of man, I am sending you to the Israelites, to a rebellious nation that has rebelled against Me; they and their ancestors have been in revolt against Me to this very day. [4] The people to whom I am sending you are obstinate and stubborn. Say to them, 'This is what the Sovereign Lord says.' [5] And whether they listen or fail to listen—for they are a rebellious people—they will know that a prophet has been among them. [6] And you, son of man, do not be afraid of them or their words. Do not be afraid, though briers and thorns are all around you and you live among scorpions. Do not be afraid of what they say or be terrified by them, though they are a rebellious people. [7] You must speak My words to them, whether they listen or fail to listen, for they are rebellious."

[9] Then I looked, and I saw a hand stretched out to me. In it was a scroll, [10] which he unrolled before me. On both sides of it were written words of lament and mourning and woe.

Ezekiel 3:11: Go now to your people in exile and speak to them. Say to them, 'This is what the Sovereign Lord says,' whether they listen or fail to listen."

[15] I came to the exiles who lived at Tel Aviv near the Kebar River. And there, where they were living, I sat among them for seven days—deeply distressed. 16. At the end of seven days the word of the Lord came to me: [17] "Son of man, I have made you a watchman for the people of Israel; so hear the word I speak and give them warning from Me.

[22] The hand of the Lord was on me there, and he said to me, "Get up and go out to the plain, and there I will speak to you." [23] So I got up and went out to the plain. And the glory of the Lord was standing there, like the glory I had seen by the Kebar River, and I fell facedown. [24] Then the Spirit came into me and raised me to my feet. He spoke to me and said: I will open your mouth and you shall say to them, 'This is what the Sovereign Lord

says.' Whoever will listen let them listen, and whoever will refuse let them refuse; for they are a rebellious people.

Ezekiel 10: Cherubim and Wheels; God's Glory Departs from the Temple: 10 I looked, and I saw the likeness of a throne of lapis lazuli above the vault that was over the heads of the cherubim. [2]The Lord said to the man clothed in linen, "Go in among the wheels beneath the cherubim. Fill your hands with burning coals from among the cherubim and scatter them over the city." And as I watched, he went in.

[3]Now the cherubim were standing on the south side of the temple when the man went in, and a cloud filled the inner court. [4]Then the glory of the Lord rose from above the cherubim and moved to the threshold of the temple. The cloud filled the temple, and the court was full of the radiance of the glory of the Lord. [5]The sound of the wings of the cherubim could be heard as far away as the outer court, like the voice of God Almighty[a] when he speaks.

[6]When the Lord commanded the man in linen, "Take fire from among the wheels, from among the cherubim," the man went in and stood beside a wheel. [7]Then one of the cherubim reached out his hand to the fire that was among them. He took up some of it and put it into the hands of the man in linen, who took it and went out. [8](Under the wings of the cherubim could be seen what looked like human hands.)

[9]I looked, and I saw beside the cherubim four wheels, one beside each of the cherubim; the wheels sparkled like topaz. [10]As for their appearance, the four of them looked alike; each was like a wheel intersecting a wheel. [11]As they moved, they would go in any one of the four directions the cherubim faced; the wheels did not turn about[b] as the cherubim went. The cherubim went in whatever direction the head faced, without turning as they went.[12] Their entire bodies, including their backs, their hands and their wings, were completely full of eyes, as were their four wheels. [13]I heard the wheels being called "the whirling wheels." [14]Each of the cherubim had four faces: One face was that of a cherub, the second the face of a human being, the third the face of a lion, and the fourth the face of an eagle.

[15]Then the cherubim rose upward. These were the living creatures I had seen by the Kebar River. [16]When the cherubim moved, the wheels beside them moved; and when the cherubim spread their wings to rise from the ground, the wheels did not leave their side. . . .[18]Then the glory of the Lord departed from over the threshold of the temple and stopped above the cherubim. [19]While I watched, the cherubim spread their wings and rose from the ground, and as they went, the wheels went with them. They stopped at the entrance of the east gate of the Lord's house, and the glory of the God of Israel was above them.

[20]These were the living creatures I had seen beneath the God of Israel by the Kebar River, and I realized that they were cherubim. [21]Each had four faces and four wings, and under their wings was what looked like human hands. [22]Their faces had the same appearance as those I had seen by the Kebar River. Each one went straight ahead.

Ezekiel 11: *God's Sure Judgment on Jerusalem is shown in verses 1-12. Then in verse 13, Ezekiel says,* "Ah, Lord! Will you make a full end of the remnant of Israel?"

The Promise of Israel's Return: [14]The word of the Lord came to me: [15]"Son of man, the people of Jerusalem have said of your fellow exiles and all the other Israelites, 'They are far away from the Lord; this land was given to us as our possession.'"

[16]"Therefore say: 'This is what the Sovereign Lord says: Although I sent them far away among the nations and scattered them among the countries, yet for a little while I have been a sanctuary for them in the countries where they have gone.'

[17]"Therefore say: 'This is what the Sovereign Lord says: I will gather you from the nations and bring you back from the countries where you have been scattered, and I will give you back the land of Israel again.'

[18]"They will return to it and remove all its vile images and detestable idols. [19]I will give them an undivided heart and put a new spirit in them; I will remove from them their heart of stone and give them a heart of flesh. [20]Then they will follow my decrees and be careful to keep My laws. They will be My people, and I will be their God. [21]But as for those whose hearts are devoted to their vile images and detestable idols, I will bring down on their own heads what they have done, declares the Sovereign Lord."

(But when the people refused to repent of their sin, the glory of the anointing of God left.)

[22]Then the cherubim, with the wheels beside them, spread their wings, and the glory of the God of Israel was above them. [23]The glory of the Lord went up from within the city and stopped above the mountain east of it. [24]The Spirit lifted me up and brought me to the exiles in Babylonia in the vision given by the Spirit of God. Then the vision I had seen went up from me, [25]and I told the exiles everything the Lord had shown me.

Chapters 25-32 emphasize judgment upon the evil nations after the fall of Jerusalem for being participants in 'the day of trouble for the descendants of Jacob.'

Ezekiel 25
The Philistines loved to boast
Of their strength and excellent sea coast.
God his vengeance upon them lay
Because they would not listen nor obey.

26. Tyrus, you no longer have a protective wall,
The Islands tremble with your fall.
The deep shall cover over thee,
Your harbor will never attract men from the sea.

28. Your heart is uplifted;
You think you are God, not man.

Of wisdom and riches you are gifted.
Your death shall be by a stranger's hand.

29. Pharaoh said, "The river is mine,
I made it for only me."
God declared, "Nothing is thine,
Behold, I bring a sword upon thee."

30. The pomp of Egypt's Strength will cease,
For the plagues against her increase.
A cloud will cover her land and its dead.
The King of Babylon erupts a fearful dread.

31. Assyria, Lebanon's tallest cedar,
Towered magnificently over the other trees.
As a world leader,
He was a nation the world envies.

32. Egypt, God will have the last word yet,
He has spread over thee a net.
Your blood will water the land,
And your flesh will fill the beast at His Command.

Chapters 33-48 speak of the hope of restoration for the people held in captivity after the fall of Jerusalem. Chapter *34 is particularly wonderful because in it we find promise of freedom of Israel from the Heathen and the <u>Promise of the Messiah, the Shepherd, and Savior!</u>*

Ezekiel 34:
The spiritual shepherd like the Pharisee, would feed himself but not the sheep.
The flock scattered and wandered aimlessly, for a watchful eye on them no one will keep.
But someday soon will come a New Shepherd, so tender, kind, and true,
He will feed the flock on His very word, and what He says He will do.

Ezekiel 34:1: The word of the Lord came to me: [2] "Son of man, prophesy against the shepherds of Israel; prophesy and say to them: 'This is what the Sovereign Lord says: Woe to you shepherds of Israel who only take care of yourselves! Should not shepherds take care of the flock?. [4] You have not strengthened the weak or healed the sick or bound up the injured. You have not brought back the strays or searched for the lost. You have ruled them harshly and brutally. [5] So they were scattered because there was no shepherd, and when they were scattered they became food for all the wild animals. [6] My sheep wandered over all the mountains and on every high hill. They were scattered over the whole earth, and no one searched or looked for them.

[7] "'Therefore, you shepherds, hear the word of the Lord: [8] As surely as I live, declares the Sovereign Lord, because My flock lacks a shepherd and so has been plundered and has become food for all the wild animals, and because My shepherds did not search for My flock but cared for themselves rather than for My flock, [9] therefore, you shepherds, hear the word of the Lord: [10] This is what the Sovereign Lord says: I am against the shepherds and will hold them accountable for My flock. I will remove them from tending the flock so that the shepherds can no longer feed themselves. I will rescue My flock from their mouths, and it will no longer be food for them.

[11] "'For this is what the Sovereign Lord says: I Myself will search for my sheep and look after them. [12] As a shepherd looks after his scattered flock when he is with them, so will I look after My sheep. I will rescue them from all the places where they were scattered on a day of clouds and darkness. [13] I will bring them out from the nations and gather them from the countries, and I will bring them into their own land. I will pasture them on the mountains of Israel, in the ravines and in all the settlements in the land. [14] I will tend them in a good pasture, and the mountain heights of Israel will be their grazing land. There they will lie down in good grazing land, and there they will feed in a rich pasture on the mountains of Israel. [15] I Myself will tend my sheep and have them lie down, declares the Sovereign Lord. [16] I will search for the lost and bring back the strays. I will bind up the injured and strengthen the weak, but the sleek and the strong I will destroy. I will shepherd the flock with justice.

[17] "'As for you, my flock, this is what the Sovereign Lord says: I will judge between one sheep and another, and between rams and goats. [18] Is it not enough for you to feed on the good pasture? Must you also trample the rest of your pasture with your feet? Is it not enough for you to drink clear water? Must you also muddy the rest with your feet? [19] Must my flock feed on what you have trampled and drink what you have muddied with your feet?

[20] "'Therefore this is what the Sovereign Lord says to them: See, I Myself will judge between the fat sheep and the lean sheep. [21] Because you shove with flank and shoulder, butting all the weak sheep with your horns until you have driven them away, [22] I will save my flock, and they will no longer be plundered. I will judge between one sheep and another.[23] I will place over them one shepherd, my servant David, and he will tend them; he will tend them and be their shepherd. [24] I the Lord will be their God, and my servant David will be prince among them. *Yes, the seed of David, Jesus will be prince among us.*

[25] "'I will make a covenant of peace with them *I will send down showers* in season; there will be showers of blessing. [27] The trees will yield their fruit and the ground will yield its crops; the people will be secure in their land. They will know that I am the Lord, when

I break the bars of their yoke and rescue them from the hands of those who enslaved them. [28] They will no longer be plundered by the nations, nor will wild animals devour them. They will live in safety, and no one will make them afraid. [29] I will provide for them a land renowned for its crops, and they will no longer be victims of famine in the land or bear the scorn of the nations. [30] Then they will know that I, the Lord their God, am with them and that they, the Israelites, are my people, declares the Sovereign Lord. [31] You are my sheep, the sheep of my pasture, and I am your God, declares the Sovereign Lord.

Ezekiel 36: *God's wonderful promises for Israel can also be for America if we turn from our wicked ways: Israel was over-run with Heathen Nations. God said in Verse 3:* This is what the Sovereign Lord says: Because they ravaged and crushed you from every side so that you became the possession of the rest of the nations and the object of people's malicious talk and slander, [4] therefore, mountains of Israel, hear the word of the Sovereign Lord: I swear with uplifted hand that the nations around you will also suffer scorn. . . . [8] "But you, mountains of Israel, will produce branches and fruit for my people Israel, for they will soon come home. [9] I am concerned for you and will look on you with favor; you will be plowed and sown, [10] and I will cause many people to live on you—yes, all of Israel. The towns will be inhabited and the ruins rebuilt. [11] I will increase the number of people and animals living on you, and they will be fruitful and become numerous. I will settle people on you as in the past and will make you prosper more than before. Then you will know that I am the Lord.

[24] "For I will take you out of the nations; I will gather you from all the countries and bring you back into your own land.

[33] "This is what the Sovereign Lord says: On the day I cleanse you from all your sins, I will resettle your towns, and the ruins will be rebuilt. [34] The desolate land will be cultivated instead of lying desolate in the sight of all who pass through it. [35] They will say, "This land that was laid waste has become like the Garden of Eden; the cities that were lying in ruins, desolate and destroyed, are now fortified and inhabited." [36] Then the nations around you that remain will know that I the Lord have rebuilt what was destroyed and have replanted what was desolate

[37] "This is what the Sovereign Lord says: Once again I will yield to Israel's plea and do this for them: I will make their people as numerous as sheep, [38] as numerous as the flocks for offerings at Jerusalem during her appointed festivals. So will the ruined cities be filled with flocks of people. Then they will know that I am the Lord."

The Picture of Restoration: You may know the Spiritual Song, "The Head Bone's Connected to the Neck Bone", etc. It comes from the reading in Ezekiel 37: The Valley of Dry Bones. In it, we see hope of restoration after the fall of Jerusalem.

Ezekiel 37:1 The hand of the LORD was on me, and he brought me out by the Spirit of the LORD and set me in the middle of a valley; it was full of bones. [2] He led me back and forth among them, and I saw a great many bones on the floor of the valley, bones that were very dry.[3] He asked me, "Son of man, can these bones live?" I said, "Sovereign LORD, you alone know."

[4] Then he said to me, "Prophesy to these bones and say to them, 'Dry bones, hear the word of the LORD! [5] This is what the Sovereign LORD says to these bones: I will make breath enter you, and you will come to life. [6] I will attach tendons to you and make flesh come upon you and cover you with skin; I will put breath in you, and you will come to life. Then you will know that I am the LORD.'"

[7] So I prophesied as I was commanded. And as I was prophesying, there was a noise, a rattling sound, and the bones came together, bone to bone. [8] I looked, and tendons and flesh appeared on them and skin covered them, but there was no breath in them. [9] Then he said to me, "Prophesy to the breath; prophesy, son of man, and say to it, 'This is what the Sovereign LORD says: Come, breath, from the four winds and breathe into these slain, that they may live.'" [10] So I prophesied as he commanded me, and breath entered them; they came to life and stood up on their feet—a vast army.

[11] Then he said to me: "Son of man, these bones are the people of Israel. They say, 'Our bones are dried up and our hope is gone; we are cut off.' [12] Therefore prophesy and say to them: 'This is what the Sovereign LORD says: My people, I am going to open your graves and bring you up from them; I will bring you back to the land of Israel. [13] Then you, my people, will know that I am the LORD, when I open your graves and bring you up from them. [14] I will put my Spirit in you and you will live, and I will settle you in your own land. Then you will know that I the LORD have spoken, and I have done it, declares the LORD."

Gog and Magog: Chapter 38: *Gog and Magog only appear here in Ezekiel and in Revelation. According to Halley (2007), in Revelation, Gog and Magog are used to represent all nations in Satan's final, furious attack on the people of God. Here in Ezekiel 38, we see the furious battle prophesied. Then in chapter 39, God will vanquish Israel's foes and will set his glory and pour out His spirit.*

Ezekiel 39: "Son of man, prophesy against Gog and say: 'This is what the Sovereign Lord says: I am against you, Gog, chief prince of Meshek and Tubal. [2] I will turn you around and drag you along. I will bring you from the far north and send you against the mountains of Israel. . . .[6] I will send fire on Magog and on those who live in safety in the coastlands, and they will know that I am the Lord.

[7] "'I will make known my holy name among my people Israel. . .[21]" I will display my glory among the nations, and all the nations will see the punishment I inflict and the hand I lay on them. [22] From that day forward the people of Israel will know that I am the Lord their God. [23] And the nations will know that the people of Israel went into exile for their sin, because they were unfaithful to me. So I hid my face from them and handed them over to their enemies, and they all fell by the sword. [24] I dealt with them according to their uncleanness and their offenses, and I hid My face from them.

[25] "Therefore this is what the Sovereign Lord says: I will now restore the fortunes of Jacob and will have compassion on all the people of Israel, and I will be zealous for My holy name. . .[27] When I have brought them back from the nations and have gathered them from the countries of their enemies, I will be proved holy through them in the sight of many nations. [28] Then they will know that I am the Lord their God, for though I sent them into exile among the nations, I will gather them to their own land, not leaving any behind. [29] I will no longer hide my face from them, for I will pour out my Spirit on the people of Israel, declares the Sovereign Lord."

Temple Area Restored and True Worship Reinstated: Ezekiel 40, 41, 42, 43, 44, 45, and 46:

Ezekiel is given the amazing vision of what the restored temple and reinstatement of true worship would be like. Chapter 40 gives the description and magnificence of the Outer Court and also describes the porches and chambers where singers gave praises and where the sons of Levi who were in charge of the altar performed their duties.

Ezekiel 40:2: In visions of God He took me to the land of Israel and set me on a very high mountain, on whose south side were some buildings that looked like a city. [3] He took me there, and I saw a man whose appearance was like bronze; He was standing in the gateway with a linen cord and a measuring rod in his hand. [4] The man said to me, "Son of man, look carefully and listen closely and pay attention to everything I am going to show you, for that is why you have been brought here. Tell the people of Israel everything you see.

In chapters 40 and 41, Ezekiel describes every detail of the wondrous temple.

The Rooms for the Priests: Chapter 42:13: Then he said to me, "The north and south rooms facing the temple courtyard are the priests' rooms, where the priests who approach the Lord will eat the most holy offerings. There they will put the most holy offerings—the grain offerings, the sin offerings[f] and the guilt offerings—for the place is holy. [14] Once the priests enter the holy precincts, they are not to go into the outer court until they leave behind the garments in which they minister, for these are holy. They are to put on other clothes before they go near the places that are for the people."

Again, I must say, "Thank you, God, that we no longer must offer animal sacrifices for sin because Jesus was our sacrifice once for all. Thank you that Jesus is also our High Priest and we need not go to a priest to rid ourselves of guilt!

Instructions for Priests are outlined in Chapter 44.

Chapters 45 to 48 involve the dividing by lot of the land to the tribes of Israel.

Remember, the theme of Ezekiel is "God acts in the events of human history so that everyone will come to know Him and find new life."

Ezekiel has stressed the need for individual responsibility and national responsibility. Let us in America not wait until we are completely in the place in which Israel found itself before we humble ourselves and receive God's blessings.

THE BOOK OF DANIEL
In Daniel, Jesus is the stranger in the fire.

Theme: God is sovereign over the kingdoms of men.

Message: Written at the time Israel was in Babylonian exile, God's people are told to be prepared for God's intervention into world affairs. (I will concentrate upon stories of Daniel and of characters that children love. You will see Bible Points that we stressed with children at church. Daniel 7-12 is prophecy, which is drawn upon in Revelation.)

BIBLE POINT: When away from home, remember what your parents taught you.

Daniel 1:1: After King Nebuchadnezzar brought sons of Israel captive to Babylon; the young men were given a special place in the king's palace. They were Daniel, Shadrach, Meshach, and Abednego.

[8] But Daniel purposed in his heart that he would not defile himself with the portion of the king's meat, nor with the wine which he drank: therefore he requested of the prince of the eunuchs that he might not defile himself. [12] Prove thy servants, I beseech thee, ten days; and let them give us pulse to eat, and water to drink. [13] Then let our countenances be looked upon before thee, and the countenance of the children that eat of the portion of the king's meat: and as thou seest, deal with thy servants.

[14] So he consented to them in this matter, and proved them ten days. [15] And at the end of ten days their countenances appeared fairer and fatter in flesh than all the children which did eat the portion of the king's meat. [17] As for these four children, God gave them knowledge and skill in all learning and wisdom: and Daniel had understanding in all visions and dreams.

[19] And the king communed with them; and among them all was found none like Daniel, Hananiah, Mishael, and Azariah: (*the Hebrew names of Shadrack, Meshack, and Abednego.*) therefore stood they before the king. [20] And in all matters of wisdom and understanding that the king enquired of them he found them ten times better than all the magicians and astrologers that were in all his realm.

Daniel Chapter 3: Bible Point: Even if I am the only one, I will serve the Lord.

Nebuchadnezzar made an image of himself of gold and the proclamation was made: Daniel 3:5: As soon as you hear the sound of the horn, flute, zither, lyre, harp, pipe and all kinds of music, you must fall down and worship the image of gold that King Nebuchadnezzar has set up. [6] Whoever does not fall down and worship will immediately be thrown into a blazing furnace."

[7] Therefore, as soon as they heard the sound of the horn, flute, zither, lyre, harp and all kinds of music, all the nations and peoples of every language fell down and worshiped the image of gold that King Nebuchadnezzar had set up. [8] At this time some astrologers[b] came forward and denounced the Jews. [9] They said to King Nebuchadnezzar. . . ."[12] But there are some Jews whom you have set over the affairs of the province of Babylon—Shadrach,

Meshach and Abednego—who pay no attention to you, Your Majesty. They neither serve your gods nor worship the image of gold you have set up."

[13] Furious with rage, Nebuchadnezzar summoned Shadrach, Meshach and Abednego. So these men were brought before the king, [14] and Nebuchadnezzar said to them, "Is it true, Shadrach, Meshach and Abednego, that you do not serve my gods or worship the image of gold I have set up? [15] Now when you hear the sound of the horn, flute, zither, lyre, harp, pipe and all kinds of music, if you are ready to fall down and worship the image I made, very good. But if you do not worship it, you will be thrown immediately into a blazing furnace. Then what god will be able to rescue you from my hand?"

[16] Shadrach, Meshach and Abednego replied to him, "King Nebuchadnezzar, we do not need to defend ourselves before you in this matter. [17] If we are thrown into the blazing furnace, the God we serve is able to deliver us from it, and he will deliver us[c] from Your Majesty's hand. [18] But even if he does not, we want you to know, Your Majesty, which <u>we will not serve your gods or worship the image of gold you have set up.</u>"

[19] Then Nebuchadnezzar was furious with Shadrach, Meshach and Abednego, and his attitude toward them changed. He ordered the furnace heated seven times hotter than usual[20] and commanded some of the strongest soldiers in his army to tie up Shadrach, Meshach and Abednego and throw them into the blazing furnace. [21] So these men, wearing their robes, trousers, turbans and other clothes, were bound and thrown into the blazing furnace.[22] The king's command was so urgent and the furnace so hot that the flames of the fire killed the soldiers who took up Shadrach, Meshach and Abednego, [23] and these three men, firmly tied, fell into the blazing furnace.

[24] Then King Nebuchadnezzar leaped to his feet in amazement and asked his advisers, "Weren't there three men that we tied up and threw into the fire?"

They replied, "Certainly, Your Majesty."

[25] He said, "Look! I see four men walking around in the fire, unbound and unharmed, and the fourth looks like a son of the gods." [26] Nebuchadnezzar then approached the opening of the blazing furnace and shouted, "Shadrach, Meshach and Abednego, servants of the Most High God, come out! Come here!"

So Shadrach, Meshach and Abednego came out of the fire, [27] and the satraps, prefects, governors and royal advisers crowded around them. They saw that the fire had not harmed their bodies, nor was a hair of their heads singed; their robes were not scorched, and there was no smell of fire on them.

[28] Then Nebuchadnezzar said, "Praise be to the God of Shadrach, Meshach and Abednego, who has sent his angel and rescued his servants! They trusted in him and defied the king's command and were willing to give up their lives rather than serve or worship any god except their own God. [29] Therefore I decree that the people of any nation or language who say anything against the God of Shadrach, Meshach and Abednego be cut into pieces and their houses be turned into piles of rubble, for no other god can save in this way."

[30]Then the king promoted Shadrach, Meshach and Abednego in the province of Babylon. Pass the Baton of Faith to the next Generation. <u>BIBLE POINT</u>: Dare to Be a Daniel!

The Story of Daniel in the Lion's Den

Daniel 6:3, KJV: Daniel was preferred above the presidents and princes, because an excellent spirit was in him, and the king wanted to set Daniel over the whole realm. *The presidents and princes wanted to find fault with Daniel, couldn't find anything wrong with Daniel because he was faithful and without error. They tricked the king into signing a petition that any man who prayed to anyone except the king would be cast into the den of lions.*

Verse 10: Now when Daniel knew that the writing was signed, he went into his house; and his windows being open in his chamber toward Jerusalem, he kneeled upon his knees three times a day, and prayed, and gave thanks before his God, as he did aforetime. [11]Then these men assembled, and found Daniel praying and making supplication before his God. [12]Then they came near, and spake before the king. . . .That Daniel, which is of the children of the captivity of Judah, regardeth not thee, O king, nor the decree

[16]Then the king commanded, and they brought Daniel, and cast him into the den of lions. Now the king spake and said unto Daniel, Thy God whom thou servest continually, he will deliver thee. [17]And a stone was brought, and laid upon the mouth of the den; and the king sealed it with his own signet, and with the signet of his lords; that the purpose might not be changed concerning Daniel.

[19]Then the king arose very early in the morning, and went in haste unto the den of lions. [20]And when he came to the den, he cried with a lamentable voice unto Daniel: and the king spake and said to Daniel, O Daniel, servant of the living God, is thy God, whom thou servest continually, able to deliver thee from the lions? [21]Then said Daniel unto the king, O king, live forever. [22]My God hath sent his angel, and hath shut the lions' mouths, that they have not hurt me: forasmuch as before him innocence was found in me; and also before thee, O king, have I done no hurt.

[23]Then was the king exceedingly glad for him, and commanded that they should take Daniel up out of the den. So Daniel was taken up out of the den, and no manner of hurt was found upon him because he believed in God. [25]Then king Darius wrote unto all people, nations, and languages, that dwell in all the earth; In every dominion of my kingdom men tremble and fear before the God of Daniel: for he is the living God, and steadfast forever, and his kingdom that which shall not be destroyed, and his dominion shall be even unto the end. [27]He delivered and rescued, and he works signs and wonders in heaven and in earth, who has delivered Daniel from the power of the lions.

Do we dare to be a Daniel? Because of one person, Daniel, the proclamation was made that all should serve God. A teacher was told by his school administration to take his Bible off his desk. He refused, and now The Fellowship of Christian Athletes is in the school, and

students can have Bible Study at noon. We need to take a stand as Christians so we can retain our rights to freedom of religion and of speech guaranteed in the first amendment.

Unity of the Scriptures: After a period of two or three years, we hear from Daniel again. After Daniel has been captive of the Babylonians, the rise of the Persian Empire will prove to be a blessing to the exiled nation of Israel. In Ezra 1:3-4 and in 2 Chronicles 36:22 to 23, Cyrus the Great encouraged people to return to Jerusalem and rebuild the temple. Much excitement existed among some of the Hebrews. But enemies discouraged plans to rebuild in Jerusalem. The same year the temple foundation is built, and restoration is begun, God brought to Daniel an amazing vision about the future, giving assurance that God will continue to rule the world. Daniel's struggles have been worthwhile.

Daniel Chapter 7 gives a prophetic revelation of four earthly kingdoms, beginning with Nebuchadnezzar's Babylon, that will one day be forever replaced by a fifth kingdom. He saw visions of the prophecy of God's everlasting kingdom of the Son of Man that will never pass away:

Daniel 7:13: In my vision at night I looked, and there before me was one like a son of man,[] coming with the clouds of heaven. He approached the Ancient of Days and was led into his presence. [14] He was given authority, glory and sovereign power; all nations and peoples of every language worshiped him. His dominion is an everlasting dominion that will not pass away, and his kingdom is one that will never be destroyed.

Daniel also saw the prophecy that the kingdom will be given to the people of the saints of the Most High, who will reign with the Most High.

Daniel 7:27 Then the sovereignty, power and greatness of all the kingdoms under heaven will be handed over to the holy people of the Most High. His kingdom will be an everlasting kingdom, and all rulers will worship and obey him.

[4] On the twenty-fourth day of the first month, as I was standing on the bank of the great river, the Tigris, [5] I looked up and there before me was a man dressed in linen, with a belt of fine gold from Uphaz around his waist. . .and his voice like the sound of a multitude.

[7] I, Daniel, was the only one who saw the vision. . . .[10] A hand touched me and set me trembling on my hands and knees. [11] He said, "Daniel, you who are highly esteemed, consider carefully the words I am about to speak to you, and stand up, for I have now been sent to you." And when he said this to me, I stood up trembling.

[12] Then he continued, "Do not be afraid, Daniel. Since the first day that you set your mind to gain understanding and to humble yourself before your God, your words were heard, and I have come in response to them. [13] But the prince of the Persian kingdom resisted me twenty-one days. Then Michael, one of the chief princes, came to help me, because I was detained there with the king of Persia. [14] Now I have come to explain to you what will happen to your people in the future, for the vision concerns a time yet to come."

[15] While he was saying this to me, I bowed with my face toward the ground and was speechless. [16] Then one who looked like a man touched my lips, and I opened my mouth

and began to speak. I said to the one standing before me, "I am overcome with anguish because of the vision, my lord, and I feel very weak. [17] How can I, your servant, talk with you, my lord? My strength is gone and I can hardly breathe."

[18] Again the one who looked like a man touched me and gave me strength. [19] "Do not be afraid, you who are highly esteemed," he said. "Peace! Be strong now; be strong." When he spoke to me, I was strengthened and said, "Speak, my lord, since you have given me strength."

[20] So he said, "Do you know why I have come to you? Soon I will return to fight against the prince of Persia, and when I go, the prince of Greece will come; [21] but first I will tell you what is written in the Book of Truth. (No one supports me against them except Michael, your prince.) *Michael is the guardian angel of Israel.*

Daniel 10:4-11:1 – the conversation between Daniel and an angel shows us what goes on in the heavenly realms. In Daniel 10:21, Michael, a prince, the guardian angel of Israel, is referred to as Daniel's people's prince or guardian. Michael is involved in spiritual warfare concerning the future of God's people. The angel tells Daniel that his own intervention in Daniel's life has made Daniel's life good under the pagan king Darius in Babylon.

The second part of the vision is futuristic and ends on the most hopeful note of all—the resurrection. We see signs of the time of the end. A time of distress such as never before; characteristics of the time at the end similar to our own generation; many going everywhere to increase in knowledge:

Daniel 12:1: "At that time Michael, the great prince who protects your people, will arise. There will be a time of distress such as has not happened from the beginning of nations until then. But at that time your people—everyone whose name is found written in the book—will be delivered. [2] Multitudes who sleep in the dust of the earth will awake: some to everlasting life, others to shame and everlasting contempt. [3] Those who are wise[a] will shine like the brightness of the heavens, and those who lead many to righteousness, like the stars for ever and ever. [4] But you, Daniel, roll up and seal the words of the scroll until the time of the end. Many will go here and there to increase knowledge."

Daniel 12:8: I heard, but I did not understand. So I asked, "My lord, what will the outcome of all this be?" [9] He replied, "Go your way, Daniel, because the words are rolled up and sealed until the time of the end. [10] Many will be purified, made spotless and refined, but the wicked will continue to be wicked. None of the wicked will understand, but those who are wise will understand.

Verse 13: Promise to Daniel: "As for you, go your way till the end. You will rest, and then at the end of the days you will rise to receive your allotted inheritance."

So ends the record of Daniel's life and his encounters with angels. We have seen Daniel as a man of prayer. Though demons may have come against him, Daniel's prayers were answered. James 5:16: The prayer of a righteous man is powerful and effective.

The 12 Minor Prophets are Hosea, Joel, Amos, Obadiah, Jonah, Micah, Nahum, Habakkuk, Zephaniah, Haggai, Zechariah, and Malachi.

THE BOOK OF HOSEA
In Hosea, Jesus is forever faithful.

Theme: God's undying love for his people.

Message: Israel was worshipping Baal and not the true God.

The Book of Hosea is a prophetic accounting of God's relentless love for His children. *(I was amazed when I assigned Hosea to a Champion for Christ when we did studies in my home. This was the first time I had really thought about and understood all Hosea must have gone through. While teaching chastity to youth, I was amazed that God told Hosea to show love over and over to a prostitute. At first I couldn't understand. Then when I realized that this was a metaphor in the themes of sin, judgment, and forgiving love, it was overwhelming to me and to the young man who reported on Hosea.)* You see, it was through the marriage of Hosea, the faithful husband, and Gomer, the adulterous wife, that God's love for the idolatrous nation of Israel is displayed

The first three chapters describe the adulterous wife and a faithful husband, symbolic of the unfaithfulness of Israel to God through idolatry. The faithful husband is symbolic of God's steadfast love. Chapters 4 through 14 contain the condemnation of Israel for the worship of Idols. God then promises eventual restoration when Israel turns to Him.

Hosea wrote this book to remind the Israelites (and us) that ours is a loving God whose loyalty to His covenant people is unwavering. (Now, we are his Covenant people.) Hosea's message is also one of warning to those who would turn their backs on God's love.

Key Verses:

Hosea 1:2, "When the LORD began to speak through Hosea, the LORD said to him, 'Go, take to yourself an adulterous wife and children of unfaithfulness, because the land is guilty of the vilest adultery in departing from the LORD.'"

Hosea 2:23: "I will plant her for Myself in the land; I will show My love to the one I called 'Not my loved one.' I will say to those called 'Not My people,' 'You are My people'; and they will say, 'You are my God.'"

Hosea 6:6, "For I desire mercy, not sacrifice, and acknowledgment of God rather than burnt offerings."

Hosea talks of judgment against the Nation that "plays the harlot" before God:

Hosea 9:12: Even if they bring up children, I will bereave them till none is left. Woe to them when I depart from them!

Hosea 10:12: Sow to yourselves in righteousness, reap in mercy; break up your fallow ground, for it is time to seek the Lord.

Hosea 13:4: Yet I am the Lord your God from the land of Egypt, and thou shall know no god but Me: for there is no savior beside Me.

Hosea 14:2-4, "Take words with you and return to the LORD. Say to Him: 'Forgive all our sins and receive us graciously, that we may offer the fruit of our lips. Assyria cannot save us; we will not mount war-horses. We will never again say "Our gods" to what our own hands have made, for in you the fatherless find compassion.' "I will heal their waywardness and love them freely, for My anger has turned away from them.'"

The last part of Hosea shows how God's love once again restores His children as He forgets their misdeeds when they turn back to Him with a repentant heart.

America, return to God. He is faithful to forgive and to heal our land if we will seek His face and will turn from our wicked ways.

Unity of the Bible: The prophetic message of Hosea foretells the coming of Israel's Messiah 700 years in the future. Hosea is quoted often in the New Testament

The last part of Hosea shows how God's love once again restores His children as He forgets their misdeeds when they turn back to Him with a repentant heart. Hosea also is a picture of how God is dishonored by our actions as his children. But when we make mistakes, if we have a sorrowful heart and promise to repent God will again show his love to us.

THE BOOK OF JOEL
In Joel, Jesus is the Spirit's Power

Theme: The Day of the Lord, a day of God's wrath and judgment.

Joel 1:3: Tell ye your children of it, let your children tell their children, and their children another generation. PASS THE BATON OF FAITH TO THE NEXT GENERATION!

Message: Judah has just been devastated by a vast horde of locusts, which destroyed everything! Joel symbolically describes the locusts as a marching human army and views all of this as divine judgment coming against the nation for her sins. Unless the people repent quickly and completely, enemy armies will devour the land as did the natural elements. The book is highlighted by two major events: The invasion of locusts and the outpouring of the Holy Spirit. The initial fulfillment of this is quoted by Peter in Acts 2 as having taken place at Pentecost.

Key Verses: Joel 1:4, "What the locust swarm has left the great locusts have eaten; what the great locusts have left the young locusts have eaten; what the young locusts have left other locusts have eaten."

The Day of the Lord: Joel 2:28 - 32
[28] "And afterward, I will pour out my Spirit on all people.
Your sons and daughters will prophesy,
your old men will dream dreams, your young men will see visions.
[29] Even on my servants, both men and women, I will pour out my Spirit in those days.
[30] I will show wonders in the heavens and on the earth, blood and fire and billows of smoke.
[31] The sun will be turned to darkness and the moon to blood
before the coming of the great and dreadful day of the Lord.
[32] And everyone who calls on the name of the Lord will be saved;
for on Mount Zion and in Jerusalem there will be deliverance.

Foreshadowings: Whenever the Old Testament speaks of judgment for sin, whether individual or national sin, the advent of Jesus Christ is foreshadowed. The prophets of the Old Testament continually warned Israel to repent, but even when they did, their repentance was limited to law-keeping and works. Their temple sacrifices were but a shadow of the ultimate sacrifice, offered once for all time, which would come at the cross (Hebrews 10:10). Joel tells us that God's ultimate judgment, which falls on the Day of the Lord, will be "great and terrible. Who can endure it?" (Joel 2:11). The answer is that we, on our own, can never endure such a moment. But if we have placed our faith in Christ for atonement of our sins, we have nothing to fear from the Day of Judgment. When we repent, God promises physical restoration, spiritual restoration, and national restoration. This speaks to us individually and as a nation! (GotQuestions.org Home)

THE BOOK OF AMOS
In Amos, Jesus is the arms that carry us.

Theme: God's judgment on Injustice

Amos 1:1 identifies the author of the Book of Amos as the Prophet Amos. The Book of Amos was likely written between 760 and 753 B.C.

Message: Amos, a shepherd and fruit picker from a Judean Village, was called of God to give the message to Israel and Judea of impending doom because of sin: neglect of God's Word, idolatry, pagan worship, greed, corrupted leadership and oppression of the poor. Amos preached on sin, separation, and sanctification. He challenges followers of God to examine themselves and their society and to confront injustice wherever it may be found. His visions from God reveal that Judgment is near. But because Israel is prosperous, they won't listen. The book ends with God's promise to Amos of future restoration of the remnant. In Amos, God roars like a lion and brings hope at the end.

Key Verses: Amos 2:4, "This is what the LORD says: 'For three sins of Judah, even for four, I will not turn back my wrath. Because they have rejected the law of the LORD and have not kept it. Hear this word, people of Israel, the word the Lord has spoken against you—against the whole family I brought up out of Egypt:

Amos 3:1: You only have I chosen of all the families of the earth; therefore I will punish you for all your sins." [3] Do two walk together unless they have agreed to do so?

Amos 4 tells Israel to prepare to meet God.

Chapter 5 warns against oppressors: There are those who hate the one who upholds justice in court and detest the one who tells the truth. [11] You levy a straw tax on the poor and impose a tax on their grain. Therefore, though you have built stone mansions, you will not live in them;

though you have planted lush vineyards, you will not drink their wine.

[12] For I know how many are your offenses and how great your sins.

There are those who oppress the innocent and take bribes and deprive the poor of justice in the courts. [13] Therefore the prudent keep quiet in such times, for the times are evil.

[14] Seek good, not evil, that you may live.

Then the Lord God Almighty will be with you, just as you say he is.

[15] Hate evil, love good; maintain justice in the courts.

Perhaps the Lord God Almighty will have mercy on the remnant of Joseph.

Amos *6 presents indictments against the complacent, lazy, materialistic, and indulgent people.*

Then in Amos 9, we again see the restoration of Israel prophesied by God through Amos.

Amos 9:14, "I will bring back my exiled people Israel; they will rebuild the ruined cities and live in them. They will plant vineyards and drink their wine; they will make gardens and eat their fruit."

Amos means "burden." Amos carried the burden of Israel's sin and of the message of the Lord. That is what Christian Americans should do.

Foreshadowings: The Book of Amos ends with a glorious promise for the future. "'I will plant Israel in their own land, never again to be uprooted from the land I have given them,' says the LORD your God" (9:15). The ultimate fulfillment of God's land promise to Abraham (Gen. 12:7; 15:7; 17:8) will occur during Christ's reign on earth (see Joel 2:26,27). Revelation 20 describes the thousand-year reign of Christ on the earth, a time of peace and joy under the perfect government of the Savior Himself. And according to the Bible, we will reign forever with Christ!

THE BOOK OF OBADIAH
In Obadiah, Jesus is the Lord our Savior.

Theme: God's judgment of proud Edom and the restoration of Israel.

Message: Edom is the land occupied by Esau, brother of Jacob. The Edomites are descendants of Esau and the Israelites are descendants of his twin brother, Jacob. A quarrel between the brothers had affected their descendants for over 1,000 years. The Edomites had taken advantage of the fall of Jerusalem to the Babylonians in 586. Edom's sins of pride now require a strong word of judgment from the Lord.. The Kingdom of Edom will be destroyed. Then the book ends with the promise of deliverance of Zion in the Last Days when the land will be restored to God's people as He rules over them. (FCA Press, 2008)

Written about 844 BC, Obadiah is the shortest book in the Old Testament, and Obadiah consists of words of a Jew to people of another nation.

Obadiah, verse 4, "Though you soar like the eagle and make your nest among the stars, from there I will bring you down," declares the LORD."

Obadiah 12, "You should not look down on your brother in the day of his misfortune, nor rejoice over the people of Judah in the day of their destruction, nor boast so much in the day of their trouble."

Obadiah 15, "The day of the LORD is near for all nations. As you have done, it will be done to you; your deeds will return upon your own head." We have heard a message from the Lord

Obadiah 20-21: The captives from Jerusalem exiled in the will return home and resettle the towns of the Negev.

[21] Those who have been rescued will go up to Mount Zion in Jerusalem

to rule over the mountains of Edom. And the Lord himself will be king!"

Foreshadowing of Christ: Verse 21 of the Book of Obadiah contains a foreshadowing of Christ.

Practical Application: God will overcome in our behalf if we will stay true to Him. Unlike Edom, we must be willing to help others in times of need. Pride is sin. We have nothing to be proud of except Jesus Christ and what He has done for us.

THE BOOK OF JONAH
In Jonah, Jesus is the great missionary.

Theme: God's love for the Gentiles, even Nineveh.

Message:. Jonah runs away from God, suffers the consequences, and then obeys God. Jonah is told by God to go to Nineveh to tell them to repent, but because Nineveh is the capital of the ruthless Assyrian Empire that threatened Israel, Jonah boards a ship and goes the other way. The miraculous encounter with the large fish reveals God's sovereignty. Jonah becomes angry with God when God blesses Nineveh after Jonah calls them to repentance.

Jonah 1: Jonah Flees From the Lord

1 The word of the Lord came to Jonah son of Amittai: [2] "Go to the great city of Nineveh and preach against it, because its wickedness has come up before me." [3] But Jonah ran away from the Lord and headed for Tarshish. He went down to Joppa, where he found a ship bound for that port. After paying the fare, he went aboard and sailed for Tarshish to flee from the Lord.

[4] Then the Lord sent a great wind on the sea, and such a violent storm arose that the ship threatened to break up. [5] All the sailors were afraid and each cried out to his own god. And they threw the cargo into the sea to lighten the ship. But Jonah had gone below deck, where he lay down and fell into a deep sleep. [6] The captain went to him and said, "How can you sleep? Get up and call on your god! Maybe he will take notice of us so that we will not perish."

[7] Then the sailors said to each other, "Come, let us cast lots to find out who is responsible for this calamity." They cast lots and the lot fell on Jonah. [8] So they asked him, "Tell us, who is responsible for making all this trouble for us? What kind of work do you do? Where do you come from? What is your country? From what people are you?"

[9] He answered, "I am a Hebrew and I worship the Lord, the God of heaven, who made the sea and the dry land."

[10] This terrified them and they asked, "What have you done?" (They knew he was running away from the Lord, because he had already told them so.)

[11] The sea was getting rougher and rougher. So they asked him, "What should we do to you to make the sea calm down for us?"

[12] "Pick me up and throw me into the sea," he replied, "and it will become calm. I know that it is my fault that this great storm has come upon you."

[13] Instead, the men did their best to row back to land. But they could not, for the sea grew even wilder than before. [14] Then they cried out to the Lord, "Please, Lord, do not let us die for taking this man's life. Do not hold us accountable for killing an innocent man, for you, Lord, have done as you pleased." [15] Then they took Jonah and threw him overboard,

and the raging sea grew calm. [16] At this the men greatly feared the Lord, and they offered a sacrifice to the Lord and made vows to him. [17] Now the Lord provided a huge fish to swallow Jonah, and Jonah was in the belly of the fish three days and three nights.

Jonah's Prayer: Chapter 2:1: From inside the fish Jonah prayed to the Lord his God. *He said he was compassed with water, weeds were wrapped around his neck. He promised to sacrifice to God with thanksgiving. 2:10: T*he Lord spake unto the fish, and it vomited Jonah upon the dry land.

Nineveh's Repentance: Jonah 3:1-5: Then the word of the Lord came to Jonah a second time: [2] "Go to the great city of Nineveh and proclaim to it the message I give you."

[3] Jonah obeyed the word of the Lord and went to Nineveh..; *He proclaimed:* Forty more days and Nineveh will be overthrown." [5] The Ninevites believed God. A fast was proclaimed, and all of them, from the greatest to the least, put on sackcloth. *(Then in the following verses, the king of Nineveh arose and repented and made the decree that all should do the same. God did not bring destruction on them.)*

Jonah's Anger at the Lord's Compassion: Jonah 4:1: But to Jonah this seemed very wrong, and he became angry. [2] He prayed to the Lord, "Isn't this what I said, Lord, when I was still at home? That is what I tried to forestall by fleeing to Tarshish. I knew that you are a gracious and compassionate God, slow to anger and abounding in love, a God who relents from sending calamity. [3] Now, Lord, take away my life, for it is better for me to die than to live." *Then in verses 5-11, God shows His love for all his creation when he made a vine grow over Jonah to protect him from the sun. When He removed the vine, Jonah grieved over the loss of the vine, and God illustrated that God grieves for all of his people, including the people and animals of Nineveh.*

Foreshadowing and Unity of the Scriptures: This is not just a story or a parable. It is a historical picture of the Messiah's resurrection and mission to all nations.. Jesus quoted Jonah's rescue as a prophetic picture of his resurrection on the "third" day in Matthew 12:40.

THE BOOK OF MICAH
In Micah, Jesus is the promise of peace.

Theme: The Impending Fall of Israel and Judah: The Messiah will be born in Bethlehem.

Message: Micah, a contemporary of the prophets Isaiah and Hosea, prophesied to both Israel and Judah. The three main ideas in Micah's message are the sins of Samaria and Jerusalem, their destruction, and the future exultation of Israel and Jerusalem. (Halley, 2007)

Key Verse: And what does the LORD require of you? To act justly and to love mercy and to walk humbly with your God. Micah 6:8

Micah 1: 1 The word of the Lord that came to Micah of Moresheth during the reigns of Jotham, Ahaz, and Hezekiah, kings of Judah—the vision he saw concerning Samaria and Jerusalem. [2] Hear, you peoples, all of you, listen, earth and all who live in it, that the Sovereign Lord may bear witness against you, the Lord from his holy temple.

<u>Judgment against Samaria and Jerusalem:</u> [3] Look! The Lord is coming from his dwelling place; he comes down and treads on the heights of the earth. [4] The mountains melt beneath him and the valleys split apart, like wax before the fire, like water rushing down a slope. [5] All this is because of Jacob's transgression, because of the sins of the people of Israel. What is Jacob's transgression? Is it not Samaria? What is Judah's high place? Is it not Jerusalem?

[6] "Therefore I will make Samaria a heap of rubble. . . . [7] All her idols will be broken to pieces;

all her temple gifts will be burned with fire; I will destroy all her images. Since she gathered her gifts from the wages of prostitutes, as the wages of prostitutes they will again be used." Because of this I will weep and wail; [9] For Samaria's plague is incurable; it has spread to Judah. It has reached the very gate of my people, even to Jerusalem itself.

<u>Judgment because of the brutality of the rulers.</u> *Micah 2 and 3 tell that the ruling class was merciless with the poor. After Micah tells of their captivity, he abruptly pictures their restoration, with God marching at their head.*

Micah 2:12-13: I will surely gather all of you, Jacob; I will surely bring together the remnant of Israel. I will bring them together like sheep in a pen, like a flock in its pasture; the place will throng with people. [13] The One who breaks open the way will go up efore them; they will break through the gate and go out. Their King will pass through before them, the Lord at their head."

In Micah 4, Micah shifts to a vision of a warless, happy, prosperous world with Zion at its head. Then again, the prophet reverted to his own troubled times and the doom of Jerusalem. He prophesied that the people would be carried away captive to Babylon!

Micah 5:2: Micah prophesied <u>that a deliverer would come from Bethlehem.</u>

"But you, Bethlehem Ephathrah, though you are small among the clans of Judah, out of you will come for Me one who will be ruler over Israel, whose origins are from of old, from ancient times." *This is just one of the many prophesies of the Messiah being sent to earth. This is the only one that tells that the birth place will be Bethlehem.*

Unity of the Scriptures: Micah 5:2 *is a prophecy of the Messiah that was quoted when the Wise Men were searching for the king born in Bethlehem (*Matthew 2:6*). These Wise Men from the East were told that from the tiny village of Bethlehem would come forth the Prince of Peace.*

Micah 6 *tells of Jehovah's controversy with his people and with their sins of ingratitude toward God, dishonesty, and idolatry and their certain punishment! But then, Micah said:*

Micah 6:8, "He has showed you, O man, what is good. And what does the LORD require of you? To act justly and to love mercy and to walk humbly with your God."

Micah 7: Prayer and Praise

[14] Shepherd your people with your staff, the flock of your inheritance, which lives by itself in a forest, in fertile pasturelands. "As in the days when you came out of Egypt, I will show them my wonders." "Who is a God like you, who pardons sin and forgives the transgression of the remnant of His inheritance? You do not stay angry forever but delight to show mercy. You will again have compassion on us; you will tread our sins underfoot and hurl all our iniquities into the depths of the sea."

[19] You will again have compassion on us; you will tread our sins underfoot

and hurl all our iniquities into the depths of the sea.

[20] You will be faithful to Jacob, and show love to Abraham,

as you pledged on oath to our ancestors in days long ago.

Always, Israel reminded God of his covenant with Father Abraham. But they must also remember that with each of God's promises comes a command—IF my people. . .

If we are obedient to Christ, we won't have to suffer the wrath of God. Also, judgment is certain if we reject His provision for sin, which is the sacrifice of his son. God will discipline the believer in Christ because He loves us. He knows that sin destroys and He wants us to be whole. The promise of restoration awaits us who remain obedient to Him.

THE BOOK OF NAHUM
In Nahum, Jesus is our strength and our shield.

Theme: The doom of Nineveh.

Message: The author is Nahum (meaning "Comforter" or "Counselor." He counsels with the City of Nineveh. Nineveh once had responded to the preaching of Jonah and turned from their evil ways to serve the Lord God Jehovah. But 150 years later, Nineveh returned to idolatry, violence and arrogance (Nahum 3:1-4). (FCA Press, 2008) Once again God sent one of His prophets to Nineveh preaching judgment in the destruction of the city and exhorting them to repentance. But the Ninevites did not heed Nahum's warning and the city was brought under the domination of Babylon. The Assyrians had become absolutely brutal in their conquests. Now Nahum was telling the people of Judah to not despair because God had pronounced judgment upon the Assyrians. (You reap what you sow!)

Key Verses: Nahum 1:7, "The LORD is good, a refuge in times of trouble. He cares for those who trust in Him."

Nahum 1:14a. "The LORD has given a command concerning you, Nineveh: 'You will have no descendants to bear your name.'"

Nahum 1:15: "Look, there on the mountains, the feet of one who brings good news, who proclaims peace!"

Foreshadowings of Christ: Paul repeats Nahum 1:15 in Romans 10:15 in regard to the Messiah and His ministry, as well as the apostles of Christ in His time.

Nahum chapter 1
God is jealous. He demands first place
In your heart and life.
In the day of trouble He will embrace
You and keep you from its strife.

Nahum chapters 1 through 3 graphically foretell the fall of Nineveh.

Nahum 1:1; The Lord is a jealous and avenging God; the Lord takes vengeance and is filled with wrath. The Lord takes vengeance on his foes and vents his wrath against His enemies.

[3] The Lord is slow to anger but great in power; the Lord will not leave the guilty unpunished.

His way is in the whirlwind and the storm, and clouds are the dust of His feet.

[4] He rebukes the sea and dries it up; he makes all the rivers run dry.

[7] The Lord is good, a refuge in times of trouble. He cares for those who trust in Him,

[8] but with an overwhelming flood He will make an end of Nineveh; and devise wicked plans.

[14]The Lord has given a command concerning you, Nineveh:
"You will have no descendants to bear your name.
I will destroy the images and idols that are in the temple of your gods.

Chapter 3
Assyria's power was at its end.
Her conquering arm cannot extend
Any further in frenzied haste.
Nineveh is laid waste.

God is patient and slow to anger. He gives every country time to proclaim Him as their Lord. But He is not mocked. Any time a country turns away from Him to serve its own motives, He steps in with judgment. Almost 220 years ago, the United States was formed as a nation guided by principles found in the Bible. In the last 50 years that has changed, and we are turning daily in the opposite direction. As Christians it is our duty to stand up for biblical principles and scriptural truth, for Truth is our country's only hope.

THE BOOK OF HABAKKUK
In Habakkuk and Zephaniah, Jesus is pleading for revival.

Theme: Faith triumphs over doubt.

Brief Summary: Written between 605 and 610 BC, the Book of Habakkuk begins with Habakkuk crying out to God for an answer to why God's chosen people are allowed to suffer in their captivity. He complained to God that His own nation was being destroyed for its *wickedness by a nation even more wicked. God said he does have a purpose in this.*

When I was a little child, people asked why God allowed a wicked man like Hitler to take over a Christian nation. My Mama said, "Because men and women and boys and girls in America are sinning against God." I understood. If America had not repented, we would not have defeated Hitler.

Habakkuk 1:1-3: Habakkuk's Complaint:

How long, Oh Lord, must I call for help, but You do not listen? Or cry out to you, 'Violence!' but You do not save. "Why do You make me look at injustice? Why do You tolerate wrongdoing? G*od's answer was that the Babylonians, drunk with the blood of nations will be destroyed, and God's people will yet fill the earth.*

The wicked hem in the righteous, so that justice is perverted. Look at the nations and watch and be utterly amazed. For I am going to do something in your days that you would not believe, even if I told you."

Habakkuk 2:2-4, "Then the Lord replied: Write down the revelation and make it plain on tablets so that a herald may run with it. For the revelation waits an appointed time; it speaks of the end and will not prove false. Though it linger, wait for it; it will certainly come and not delay. See, he is puffed up; his desires are not upright - but the righteous will live by his faith." (*This is quoted many times in the New Testament.*)

Habakkuk 2:14: For the earth will be filled with the knowledge of the glory of the Lord as the waters that cover the sea.

Habakkuk, after talking with God, writes a prayer expressing his strong faith in God, even through these trials (Habakkuk 3:1-19). *Habakkuk prayed that God would do miracles for his people that he had seen in the past. He ended with the confidence in the security of God's people. The lesson is:*

The righteous shall lie by faith. Faith is the ability to trust God in the middle of despair and to not doubt the glorious future of His Children. (That is us!) We must remember that God has all things under control. We need to be still and know that He is God.

Habakkuk 3:19, "The Sovereign Lord is my strength; He makes my feet like the feet of a deer, He enables me to go on the heights."

Sometimes we have to be tested in order to be set apart so we can go to greater heights. We can't appreciate the mountains until we have been through the valley.

THE BOOK OF ZEPHANIAH
Theme: The Coming Day of the Lord

Message: Likely written between 735 and 725 B.C., Zephaniah's message of gloom and doom and also encouragement contains three major doctrines: 1) God is sovereign over all nations. 2) The wicked will be punished and the righteous will be vindicated on the Day of Judgment. 3) God blesses those who repent and trust in Him. FCA, God's Game Plan (2008).

Key Verses: 3:17: The LORD your God is with you, he is mighty to save. He will take great delight in you, he will quiet you with his love, he will rejoice over you with singing."

Zephaniah 2:3: Seek the Lord all you humble of the land, you who do what he commands. Seek righteousness, seek humility; perhaps you will be sheltered on the day of the LORD's anger.

God is compassionate, but when all His warnings are ignored, judgment is to be expected.

Zephaniah 2:11: The LORD will be awesome to them when He destroys all the gods of the earth.

Distant nations will bow down to Him, all of them in their own lands. [13] He will stretch out his hand against the north and destroy Assyria leaving Nineveh utterly desolate and dry as the desert.

But hope is given when people turn from their sins. Also, hope when the Day of the Lord comes. The final blessings on Zion pronounced in 3:14-20 are largely unfulfilled. Some will not be fulfilled until the second coming of Christ. Our punishment can only be taken away through Christ, who died for His people.

Zechariah 3:9: "Then will I purify the lips of the peoples, that all of them may call on the name of the LORD and serve him shoulder to shoulder. 11 On that day you will not be put to shame for all the wrongs you have done to me, because I will remove from this city those who rejoice in their pride. 14 Be glad and rejoice with all your heart, O Daughter of Jerusalem! 15The LORD has taken away your punishment, he has turned back your enemy.

Prophecy of the Coming Messiah: The LORD, the King of Israel, is with you; never again will you fear any harm. 3:16: On that day they will say to Jerusalem, "Do not fear, O Zion; do not let your hands hang limp. 17 The LORD your God is with you, he is mighty to save. He will take great delight in you, He will quiet you with his love, He will rejoice over you with singing." 20 At that time I will gather you; at that time I will bring you home.

This prophet of 8th century B.C. could stand in our pulpits today and deliver the same message of judgment of the wicked and hope for the faithful. Zephaniah reminds us that God's people will not escape punishment when they sin willfully. Punishment may be painful, but I pray that his punishment of Americans will be redemptive. Perhaps it will pull us back to our senses. God does not forget the faithful remnant.

THE BOOK OF HAGGAI
In Haggai, Jesus restores a lost heritage.

Theme: Make the rebuilding of the temple your priority. Rebuilding the Nation. The blessing is in the doing.

Message: In 520 BC, upon the return of the Jews from Babylonian exile, Hagaii called the people to restore their lost heritage and to rebuild the temple while they were rebuilding Jerusalem.

Haggai 1
It is time to build in haste
For the temple lies in waste.
Everyone's home is in good repair,
But to God's house they had no money or time to spare.

^{Haggai 1:3} Then the word of the Lord came through the prophet Haggai: ⁴"Is it a time for you yourselves to be living in your paneled houses, while this house remains a ruin?"⁵ Now this is what the Lord Almighty says: "Give careful thought to your ways. ⁶You have planted much, but harvested little. You eat, but never have enough. You drink, but never have your fill. You put on clothes, but are not warm. You earn wages, only to put them in a purse with holes in it."

⁷This is what the Lord Almighty says: "Give careful thought to your ways. ⁸Go up into the mountains and bring down timber and build My house, so that I may take pleasure in it and be honored," says the Lord. ⁹"You expected much, but see, it turned out to be little. What you brought home, I blew away. Why?" declares the Lord Almighty. "Because of my house, which remains a ruin, while each of you is busy with your own house. ¹⁰ Therefore, because of you the heavens have withheld their dew and the earth its crops. ¹¹ I called for a drought on the fields and the mountains, on the grain, the new wine, the olive oil and everything else the ground produces, on people and livestock, and on all the labor of your hands."

¹³Then Haggai, the Lord's messenger, gave this message of the Lord to the people: "I am with you," declares the Lord.

The Lord stirred up the spirit of Zerubbabel son of Shealtiel, governor of Judah. . .and the spirit of the whole remnant of the people. They came and began to work on the house of the Lord Almighty, their God. . .

Haggai 2
Who is left that saw this house in her first glory?
We love to hear old timers tell their story,

How great the church once had been.
Every tale starts, "Remember when?"

Haggai 2:9, "'The glory of this present house will be greater than the glory of the former house,' says the LORD Almighty. 'And in this place I will grant peace,' declares the LORD Almighty."

Foreshadowings: As with most of the books of the Minor Prophets, Haggai ends with promises of restoration and blessing. In the last verse, Haggai 2:23, God uses a distinctly Messianic title in reference to Zerubbabel, "My Servant" (Compare 2 Samuel 3:18; 1 Kings 11:34; Isaiah 42:1–9; Ezekiel 37:24,25). Through Haggai, God promises to make him like a signet ring, which was a symbol of honor, authority, and power. Zerubbabel, as God's signet ring, represents the house of David and the resumption of the messianic line interrupted by the Exile. Zerubbabel reestablished the Davidic line of kings which would culminate in the millennial reign of Christ. Zerubbabel appears in the line of Christ on both side (Matt. 1:12) and Mary's side (Luke 3:27). www.messiahrevealed.org/haggai.html) Most of us face common problems.

When we face problems like those in Haggai, we, too, must first examine our priorities, reject a defeatist attitude when we encounter discouraging circumstances, confess our failures and seek to live pure lives, and know that God will abundantly bless us as we faithfully serve Him.

THE BOOK OF ZECHARIAH
In Zechariah, Jesus is our fountain.

Theme: Rebuilding the Temple: Visions of the Coming Messiah and His Universal Kingdom.

Message: The book of Zechariah is second only to Isaiah in its abundance of prophecies concerning the Messiah. Zechariah was a younger contemporary of Hagaii. He was one of 50,000 exiles who were allowed to leave Babylonian captivity to resettle their homeland. Zechariah, along with Hagaii was commissioned by God to rouse the people from their indifference and challenge them to rebuild the temple. He tried to encourage them by reminding them of God's promises that he would restore and bless them and by reminding them of the promised Messiah who would inhabit it.

In Zechariah 1, the opening message warns that the people are returning to the disobedient ways of their forefathers and calls for repentance.

Zechariah 1:2: The Lord was very angry with your ancestors. [3] Therefore tell the people: This is what the Lord Almighty says: 'Return to Me,' declares the Lord Almighty, 'and I will return to you, 'says the Lord Almighty. [4] Do not be like your ancestors, to whom the earlier prophets proclaimed: This is what the Lord Almighty says: 'Turn from your evil ways and your evil practices.' But they would not listen or pay attention to me, declares the Lord.

According to Halley (2007), Zechariah was given the visions for comfort of those who had returned from exile to the land promised to them by Abraham. Some have been fulfilled, but most await the Second Advent of Jesus. Visions include reassuring words to the exiles by revealing God's purpose in the future of His chose people.

The Vision of the Horses: Zechariah 1:7-17. Under Persian Rule of King Darius was to come a time when rebuilding could take place and Jerusalem could prosper. Zech. 1:16-17: "Therefore this is what the Lord says: 'I will return to Jerusalem with mercy, and there My house will be rebuilt. And the measuring line will be stretched out over Jerusalem,' declares he Lord Almighty. [17] "Proclaim further: This is what the Lord Almighty says: 'My towns will again overflow with prosperity, and the Lord will again comfort Zion and choose Jerusalem.'"

Vision of the Four Horns and Four Craftsmen: Zechariah 1:18-21 details the judgment of the nations who persecuted Israel and builds upon God's promise to comfort His people. 18. Then I looked up, and there before me were four horns. [19] I asked the angel who was speaking to me, "What are these?" He answered me, "These are the horns that scattered Judah, Israel and Jerusalem." [20] Then the Lord showed me four craftsmen. [21] I asked, "What are these coming to do?" He answered, "These are the horns that scattered Judah so that no one could raise their head, but the craftsmen have come to terrify them and throw down these horns of the nations who lifted up their horns against the land of Judah to scatter its people."

Caution, America! God has always blessed America when we bless and stand for Israel. Those nations were destroyed who did not. Remember how Hitler murdered 6,000,000 Jews during World War II and how God blessed America? Right now, in 2013 and 2014, in all the middle East Crises, are we going to stand up for Israel or for the Muslim Nations?

The Vision of the Man with the Measuring Line: Zechariah 3:1-13 builds on God's promise to comfort His people. The scope of this vision extends beyond the time of Zechariah to the rule of the Messiah on Earth. Verses 3-5 show that God will be a protective wall of fire around Jerusalem. 8. For this is what the LORD Almighty says: "After the Glorious One has sent me against the nations that have plundered you—for whoever touches you touches the apple of his eye—⁹ I will surely raise my hand against them so that their slaves will plunder them. Then you will know that the LORD Almighty has sent me.

¹⁰ "Shout and be glad, Daughter Zion. For I am coming, and I will live among you," declares the LORD. ¹¹ "Many nations will be joined with the LORD in that day and will become my people. I will live among you and you will know that the LORD Almighty has sent me to you.¹² The LORD will inherit Judah as his portion in the holy land and will again choose Jerusalem. ¹³ Be still before the LORD, all mankind, because He has roused himself from His holy dwelling."

The Vision of Joshua the High Priest: Zechariah 3:1-10 details the restoration of a priestly nation, Israel. Verses 1-5 reveal the vision, and the significance is given in verses 6-10. Verses 1-5 tell of Joshua, the high priest, standing dressed in filthy clothes. An angel tells him to take off his filthy clothes. The Lord promised to take away his sin and put fine garments on him.

⁶ "This is what the LORD Almighty says: 'If you will walk in obedience to Me and keep My requirements, then you will govern My house and have charge of My courts, and I will give you a place among these standing here.

⁸ "'Listen, High Priest Joshua, you and your associates seated before you, who are men symbolic of things to come: I am going to bring my servant, the Branch. ⁹ See, the stone I have set in front of Joshua!. . .' says the LORD Almighty, 'and I will remove the sin of this land in a single day. ¹⁰ "'In that day each of you will invite your neighbor to sit under your vine and fig tree,' declares the LORD Almighty." *The branch is Jesus. The "stone" is always a reference to the Messiah. Here He is the foundation stone.*

The Vision of the Gold Lampstand and the two Olive Trees: Zech. 4:1-14: The candlestick is a symbolic representation of the light-bearing qualities of God's house. We are shown that the Lord will empower Israel by His Spirit. (verse 10) "This is the word of the Lord to Zerubbabel: 'Not by might nor by power, but by my Spirit,' says the Lord Almighty.

The Vision of the Flying Scroll: Zech. 5:1-4: This depicts the word of God which has been disobeyed. Dishonesty is cursed. ³ And he said to me, "This is the curse that is going out over the whole land; for according to what it says on one side, every thief will be banished, and according to what it says on the other, everyone who swears falsely will be banished.

The Flying Basket:: Zech. 5:5-11 focuses on the removal of the whole sinful system from Israel before the kingdom comes..

The Four Chariots: Zech. 6:1-8:23: God's judgment on the nations just prior to the establishment of the Messianic Kingdom. Also, God's promise for the faithful.

Zech 8:3:[3] This is what the Lord says: "I will return to Zion and dwell in Jerusalem. Then Jerusalem will be called the Faithful City, and the mountain of the Lord Almighty will be called the Holy Mountain." [7] This is what the Lord Almighty says: "I will save My people from the countries of the east and the west. [8] I will bring them back to live in Jerusalem; they will be My people, and I will be faithful and righteous to them as their God."

[9] This is what the Lord Almighty says. . . .11. Now I will not deal with the remnant of this people as I did in the past," declares the Lord Almighty. 14. Just as I had determined to bring disaster on you and showed no pity when your ancestors angered Me, so now I have determined to do good again to Jerusalem and Judah. Do not be afraid. [16] These are the things you are to do: Speak the truth to each other, and render true and sound judgment in your courts; [17] do not plot evil against each other, and do not love to swear falsely. I hate all this," declares the Lord. . . .Therefore love truth and peace."

[20] This is what the Lord Almighty says: "Many peoples and the inhabitants of many cities will yet come, [21] and the inhabitants of one city will go to another and say, 'Let us go at once to entreat the Lord and seek the Lord Almighty. I myself am going.'

Unity of the scriptures: MacArthur (2005) gives 27 different scriptures for God's promises to regather dispersed Israel for the Millennial Kingdom. (p 1065)

Part 2, chapters 9-14, was written 40 years later. Zechariah tries to instill a desire for rebuilding the temple as they see that this will result in a transformation of God's people into a holy nation. Chapters 9-11 are oracles from God concerning neighboring nations. Chapters 12-14 are messages from God concerning Israel.

Zechariah 9:1-8:The word of the Lord is against the land of Hadrak and will come to rest on Damascus—for the eyes of all people and all the tribes of Israel are on the Lord—and I will put an end to the pride of the Philistines. [7] I will take the blood from their mouths, the forbidden food from between their teeth. Those who are left will belong to our God and become a clan in Judah, and Ekron will be like the Jebusites. [8] But I will encamp at my temple to guard it against marauding forces. Never again will an oppressor overrun my people, or now I am keeping watch.

Zech. 12:1: The Lord, who stretches out the heavens, who lays the foundation of the earth, and who forms the human spirit within a person, declares: [2] "I am going to make Jerusalem a cup that sends all the surrounding peoples reeling. Judah will be besieged as well as Jerusalem.[3] On that day, when all the nations of the earth are gathered against her,

I will make Jerusalem an immovable rock for all the nations. . . .[9] On that day I will set out to destroy all the nations that attack Jerusalem.

Mourning for the One They Pierced *(The one who was pierced is always Jesus, throughout scriptures.)* [10] "And I will pour out on the house of David and the inhabitants of Jerusalem a spirit[a] of grace and supplication. They will look on Me, the one they have pierced, and they will mourn for Him as one mourns for an only child.

Zechariah 13:1: "On that day a fountain will be opened to the house of David and the inhabitants of Jerusalem, to cleanse them from sin and impurity. [2] "On that day, I will banish the names of the idols from the land, and they will be remembered no more," declares the Lord Almighty.

[8] In the whole land, "declares the Lord, "two-thirds will be struck down and perish; yet one-third will be left in it. [9] This third I will put into the fire; I will refine them like silver and test them like gold. They will call on My name and I will answer them;

I will say, 'They are My people,' and they will say, 'The Lord is our God.'"

The Lord Comes and Reigns

14:1: A day of the Lord is coming, Jerusalem, when your possessions will be plundered and divided up within your very walls. [2] I will gather all the nations to Jerusalem to fight against it; the city will be captured, the houses ransacked, and the women raped. Half of the city will go into exile, but the rest of the people will not be taken from the city. [3] Then the Lord will go out and fight against those nations, as he fights on a day of battle. [4] On that day his feet will stand on the Mount of Olives, east of Jerusalem, and the Mount of Olives will be split in two from east to west, forming a great valley, with half of the mountain moving north and half moving south.[5] You will flee by my mountain valley, for it will extend to Azel. You will flee as you fled from the earthquake[e] in the days of Uzziah king of Judah. Then the Lord my God will come and all the holy ones with him.

[6] On that day there will be neither sunlight nor cold, frosty darkness. [7] It will be a unique day—a day known only to the Lord—with no distinction between day and night. When evening comes, there will be light. [8] On that day living water will flow out from Jerusalem, half of it east to the Dead Sea and half of it west to the Mediterranean Sea, in summer and in winter.

[9] The Lord will be king over the whole earth. On that day there will be one Lord, and His name the only name.

Zechariah's prophecies forecast the doctrines of the coming Messiah's atoning death for sin, His deity, and His universal kingdom.

THE BOOK OF MALACHI
In Malachi, Jesus is the son of righteousness rising with healing in His wings

Theme: Repentance is the cure for spiritual indifference.

From the rising of the sun to the going down of the same, my name shall be great among the Gentiles. Malachi 1:11

Message: Malachi, probably the last prophet before the coming of the Messiah, uses a question-and-answer form of dialog to develop the theme. (Constable, T. L. 2013) Malachi prophesied at a time when Israel lapsed into spiritual indifference. Biblical history tells us that the exiles had returned from Babylonia and finished building the temple in 516 BC. Temple worship was restored by Ezra in 458 AB. Then in 445 BC, Nehemiah returned to Jerusalem, rebuilt the walls, and brought many religious reforms. After all these successes, the people lapsed into spiritual decay. They intermarried with idolatrous neighbors. They just settled down to wait for the return of the Messiah, but Malachi assured them He would come, but it would mean judgment rather than glory for them.

Malachi 1:1: KJV: The burden of the word of the LORD to Israel by Malachi. 2 I have loved you, saith the LORD. I:6: A son honoureth his father, and a servant his master: if then I be a father, where is mine honour? And if I be a master, where is my fear? Saith the LORD of hosts unto you, O priests, that despise my name. And ye say,

Question: Wherein have we despised thy name? 7 Ye offer polluted bread upon mine altar; and ye say, Wherein have we polluted thee?

Question: Wherein have we polluted thee? In that ye say, The table of the LORD is contemptible.

Answer: Mal 1:8 And if ye offer the blind for sacrifice, is it not evil? And if ye offer the lame and sick, is it not evil? Ye priests, this commandment is for you. 2 If ye will not hear, and if ye will not lay it to heart, to give glory unto my name, saith the LORD of hosts, I will even send a curse upon you, and I will curse your blessings: 4 And ye shall know that I have sent this commandment unto you, that my covenant might be with Levi, saith the LORD of hosts. 5 My covenant was with him of life and peace; and I gave them to him for the fear wherewith he feared Me, and was afraid before My name. 6 The law of truth was in His mouth, and iniquity was not found in His lips: He walked with me in peace and equity, and did turn many away from iniquity. 7For the priest's lips should keep knowledge, and they should seek the law at his mouth: for he is the messenger of the LORD of hosts. 8 But ye are departed out of the way; ye have caused many to stumble at the law; ye have corrupted the covenant of Levi, saith the LORD of hosts.

Question: Wherein have we wearied the Lord?

Answer 2:17: Ye have wearied the LORD with your words. Yet ye say, Wherein have we wearied him? When ye say, every one that doeth evil is good in the sight of the LORD, and he delighteth in them; or, where is the God of judgment?

Prophecy of John the Baptist, the messenger who will prepare the way for the Messiah.

3:1: Behold, I will send my messenger, and he shall prepare the way before me: and the Lord, whom ye seek, shall suddenly come to his temple, even the messenger of the covenant, whom ye delight in: behold, He shall come, saith the LORD of hosts. 2 But who may abide the day of His coming? And who shall stand when He appeared? for he is like a refiner's fire, and like fullers ' soap: 3 And He shall sit as a refiner and purifier of silver: and He shall purify the sons of Levi, and purge them as gold and silver, that they may offer unto the LORD an offering in righteousness. 4Then shall the offering of Judah and Jerusalem be pleasant unto the LORD, as in the days of old, and as in former years. 5 And I will come near to you to judgment; Return unto me, and I will return unto you, saith the LORD of hosts.

Question: Malachi 3:8: Wherein shall we return? Will a man rob God? But ye say, Wherein have we robbed thee? (*God's answer includes a great Promise!*)

Answer: In tithes and offerings. 9 Ye are cursed with a curse: for ye have robbed me, even this whole nation. 10 Bring ye all the tithes into the storehouse, that there may be meat in Mine house, and prove Me now herewith, saith the LORD of hosts, if I will not open you the windows of heaven, and pour you out a blessing, that there shall not be room enough to receive it.

Question: What have we spoken so much against thee? It is vain to serve God; and what profit is it that we have kept his ordinance?

God's Answer: Mal. 3:16:. . .And a book of remembrance was written before him for them that feared the LORD, and that thought upon his name. 17 And they shall be Mine, says the LORD of hosts, in that day when I make up my jewels; and I will spare them, as a man spares his own son that serve him. 18 Then shall ye return, and discern between the righteous and the wicked, between him that serveth God and him that serveth him not.

Mal 4: 4 Remember ye the Law of Moses my servant, which I commanded unto him in Horeb for all Israel, with the statutes and judgments. 5 Behold, I will send you Elijah the prophet before the coming of the great and dreadful day of the LORD: 6And he shall turn the heart of the fathers to the children, and the heart of the children to their fathers.

Thus, God's answer is that they should keep the commandments given to Moses. Then he gives hope of the Messiah, who is often called Elijah. He will restore the hearts of people within the home. The home is the first institution planned by God.

The Old Testament: Revisited and Summarized

According to Halley (2007), there is the story of the Old Testament, and there is "The Story Behind the Story." The first three chapters of Genesis tell of creation that was good and harmonious, but harmony was destroyed when Adam and Eve sinned. As a result, we all have sinned. The rest of the Bible tells what God has done to again set things right. God promised that a descendent of Eve would bring salvation. That was Jesus.

The next part of Genesis told of the time of the Patriarchs, Abraham, Isaac, Jacob, and Joseph.. God made a covenant with Abraham that through their descendants, the whole world would be blessed. The promised Messiah, Redeemer would come. Later, on Mount Sinai, God made another covenant with Israel, the descendants of Abraham. Part of the covenant was the warning that disobedience would bring disaster, and obedience to God's laws will bring blessings. Much of the remainder of the Old Testament shows the Israelites going through being blessed and cursed, depending upon their following God's precepts as individuals and as a nation.

The periods of time after the Israelites got to the Promised Land include the time of the Judges, the time they wanted a King, which resulted in a Monarchy and the Divided Kingdom. Then came the Babylonian Exile and the Return from Exile. During all this time, prophets from God were warning Kings and the people to follow God's commandments, but they did not. The terrible experience of the exile in Babylon brought about a focus that God had not abandoned them and that He would fulfill His promise of sending the Messiah.

The 400 Years between the Testaments

After the Babylonian exile, the Jews returned to Jerusalem. God prepared the world for the coming Messiah. During the time between the testaments, the Romans, rather than the Persians, become the great world power. The Romans provided a stable government, world-wide peace, and a system of roads so Christians could evangelize the world. The Greek Empire gave the then known world a common language – Greek. This all made it possible for the rapid spread of the Gospel of Jesus Christ (Halley, 2000, pp. 16 and 17).

Yes, the time had come for Jesus to be born. That single solitary life that has influenced the world more than any other! "The Christian Church has made more changes on Earth for the good than any other movement or force in history." (Kennedy, 1994, p. 3)

Fulfilled Prophecy: Jesus is the Promised Messiah!

Genesis 3:15 says He would be the seed of Woman and is fulfilled in Galatians 4:4.

Genesis 12:3 says he will be the descendent of Abraham. Fulfilled in Matthew 1:1

Genesis 17:18: He will be the descendent of Isaac. See Luke 3:34

Numbers 24:17: The Seed of Jacob. Luke Matthew 1:2

Genesis 49:10: From the tribe of Judah: Luke 3:33

Isaiah 9:7: The heir to the throne of David. Luke 1:32, 33

Micah 5:2: Born in Bethlehem: Luke 2:4, 5, 7

Daniel 9:25: Time for His birth. Luke 2:1,2

Isaiah 7:14: To be born of a virgin. Luke 1:26-31

Jeremiah 31:15: Slaughter of the innocents. Matthew 2:16-18

Hosea 11:1: flight into Egypt: Matthew 2:14,15

Malachi 3:1: Proceeded by a forerunner. Luke 7:24, 27

Psalm 2:7: Declared the Son of God. Mathew 3:17

Isaiah 9:1, 2: Galilean Ministry. Matthew 4:13-16

Deuteronomy 18:15: a prophet. Acts 3:26

Isaiah 61:1: To heal the brokenhearted: Luke 4:18, 19

Isaiah 53:3: Rejected by his own people, the Jews. John 1:11

Psalm 110:4: Priest after the order of Melchizedek. Hebrews 5:5,6

Zechariah 9:9: Triumphal Entry: Mark 11:7:8

Psalm 41:9: Betrayed by Friend: Luke 22:47

Zechariah 11:12: Sold for 30 pieces of silver: Matthew 26:15

Psalm 35:11: Accused by false witnesses: Mark 14:57

Isaiah 53:7: Silent to accusations: Mark 15:4, 5

Isaiah 56:6 Spat upon and smitten: Matthew 26:6

Psalm 35:19: Hated without reason: John 15:24, 25

Isaiah 53:5: Vicarious sacrifice: Romans 5:6, 8

Isaiah 53:12: Crucified with malefactors: Mark 15:27

Zechariah 12:10: Pierced through hands and feet: John 20:27

Psalm 22:7, 8: Scorned and mocked: Luke 23:35

Psalm 69:21: Given vinegar and gall: Matthew 27:34

Psalm 109:4: Prayer for enemies: Luke 23:34

Psalm 22:17: Soldiers gambled for his coat: Matthew 27:35

Psalm 34:26: No bones broken: John 19:32, 33

Zechariah 12:10: His side pierced: John 19:34

Isaiah 53:9: Buried with the rich: Matthew 27:57-60

Psalm 16:10 & 4; 15: To be resurrected: Mark 16:6, 7

Psalm 68:18: Ascension to God's right hand: Mark 16:19; I Cor. 15:4; Eph. 4:8

PROPHECY

Too many prophecies have already been fulfilled for us to say they just happened by chance. History confirms the undeniable fact that a Man named Jesus lived, and the Word of God reveals exactly who He was, and why He lived, died, and rose again. Prophecies already fulfilled give absolute proof that prophecies not yet fulfilled will be brought to pass exactly as prophesied. Jesus Christ is the Capstone of the Pyramid of Prophecy. If Jesus were removed from the Bible, we would have no Bible. <u>More than half of prophecies concerning Jesus are yet to be fulfilled</u>. (Green, 1970) Jesus' first coming demands his second coming.

We will discuss the prophecies yet to be fulfilled when they are discussed in the New Testament- in the Gospels, the Epistles, and especially in the prophetic book of Revelation.

THE NEW TESTAMENT

The First Four Books of the New Testament are called *The Gospels*.

In Matthew, Mark, Luke, and John, Jesus is God, Man, Messiah.

The four Gospels tell the story of Jesus' birth, childhood, earthly ministry, and death, burial, and resurrection. Jesus, Himself, testifies of his Messiahship and the unity of the Bible, when he quotes from the prophecies of the Old Testament. The Scarlet Thread Continues!

According to Halley (2007), the Four Gospels were written by four different men who reflected their own personalities and wrote from different perspectives. Matthew shows Jesus as the Messiah, who fulfills the Old Testament prophecies. Mark presents Jesus, the Wonderful, who was rejected, suffered, and died as the essential part of His mission. Luke presents Jesus the Son of Man. John shows Jesus the Son of God, the creator.

Using scriptures, I will recount <u>the life of Jesus</u> on earth while <u>harmonizing the four Gospels</u>, beginning with Jesus' birth and ending with His glorious resurrection and ascension!

THE GENEALOGY AND BIRTH OF JESUS

Matthew 1:1-2: The book of the generation of Jesus Christ, the son of David, the son of Abraham. Abraham begat Isaac; and Isaac begat Jacob; and Jacob begat Joseph, and his brethren.

Matthew 1:17: So all the generations from Abraham to David are fourteen generations; and from David unto the carrying away into Babylon are fourteen generations; and from the carrying away unto Babylon unto Christ are fourteen generations.

(I am writing this during the Christmas Season. How exciting to think that time is marked by the birth of Jesus. About 2012 years ago, Jesus was sent to Earth by God!)

Matthew 1:18: Now the birth of Jesus Christ was on this wise: When his mother, Mary was espoused to Joseph, before they came together, she was found with child of the Holy Ghost.

Matthew 1:20b-21, KJV: The angel of the Lord said, "Fear not to take unto thee, Mary thy wife, for that which is conceived in her is of the Holy Ghost. And she shall bring forth a son, and thou shalt call his Name Jesus, for he shall save his people from their sins."

(After writing and producing several church and school Christmas programs, I realized Chapter 2 of Luke would be easy to memorize. What a miracle and wonder Jesus' birth is! God sent Jesus from the glories of Heaven as a baby in a manger, born of a Virgin, to die for our sins.

Luke 2:1, 3-20, KJV: And it came to pass in those days, that there went out a decree from Caesar Augustus, that all the world should be taxed. [3] And all went to be taxed, every one into his own city. [4] And Joseph also went up from Galilee, out of the city of Nazareth, into Judaea, unto the city of David, which is called Bethlehem; (because he was of the house and lineage of David:) [5] To be taxed with Mary his espoused wife, being great with child.

[6] And so it was, that, while they were there, the days were accomplished that she should be delivered. [7] And she brought forth her firstborn son, and wrapped him in swaddling clothes, and laid him in a manger; because there was no room for them in the inn.

[8] And there were in the same country shepherds abiding in the field, keeping watch over their flock by night. And, lo, the angel of the Lord came upon them, and the glory of the Lord shone round about them: and they were sore afraid. [10] And the angel said unto them, Fear not: for, behold, I bring you good tidings of great joy, which shall be to all people. [11] For unto you is born this day in the city of David a Savior, which is Christ the Lord. [12] And this *shall be* a sign unto you; Ye shall find the babe wrapped in swaddling clothes, lying in a manger.

[13] And suddenly there was with the angel a multitude of the heavenly host praising God, and saying, [14] Glory to God in the highest, and on earth peace, good will toward men. [15] And it came to pass, as the angels were gone away from them into heaven, the shepherds said one to another, Let us now go even unto Bethlehem, and see this thing which is come to pass, which the Lord hath made known unto us.

[16] And they came with haste, and found Mary, and Joseph, and the babe lying in a manger. . . .[20] And the shepherds returned, glorifying and praising God for all the things that they had heard and seen, as it was told unto them.

Matthew Chapter 2, KJV: After Jesus was born in Bethlehem in Judea, during the time of King Herod, Magi from the East came to Jerusalem [2] and asked, "Where is the one who has been born king of the Jews? We saw his star when it rose and have come to worship him."

[3] When King Herod heard this he was disturbed, and all Jerusalem with him. [4] When he had called together all the people's chief priests and teachers of the law, he asked them where the Messiah was to be born. [5]"In Bethlehem in Judea," they replied, "for this is what the prophet has written:

Micah 5:2: "But you, Bethlehem, in the land of Judah, are by no means least among the rulers of Judah; for out of you will come a ruler who will shepherd my people Israel."

The Unity of the Scriptures: *Micah 5:2 shows prophecy of the birth of Jesus in Bethlehem from the Old Testament fulfilled and shows the unity of the scriptures. How many Wise Men (Magi) came to Jerusalem? Probably many, because all Jerusalem was disturbed when they entered their city.*

[7]Then Herod called the Magi secretly and found out from them the exact time the star had appeared. [8]He sent them to Bethlehem and said, "Go and search carefully for the child. As soon as you find him, report to me, so that I too may go and worship him."

[9]After they had heard the king, they went on their way, and the star they had seen when it rose went ahead of them until it stopped over the place where the child was. [10]When they saw the star, they were overjoyed.[11]On coming to the house, they saw the child with his mother Mary, and they bowed down and worshiped him. Then they opened their treasures and presented him with gifts of gold, frankincense and myrrh. [12]And having been warned in a dream not to go back to Herod, they returned to their country by another route.

(In *Matthew 2:16-18 Herod had all baby boys under 2 years killed to be certain he killed Baby Jesus—that the prophecy by Jeremiah might be fulfilled. Also, in verse 23, we see Jesus fulfilling the prophecy that Jesus would be raised in Nazareth. God miraculously saved Jesus, for He was sent to Earth for a purpose.)*

JESUS' CHILDHOOD

Luke 2:40, KJV: And the child grew, and waxed strong in spirit, filled with wisdom: and the grace of God was upon Him.

[41] Now his parents went to Jerusalem every year at the feast of the Passover. [42] And when he was twelve years old, they went up to Jerusalem after the custom of the feast.

[46]. . .They found him in the temple, sitting in the midst of the doctors, both hearing them and asking them questions. [47] And all that heard him were astonished at his understanding and answers. [48] And when they saw him, they were amazed: and his mother said unto him, Son, why hast thou thus dealt with us? Behold, thy father and I have sought thee sorrowing.

[49] And he said unto them, How is it that ye sought me? Wist ye not that I must be about my Father's business? *Even Jesus' earthly parents didn't understand.*

[51] And he went down with them, and came to Nazareth, and was subject unto them: but his mother kept all these sayings in her heart. [52] And Jesus increased in wisdom and stature, and in favor with God and man.

(We should teach children and aid them to grow in the ways that Jesus grew in Luke *2:52. They would then grow mentally, physically, spiritually, and socially.)*

JESUS, THE WORD, CREATOR, GOD, AND LIGHT OF THE WORLD JOHN 1:1-15, KJV (*I memorized and said this for a Youth Halloween Party at my house to show the difference in darkness and Light and to show that Jesus came as the light of the world. Jesus, the Word and the light is God and is the Creator!)*

1 In the beginning was the Word, and the Word was with God, and the Word was God. [2]The same was in the beginning with God. [3]All things were made by him; and without him was not anything made that was made. [4]In him was life; and the life was the light of men. [5]And the light shineth in darkness; and the darkness comprehended it not.

⁶There was a man sent from God, whose name was John. ⁷The same came for a witness, to bear witness of the Light that all men through him might believe. ⁸He was not that Light, but was sent to bear witness of that Light.

⁹That was the true Light, which lighteth every man that cometh into the world. ¹⁰He was in the world, and the world was made by him, and the world knew him not. ¹¹He came unto his own, and his own received him not. ¹²But as many as received him, to them gave he power to become the sons of God, even to them that believe on his name: ¹³Which were born, not of blood, nor of the will of the flesh, nor of the will of man, but of God. ¹⁴And the Word was made flesh, and dwelt among us, (and we beheld his glory, the glory as of the only begotten of the Father,) full of grace and truth.

¹⁵John bare witness of him, and cried, saying, This was he of whom I spake, He that cometh after me is preferred before me: for he was before me.

THE BAPTISM OF JESUS BY JOHN THE BAPTIST

John 1:29, KJV: John saw Jesus coming unto him, and saith, "Behold the Lamb of God, which taketh away the sin of the world. John 1:30: This is he of whom I said, After me cometh a man which is preferred before me.

Mark 8:9, KJV: Jesus came from Nazareth of Galilee, and was baptized of John in Jordan. And coming up out of the water, he saw the heavens opened, and the Spirit like a dove descending upon him: And there came a voice from heaven, saying, Thou art my beloved son in whom I am well-pleased.

THE TEMPTATION OF JESUS

In Matthew 4 and in Luke 4, we find the account of Jesus's temptation by Satan. After 40 days in the wilderness, Satan tempted Jesus three times, and each time Jesus quoted God's Word: "It is written."

Matthew 4:1-4: Then Jesus was led by the Spirit into the wilderness to be tempted by the devil. ²After fasting forty days and forty nights, he was hungry. ³The tempter came to him and said, "If you are the Son of God, tell these stones to become bread."

⁴Jesus answered, "It is written: 'Man shall not live on bread alone, but on every word that comes from the mouth of God." *This is the model for us. We answer temptation by quoting the scripture that is hidden in our hearts.*

THE MINISTRY OF JESUS:

Jesus chose 12 special helpers. Matthew 10:2-4: Now the names of the 12 apostles are these: The first, Simon, who is called Peter, and Andrew his brother; James the son of Zebedee, and John his brother. Philip, and Bartholomew, Thomas, and Matthew the publican; James the son of Alphaeus, and Thaddaeus; Simon the Canaanite, and Judas Iscariot, who betrayed Jesus

THE SERMON ON THE MOUNT: Matthew 5, 6, and 7. Please *read the entire sermon.* I am including what I have memorized, the most memorable for you. All is amazing!

The Beatitudes: Matthew 5:1-12, KJV: *Blessed means "Happy." Isn't Jesus' way of thinking wonderful and very different than expected!*

1 And seeing the multitudes, he went up into a mountain: and when he was set, his disciples came unto him: [2] And he opened his mouth, and taught them, saying,

[3] Blessed are the poor in spirit: for theirs is the kingdom of heaven.

[4] Blessed are they that mourn: for they shall be comforted.

[5] Blessed are the meek: for they shall inherit the earth.

[6] Blessed are they which do hunger and thirst after righteousness: for they shall be filled.

[7] Blessed are the merciful: for they shall obtain mercy.

[8] Blessed are the pure in heart: for they shall see God.

[9] Blessed are the peacemakers: for they shall be called the children of God.

[10] Blessed are they which are persecuted for righteousness' sake: for theirs is the kingdom of heaven.

[11] Blessed are ye, when men shall revile you, and persecute you, and shall say all manner of evil against you falsely, for my sake. [12] Rejoice, and be exceeding glad: for great is your reward in heaven: for so persecuted they the prophets which were before you.

[13] Ye are the salt of the earth: but if the salt has lost his savor, wherewith shall it be salted? it is thenceforth good for nothing, but to be cast out, and to be trodden under foot of men.

[14] Ye are the light of the world. A city that is set on a hill cannot be hid. [15] Neither do men light a candle, and put it under a bushel, but on a candlestick; and it gives light unto all that are in the house. [16] Let your light so shine before men, that they may see your good works, and glorify your Father which is in heaven.

Matthew 5: 38-48, KJV: Ye have heard that it hath been said, an eye for an eye, and a tooth for a tooth: But I say unto you, that ye resist not evil: but whosoever shall smite thee on thy right cheek, turn to him the other also. . . .Ye have heard that it hath been said, Thou shalt love thy neighbor, and hate thine enemy. But I say unto you, Love your enemies, bless them that curse you, do good to them that hate you, and pray for them which despitefully use you, and persecute you.

Matthew 6:9-15, KJV: The Lord's Prayer: After this manner therefore pray ye: Our Father which art in heaven, Hallowed be thy name. [10] Thy kingdom come, Thy will be done in earth, as it is in heaven. [11] Give us this day our daily bread. [12] And forgive us our debts, as we forgive our debtors. [13] And lead us not into temptation, but deliver us from evil: For thine is the kingdom, and the power, and the glory, forever. Amen.

[14] For if ye forgive men their trespasses, your heavenly Father will also forgive you: [15] But if ye forgive not men their trespasses, neither will your Father forgive your trespasses.

Matthew 6:19, KJV: Lay not up for yourselves treasures upon earth, where moth and rust doth corrupt, and where thieves break through and steal: [20] But lay up for yourselves treasures in heaven, where neither moth nor rust doth corrupt, and where thieves do not break through nor steal: [21] For where your treasure is, there will your heart be also.

[25] Therefore I say unto you, Take no thought for your life, what ye shall eat, or what ye shall drink; nor yet for your body, what ye shall put on. Is not the life more than meat, and the body than raiment? [30] Wherefore, if God so clothe the grass of the field, which today is, and tomorrow is cast into the oven, shall he not much more clothe you, O ye of little faith?

[33] But seek ye first the kingdom of God, and his righteousness; and all these things shall be added unto you.

Matthew 7:7-14, KJV: Ask, and it shall be given you; seek, and ye shall find; knock, and it shall be opened unto you: [8] For every one that asketh receiveth; and he that seeketh findeth; and to him that knocketh it shall be opened. [9] Or what man is there of you, whom if his son ask bread, will he give him a stone? [10] Or if he ask a fish, will he give him a serpent? [11] If ye then, being evil, know how to give good gifts unto your children, how much more shall your Father which is in heaven give good things to them that ask him? The Golden Rule: [12] Therefore all things whatsoever ye would that men should do to you, do ye even so to them: for this is the law and the prophets.

[13] Enter ye in at the strait gate: for wide is the gate, and broad is the way, that leadeth to destruction, and many there be which go in thereat: 14. Because strait is the gate, and narrow is the way, which leadeth unto life, and few there be that find it.

John 3:16 is said to be "The Gospel in a Nutshell." The following gives the whole context for it. Jesus recalls from the book of Exodus when Moses lifted up the serpent in the wilderness and those who looked at the serpent were healed. Jesus said that when we look to Jesus, we will be healed of sin. John 3 is where the term, "Born again" originates.

John Chapter 3, KJV: [1] There was a man of the Pharisees, named Nicodemus, a ruler of the Jews: [2] The same came to Jesus by night, and said unto him, Rabbi, we know that thou art a teacher come from God: for no man can do these miracles that thou doest, except God be with him.

[3] Jesus answered and said unto him, Verily, verily, I say unto thee, except a man be born again, he cannot see the kingdom of God. [7] Marvel not that I said unto thee, Ye must be born again. [8] The wind bloweth where it listeth, and thou hearest the sound thereof, but canst not tell whence it cometh, and whither it goeth: so is every one that is born of the Spirit.

[14] And as Moses lifted up the serpent in the wilderness, even so must the Son of man be lifted up: 15. That whosoever believeth in him should not perish, but have eternal life. 16 For God so loved the world, that he gave his only begotten Son, that whosoever believeth in him should not perish, but have everlasting life.

[17] For God sent not his Son into the world to condemn the world; but that the world through him might be saved. [18] He that believeth on him is not condemned: but he that believeth not is condemned already, because he hath not believed in the name of the only begotten Son of God.

John Chapter 10, KJV: [7] Then said Jesus unto them again, Verily, verily, I say unto you, I am the door of the sheep. [8] All that ever came before me are thieves and robbers: but the sheep did not hear them. 9 I am the door: by me if any man enter in, he shall be saved, and shall go in and out, and find pasture. *(The Champions' key verse is 10:)* [10] The thief cometh not, but for to steal, and to kill, and to destroy: I am come that they might have life, and that they might have it more abundantly. [11] I am the good shepherd: the good shepherd gives his life for the sheep.

[14] I am the good shepherd, and know my sheep, and am known of mine. [17] Therefore doth my Father love me, because I lay down my life, that I might take it again. [18] No man taketh it from me, but I lay it down of myself. I have power to lay it down, and I have power to take it again. This commandment have I received of my Father.

(The Security of the Believer)[27] My sheep hear my voice, *(If we are His sheep, we will hear his voice and follow Him.)* and I know them, and they follow me: [28] And I give unto them eternal life; and they shall never perish, neither shall any man pluck them out of my hand. [29] My Father, which gave them me, is greater than all; and no man is able to pluck them out of my Father's hand. [30] I and my Father are one.

THE PARABLES:

Jesus taught in parables, stories about earthly things to help people understand about Heavenly things. And that is what Jesus did; in his parables he would compare an aspect of everyday life with a truth about the kingdom of God. The word pictures painted by Jesus in his parables are just as clear today as they were two thousand years ago. There are a total of 33 different parables recorded in Matthew, Mark, and Luke.

Some of my favorite parables especially for working with children are:

The Wise and the Foolish Builders: We know the song, "The Wise Man Built His House upon the Rock." Jesus is the strong foundation for a life.

Matthew 7:24-27, KJV: [24] Therefore whosoever hears these sayings of mine, and doeth them, I will liken him unto a wise man, which built his house upon a rock: [25] And the rain descended, and the floods came, and the winds blew, and beat upon that house; and it fell not: for it was founded upon a rock.[26] And every one that hears these sayings of mine, and doeth them not, shall be likened unto a foolish man, which built his house upon the sand: [27] And the rain descended, and the floods came, and the winds blew, and beat upon that house; and it fell: and great was the fall of it.

<u>With children, I love doing three parables about three lost items</u>. They are the parable of the lost sheep, the lost coin, and the lost son. In all three, we see rejoicing when each is found, just like the rejoicing of Jesus and the angels in Heaven when one lost soul is found and is saved for heaven! Children love to think about angels rejoicing over them in heaven when they are saved!

<u>The Parable of The Lost Sheep: Matthew 18:12-14:</u> [12] "What do you think? If a man owns a hundred sheep, and one of them wanders away, will he not leave the ninety-nine on the hills and go to look for the one that wandered off? [13] And if he finds it, truly I tell you, he is happier about that one sheep than about the ninety-nine that did not wander off. [14] In the same way your Father in heaven is not willing that any of these little ones should perish.

The story of a shepherd seeking one little lost lamb in a storm is very touching for children. <u>All of us who need the Lord are as little lost lambs!</u>

<u>Luke 15:11-32: The Parable of the Lost Son</u> (The Prodigal Son)

[11] Jesus continued: "There was a man who had two sons. [12] The younger one said to his father, 'Father, give me my share of the estate.' So he divided his property between them.

[13] "Not long after that, the younger son got together all he had, set off for a distant country and there squandered his wealth in wild living. [14] After he had spent everything, there was a severe famine in that whole country, and he began to be in need. [15] So he went and hired himself out to a citizen of that country, who sent him to his fields to feed pigs. [16] He longed to fill his stomach with the pods that the pigs were eating, but no one gave him anything.

[17] "When he came to his senses, he said, 'How many of my father's hired servants have food to spare, and here I am starving to death! [18] I will set out and go back to my father and say to him: Father, I have sinned against heaven and against you. [19] I am no longer worthy to be called your son; make me like one of your hired servants.' [20] So he got up and went to his father.

"But while he was still a long way off, his father saw him and was filled with compassion for him; he ran to his son, threw his arms around him and kissed him. [21]" The son said to him, 'Father, I have sinned against heaven and against you. I am no longer worthy to be called your son.'

[22] "But the father said to his servants, 'Quick! Bring the best robe and put it on him. Put a ring on his finger and sandals on his feet. [23] Bring the fattened calf and kill it. Let's have a feast and celebrate. [24] For this son of mine was dead and is alive again; he was lost and is found.' So they began to celebrate. (*The older son was angry because a celebration was planned for the brother because he, himself, had been faithful all of his life, but when the prodigal son who had squandered all his goods returned, they rejoiced and had a party.*)

His Father said, "My son, you are always with me, and everything I have is yours. [32] But we had to celebrate and be glad, because this brother of yours was dead and is alive again; he was lost and is found." *Just as there was rejoicing over the return of the prodigal son, there is rejoicing in heaven as the Heavenly Father receives the worst of sinners home!*

Parable of the Lost Coin: Luke 15:8. Or what woman, having ten silver coins, if she loses one coin, does not light a lamp, sweep the house, and search carefully until she finds it? 9 And when she has found it, she calls her friends and neighbors together, saying, 'Rejoice with me, for I have found the piece which I lost!' 10 Likewise, I say to you, there is joy in the presence of the angels of God over one sinner who repents. (*In this parable, the coin that is found represents us. We are that one sinner who repents and that causes heaven to rejoice. Our granddaughter, Halle Grace (age 5 ½) told us she just recently asked Jesus into her heart. I told her of the joy in Heaven among Jesus and the angels. I also remarked that Halle's heart was good soil for the Word like in the following parable of The Sower in Luke 8:5-8.)*

[5]"A sower went out to sow his seed. And as he sowed, some fell along the path and was trampled underfoot, and the birds of the air devoured it. [6]And some fell on the rock, and as it grew up, it withered away, because it had no moisture. [7]And some fell among thorns, and the thorns grew up with it and choked it. [8]And some fell into good soil and grew and yielded a hundredfold. "As he said these things, he called out, "He who has ears to hear, let him hear."

Sometimes Jesus would explain the parables to his disciples after he had told them to the crowds as in the Parable of the Sower: Luke 8:9-15.

[9]And when his disciples asked him what this parable meant, [10]he said, "To you it has been given to know the secrets of the kingdom of God, but for others they are in parables, so that 'seeing they may not see, and hearing they may not understand.' [11]Now the parable is this: The seed is the word of God. [12]The ones along the path are those who have heard; then the devil comes and takes away the word from their hearts, so that they may not believe and be saved. [13]And the ones on the rock are those who, when they hear the word, receive it with joy. But these have no root; they believe for a while, and in time of testing fall away.[14]And as for what fell among the thorns, they are those who hear, but as they go on their way they are choked by the cares and riches and pleasures of life, and their fruit does not mature. [15]As for that in the good soil, they are those who, hearing the word, hold it fast in an honest and good heart, and bear fruit with patience.

(*We must prepare our hearts and those of our children to be good soil that will listen, hear, and bear fruit. Today, so many outside influences choke out the word like the seed that fell among thorns and make it impossible for us to concentrate on things of the Lord.*

In The Parable of The Pharisee and the Publican, Jesus teaches us to pray in an humble way:

Luke 18:9-14: *He also told this parable to those who trusted in themselves that they were righteous, and treated others with contempt:* 10 "Two men went up into the temple to pray, one a Pharisee and the other a tax collector. 11 The Pharisee, standing by himself, prayed thus: 'God, I thank you that I am not like other men, extortioners, unjust, adulterers, or even like this tax collector.12 I fast twice a week; I give tithes of all that I get.' 13 But the tax collector, standing far off, would not even lift up his eyes to heaven, but beat his breast, saying, 'God, be merciful to me, a sinner!' 14 I tell you, this man went down to his house justified, rather than the other. For everyone who exalts himself will be humbled, but the one who humbles himself will be exalted."

The Good Samaritan: Luke 10:30-37, KJV

(Jesus teaches us who our neighbor is. Anyone who needs our help is our neighbor. Also, this parable teaches us that those of other cultures are our neighbors.)

[30] And Jesus answering said, A certain man went down from Jerusalem to Jericho, and fell among thieves, which stripped him of his raiment, and wounded him, and departed, leaving him half dead. [31] And by chance there came down a certain priest that way: and when he saw him, he passed by on the other side. [32] And likewise a Levite, when he was at the place, came and looked on him, and passed by on the other side.

[33] But a certain Samaritan, as he journeyed, came where he was: and when he saw him, he had compassion on him, [34] and went to him, and bound up his wounds, pouring in oil and wine, and set him on his own beast, and brought him to an inn, and took care of him. And on the morrow when he departed, he took out two pence, and gave them to the host, and said unto him, Take care of him; and whatsoever thou spendest more, when I come again, I will repay thee.

[36] Which now of these three, thinkest thou, was neighbour unto him that fell among the thieves? [37] And he said, He that shewed mercy on him. Then said Jesus unto him, Go, and do thou likewise." *(Some say "A picture is worth a thousand words." But it seems that Jesus painted that picture with words! "Go, and do thou likewise.")*

JESUS MINISTERED TO THE NEEDS OF PEOPLE: Jesus' ministry also included ministering to the many needs of people. He healed the sick wherever he went:

Luke 4:18-19

[18] "The Spirit of the LORD *is* upon Me, because He has anointed Me

To preach the gospel to *the* poor; He has sent Me to heal the brokenhearted,

To proclaim liberty to *the* captives and recovery of sight to *the* blind,

To set at liberty those who are oppressed; [19] To proclaim the acceptable year of the LORD.

THE UNITY OF THE SCRIPTURES: Prophecy Fulfilled:

Look at Isaiah 61:1-2 and see a prophecy or foreshadowing of the coming Messiah. It is the same scripture as found in Luke 4. Jesus is the promised Messiah!

Luke 4:40 When the sun was setting, all those who had any that were sick with various diseases brought them to Him; and He laid His hands on every one of them and healed them. Luke 5:15 Yet the news about him spread all the more, so that crowds of people came to hear him and to be healed of their sicknesses.

Luke 5:17 One day as he was teaching, Pharisees and teachers of the law, who had come from every village of Galilee and from Judea and Jerusalem, were sitting there. And the power of the Lord was present for him to heal the sick. Luke 6:19: And the whole multitude sought to touch Him, for power went out from Him and healed them all

Mark 10:46; Jesus and his disciples went to Jericho. And as they were leaving, they were followed by a large crowd. A blind beggar by the name of Bartimaeus son of Timaeus was sitting beside the road. [47] When he heard that it was Jesus from Nazareth, he shouted, "Jesus, Son of David, have pity on me!" [48] Many people told the man to stop, but he shouted even louder, "Son of David, have pity on me!" [49] Jesus stopped and said, "Call him over!"

They called out to the blind man and said, "Don't be afraid! Come on! He is calling for you." [50] The man threw off his coat as he jumped up and ran to Jesus. [51] Jesus asked, "What do you want me to do for you?" The blind man answered, "Master, I want to see!" [52] Jesus told him, "You may go. Your eyes are healed because of your faith." Right away the man could see, and he went down the road with Jesus.

Matthew 4:23 And Jesus went about all Galilee, teaching in their synagogues, preaching the gospel of the kingdom, and healing all kinds of sickness and all kinds of disease among the people. Matthew 4:24 Then His fame went throughout all Syria; and they brought to Him all sick people who were afflicted with various diseases and torments, and those who were demon-possessed, epileptics, and paralytics; and He healed them.

Matthew 9:27 When Jesus departed from there, two blind men followed Him, crying out and saying, "Son of David, have mercy on us!" Matthew 9:35 Then Jesus went about all the cities and villages, teaching in their synagogues, preaching the gospel of the kingdom, and healing every sickness and every disease among the people. Matthew 10:1 And when He had called His twelve disciples to Him, He gave them power over unclean spirits, to cast them out, and to heal all kinds of sickness and all kinds of disease.

John 10:38 But if I do it, even though you do not believe me, believe the miracles, that you *may* know and understand that the Father is in me, and I in the Father." John 14:11 Believe me when I say that I am in the Father and the Father is in me; or at least believe on the evidence of the works I do.

Mark 11:24 "Therefore I say to you whatever things you ask when you pray, believe that you receive them, and you will have them." Mark 16:17-18 "And these signs shall follow them that believe; In my name. . .they shall lay hands on the sick, and they shall recover."

Matthew 9:18-26: Jesus also raised the dead. Because of the faith of a ruler, He brought his daughter back to life. [26] And the fame hereof went abroad into all that land.

Jesus' Love showed through in all He did: Jesus said, "Let the little children come unto me and forbid them not, for of such is the kingdom of heaven."

JESUS PERFOMED MIRACLES

Many of Jesus' miracles involved the healing of people. During his earthly ministry, <u>Jesus Christ</u> touched and transformed countless lives. The four <u>Gospels</u> record 37 miracles of Jesus. Some of his miracles, other than those of healing were:

Driving out an evil spirit in Mark 1:1-21-27; Miraculous Catch of Fish in Luke 5:1-11; casting out demons and putting them in a herd of pigs in Mark 5:1-20; Turning water into wine in John 2:1-11; Raising Jairus' Daughter to Life in Matthew 9:18, 23-26; The feeding of 4,000 in ark 8:1-13; the feeding of 5,000; raising the Widow's son in Nan in Luke 7:11-17; Jesus withers the fig tree in Matthew 21:18-20; Cleanses ten lepers: Luke 17:11-19

The closing verse of John's Gospel says, "Jesus did many other things as well. If every one of them were written down, I suppose that even the whole world would not have room for the books that would be written.

Jesus Walks on Water: Matthew 14:22-33: Immediately Jesus made the disciples get into the boat and go on ahead of him to the other side, while he dismissed the crowd. [23] After he had dismissed them, he went up on a mountainside by himself to pray. Later that night, he was there alone, [24] and the boat was already a considerable distance from land, buffeted by the waves because the wind was against it.

[25] Shortly before dawn Jesus went out to them, walking on the lake. [26] When the disciples saw him walking on the lake, they were terrified. "It's a ghost," they said, and cried out in fear.

[27] But Jesus immediately said to them: "Take courage! It is I. Don't be afraid."

[28] "Lord, if it's you," Peter replied, "tell me to come to you on the water." [29] "Come," he said.

Then Peter got down out of the boat, walked on the water and came toward Jesus. [30] But when he saw the wind, he was afraid and, beginning to sink, cried out, "Lord, save me!" [31] Immediately Jesus reached out his hand and caught him. "You of little faith," he said, "why did you doubt?" [32] And when they climbed into the boat, the wind died down. [33] Then those who were in the boat worshiped him, saying, "Truly you are the Son of God."

<u>*Yet the Jewish leaders, Scribes, Pharisees, and Sadducees hated Jesus and constantly tried to get rid of Him.*</u> *Throughout Jesus' ministry, they tried to find wrong he had done. They criticized Him when he healed; they questioned all His teachings; they criticized Jesus for dining with sinners; they tried to turn the people against Jesus. The Sanhedrin was the Jewish High Court, and as the Passover time approached, members had met to conspire against Jesus and to plan to arrest and try Him. At Passover, tens of thousands of Jews came to Jerusalem to the Temple to bring blood sacrifices and to offer them for their sins. It was during this time that Jesus instituted the Lord's Supper, and that Jesus was arrested, tried, and crucified.*

The Passover and the Lord's Supper

We must remember that Jesus was God. But He was also man, and he suffered like we do. What a heavy burden he carried! Most are familiar with the Passover Supper and the Lord's Supper. It was at the time of the observance of the Passover (when the death angel passed over the homes that had the blood on the door in the days of Moses) that Jesus died. The Passover is still observed by Jews today. Those who are Messianic Jews, those who accepted Jesus as the Messiah, find the Passover to, indeed, be a blessed occasion. They see the whole story – the blood, the scarlet thread leading to Jesus, who died and shed his blood for the remission of our sins!

The Scarlet Thread: At the Passover supper, Jesus instituted the Lord's Supper:

Luke 22:19: And Jesus took the bread and gave thanks and broke it and gave it unto them, saying, "This is my body which is given for you: this do in remembrance of me. 20. Likewise also the cup after supper saying, "This cup is the new testament in my blood, which is shed for you." (*Then Jesus said his betrayer was near and they left the supper and Jesus gave his last words to them, which are in John 14, 15, 16, and 17. These were favorites, for which I made a unit when I taught the young married class. These were the last teachings of Jesus before he was arrested and crucified. The richness of these chapters was so amazing that I memorized much of them!*)

THE TRINITY: John 14, KJV (*Jesus teaches us about all three members of THE TRINITY: The Father, the Son, and the Holy Spirit. Verse 6 shows that Jesus is the only way to Heaven!*)

1 Let not your heart be troubled: ye believe in God, believe also in me. 2 In my Father's house are many mansions: if it were not so, I would have told you. I go to prepare a place for you. 3 And if I go and prepare a place for you, I will come again, and receive you unto myself; that where I am, there ye may be also. 4 And whither I go ye know, and the way ye know. 5 Thomas saith unto him, Lord, we know not whither thou goest; and how can we know the way? 6 Jesus saith unto him, I am the way, the truth, and the life: no man cometh unto the Father, but by me.

7 If ye had known me, ye should have known my Father also: and from henceforth ye know him, and have seen him. 13 And whatsoever ye shall ask in my name, that will I do, that the Father may be glorified in the Son. 14 If ye shall ask any thing in my name, I will do it. 15 If ye love me, keep my commandments.

PROPHECY: *The disciples asked Jesus what the signs of his coming and the end of the world would be and* Jesus answered: "Watch out that no one deceives you. [5] For many will come in my name, claiming, 'I am the Messiah,' and will deceive many. [6] You will hear of wars and rumors of wars, but see to it that you are not alarmed. Such things must happen, but the end is still to come. [7] Nation will rise against nation, and kingdom against kingdom.

There will be famines and earthquakes in various places. [8] All these are the beginning of birth pains.

[9] "Then you will be handed over to be persecuted and put to death, and you will be hated by all nations because of me. [10] At that time many will turn away from the faith and will betray and hate each other, [11] and many false prophets will appear and deceive many people. [12] Because of the increase of wickedness, the love of most will grow cold, [13] but the one who stands firm to the end will be saved. [14] And this gospel of the kingdom will be preached in the whole world as a testimony to all nations, and then the end will come. Matthew 24:4-14

THE JUDGMENT: Matthew 25:31-46: "When the Son of Man comes in his glory, and all the angels with him, he will sit on his glorious throne. [32] All the nations will be gathered before him, and he will separate the people one from another as a shepherd separates the sheep from the goats. [33] He will put the sheep on his right and the goats on his left.

[34] "Then the King will say to those on his right, 'Come, you who are blessed by my Father; take your inheritance, the kingdom prepared for you since the creation of the world. [35] For I was hungry and you gave me something to eat, I was thirsty and you gave me something to drink, I was a stranger and you invited me in, [36] I needed clothes and you clothed me, I was sick and you looked after me, I was in prison and you came to visit me.'

[37] "Then the righteous will answer him, 'Lord, when did we see you hungry and feed you, or thirsty and give you something to drink? [38] When did we see you a stranger and invite you in, or needing clothes and clothe you? [39] When did we see you sick or in prison and go to visit you?' [40] "The King will reply, 'Truly I tell you, whatever you did for one of the least of these brothers and sisters of mine, you did for me.'

[41] "Then he will say to those on his left, 'Depart from me, you who are cursed, into the eternal fire prepared for the devil and his angels. [42] For I was hungry and you gave me nothing to eat, I was thirsty and you gave me nothing to drink, [43] I was a stranger and you did not invite me in, I needed clothes and you did not clothe me, I was sick and in prison and you did not look after me.' [44] "They also will answer, 'Lord, when did we see you hungry or thirsty or a stranger or needing clothes or sick or in prison, and did not help you?'

[45] "He will reply, 'Truly I tell you, whatever you did not do for one of the least of these, you did not do for me.' [46] "Then they will go away to eternal punishment, but the righteous to eternal life."

PROMISE OF THE HOLY SPIRIT: John 14:16, KJV: And I will pray the Father, and he shall give you another Comforter, that he may abide with you forever; 17 Even the Spirit of truth; whom the world cannot receive, because it seeth him not, neither knoweth him: but ye know him; for he dwelleth with you, and shall be in you. 18 I will not leave you comfortless: I will come to you.

26 But the Comforter, which is the Holy Ghost, whom the Father will send in my name, he shall teach you all things, and bring all things to your remembrance, whatsoever I

have said unto you. 27 Peace I leave with you, my peace I give unto you: not as the world giveth, give I unto you. Let not your heart be troubled, neither let it be afraid. (*Wow! What a promise!*)

THE HOLY SPIRIT: *According to* The Baptist Faith and Message *(2000), The Holy Spirit, as the third in the God-Head Trinity, has many roles. His main role is to exalt Christ. He inspired the writing of the scriptures, and He helps us understand the Truth. He convicts men of sin and calls them to the Savior. He seals the believer until the day of final redemption.*

John Chapter 15, KJV: 1 I am the true <u>vine</u>, and my Father is the <u>husbandman</u>. 4 Abide in me, and I in you. As the <u>branch</u> cannot bear <u>fruit</u> of itself, except it abide in the <u>vine</u>; no more can ye, except ye abide in me. 5 I am the <u>vine</u>, ye are the branches: He that abideth in me, and I in him, the same bringeth forth much <u>fruit</u>: for without me ye can do nothing. <u>7 If ye abide in me, and my words abide in you, ye shall ask what ye will, and it shall be done unto you.</u> (*This is the promise that was my New Year's Resolution for 2 years in a row.*)

10 If ye keep my commandments, ye shall abide in my love; even as I have kept my Father's commandments, and abide in his love. 12 This is my commandment, that ye love one another, as I have loved you. 13 Greater love hath no man than this that a man lay down his life for his friends. 17 These things I command you, that ye love one another.

John Chapter 16, KJV: 7. Nevertheless I tell you the truth; it is expedient for you that I go away: for if I go not away, the Comforter will not come unto you; but if I depart, I will send him unto you. 8 And when he is come, he will reprove the world of sin, and of righteousness, and of judgment: 13 Howbeit when he, the Spirit of truth, is come, he will guide you into all truth: for he shall not speak of himself; but whatsoever he shall hear, that shall he speak: and he will shew you things to come.

23 Verily, verily, I say unto you, whatsoever ye shall ask the Father in my name, he will give it you. 26 At that day ye shall ask in my name: and I say not unto you, that I will pray the Father for you: 27 For the Father himself loveth you, because ye have loved me, and have believed that I came out from God.

32 Behold, the hour cometh, yea, is now come, that ye shall be scattered, every man to his own, and shall leave me alone: and yet I am not alone, because the Father is with me. 33 These things I have spoken unto you, that in me ye might have peace. In the world ye shall have tribulation: but be of good cheer; I have overcome the world.

John Chapter 17, KJV: (*Jesus' Prayer in the Garden of Gethsemane just before He is arrested. Here we see the humanity of Christ as well as his Deity. Christ's dual nature is what makes the Gospels so interesting. Christ's ability to suffer, to feel human pain, is crucial to the Gospels.*)

1 These words spoke <u>Jesus</u>, and lifted up his eyes to heaven, and said, Father, the hour is come; glorify thy Son, that thy Son also may glorify thee: 2 As thou hast given him power over all flesh, that he should give eternal life to as many as thou hast given him.

3 And this is life eternal, that they might know thee the only true God, and Jesus Christ, whom thou hast sent.

4 I have glorified thee on the earth: I have finished the work which thou gave me to do. 8 For I have given unto them the words which thou gave me; and they have received them, and have known surely that I came out from thee, and they have believed that thou didst send me.

(Jesus prayed for us who have believed on him!)

9 I pray for them: I pray not for the world, but for them which thou hast given me; for they are thine. 13 And now come I to thee; and these things I speak in the world, that they might have my joy fulfilled in themselves. 14 I have given them thy word; and the world hath hated them, because they are not of the world, even as I am not of the world.

15 I pray not that thou should not take them out of the world, but that thou should keep them from the evil. 16 They are not of the world, even as I am not of the world. 17 Sanctify them through thy truth: thy word is truth. 18 As thou hast sent me into the world, even so have I also sent them into the world. 19 And for their sakes I sanctify myself, that they also might be sanctified through the truth.

20 Neither pray I for these alone, but for them also which shall believe on me through their word;. . . .23 I in them, and thou in me, that they may be made perfect in one; and that the world may know that thou hast sent me, and hast loved them, as thou hast loved me. 26 And I have declared unto them thy name, and will declare it: that the love wherewith thou hast loved me may be in them, and I in them.

(Dear Jesus, I pray that each of us will have the love with which Jesus loved us. If we did, how different our lives, our families, and our nation would be! Thank you for sharing this prayer in your Word!)

THE DEATH, BURIAL, AND RESURRECTION OF JESUS: You can read of the arrest, trial, death, burial, and resurrection of Jesus in the last few chapters of each of the four Gospels.

(I will tell the story of the crucifixion and the resurrection from the books of Matthew, Mark, Luke, and John. Also, having just read The Trial of Jesus by Arthur Michelson, a Jewish Rabbi who converted from Judaism and Law to Christ and Grace, I want to tell some of the history from his point of view.)

First, Dr. Michelson recalled the prophecies of the Old Testament about the Messiah that show without a doubt that Jesus is that Messiah. He used the work of the Trinity in his argument that Jesus, the Messiah, died for our sins. He also told this amazing statistic from Josephus, the Jewish historian. At one Passover, no less than 256,500 lambs were killed in Jerusalem. This disgusting sight and smell must have reminded them of how God hates sin! Then what is so amazing is all the facts Jews knew about the Jewish Laws, the court system, the Sanhedrin, the Pentateuch, and the Talmud! Michelson showed how the trial of Jesus from beginning to end was illegal, and that is the reason there is no record of it outside of the Gospels. In violation of Jewish law Jesus was murdered by an unprincipled, unscrupulous, and jealous hierarchy. But Jesus had to die in order to make the everlasting atonement according to Leviticus 17:11.

Yes, many tricks were tried during the night on Thursday night. Also, Jesus was beaten and bruised (like in the movie, *The Passion of Christ and in the Isaiah prophecy.*). Isaiah 53 says in verses 3-7 "He would be wounded for our transgressions, he would be brought as a lamb to the slaughter, yet he would not open his mouth." *All of this came true when Jesus was tried, beaten, and crucified*

Read of the betrayal of Jesus by Judas on Matthew 27. Also, the questioning of Jesus by Pilate is in chapter 27. Of course no fault could be found in Jesus because Jesus is the only person who never sinned! But the large crowd demanded Jesus be crucified! The shameful way Jesus was treated is also in Matthew 27, Mark 15, and John 19. We are reminded many times of the fulfilled prophecy from the Old Testament.

JESUS IS CRUCIFIED: [22] They brought Jesus to the place called Golgotha (which means "the place of the skull"). [23] Then they offered him wine mixed with myrrh, but he did not take it. [24] And they crucified him. Dividing up his clothes, they cast lots to see what each would get his robe. [25] It was nine in the morning when they crucified him. [26] The written notice of the charge against him read: The King of the Jews.

[27] They crucified two rebels with him, one on his right and one on his left. [29] Those who passed by hurled insults at him, shaking their heads and saying, "So! You who are going to destroy the temple and build it in three days, [30] come down from the cross and save yourself!" [31] In the same way the chief priests and the teachers of the law mocked him among themselves. "He saved others," they said, "but he can't save himself! [32] Let this Messiah, this king of Israel, come down now from the cross, that we may see and believe." Those crucified with him also heaped insults on him. But through it all, Jesus prayed while suffering on the cross, "Father, forgive them for they know not what they do." Luke 23:34

THE DEATH OF JESUS" [33] At noon, darkness came over the whole land until three in the afternoon. [34] And at three in the afternoon Jesus cried out in a loud voice, *"Eloi, Eloi, lema sabachthani?"* (which means "My God, my God, why have you forsaken me?)

[37] With a loud cry, Jesus breathed his last.

[38] The curtain of the temple was torn in two from top to bottom. [39] And when the centurion, who stood there in front of Jesus, saw how he died, he said, "Surely this man was the Son of God!"

Matthew 27:22 "What shall I do, then, with Jesus who is called the Messiah?" Pilate asked.

They all answered, "Crucify him! [23] "Why? What crime has he committed?" asked Pilate. But they shouted all the louder, "Crucify him!" [24] When Pilate saw that he was getting nowhere, but that instead an uproar was starting, he took water and washed his hands in front of the crowd. "I am innocent of this man's blood," he said. "It is your responsibility!"

(Jesus was sentenced to death on the cross, the most horrible death designed for only the worse of criminals. He was forced to try to carry his own cross.)

Mark 15:16: The soldiers led Jesus away into the palace (that is, the Praetorian) and called together the whole company of soldiers. [17] They put a purple robe on him, then twisted together a crown of thorns and set it on him. [18] And they began to call out to him, "Hail, king of the Jews!" [19] Again and again they struck him on the head with a staff and spit on him. Falling on their knees, they paid homage to him. [20] And when they had mocked him, they took off the purple robe and put his own clothes on him. Then they led him out to crucify him.

Matthew 27:33 They came to a place called Golgotha (which means "the place of the skull"). 35. After they had nailed Him to the cross, the soldiers gambled for his clothes by throwing dice.[38] Two rebels were crucified with him, one on his right and one on his left. [39] Those who passed by hurled insults at him, shaking their heads [40] and saying, "You who are going to destroy the temple and build it in three days, save yourself! Come down from the cross, if you are the Son of God!" [41] In the same way the chief priests, the teachers of the law and the elders mocked him. [42] "He saved others," they said, "but he can't save himself! He's the king of Israel! Let him come down now from the cross, and we will believe in him. [43] He trusts in God. Let God rescue him now if he wants him, for he said, 'I am the Son of God.'"[44] In the same way the rebels who were crucified with him also heaped insults on him.

But while on the cross, Jesus forgave the rebel on the cross who came to believe on him and he forgave all those who were crucifying Him. To the rebel, he replied, "I say to you, today you will be with me in Paradise." Luke 23:43

In Luke 23:34, Jesus said, "Father, forgive them for they do not know what they do."

[45] From noon until three in the afternoon darkness came over all the land. [46] About three in the afternoon Jesus cried out in a loud voice, "Eli, Eli lema sabachthani?" (Which means, "My God, my God, why have you forsaken me?") [50] And when Jesus had cried out again in a loud voice, he gave up his spirit. [51] At that moment the curtain of the temple was torn in two from top to bottom. The earth shook, the rocks split [52] and the tombs broke open. The bodies of many holy people who had died were raised to life. [53] They came out of the tombs after Jesus' resurrection and went into the holy city and appeared to many people.

[54] When the centurion and those with him who were guarding Jesus saw the earthquake and all that had happened, they were terrified, and exclaimed, "Surely he was the Son of God!"

The Scarlet Thread: Jesus' blood was shed for us on the cross. Jesus was foreordained to crucifixion by God from the foundation of the world. Now we can have atonement for our sins. In the Old Testament, the sacrifice of an animal atoned for the person's sin. Jesus' life was offered as a substitute for our death and atoned for our sins. The just died for the unjust.

Death on the cross is a hideous thing! But why do we now wear beautiful crosses? Because the meaning of a cross was transformed! This is the greatest story ever told. This is the culmination of everything taught in the Old Testament. The Devil was sure he was victorious, but that wasn't the end. Jesus was resurrected from the Grave!

THE RESURRECTION: *According to Henry M. Morris, Ph.D. (1984) the bodily resurrection of Jesus Christ from the dead is the crowning proof of Christianity. If the resurrection did not take place then Christianity is a false religion. If it did take place, then Christ is God and the Christian faith is absolute truth.*

The story of the resurrection is the heart of the New Testament. Jesus provided reliable living witness to His Resurrection and inspired his disciples to spread the Word, which he had given to them. All four Gospels describe these events with great dramatic effect! The unique bodily resurrection of Jesus Christ is clear proof that He is God, as well as man, because only God could conquer death. The great Creator became the Son of Man that He might die for man's sin but He also remained God, and death could not hold Him!

THE ASCENSION OF JESUS: *Though Jesus had told his disciples what would happen, it was hard for them to believe he had risen. After Jesus arose from the grave, he appeared many times on earth before he ascended and went back to Heaven. Before he departed, he gave* the Great Commission *in Matthew 28:18-20 to go and teach all nations to observe all Jesus has commanded us to do. Then Jesus came to them and said,* "All authority in heaven and on earth has been given to me. [19] Therefore go and make disciples of all nations, baptizing them in the name of the Father and of the Son and of the Holy Spirit, [20] and teaching them to obey everything I have commanded you. And surely I am with you always, to the very end of the age."

In *John 14:23-29,* Jesus imparted the power of the Holy Spirit to his disciples by breathing on them. *The Bible comes full circle, back to the point in Genesis when God breathed life into Adam. But now Jesus is granting* eternal *life. My sister, Marilyn Kay Gage, sums up the story of the death and resurrection of Jesus in her poetry.*

Darkness fell across the land,
When the Lord of the Universe died.
Religious leaders formed a jeering band,
As cheerleaders for the Devil's side.

The curtain was split;
That included the Holiest Place.
I need no priest to transmit
My prayers and plead before God my case.

When I am lifted upon the cross,
I will draw all men with lives so hollow —
A spiritual magnet for the lost
To take up their cross and follow.

"For whom am I to pray?" I ask myself every day.
"For family, friends, pastor and Kay."
Christ as the one crucified, To the Father He cried,
"Forgive them." In agony He died.

With the bruises of Jesus the Lord was satisfied.
Through his wounds I am justified.
For my sins Christ was crucified.
I can live forever in a body glorified!

His side was pierced
By a Roman soldier hard and fierce.
I cannot claim innocence, I am guilty.
My sins nailed Christ to that tree.

There are always two mountains, to every one valley,
Because of Calvary's fountain, we can from our depressions rally.
Because Christ died at Calvary, I won't have to pay fare or fee.
Angels will come and carry me, to that heavenly place I'll ever be.

Joseph of Arimathaea boldly went, asking Pilate for his consent.
The body of Jesus he did crave, to place in a newly hewn grave.
The two Mary's and Salome brought spices for embalming they had bought;
They worried how they would move the stone, but when they arrived, the stone was gone.

The Tomb was empty; all could see.
The grave cannot be the final prison for Christ nor me.
The Lord is risen indeed! He conquered death and the grave,
Providing for my every need, eternal life He gave.

Christ arose from the grave in bodily form,
Not as a ghost, dim.
His followers' hearts felt strangely warm,
As he talked to them.

If I could have believed without having seen,
More blessed I would have been.
My name could be "Thomas" for I always doubt;
It's my most convenient sin I keep about.
The spirit is upon me to go forth and tell,
"Jesus died at Calvary, but lives again. All is well!

Truths about Jesus Christ

1. Jesus forgives sins. Mark 2:10 *The Son of Man has authority on earth to forgive sins.*

2. Jesus performed miracles. John 10:32: I have shown you many great miracles from the Father.

3. Jesus came from the Father. John 16:28: I came from the Father and entered the world, now I am leaving the world and going back to the Father.

4. Jesus was God also became fully man. Philippians 2;4-11: In your attitude with one another, have the same mindset as Christ Jesus: [6] Who, being in very nature God, did not consider equality with God something to be used to his own advantage; [7] rather, he made himself nothing by taking the very nature of a servant, being made in human likeness. [8] And being found in appearance as a man, he humbled by becoming obedient to death—even death on a cross!

5. Jesus is the Messiah. John 4:25-26: The Samaritan woman said, "I know that Messiah (called Christ) is coming. When he comes he will explain everything to us." Then Jesus declared, "I who speak to you am He."

6. Jesus came to give spiritual life. John 10:10: I have come that they may have life, and have it more abundantly.

7. Jesus gives us the right to become God's children. John 1:12: To all who received him, to those who believed in his name, he gave the right to become the children of God.

8. Jesus bestows eternal life. John 10:38: I give them eternal life.

9. Jesus keeps us in eternal life. John 10:28: They shall never perish because no one can snatch them out of my hand.

10. Jesus death was a ransom for our sins. Matthew 29:28: The Son of man gave His life as a ransom for sins.

11. Jesus died for us while we were still sinners. Romans 5:8: But God demonstrated His own love for us in that while we were still sinners, Christ died for us.

12. Jesus rose from the dead. Acts 2:24: But God raised him from the dead.

Jesus is either God, or He is not good. Anselm
(*I did not write the above. I got it from a long pamphlet, which doesn't tell who published or wrote it. The Title was* Fifteen Truths about Jesus.)

If Jesus Had Never Been Born

According to D. James Kennedy and Jerry Newcomb, (1994), *What if Jesus Had Never Been Born*, "Jesus Christ has changed virtually every aspect of human life. The Christian Church has made more changes than any other movement in history." (p. 3)
Contributions of Christianity include:

- High regard for human life.
- The elevation of women.
- Benevolence and charity; the Good Samaritan ethic.
- The abolition of slavery, both in antiquity and in modern times.
- The civilizing of many barbarian and primitive cultures.
- Literacy and education of the masses.
- Higher standards of justice; Civil Liberties
- Capitalism, Free Enterprise. Representative Government,
- Most universities were started by Christians for Christian purposes.
- The codifying and setting to writing of many of the world's languages.
- Inspiration for the greatest works of art, music, and literature.
- Countless lives transformed from liabilities into assets to society because of the Gospel.
- eternal salvation of countless souls! (The primary goal of Christianity)

"When Christ took upon himself the form of man, He imbued mankind with a dignity and inherent value that had never been dreamed of before. Christ's influence on the world is immeasurable." (p. 4) All the little things Jesus did transformed the history of mankind.

THE BOOK OF ACTS
In Acts, Jesus Is fire from Heaven.

Theme: The Formation and Spread of the Church. The Gospel (the good news of Jesus Christ) is also for the Gentiles. The Life and Work of Paul.

Key Verses in Acts. Salvation is found in no one else, for there is no other name under heaven given to men by whom we must be saved. Acts 4:13

What must I do to be saved? They replied, "Believe in the Lord Jesus Christ, and you will be saved – you and your household. Acts 16:30-31

The Message of Acts

The Book of Acts tells of the Acts of the Holy Spirit and the Acts of the Apostles, primarily of the Apostle Peter and Paul. In Acts 1, Luke, the author, retells Jesus giving the great commission before he arose and went to heaven. Here, Jesus gave instruction to his followers to wait until they were empowered with the Holy Spirit before going to all of their own city, country, and the whole world to spread the Gospel.

Jesus' life and death have created the Church, and we see the spread of the church to parts of the entire known world.

On the day of Pentecost, Jesus came in the form of fire when the Holy Spirit descended upon the apostles in Chapter 2 of Acts. The Holy Spirit gave great power and 3000 souls were saved, baptized, and added to the church that same day. The same Gospel story is told over and over in Acts – by Peter, Stephen, and Paul. In Acts, we see the Gospel given to the Gentiles, and the Gentiles are accepted into the Church of Jesus Christ, along with the Jews. Paul was called to go to the Gentiles, as well as to the Jews, and Paul went on three long missionary journeys preaching and starting churches. His work has affected the whole Western World even to today.

Paul constantly fought persecution, being beaten and put in jail several times. The larger bulk of the Epistles (letters) written to churches were written by Paul. Acts is the bridge between the Gospel of Jesus Christ and the Epistles.

When we say we attend a New Testament Church, we are implying that our church was patterned after that Church in Acts and that its founder is Jesus Christ.

I want to whet your appetite so you will long to read all the wonderful, exciting stories of history in the Book of Acts. Luke had already written the book of Luke telling the life of Jesus and now will write a second "treatise." This first part of the first chapter tells us so much!

Jesus was on earth 40 days after his resurrection, showing himself to many people. Infallible proofs exist to this fact. Jesus said that the Holy Spirit would come soon. Jesus said that no one knows when Jesus will come again to Earth. But their part was to be witnesses of Jesus from Jerusalem, to Judaea, to Samaria, and to all the earth. Then Jesus was taken up into Heaven. An angel promised that Jesus will come again to Earth.

Acts Chapter 1:1: In my former book, Theophilus, I wrote about all that Jesus began to do and to teach[2] until the day he was taken up to heaven, after giving instructions through the Holy Spirit to the apostles he had chosen. [3]After his suffering, he presented himself to them and gave many convincing proofs that he was alive. He appeared to them over a period of forty days and spoke about the kingdom of God. [4]On one occasion, while he was eating with them, he gave them this command: "Do not leave Jerusalem, but wait for the gift my Father promised, which you have heard me speak about. [5]For John baptized with water, but in a few days you will be baptized with the Holy Spirit."

[6]Then they gathered around him and asked him, "Lord, are you at this time going to restore he kingdom to Israel?"

Jesus gave the Great Commission, but he said for them to wait until they received power from the Holy Spirit before going to their own city, all of their own country, and to all of the world.

[7]He said to them: "It is not for you to know the times or dates the Father has set by his own authority. [8]But you will receive power when the Holy Spirit comes on you; and you will be my witnesses in Jerusalem, and in all Judea and Samaria, and to the ends of the earth."

[9]After he said this, he was taken up before their very eyes, and a cloud hid him from their sight.

[10]They were looking intently up into the sky as he was going, when suddenly two men dressed in white stood beside them. "Men of Galilee," they said, "why do you stand here looking into the sky? This same Jesus, who has been taken from you into heaven, will come back in the same way you have seen him go into heaven."

One hundred twenty of Jesus' followers continued to pray in an upper room, waiting, as commanded by their Lord. The Holy Spirit came in Chapter 2 of Acts, KJV:

And when the day of Pentecost was fully come, they were all with one accord in one place.

2 And suddenly there came a sound from heaven as of a rushing mighty wind, and it filled all the house where they were sitting. 3 And there appeared unto them cloven tongues like as of fire, and it sat upon each of them. 4 And they were all filled with the Holy Ghost, and began to speak with other tongues, as the Spirit gave them utterance.

5 And there were dwelling at Jerusalem Jews, devout men, out of every nation under heaven. 6 Now when this was noised abroad, the multitude came together, and were confounded, because that every man heard them speak in his own language.

Verses 7 through 12 tell of tongues from all the known world being spoken so that everyone could hear the gospel in his own language. Some said they must be drunk with wine. But Peter, speaking in the language of the Hebrews, explained what was happening.

Peter, the one who had been very weak and who had denied Jesus in the past, was filled with great power! He declared that these are not drunk, but this is a fulfillment of the prophecy from the prophet, Joel:

The Unity of the Bible.: 16 But this is that which was spoken by the prophet Joel; 17 And it shall come to pass in the last days, saith God, I will pour out of my Spirit upon all flesh. 19 And I will shew wonders in heaven above. 20 The sun shall be turned into darkness, and the moon into blood, before the great and notable day of the Lord come:

Then empowered by the Holy Spirit, the usually weak Peter preached to them Jesus. He told that they had crucified him and that he was raised from the dead. He reminded them that David had prophesied this.

Acts 2:22, KJV: Ye men of Israel, hear these words; Jesus of Nazareth, a man approved of God among you by miracles and wonders and signs, which God did by him in the midst of you, as ye yourselves also know: 23 Him, being delivered by the determinate counsel and foreknowledge of God, ye have taken, and by wicked hands have crucified and slain: 24 Whom God hath raised up, having loosed the pains of death.

(In the next verses, Peter tells about David seeing Jesus raised and exalted at the right hand of God.) 32 This Jesus hath God raised up, whereof we all are witnesses. 33 Therefore being by the right hand of God exalted, and having received of the Father the promise of the Holy Ghost, he hath shed forth this, which ye now see and hear. . . .

36 Therefore let all the house of Israel know assuredly, that God hath made the same Jesus, whom ye have crucified, both Lord and Christ. 37 Now when they heard this, they were pricked in their heart, and said unto Peter and to the rest of the apostles, Men and brethren, what shall we do?

38 Then Peter said unto them, Repent, and be baptized every one of you in the name Of Jesus Christ for the remission of sins, and ye shall receive the gift of the Holy Ghost. 41 Then they that gladly received his word were baptized: and the same day there were.added unto them about three thousand souls.

The Church in Jerusalem:42 And they continued steadfastly in the apostles' doctrine and fellowship, and in breaking of bread, and in prayers. 46 And they, continuing daily with one accord in the temple, and breaking bread from house to house, did eat their meat with gladness and singleness of heart,47 Praising God, and having favor with all the people. And the Lord added to the church daily such as should be saved.

The church was persecuted from the beginning. The apostles were constantly threatened with being put in jail. When Peter and John healed the lame man at the temple (chapter 3) Peter said they didn't heal him and pointed them to Jesus, the one they denied and crucified. In verses 22 to 26, he reminded them of the prophecies of Moses and Samuel, and told them that they are the seed of Abraham, to whom the promise of God's son, Jesus, was given.

How very powerful Chapter 4 is! When Peter preached the resurrected Jesus, after healing the man at the temple gate, 5000 were saved. Peter and John were put into jail.

Acts 4:7, KJV: They had Peter and John brought before them and began to question them: "By what power or what name did you do this?"

Peter Speaks. [8] Then Peter, filled with the Holy Spirit, said to them: "Rulers and elders of the people! It is by the name of Jesus Christ of Nazareth, whom you crucified but whom God raised from the dead, that this man stands before you healed. [11] Jesus is 'the stone you builders rejected, which has become the cornerstone.' [12] Salvation is found in no one else, for there is no other name under heaven given to mankind by which we must be saved."

[13] When they saw the courage of Peter and John and realized that they were unschooled, ordinary men, they were astonished and they took note that these men had been with Jesus. [18] Then they called them in again and commanded them not to speak or teach at all in the name of Jesus. [19] But Peter and John replied, "Which is right in God's eyes: to listen to you, or to him? You be the judges! [20] As for us, we cannot help speaking about what we have seen and heard."

In Chapter 5, The Apostles healed many; the apostles were persecuted and jailed; they continued preaching Jesus.

[12] The apostles performed many signs and wonders among the people. 14. More and more men and women believed in the Lord and were added to their number. [17] Then the high priest and all his associates, who were members of the party of the Sadducees, were filled with jealousy. [18] They arrested the apostles and put them in the public jail. [19] But during the night an angel of the Lord opened the doors of the jail and brought them out.

[27] The apostles were brought in and made to appear before the Sanhedrin to be questioned by the high priest. [28] "We gave you strict orders not to teach in this name," he said. "Yet you have filled Jerusalem with your teaching and are determined to make us guilty of this man's blood."

[29] Peter and the other apostles replied: "We must obey God rather than human beings! [30] The God of our ancestors raised Jesus from the dead—whom you killed by hanging him on a cross. [31] God exalted him to his own right hand as Prince and Savior that he might bring Israel to repentance and forgive their sins. [32] We are witnesses of these things, and so is the Holy Spirit, whom God has given to those who obey him."

[33] When they heard this, they were furious and wanted to put them to death. [34] But a Pharisee named Gamaliel, a teacher of the law. . . .addressed the Sanhedrin: Leave these men alone! Let them go! For if their purpose or activity is of human origin, it will fail. [39] But if it is from God, you will not be able to stop these men; you will only find yourselves fighting against God."

[40] His speech persuaded them. They called the apostles in and had them flogged. Then they ordered them not to speak in the name of Jesus, and let them go. [41] The apostles left the Sanhedrin, rejoicing because they had been counted worthy of suffering disgrace for the Name. [42] Day after day, in the temple courts and from house to house, they never stopped teaching and proclaiming the good news that Jesus is the Messiah.

(What a lesson for us today. If our church were truly a New Testament Church. . .Will we be ready to proclaim Jesus amid persecution? Do we proclaim Jesus now, though no threat of persecution?)

In chapter 6, seven deacons were chosen by the church. One of these was Stephen, When Stephen preached of Jesus, he was accused of blasphemous words against Moses and against God. Stephen was brought before the council and his sermon tells the whole story of the Old Testament through the time of Jesus. Stephen's face was as the face of an angel as he said in Acts Chapter 7, KJV: To this he replied: "Brothers and fathers, listen to me! The God of glory appeared to our father Abraham. . . . .[3] 'Leave your country and your people,' God said, 'and go to the land I will show you. God sent him to this land where you are now living. . . .But God promised him that he and his descendants after him would possess the land.

Then Stephen told of how God told Abraham that his descendants would be enslaved in another land but that they would be brought back to this land to worship him. He recounted the story of Isaac, of Jacob, father of the 12 patriarchs who became the names of the 12 tribes of Israel. He even told the whole story of Joseph, who was sold as a slave into Egypt, of the Israelites being brought to Egypt, and of Moses being called by God to be the deliverer who would bring them back to the Promised Land.

Please read chapter 7. It tells the history of the Israelites, of the Bible, and of prophecies of Jesus Christ. Stephen recounted the times when Israel had turned from God and when they had turned to Him. He told of David and of Solomon. He told of how the forefathers had persecuted the prophets: Stephen continued:

51 "You stiff-necked people! Your hearts and ears are still uncircumcised. You are just like your ancestors: You always resist the Holy Spirit! 52 Was there ever a prophet your ancestors did not persecute? They even killed those who predicted the coming of the Righteous One. And now you have betrayed and murdered him—53 you who have received the law that was given through angels but have not obeyed it."

The Stoning of Stephen: 54 When the members of the Sanhedrin heard this, they were furious and gnashed their teeth at him. 55 But Stephen, full of the Holy Spirit, looked up to heaven and saw the glory of God, and Jesus standing at the right hand of God. 56 "Look," he said, "I see heaven open and the Son of Man standing at the right hand of God."

57 At this they covered their ears and, yelling at the top of their voices, they all rushed at him, 58 dragged him out of the city and began to stone him. Meanwhile, the witnesses laid their coats at the feet of a young man named Saul.

59 While they were stoning him, Stephen prayed, "Lord Jesus, receive my spirit." 60 Then he fell on his knees and cried out, "Lord, do not hold this sin against them." When he had said this, he fell asleep. *(This is the same thing Jesus said when he was crucified. "Father, forgive them for they know not what they do.")*

[54] When the members of the Sanhedrin heard this, they were furious and gnashed their teeth at him.[55] But Stephen, full of the Holy Spirit, looked up to heaven and saw the glory of God, and Jesus standing at the right hand of God. [56] "Look," he said, "I see heaven open and the Son of Man standing at the right hand of God." (*Stephen saw Jesus, who welcomed him to Heaven!*}

[57] At this they covered their ears and, yelling at the top of their voices, they all rushed at him, [58] dragged him out of the city and began to stone him. Meanwhile, the witnesses laid their coats at the feet of a young man named Saul.

[59] While they were stoning him, Stephen prayed, "Lord Jesus, receive my spirit." [60] Then he fell on his knees and cried out, "Lord, do not hold this sin against them." When he had said this, he fell asleep.

(*Stephen was the first Christian Martyr! Stephen's sermon tells the whole story of prophecies of Jesus and of his death. It also leads us to the main earthly character of Acts – Saul of Tarsus, or Paul. Chapter 8 and 9 tell us that Saul persecuted Christians.*

Acts 8:1-3, KJV: And Saul consented unto Stephen's death. On that day a great persecution broke out against the church in Jerusalem, and all except the apostles were scattered throughout Judea and Samaria. [2] Godly men buried Stephen and mourned deeply for him. [3] But Saul began to destroy the church. Going from house to house, he dragged off both men and women and put them in prison.

The Dispersion of the Church: The church in Jerusalem had become a formidable movement. Now in the providence of God, this persecution started the missionary work of the church. The people had listened to the apostles long enough to have learned the whole story of Jesus, His death, and resurrection. Verse 4 says: [4] Those who had been scattered preached the word wherever they went. (*Persecution caused the Word to spread. Will we have to be persecuted so we will spread the Word?*)

Also in Chapter 8 is the account of the Deacon, Phillip. The Spirit told Philip in Acts 8:29, to go to a chariot in which an eunuch of great authority from Ethiopia was reading from the Old Testament in the book of Isaiah.

Unity of the scriptures: *Phillip explained Isaiah 53:7 and told him that the person* "who was led as a sheep to the slaughter and like a lamb dumb before his shearer, yet he opened not his mouth" *was a prophecy of Jesus. Then he preached to him Jesus, who was the Lamb of God.*

The Conversion of Saul: Before his conversion, Saul was a person who captured believers in Jesus and took them to jail. After his conversion, he began to preach the Gospel wherever he went. God had a plan for Saul's life to carry Jesus' name to people who didn't know Him.

(*Acts chapter 9 tells of the conversion of Saul on the road to Damascus. As Saul traveled to get letters giving permission to slaughter Jesus' disciples, a light blinded him, and he had an encounter with Jesus Christ, the one he was persecuting!*)

[3] As he neared Damascus on his journey, suddenly a light from heaven flashed around him. [4] He fell to the ground and heard a voice say to him, "Saul, Saul, why do you persecute me?" [5] "Who are you, Lord?" Saul asked. "I am Jesus, whom you are persecuting," he replied. [6] "Now get up and go into the city, and you will be told what you must do."

(Now Saul will become Paul, the one who would go on Missionary journeys and who would be persecuted for his faith in Jesus Christ. He would write most of the Epistles of the New Testament! How Jesus does change lives! Throughout the rest of the book of Acts, Paul will retell the same story of Jesus of Nazareth, who was crucified and is resurrected and who will come again. But Paul usually begins by telling of his personal experience with Jesus and of his conversion. This is exactly what we should do!)

The first 12 chapters of Acts report events between the time of Jesus' last meeting with his disciples and the beginning of Paul's work as a Christian missionary. The remaining sixteen chapters describe Paul's activities, beginning with his mission to the church at Antioch and ending with his residence in Rome as a prisoner of the Roman government. Acts tell us of four missionary journeys made by Paul.

Paul's First Missionary Journey: Acts 13:1, KJV: Now there were in the church that was at Antioch certain prophets and teachers. . . .2 As they ministered to the Lord, and fasted, the Holy Ghost said, Separate me Barnabas and Saul for the work whereunto I have called them. 3 And when they had fasted and prayed, and laid *their* hands on them, they sent *them* away. 4 So they, being sent forth by the Holy Ghost. . .they preached the word of God in the synagogues of the Jews.

Paul always reminded the Jews of their wonderful history as God's chosen people. Then he showed that Jesus is of the seed of Abraham, and of David. Then he preached to them the promised Savior of Israel.

5 And after the reading of the law and the prophets the rulers of the synagogue sent unto them, saying, *Ye* men *and* brethren, if ye have any word of exhortation for the people, say on. 16 Then Paul stood up, and beckoning with *his* hand said, Men of Israel, and ye that fear God, give audience. 17 The God of this people of Israel chose our fathers, and exalted the people when they dwelt as strangers in the land of Egypt, and with an high arm brought he them out of it. 18 And about the time of forty years suffered he their manners in the wilderness. 19 And when he had destroyed seven nations in the land of Canaan, he divided their land to them by lot. 20 And after that he gave *unto them* judges about the space of four hundred and fifty years, until Samuel the prophet.

21 And afterward they desired a king: and God gave unto them Saul. . . .by the space of forty years. 22 And when he had removed him, he raised up unto them David to be their king; to whom also he gave testimony, and said, I have found David the *son* of Jesse, a man after mine own heart, which shall fulfill all my will. 23 Of this man's seed hath God according to *his* promise raised unto Israel a Savior, Jesus:

24 When John had first preached before his coming the baptism of repentance to all the people of Israel. 25 And as John fulfilled his course, he said, whom think ye that I am? I am not *he*. But, behold, there cometh one after me, whose shoes of *his* feet I am not worthy to loose. 26 Men *and* brethren, children of the stock of Abraham, and whosoever among you feareth God, to you is the word of this salvation sent. 27 For they that dwell at Jerusalem, and their rulers, because they knew him not, nor yet the voices of the prophets which are read every sabbath day, they have fulfilled *them* in condemning *him*. 28 And though they found no cause of death *in him,* yet desired they Pilate that he should be slain.

29 And when they had fulfilled all that was written of him, they took *him* down from the tree, and laid *him* in a sepulcher. 30 But God raised him from the dead: 31 And he was seen many days of them which came up with him from Galilee to Jerusalem, who are his witnesses unto the people. 32 And we declare unto you glad tidings, how that the promise which was made unto the fathers, 33 God hath fulfilled the same unto us their children, in that he hath raised up Jesus again; as it is also written in the second psalm, Thou art my Son, this day have I begotten thee. 35 Wherefore he saith also in another *psalm,* Thou shalt not suffer thine Holy One to see corruption. 36 For David, after he had served his own generation by the will of God, fell on sleep, and was laid unto his fathers, and saw corruption: 37 But he, whom God raised again, saw no corruption.

13:38 KJV: Be it known unto you therefore, men *and* brethren, that through this man is preached unto you the forgiveness of sins: 39 And by him all that believe are justified from all things, from which ye could not be justified by the Law of Moses.

42 And when the Jews were gone out of the synagogue, the Gentiles besought that these words might be preached to them the next Sabbath. 43 Now when the congregation was broken up, many of the Jews and religious proselytes followed Paul and Barnabas: who, speaking to them, persuaded them to continue in the grace of God.

Upon opposition from the Jews, Paul turned to the Gentiles, making the Jews envious.

13:44: And the next Sabbath day came almost the whole city together to hear the word of God. 45 But when the Jews saw the multitudes, they were filled with envy, and spake against those things which were spoken by Paul, contradicting and blaspheming. 46 Then Paul and Barnabas waxed bold, and said, It was necessary that the word of God should first have been spoken to you: but seeing ye put it from you, and judge yourselves unworthy of everlasting life, lo, we turn to the Gentiles. 47 For so hath the Lord commanded us, *saying,* I have set thee to be a light of the Gentiles, that thou shouldest be for salvation unto the ends of the earth. 48 And when the Gentiles heard this, they were glad, and glorified the word of the Lord: and as many as were ordained to eternal life believed. 49 And the word of the Lord was published throughout all the region.

<u>*Rejoicing While Persecuted:*</u> 13:50 But the Jews stirred up the devout and honorable women, and the chief men of the city, and raised persecution against Paul and Barnabas, and expelled them out of their coasts. 51 But they shook off the dust of their feet against

them, and came unto Iconium. 52 And the disciples were filled with joy, and with the Holy Ghost. (*Remember the Beatitudes in the Sermon on the Mount. "Blessed are those who are persecuted for Righteousness sake for theirs is the Kingdom of Heaven. Rejoice and be exceedingly glad for great is your reward in heaven."*)

Acts 14:1 KJV: And it came to pass in Iconium that they went both together into the synagogue of the Jews, and so spake, that a great multitude both of the Jews and also of the Greeks believed. 2 But the unbelieving Jews stirred up the Gentiles, and made their minds evil affected against the brethren. 3 Long time therefore abode they speaking boldly in the Lord, which gave testimony unto the word of his grace, and granted signs and wonders to be done by their hands. 4 But the multitude of the city was divided: and part held with the Jews, and part with the apostles. 5 And when there was an assault made both of the Gentiles, and also of the Jews with their rulers, to use *them* despitefully, and to stone them, 6 They were aware of *it,* and fled unto Lystra and Derbe, cities of Lycaonia, and unto the region that lieth round about: 7 And there they preached the Gospel.

Also in chapter 14, when Paul healed a man at Lystra, people wanted to worship Paul and Barnabas as though they were gods! Then when Paul said they were men just like they were and gave to Jesus the glory, they stoned Paul and put him out of the city, supposing he was dead. Then in verse 20:

Acts 14:20, KJV: Howbeit, as the disciples stood round about him, he rose up, and came into the city: and the next day he departed with Barnabas to Derbe. . . .Confirming the souls of the disciples, *and* exhorting them to continue in the faith, and that we must through much tribulation enter into the kingdom of God. 23And when they had ordained them elders in every church, and had prayed with fasting, they commended them to the Lord, on whom they believed. . . .

26 And thence sailed to Antioch, from whence they had been recommended to the grace of God for the work which they fulfilled. 27 And when they were come, and had gathered the church together, they rehearsed all that God had done with them, and how he had opened the door of faith unto the Gentiles. 28 And there they abode long time with the disciples. *Antioch is the first place where believers in Christ were called Christians.*

Acts 15:1: KJV: And certain men which. . .taught the brethren and said, Except ye be circumcised after the manner of Moses, ye cannot be saved..*Here begins the battle between Law and Grace, or between Works and Grace. When we look at the Epistles written to the Galatians and Ephesians, we see that truly Paul did address this battle. When Paul wrote to the Galatians in chapter 3:24-25, he said, [24] So the law was our guardian until Christ came that we might be justified by faith. [25] Now that this faith has come, we are no longer under a guardian. [26] So in Christ Jesus you are all children of God through faith, [27] for all of you who were baptized into Christ have clothed yourselves with Christ. [28] There is neither Jew nor Gentile, neither slave nor free, nor is there male and female, for you are all one in*

Christ Jesus. [29] *If you belong to Christ, then you are Abraham's seed, and heirs according to the promise.*

Paul's Second Missionary Journey: Acts 15:36-18:23: KJV

Acts 15:36 And some days after Paul said unto Barnabas, Let us go again and visit our brethren in every city where we have preached the word of the Lord, *and see* how they do. 37 And Barnabas determined to take with them John, whose surname was Mark. 38 But Paul thought not good to take him with them, who departed from them from Pamphylia, and went not with them to the work. . . .Barnabas took Mark, and sailed unto Cyprus; 40 And Paul chose Silas, and departed, being recommended by the brethren unto the grace of God. 41 And he went through Syria and Cilicia, confirming the churches.

4 And as they went through the cities, they delivered them the decrees for to keep, that were ordained of the apostles and elders which were at Jerusalem. 5 And so were the churches established in the faith, and increased in number daily.

(My Uncle Floyd Hubbard taught a lesson at our Hubbard Reunion called "What If?" What if Paul had not been called to Macedonia (to Western Europe and to the Gentiles?) Our Nation of America would be totally different! (Be sure to look at a map of the known world around the Mediterranean Sea and see where all three of Paul's Missionary Journeys took him.)

9 And a vision appeared to Paul in the night; there stood a man of Macedonia, and prayed, saying, Come over into Macedonia, and help us. 10 And after he had seen the vision, immediately we endeavored to go into Macedonia, assuredly gathering that the Lord had called us for to preach the gospel unto them.

Acts 16:16:KJV: And it came to pass, as we went to prayer, a certain damsel possessed with a spirit of divination met us, which brought her masters much gain by soothsaying: 17 The same followed Paul and us, and cried, saying, These men are the servants of the most high God, which show unto us the way of salvation. 18 And this did she many days. But Paul, being grieved, turned and said to the spirit, I command thee in the name of Jesus Christ to come out of her. And he came out the same hour.

Paul and Silas are again put into jail: 16:19 And when her masters saw that the hope of their gains was gone, they caught Paul and Silas, and drew *them* into the marketplace unto the rulers, 20 And brought them to the magistrates, saying, These men, being Jews, do exceedingly trouble our city, 21 And teach customs, which are not lawful for us to receive, neither to observe, being Romans. 22 And the multitude rose up together against them: and the magistrates rent off their clothes, and commanded to beat *them*. 23 And when they had laid many stripes upon them, they cast *them* into prison, charging the jailer to keep them safely: 24 Who, having received such a charge, thrust them into the inner prison, and made their feet fast in the stocks.

An Angel miraculously releases Paul and Silas from Prison

16:25 And at midnight Paul and Silas prayed, and sang praises unto God: and the prisoners heard them. 26 And suddenly there was a great earthquake, so that the foundations of the prison were shaken: and immediately all the doors were opened, and every one's bands were loosed. 27 And the keeper of the prison awaking out of his sleep, and seeing the prison doors open, he drew out his sword, and would have killed himself, supposing that the prisoners had been fled. 28 But Paul cried with a loud voice, saying, Do thyself no harm: for we are all here. 29 Then he called for a light, and sprang in, and came trembling, and fell down before Paul and Silas,

30 And brought them out, and said, Sirs, what must I do to be saved? 31 And they said, Believe on the Lord Jesus Christ, and thou shalt be saved, and thy house. 32 And they spake unto him the word of the Lord, and to all that were in his house. 33 And he took them the same hour of the night, and washed *their* stripes; and was baptized, he and all his, straightway. 34 And when he had brought them into his house, he set meat before them, and rejoiced, believing in God with all his house. 40 And they went out of the prison, and entered into *the house of* Lydia: and when they had seen the brethren, they comforted them, and departed.

Acts 17:1: KJV: Now when they had passed through Amphipolis and Apollonia, they came to Thessalonica, where was a synagogue of the Jews: 2 And Paul, as his manner was, went in unto them, and three Sabbath days reasoned with them out of the scriptures, 3 Opening and alleging, that Christ must needs have suffered, and risen again from the dead; and that this Jesus, whom I preach unto you, is Christ. 4 And some of them believed, and consorted with Paul and Silas; and of the devout Greeks a great multitude, and of the chief women not a few.

The Gospel met opposition:. 17:5 But the Jews which believed not set all the city on an uproar, and assaulted the house of Jason, and sought to bring them out to the people.

17:11 These were more noble than those in Thessalonica, in that they received the word with all readiness of mind, and searched the scriptures daily, whether those things were so. 12 Therefore many of them believed; also of honorable women which were Greeks, and of men, not a few. 13 But when the Jews of Thessalonica had knowledge that the word of God was preached of Paul at Berea, they came thither also, and stirred up the people.

Paul went to Athens, Greece: 17:16 While Paul was waiting for them in Athens, he was greatly distressed to see that the city was full of idols. [17] So he reasoned in the synagogue with both Jews and God-fearing Greeks, as well as in the marketplace day by day with those who happened to be there. [18] A group of Epicurean and Stoic philosophers began to debate with him. Some of them asked, "What is this babbler trying to say?" Others remarked, "He seems to be advocating foreign gods." They said this because Paul was preaching the good news about Jesus and the resurrection. [19] Then they took him and brought him to a meeting of the Areopagus, where they said to him, "May we know what this new teaching is that you are presenting? [20] You are bringing some strange ideas to our ears, and we would like to know what they mean." [21] (All the Athenians and the foreigners who lived there spent their time doing nothing but talking about and listening to the latest ideas.)

[22] Paul then stood up in the meeting of the Areopagus and said: "People of Athens! I see that in every way you are very religious. [23] For as I walked around and looked carefully at your objects of worship, I even found an altar with this inscription: to an unknown god. So you are ignorant of the very thing you worship—and this is what I am going to proclaim to you.

[24] "The God who made the world and everything in it is the Lord of heaven and earth and does not live in temples built by human hands. [25] And he is not served by human hands, as if he needed anything. Rather, he himself gives everyone life and breath and everything else. [26] From one man he made all the nations, that they should inhabit the whole earth; and he marked out their appointed times in history and the boundaries of their lands. [27] God did this so that they would seek him and perhaps reach out for him and find and have him, though he is not far from any one of us. [28] 'For Him we live and move our being.' As some of your own poets have said, 'We are his offspring.'[1]

[29] "Therefore since we are God's offspring, we should not think that the divine being is like gold or silver or stone—an image made by human design and skill. [30] In the past God overlooked such ignorance, but now he commands all people everywhere to repent. [31] For he has set a day when he will judge the world with justice by the man he has appointed. He has given proof of this to everyone by raising him from the dead."

[32] When they heard about the resurrection of the dead, some of them sneered, but others said, "We want to hear you again on this subject." [33] At that, Paul left the Council. [34] Some of the people became followers of Paul and believed.

Please note the following sermon. It was preached in Athens, home of the great philosophers of the golden age of Greece. It was also a pluralistic society where many Gods were worshipped.

Corinth, in Greece, was one of the great cities of the Roman Empire. Paul stayed there a year and a half and established a great church there. Silas and Timothy came from Macedonia and joined them in Corinth. Paul continued to try to convince the Jews there that Jesus was the promised Messiah.

18:4, KJV: And he reasoned in the synagogue every Sabbath, and persuaded the Jews and the Greeks. 5 And when Silas and Timotheus were come from Macedonia, Paul was pressed in the spirit, and testified to the Jews *that* Jesus *was* Christ. 6 And when they opposed themselves, and blasphemed, he shook *his* raiment, and said unto them, Your blood *be* upon your own heads; I *am* clean: from henceforth I will go unto the Gentiles. 7 And he departed thence. *(Paul said he must go to Jerusalem to keep the feast. Then he began his third Missionary Journey.)*

<u>Paul's Third Missionary Journey</u> began in Acts 18:23, KJV: He departed, and went over *all* the country of Galatia and Phrygia in order, strengthening all the disciples.

Paul did the most miraculous work in his entire wonderful career in Ephesus. Large numbers of worshippers of Diana became Christians! Ephesus rapidly became the leading center of the Christian world. Churches were established in a 100 mile radius of Ephesus. Paul shook the mighty city to its foundations. Magicians who pretended to work miracles were so awed by Christianity that they made bonfire and burned their books of magic

*Also, Paul was able to convince Jews that Jesus was the Messiah, with the help of Apollos, a Jew. Acts 18:*28: KJV: For he mightily convinced the Jews, *and that* publicly, showing by the scriptures that Jesus was the Christ.

Acts 19:17b: KJV: and the name of the Lord Jesus was magnified. 18 And many that believed came, and confessed, and showed their deeds. 19 Many of them also which used curious arts brought their books together, and burned them before all *men:* and they counted the price of them, and found *it* fifty thousand *pieces* of silver. 20 So mightily grew the word of God and prevailed.

19:21 After these things were ended, Paul purposed in the spirit, when he had passed through Macedonia and Achaia, to go to Jerusalem, saying, After I have been there, I must also see Rome. 22 So he sent into Macedonia two of them that ministered unto him, Timotheus and Erastus; but he himself stayed in Asia for a season. 23 And the same time there arose no small stir about that way.

24 For a certain *man* named Demetrius, a silversmith, which made silver shrines for Diana, brought no small gain unto the craftsmen; 25 Whom he called together with the workmen of like occupation, and said, Sirs, ye know that by this craft we have our wealth. 26 Moreover ye see and hear, that not alone at Ephesus, but almost throughout all Asia, this Paul hath persuaded and turned away much people, saying that they be no gods, which are made with hands: 27 So that not only this our craft is in danger to be set at nought; but also that the temple of the great goddess Diana should be despised, and her magnificence should be destroyed, whom all Asia and the world worships.

28 And when they heard *these sayings,* they were full of wrath, and cried out, saying, "Great *is* Diana of the Ephesians." 29 And the whole city was filled with confusion: and having caught Gaius and Aristarchus, men of Macedonia, Paul's companions in travel, they rushed with one accord into the theatre. 30 And when Paul would have entered in unto the people, the disciples suffered him not.

Acts 20:1 And after the uproar was ceased, Paul called unto *him* the disciples, and embraced *them,* and departed for to go into Macedonia. 2 And when he had gone over those parts, and had given them much exhortation, he came into Greece. 3 And *there* abode three months. And when the Jews laid wait for him, as he was about to sail into Syria, he purposed to return through Macedonia.

Paul's Farewell Address: Acts 20:16. . .He hasted, if it were possible for him, to be at Jerusalem the day of Pentecost. 17 And from Miletus he sent to Ephesus, and called the elders of the church. 18 And when they were come to him, he said unto them, Ye know, from the first day that I came into Asia, after what manner I have been with you at all seasons, 19 Serving the Lord with all humility of mind, and with many tears, and temptations, which befell me by the lying in wait of the Jews: 21 Testifying both to the Jews, and also to the Greeks, repentance toward God, and faith toward our Lord Jesus Christ. 22 And now, behold, I go bound in the spirit unto Jerusalem, not knowing the things that shall befall me there: 23 Save that the Holy Ghost witnesseth in every city, saying that bonds and afflictions abide me. 24 But none of these things move me, neither count I my life dear unto myself, so that I might finish my course with joy, and the ministry, which I have received of the Lord Jesus, to testify the gospel of the grace of God.

Acts 20:29: Take heed therefore unto yourselves, and to all the flock, over which the Holy Ghost hath made you overseers, to feed the church of God, which he hath purchased with his own blood. 29 For I know this, that after my departing shall grievous wolves enter in among you, not sparing the flock. 32 And now, brethren, I commend you to God, and to the word of his grace, which is able to build you up, and to give you an inheritance among all them which are sanctified. 35 I have shown you all things, how that so laboring ye ought to support the weak, and to remember the words of the Lord Jesus, how he said, It is more blessed to give than to receive.

20:36 And when he had thus spoken, he kneeled down, and prayed with them all. 37 And they all wept sore, and fell on Paul's neck, and kissed him, 38 Sorrowing most of all for the words which he spake, that they should see his face no more. And they accompanied him unto the ship.

And they besought him not to go up to Jerusalem. 13 Then Paul answered, "What mean ye to weep and to break mine heart? for I am ready not to be bound only, but also to die at Jerusalem for the name of the Lord Jesus." 14 And when he would not be persuaded, we ceased, saying, The will of the Lord be done.

Rejoicing in Jerusalem: Acts 21: 17: [17] And when we were come to Jerusalem, the brethren received us gladly. [18] And the day following Paul went in with us unto James; and all the elders were present. [19] And when he had saluted them, he declared particularly what things God had wrought among the Gentiles by his ministry. [20] And when they heard it, they glorified the Lord, and said unto him, Thou seest, brother, how many thousands of Jews there are which believe; and they are all zealous of the law:

But Jews from Asia stirred up the people against Paul: In Acts 22:27-40, KJV: we read that the people went to kill Paul, but he was rescued by the chief captain of the Romans. The multitude cried, "Away with Him." Paul asked if he could speak to the people. When there was great silence, he spoke to them in the Hebrew tongue, saying,

Men, brethren, and fathers, hear ye my defense *which I make* now unto you. [3] I am verily a man *which am* a Jew, born in Tarsus, *a city* in Cilicia, yet brought up in this city at the feet of Gamaliel, *and* taught according to the perfect manner of the law of the fathers, and was zealous toward God, as ye all are this day.

[4] And I persecuted this way unto the death, binding and delivering into prisons both men and women. [5] As also the high priest doth bear me witness, and all the estate of the elders: from whom also I received letters unto the brethren, and went to Damascus, to bring them which were there bound unto Jerusalem, for to be punished.

Paul again gave his personal testimony. He told of his experience on the road to Damascus when he came to believe that Jesus was the promised Messiah in Acts 22:3-21. Paul was told that he is chosen to be a witness of his conversion to others. When he testified of his experiences –

Acts 22:23: And as they cried out, and cast off *their* clothes, and threw dust into the air, [24] The chief captain commanded him to be brought into the castle, and bade that he should be examined by scourging; that he might know wherefore they cried so against him. [25] And as they bound him with thongs, Paul said unto the centurion that stood by, Is it lawful for you to scourge a man that is a Roman, and uncondemned? [26] When the centurion heard *that*, he went and told the chief captain, saying, Take heed what thou doest: for this man is a Roman. [27] Then the chief captain came, and said unto him, tell me, art thou a Roman? He said, yea.

When they learned he was born a Roman Citizen, who had done nothing wrong, they would have nothing to do with sentencing him and turned him over to the Sanhedrin, the same council who had tried Jesus! The same Ananias, the High Priest, commanded that they smite Paul on the mouth.

In Acts 23:6 KJV: *Paul perceived that some of the council were Pharisees and some were Sadducees, Paul said he was a Pharisee and believed in the resurrection from the dead. The two sects fought against each other. Seeing the dissension, the chief captain feared that Paul would be pulled to pieces and they took him and brought him into the castle.*

Acts 23:11: And the night following the Lord stood by him, and said, Be of good cheer, Paul: for as thou hast testified of me in Jerusalem, so must thou bear witness also at Rome.

Now Paul has all assurance that he will go to Rome, although the conspiracy to kill him continued. Verses 12-15 tell us that over 40 men said they would neither eat nor drink until they had slain Paul. They lay in wait for Paul to come out of the Castle. But Paul's sister's son heard of it and he went into the castle and told Paul. The young boy then told the chief captain that the Jews were going to kill Paul tomorrow when he went into the council.

Then the miraculous hand of God was at work: Acts 23:23: And he (the Chief Captain) called unto him two centurions, saying, Make ready two hundred soldiers to go to Caesarea, and horsemen threescore and ten, and spearmen two hundred, at the third hour of the night; [24] And provide them beasts, that they may set Paul on, and bring him safe unto Felix the governor.

[25] And he wrote a letter after this manner: [27] This man was taken of the Jews, and should have been killed of them: then came I with an army, and rescued him, having understood that he was a Roman. [28] And when I would have known the cause wherefore they accused him, I brought him forth into their council: [29] Whom I perceived to be accused of questions of their law, but to have nothing laid to his charge worthy of death or of bonds. (*So like the trial of Jesus*)

[31] Then the soldiers, as it was commanded them, took Paul, and brought him by night to Antipatris. *Ananias the high priest appeared to Felix and made accusations of Paul. In Acts 24:10*, Paul said, "I do the most cheerfully answer for myself."

Acts 24:14:KJV: But this I confess unto thee, that after the way which they call heresy, so worship I the God of my fathers, believing all things which are written in the law and in the prophets: [15] And have hope toward God, which they themselves also allow, that there shall be a resurrection of the dead, both of the just and unjust. [16] And herein do I exercise myself, to have always a conscience void to offence toward God, and toward men. [17] Now after many years I came to bring alms to my nation, and offerings.

Then Paul told of how he was falsely accused and that they had nothing against him. Then after a few days, Felix and his wife called Paul and asked him to explain to him his faith in Christ. Acts 24:25: [5] *And as he reasoned of righteousness, temperance, and judgment to come, Felix trembled, and answered, Go thy way for this time; when I have a convenient season, I will call for thee.* [27] *But after two years Porcius Festus came into Felix' room: and Felix, willing to shew the Jews a pleasure, left Paul bound.*

In Chapter 25, we see that the high priest asked Festus to bring Paul to Jerusalem, as they lay in wait to kill him. But Festus didn't allow this to happen and sat in judgment over Paul, himself. At the end of talking with Festus, Paul would not go back to the Jewish Council, and he said, I Appeal to Caesar.

Paul was then sent to King Agrippa. In his defense, Paul again gave his testimony of his salvation on the road to Damascus to persecute Christians. He told that he was obedient to the heavenly vision:

Acts 26:22-23, KJV: Having therefore obtained help of God, I continue unto this day, witnessing both to small and great, saying none other things than those which the prophets and Moses did say should come: [23] That Christ should suffer, and that he should be the first that should rise from the dead, and should shew light unto the people, and to the Gentiles.

When Paul had witnessed to King Agrippa, Paul asked him if he believed the prophets.

Acts 26:28, KJV: Then Agrippa said unto Paul, Almost you persuade me to be a Christian. (*This is the sad answer many people give to the gospel.*)

29. And Paul said, I would to God, that not only thou, but also all that hear me this day, were both almost, and altogether such as I am, except these bonds. . . .Then they talked

between themselves, saying, this man doeth nothing worthy of death or of bonds. [32] Then said Agrippa unto Festus, This man might have been set at liberty, if he had not appealed unto Caesar.

Paul Sails for Rome and begins his fourth missionary journey

27:1 And when it was determined that we should sail into Italy, they delivered Paul and certain other prisoners unto *one* named Julius, a centurion of Augustus' band.

(The trip to Rome began in the early fall of AD 60. The three winter months were spent in Malta. They arrived in Rome in the early spring of AD 61. The voyage was made in three different ships. We are told that the account of this voyage has given the best historical account of sailing of that period. They met with fierce winds and were driven off course. Read Acts 27 for the exciting account of sailing in tempestuous winds, of ship wreck, and of God's intervention. When all hope of survival was gone, Paul stood forth and said:)

Acts 27:22, KJV: Be of good cheer, for there shall be no loss of any man's life among you, but of the ship. *(Then he told them that God had promised that he would be brought safely to Rome to appeal to Caesar. And all 276 people escaped safely to land.)*

Chapter 28 tells of the 3 months after the ship wreck that they spent at Melita, among barbarous people. Through Miracles of God, they were treated well. Paul told the story of Jesus Christ wherever they went.

Acts 28:16, KJV: And when we came to Rome, the centurion delivered the prisoners to the captain of the guard: but Paul was suffered to dwell by himself with a soldier that kept him. (Paul was in Rome at least 2 years; and though a prisoner, he was allowed to live in his own rented house and to preach the Gospel as he pleased.)

Verse 17: And it came to pass, that after three days Paul called the chief of the Jews together: and when they were come together, he said unto them, Men *and* brethren: *Then he told them the same story of Jesus and of his experiences.*

Verses 30 and 31: And Paul dwelt two whole years in his own hired house, and received all that came in unto him, preaching the kingdom of God, and teaching those things which concern the Lord Jesus Christ, with all confidence, no man forbidding him.

Acts is more exciting than any historical novel because it is all true and is much more intriguing. While in Rome under house arrest, Paul wrote the letters to the Ephesians, Philippians, Colossians, and Philemon. It is generally accepted that Paul was acquitted about AD 62. Paul made a fourth missionary journey to Spain, Greece, and Asia Minor, during which time he wrote the letters to Titus and Timothy. He was arrested again, taken back to Rome, and beheaded in AD 67.

Paul's ministry lasted 30 years. To say he was the greatest missionary who ever lived is an understatement. The impact he had upon history, through the guidance of the Holy Spirit, we will understand more fully in the future! His suffering was unbelievable. I believe it was the Holy Spirit who gave him strength to live to bring thousands to Christ while per-secuted, imprisoned, mobbed, beaten, and stoned and left for dead. The Book of Acts is the book of the acts of the Holy Spirit and the acts of the apostles, especially the Apostle Paul.

The Epistles – (The Living Letters)

THE BOOK OF ROMANS
Jesus is the grace of God.

Theme. Being right with God through Faith in Christ

Message: Romans, written by Paul, focuses on the question of how God will judge each of us on the final day. According to Greene (1962), Romans was the sixth of the *Living Letters* to be written. It is just as meaningful for us today. Will we be judged on the basis of how "good" we are and how well we have kept the law? No, but we can have assurance of right standing with God through our faith in what God's grace has done for us through Christ's sacrificial death.. Many times, Paul said his message was one of redemption, one of "the cross." Paul ends his message to the Romans with practical instructions for living a Christian life of faith.

In Romans 1 through 3:20*: KJV The whole world is equally guilty before God.*

Romans 1:1 Paul, a servant of Christ Jesus, called to be an apostle and set apart for the gospel of God—[2] the gospel he promised beforehand through his prophets in the Holy Scriptures[3] regarding his Son, who as to his earthly life was a descendant of David, [4] and who through the Spirit of holiness was appointed the Son of God in power by his resurrection from the dead: Jesus Christ our Lord. [5] Through him we received grace and apostleship to call all the Gentiles to the obedience that comes from faith for his name's sake. [6] And you also are among those Gentiles who are called to belong to Jesus Christ.

[7] To all in Rome who are loved by God and called to be his holy people: Grace and peace to you from God our Father and from the Lord Jesus Christ. [8] First, I thank my God through Jesus Christ for all of you, because your faith is being reported all over the world. [9] God, whom I serve in my spirit in preaching the gospel of his Son, is my witness how constantly I remember you [10] in my prayers at all times. . . .

[14] I am obligated both to Greeks and non-Greeks, both to the wise and the foolish. [15] That is why I am so eager to preach the gospel also to you who are in Rome. . . .[16] For I am not ashamed of the gospel, because it is the power of God that brings salvation to everyone who believes: first to the Jew, then to the Gentile. [17] For in the gospel the righteousness of God is revealed—a righteousness that is by faith from first to last, just as it is written: "The righteous will live by faith."

God's Wrath Against Sinful Humanity: Romans 1:18: The wrath of God is being revealed from heaven against all the godlessness and wickedness of people, who suppress the truth by their wickedness, [19] since what may be known about God is plain to them, because God has made it plain to them. [20] For since the creation of the world God's invisible qualities—his eternal power and divine nature—have been clearly seen, being understood from what has been made, so that people are without excuse.

[21] For although they knew God, they neither glorified him as God nor gave thanks to him, but their thinking became futile and their foolish hearts were darkened. [22] Although they claimed to be wise, they became fools [23] and exchanged the glory of the immortal God for images made to look like a mortal human being and birds and animals and reptiles. [24] Therefore God gave them over in the sinful desires of their hearts to sexual impurity for the degrading of their bodies with one another. [25] They exchanged the truth about God for a lie, and worshiped and served created things rather than the Creator—who is forever praised. Amen.

[26] Because of this, God gave them over to shameful lusts. Even their women exchanged natural sexual relations for unnatural ones. [27] In the same way the men also abandoned natural relations with women and were inflamed with lust for one another. Men committed shameful acts with other men, and received in themselves the due penalty for their error.

[28] Furthermore, just as they did not think it worthwhile to retain the knowledge of God, so God gave them over to a depraved mind, so that they do what ought not to be done. [29] They have become filled with every kind of wickedness, evil, greed and depravity. They are full of envy, murder, strife, deceit and malice. They are gossips, [30] slanderers, God-haters, insolent, arrogant and boastful; they invent ways of doing evil; they disobey their parents; [31] they have no understanding, no fidelity, no love, no mercy. [32] Although they know God's righteous decree that those who do such things deserve death, they not only continue to do these very things but also approve of those who practice them.

Does this sound familiar? Does this sound like it was written today? It hasn't always been like this in America. According to Ricky McGee (2012) in From Bibles to Bullets to Bankruptcy, *the principles this nation of immigrants was founded and built upon were biblical principles. God blessed America beyond that of all nations in history. People have flocked to America for freedom. But what happened? According to Dr. Ricky McGee, the American Public School System became a religion-free zone. When prayer was taken out of the schools, our nation went from Bibles to bullets to bankruptcy. The fall in America Began in the Classroom. I taught from 1959 through 2005 in our classrooms and watched our fall every step of the way. What must we do? Now we, like Paul must say:*

Romans 1:16: I am not ashamed of the gospel, because it is the power of God for the salvation of everyone who believes: first for the Jew, then for the Gentile.

We must stand for religious freedom. The First Amendment to the Constitution guarantees us freedom of speech and of religion.

The First Amendment to the United States Constitution prohibits the making of any law respecting an establishment of religion, impeding the free exercise of religion, abridging the freedom of speech, infringing on the freedom of the press, interfering with the right to peaceably assemble or prohibiting the petitioning for a governmental redress of grievances. It was adopted on December 15, 1791, as one of the ten amendments that comprise the Bill of Rights. (Wikipedia)

While we can, we *must tell others how to be saved*. *We can use the* Roman Road to Salvation.

The Roman Road: *This is the term for the scriptures from Romans often used to show the way a person can be saved and be made right with God. Halle Grace, our granddaughter who is in kindergarten, is memorizing these now:*

Romans 3:2, KJV; For all have sinned and come short of the glory of God.

Romans 6:23, KJV: For the wages of sin is death; but the gift of God is eternal life, through Jesus Christ our Lord.

Romans 5:8, KJV: But God commended his love toward us, in that, while we were yet sinners, Christ died for us.

Romans 10:9-10, KJV: If thou shalt confess with thy mouth the Lord Jesus and shall believe in thine heart that God hath raised him from the dead, thou shalt be saved. For with the heart man believes unto righteousness, and with the mouth confession is made unto salvation.

Other favorites and a few of the most important scriptures are:

Romans 5, KJV: *summarizes God's love for us when we were sinners. It shows that by the disobedience of one man, Adam, sin entered the world and that by obedience of Jesus all can be made righteous.*

Therefore being justified by faith, we have peace with God through our Lord Jesus Christ: [2] By whom also we have access by faith into this grace wherein we stand, and rejoice in hope of the glory of God.

[6] For when we were yet without strength, in due time Christ died for the ungodly. [8] But God commendeth his love toward us, in that, while we were yet sinners, Christ died for us.

Romans 5:14-21, KJV: Paul says, "Nevertheless death reigned from Adam until Moses, even over those who had not sinned in the likeness of the offense of Adam, who is a type of Him who was to come. But the free gift is not like the transgression. For if by the transgression of the one the many died, much more did the grace of God and the gift by the grace of the one Man, Jesus Christ, abound to the many. The gift is not like that which came through the one who sinned; for on the one hand the judgment arose from one transgression resulting in condemnation, but on the other hand the free gift arose from many transgressions resulting in justification. For if by the transgression of the one, death reigned through the one, much more those who receive the abundance of grace and of the gift of righteousness will reign in life through the One, Jesus Christ.

Romans 5:12: [12] Wherefore, as by one man sin entered into the world, and death by sin; and so death passed upon all men, for that all have sinned. . . .[19] For as by one man's disobedience many were made sinners, so by the obedience of one shall many be made righteous.

Romans 8 is one of the best-loved chapters of the Bible. *Verses 1-11 instruct us that we have a new life and a new nature, with the indwelling of the Holy Spirit.*

Romans 8:18, KJV: Present Suffering and Future Glory: [18] I consider that our present sufferings are not worth comparing with the glory that will be revealed in us.

Remember in Genesis, the seed plot of the Bible, how everything that God had made was very good. Then sin brought corruption on earth. Now see what we are told about the creation and earth in Romans: Romans 8 KJV: [19] For the creation waits with eager longing for the revealing of the sons of God. [20] For the creation was subjected to futility, not willingly, but because of him who subjected it, in hope [21] that the creation itself will be set free from its bondage to corruption and obtain the freedom of the glory of the children of God. [22] For we know that the whole creation has been groaning together in the pains of childbirth until now. [23] And not only the creation, but we ourselves, who have the first fruits of the Spirit, groan inwardly as we wait eagerly for adoption as sons, the redemption of our bodies.

Unity of the Scriptures: The Earth is now under the curse of sin. But the time will come when we will have a New Earth, when the Earth will be restored to its original state (Revelation, chapters 21-22), The New Earth will be God's dwelling place; it will be fashioned for resurrected people to live there (Alcorn, 2004). How we can look forward to future glory on the New Earth!

Romans 8:31-39, KJV: *Nothing can separate us from the love of Christ* [1] What, then, shall we say in response to these things? If God is for us, who can be against us? [32] He who did not spare his own Son, but gave him up for us all—how will he not also, along with him, graciously give us all things? [33] Who will bring any charge against those whom God has chosen? It is God who justifies. [34] Who then is the one who condemns? No one. Christ Jesus who died—more than that, who was raised to life—is at the right hand of God and is also interceding for us. [35] Who shall separate us from the love of Christ? Shall trouble or hardship or persecution or famine or nakedness or danger or sword?

[37] No, in all these things we are more than conquerors through him who loved us. [38] For I am convinced that neither death nor life, neither angels nor demons, neither the present nor the future, nor any powers, [39] neither height nor depth, nor anything else in all creation, will be able to separate us from the love of God that is in Christ Jesus our Lord.

Romans 12: After Paul has insisted that our standing with God is dependent on the Mercy of Christ and not on our good works, he shows that the mercy of God compels us to want to have a transformed life. We are admonished to not be conformed to this world but to be transformed by the renewing of our minds. We are told to give our bodies a living sacrifice. The last part of chapter 12 shows love in action. My husband, Dale, and I have read this chapter together many times as a reminder of what we should do daily.

12:1, KJV: Therefore, I urge you, brothers and sisters, in view of God's mercy, to offer your bodies as a living sacrifice, holy and pleasing to God—this is your true and proper worship. [2] Do not conform to the pattern of this world, but be transformed by the renewing of your mind. Then you will be able to test and approve what God's will is—his good, pleasing and perfect will.

[9] Love must be sincere. Hate what is evil; cling to what is good. [10] Be devoted to one another in love. Honor one another above yourselves. [11] Never be lacking in zeal, but keep your spiritual fervor, serving the Lord. [12] Be joyful in hope, patient in affliction, faithful in prayer. [13] Share with the Lord's people who are in need. Practice hospitality. [14] Bless those who persecute you; bless and do not curse. [15] Rejoice with those who rejoice; mourn with those who mourn. [16] Live in harmony with one another. [17] Do not repay anyone evil for evil. Be careful to do what is right in the eyes of everyone. [18] If it is possible, as far as it depends on you, live at peace with everyone. [19] Do not take revenge, my dear friends, but leave room for God's wrath, for it is written: "It is mine to avenge; I will repay," says the Lord. [20] On the contrary: If your enemy is hungry, feed him; if he is thirsty, give him something to drink. In doing this, you will heap burning coals on his head. [21] Do not be overcome by evil, but overcome evil with good.

Chapter 13 reminds us to be obedient to civil law and tells us that civil government is established by God. Chapter 14 admonishes us not to judge each other. Chapter 14 reminds the stronger Christians to support the weaker Christians.

Romans 15, KJV tells of his ministry to the Gentiles. I glory in Christ Jesus in my service to God. [18] I will not venture to speak of anything except what Christ has accomplished through me in leading the Gentiles to obey God by what I have said and done—So from Jerusalem all the way around to Illyricum, I have fully proclaimed the gospel of Christ. [20] It has always been my ambition to preach the gospel where Christ was not known.

Paul arrived in Rome 2 years after he wrote the Letter to the Romans Paul's mission was to carry the name of Christ to all the known world. How glad we are that he worked his way westward, which means Western Europe came to have Christ. Western Europe settled America! Therefore, we have experienced life in the greatest country of all times.

THE BOOK OF I CORINTHIANS

In I & II Corinthians, Jesus is the power of love.

Theme: Christian Lifestyle in a pagan society

Message*: Corinth was a wealthy, young pagan city. New Christians were having a difficult time. It was a center of luxury, art, and philosophy for the Roman Empire. Paganism was mounting an attack on Christianity. Paul had received letters asking him questions about marriage, sex, and other matters. Paul begged for there to be no division among Christians. Paul taught them that Christ is the power and the wisdom.*

I Corinthians 1: Paul, an apostle of Christ Jesus by the will of God, and Timothy our brother, To the church of God in Corinth, together with all his holy people throughout Achaia: [2] Grace and peace to you from God our Father and the Lord Jesus Christ. [3] Praise be to the God and Father of our Lord Jesus Christ, the Father of compassion and the God of all comfort, [4] who comforts us in all our troubles, so that we can comfort those in any trouble with the comfort we ourselves receive from God. [5] For just as we share abundantly in the sufferings of Christ, so also our comfort abounds through Christ.

Chapter 2: God's Wisdom Revealed by the Spirit.: When I came to you, I did not come with eloquence or human wisdom as I proclaimed to you the testimony about God. [2] For I resolved to know nothing while I was with you except Jesus Christ and him crucified. [3] I came to you in weakness with great fear and trembling. [4] My message and my preaching were not with wise and persuasive words, but with a demonstration of the Spirit's power, so that your faith might not rest on human wisdom, but on God's power.

[6] We do, however, speak a message of wisdom among the mature, but not the wisdom of this age or of the rulers of this age, who are coming to nothing. [7] No, we declare God's wisdom, a mystery that has been hidden and that God destined for our glory before time began. [8] None of the rulers of this age understood it, for if they had, they would not have crucified the Lord of glory. [9] However, as it is written:

"What no eye has seen, what no ear has heard, and what no human mind has conceived"—
the things God has prepared for those who love him—
(*What motivation and a blessing for us as we look forward to Heaven!*)

I Corinthians 6 rebukes immoral church members. [15] Do you not know that your bodies are members of Christ himself? Shall I then take the members of Christ and unite them with a prostitute? Never! [16] Do you not know that he who unites himself with a prostitute is one with her in body? For it is said, "The two will become one flesh." [17] But whoever is united with the Lord is one with him in spirit.

[18] Flee from sexual immorality. All other sins a person commits are outside the body, but whoever sins sexually, sins against their own body. [19] Do you not know that your bodies are temples of the Holy Spirit, who is in you, whom you have received from God? You are not your own; [20] you were bought at a price. Therefore honor God with your bodies.

(Please, precious ones, adhere to the above. It will bring happiness if you do. Not keeping God's laws brings much unhappiness. Remember the following promise from God about temptation.)

I Corinthians 10:13: No temptation has overtaken you except what is common to mankind. And God is faithful; he will not let you be tempted beyond what you can bear. But when you are tempted he will also provide a way out so that you can endure it.

The Love Chapter of the Bible: I Corinthians Chapter 13, KJV: *I memorized all of this when I was in the Bible Contest at the huge" Chickasha Junior High School. I won second in the finals, which was held in the auditorium before the whole large student body. I received a quarter for my prize! Because I learned it when I was very young, this "Love Chapter of the Bible" has always been hidden in my heart.*

Though I speak with the tongues of men and of angels, and have not charity, I am become as sounding brass, or a tinkling cymbal. [2] And though I have the gift of prophecy, and understand all mysteries, and all knowledge; and though I have all faith, so that I could remove mountains, and have not charity, I am nothing. [3] And though I bestow all my goods to feed the poor, and though I give my body to be burned, and have not charity, it profiteth me nothing.

[4] Charity suffereth long, and is kind; charity envieth not; charity vaunteth not itself, is not puffed up, [5] Doth not behave itself unseemly, seeketh not her own, is not easily provoked, thinketh no evil; [6] Rejoiceth not in iniquity, but rejoiceth in the truth; [7] Beareth all things, believeth all things, hopeth all things, endureth all things.

[8] Charity never faileth: but whether there be prophecies, they shall fail; whether there be tongues, they shall cease; whether there be knowledge, it shall vanish away. [9] For we know in part, and we prophesy in part. [10] But when that which is perfect is come, then that which is in part shall be done away. [11] When I was a child, I spake as a child, I understood as a child, I thought as a child: but when I became a man, I put away childish things.

[12] For now we see through a glass, darkly; but then face to face: now I know in part; but then shall I know even as also I am known. [13] And now abideth faith, hope, charity, these three; but the greatest of these is charity.

Proofs of Jesus 'Resurrection and the Importance of the Resurrection: Chapter 15:3: Christ died for our sins according to the Scriptures, [4] that he was buried, that he was raised on the third day according to the Scriptures, [5] and that he appeared to Cephas, and then to the Twelve. [6] After that, he appeared to more than five hundred of the brothers and sisters at the same time, most of whom are still living, though some have fallen asleep. [7] Then he appeared to James, then to all the apostles, [8] and last of all he appeared to me also.

[12] But if it is preached that Christ has been raised from the dead, how can some of you say that there is no resurrection of the dead? [13] If there is no resurrection of the dead, then not even Christ has been raised. [14] And if Christ has not been raised, our preaching is useless and so is your faith. [15] More than that, we are then found to be false witnesses about

God, for we have testified about God that he raised Christ from the dead. But he did not raise him if in fact the dead are not raised. [16] For if the dead are not raised, then Christ has not been raised either. [17] And if Christ has not been raised, your faith is futile; you are still in your sins. [18] Then those also who have fallen asleep in Christ are lost. [19] If only for this life we have hope in Christ, we are of all people most to be pitied.

[20] But Christ has indeed been raised from the dead, the firstfruits of those who have fallen asleep. [21] For since death came through a man, the resurrection of the dead comes also through a man. [22] For as in Adam all die, so in Christ all will be made alive[l]

Resurrection of our bodies: We will not all sleep, but we will all be changed—[52] in a flash, in the twinkling of an eye, at the last trumpet. For the trumpet will sound, the dead will be raised imperishable, and we will be changed. [53] For the perishable must clothe itself with the imperishable, and the mortal with immortality. [54] When the perishable has been clothed with the imperishable, and the mortal with immortality, then the saying that is written will come true: "Death has been swallowed up in victory. [55] "Where, O death, is your victory? Where, O death, is your sting?"[li]

[56] The sting of death is sin, and the power of sin is the law. [57] But thanks be to God! He gives us the victory through our Lord Jesus Christ. [58] Therefore, my dear brothers and sisters, stand firm. Let nothing move you. Always give yourselves fully to the work of the Lord, because you know that your labor in the Lord is not in vain. (*What a living letter for us today!*)

THE BOOK OF II CORINTHIANS
Theme: The strength of weakness

Paul reveals much feeling because of all that has happened in Corinth. He will fight to wrest the Corinthians from the corrupting influence of false teachers. He was an apostle called by God to bring people into the kingdom of God. In Chapters 2 and 3, he shows the superiority of the New Covenant under Christ over the Old Covenant under the law.

Chapter 4 encourages those who are suffering: [5] for what we preach is not ourselves, but Jesus Christ as Lord, and ourselves as your servants for Jesus' sake. [6] For God, who said, "Let light shine out of darkness." He made his light shine in our hearts to give us the light of the knowledge of God's glory displayed in the face of Christ.

[7] But we have this treasure in jars of clay to show that this all-surpassing power is from God and not from us. [8] We are hard pressed on every side, but not crushed; perplexed, but not in despair; [9] persecuted, but not abandoned; struck down, but not destroyed.

Other meaningful verses include:

Awaiting the New Body: II Cor. 5:1: For we know that if the earthly tent we live in is destroyed, we have a building from God, an eternal house in heaven, not built by human hands. [2] Meanwhile we groan, longing to be clothed instead with our heavenly dwelling, [6] Therefore we are always confident and know that as long as we are at home in the body we are away from the Lord. . . .[10] For we must all appear before the judgment seat of Christ, so that each of us may receive what is due us for the things done while in the body, whether good or bad.

[14] For Christ's love compels us, because we are convinced that one died for all, and therefore all died.[15] And he died for all, that those who live should no longer live for themselves but for him who died for them and was raised again.

Be reconciled to God: [17] Therefore, if anyone is in Christ, the new creation has come: The old has gone, the new is here! [18] All this is from God, who reconciled us to himself through Christ. . .We implore you on Christ's behalf: Be reconciled to God. [21] God made him who had no sin to be sin for us, so that in him we might become the righteousness of God.

2 Cor. 6:14: Be ye not unequally yoked together with unbelievers: for what fellowship hath righteousness with unrighteousness?

2 Corinthians 9:7: Every man according as he purposeth in his heart, so let him give; not grudgingly or of necessity, for God loveth a cheerful giver.

2 Cor. 10: 4-5: [4] For the weapons of our warfare are not carnal, but mighty through God to the pulling down of strong holds; 5 Casting down imaginations, and every high thing that exalteth itself against the knowledge of God, and bringing into captivity every thought to the obedience of Christ.

II Cor 11:22-30: (*Here, Paul shows his weaknesses and strength in suffering, This is also a good summary of Paul's life as a missionary for Christ.*)

[22] Are they Hebrews? So am I. Are they Israelites? So am I. Are they Abraham's descendants? So am I. [23] Are they servants of Christ? (I am out of my mind to talk like this.) I am more. I have worked much harder, been in prison more frequently, been flogged more severely, and been exposed to death again and again. [24] Five times I received from the Jews the forty lashes minus one. [25] Three times I was beaten with rods, once I was pelted with stones, three times I was shipwrecked, I spent a night and a day in the open sea,

[26] I have been constantly on the move. I have been in danger from rivers, in danger from bandits, in danger from my fellow Jews, in danger from Gentiles; in danger in the city, in danger in the country, in danger at sea; and in danger from false believers. [27] I have labored and toiled and have often gone without sleep; I have known hunger and thirst and have often gone without food; I have been cold and naked. [28] Besides everything else, I face daily the pressure of my concern for all the churches. [29] Who is weak, and I do not feel weak? Who is led into sin, and I do not inwardly burn?

[30] If I must boast, I will boast of the things that show my weakness. [31] The God and Father of the Lord Jesus, who is to be praised forever.

2 Cor 12:9: (*Paul revealed what Christ had said to him:*) My Grace is sufficient for you, for my strength is made perfect in weakness.

THE BOOK OF GALATIANS
In Galatians, Jesus is the freedom from the curse of sin.

The Theme: Justification by Faith alone

The Background: Paul was angry because the Galatians were adding to the message of Jesus Christ. The Gospel asserted that you are saved by grace, through faith. The Galatians were saying "You must be circumcised." Paul feared this would be the first step back into keeping the whole law and being saved by works rather than salvation being a free gift.

Key Verses: *Chapter 2:16, 20, 21*: No person is justified by the works of Law but through faith in Christ Jesus, even we have believed in Christ Jesus, that we may be justified by faith in Christ, and not by the works of Law; since by the works of Law shall no person be justified.

20 I have been crucified with Christ; and it is no longer I who live, but Christ lives in me; and the life that I now live in the flesh I live by faith in the Son of God, who loved me and delivered himself up for me.

Galatians 3:6-9: Just as Abraham "believed God, and it was accounted to him for righteousness." [7] Therefore know that *only* those who are of faith are sons of Abraham. [8] And the Scripture, foreseeing that God would justify the Gentiles by faith, preached the gospel to Abraham beforehand, *saying,* "In you all the nations shall be blessed." [9] So then those who *are* of faith are blessed with believing Abraham.

Galatians 3:11-14: [11] Clearly no one who relies on the law is justified before God, because "the righteous will live by faith." [12] The law is not based on faith; on the contrary, it says, "The person who does these things will live by them." [13] Christ redeemed us from the curse of the law by becoming a curse for us, for it is written: "Cursed is everyone who is hung on a tree."[14] He redeemed us in order that the blessing given to Abraham might come to the Gentiles through Christ Jesus, so that by faith we might receive the promise of the Spirit.

The Law and the Promise: Galatians 3:16-21: The promises were spoken to Abraham and to his seed. [18] For if the inheritance depends on the law, then it no longer depends on the promise; but God in his grace gave it to Abraham through a promise. [19] Why, then, was the law given at all? It was added because of transgressions until the Seed to whom the promise referred had come. [21] Is the law, therefore, opposed to the promises of God? Absolutely not! For if a law had been given that could impart life, then righteousness would certainly have come by the law. [22] But Scripture has locked up everything under the control of sin, so that what was promised, being given through faith in Jesus Christ, might be given to those who believe.

[24] So the law was our school master until Christ came that we might be justified by faith. [25] Now that this faith has come, we are no longer under a schoolmaster. [26] So in Christ Jesus you are all children of God through faith, [27] for all of you who were baptized into Christ

have clothed yourselves with Christ. [28] There is neither Jew nor Gentile, neither slave nor free, nor is there male and female, for you are all one in Christ Jesus. [29] If you belong to Christ, then you are Abraham's seed, and heirs according to the promise.

Galatians 3
I am no longer subject to the schoolmaster law.
Its tutorship had to withdraw.
I have graduated and with diploma in hand
Faith came, and I am one in Christ Jesus grand.

Yes, Jews and Gentiles come to Christ in the same way, by grace, through faith in Jesus!

Chapter 4:4-7: But when the set time had fully come, God sent his Son, born of a woman, born under the law, [5] to redeem those under the law, that we might receive adoption to sonship. [6] Because you are his sons, God sent the Spirit of his Son into our hearts, the Spirit who calls out, "Abba Father." [7] So you are no longer a slave, but God's child; and since you are his child, God has made you also an heir. *What a promise! We are heirs with Christ because we are God's children!*

Galatians 4
When the heir is only a child,
He is no different than a bond servant.
He is under tutors until the appointed time
As we were in bondage of the world's elements
Then heirs of God through Christ to a life sublime.

Chapter 5:14, KJV: For all the law is fulfilled in one word, even in this; Thou shalt love thy neighbor as thyself. *Freedom in Christ does not mean license to continue in sin. Those who follow the desires of the sinful nature cannot be saved.* 16 This I say then, Walk in the Spirit, and ye shall not fulfill the lust of the flesh. . .18 but if ye be led of the Spirit, ye are not under the law. [19] The acts of the flesh are obvious: sexual immorality, impurity and debauchery; [20] idolatry and witchcraft; hatred, discord, jealousy, fits of rage, selfish ambition, dissensions, factions [21] and envy; drunkenness, orgies, and the like. I warn you, as I did before, that those who live like this will not inherit the kingdom of God.

[22] But the fruit of the Spirit is love, joy, peace, forbearance, kindness, goodness, faithfulness, [23] gentleness and self-control. Against such things there is no law. 24 And they that are Christ's have crucified the flesh with affections and lusts. 25 If we live in the Spirit, let us also walk in the Spirit.

Chapter 6:2: KJV: Bear ye one another's burdens, and so fulfill the law of Christ. Galatians 6:7: Be not deceived; God is not mocked: for whatsoever a man soweth, that shall he also reap. 8 For he that soweth to his flesh shall of the flesh reap corruption; but he that soweth to the Spirit shall of the Spirit reap life everlasting. 9 And let us not be weary in well doing: for in due season we shall reap, if we faint not. 10 As we have therefore opportunity, let us do good unto all men, especially unto them who are of the household of faith.

14 But God forbid that I should glory, save in the cross of our Lord Jesus Christ, by whom the world is crucified unto me, and I unto the world. [15] Neither circumcision nor uncircumcision means anything; what counts is the new creation. [16] Peace and mercy to all who follow this rule—to the Israel of God.

Thus, Paul showed the Galatians that it was not by works of the law that we are justified. Salvation is a free gift made possible by what Jesus did on the cross.

THE BOOK OF EPHESIANS
In Ephesians, Jesus is our glorious treasure

The Theme: God's new society

While in prison, Paul wrote to the Ephesians after receiving disturbing news about them. Jesus created the church, a new social order of love and unity. Paul shows how God, out of love, calls people to be reconciled to Christ and to each other.

I will tell you my favorite scriptures and why I love them. May this whet your appetite to read all of Ephesians.

Ephesians 1:3, 7, 13, KJV: Blessed be the God and Father of our Lord Jesus Christ, who hath blessed us with all spiritual blessings in heavenly places in Christ: [7] In whom we have redemption through his blood, the forgiveness of sins, according to the riches of his grace. 13: In whom ye also trusted, after that ye heard the word of truth, the gospel of your salvation: in whom also after that ye believed, ye were sealed with that Holy Spirit of promise. *This shows that we have security as a believer.*

Ephesians 2: 8-9, KJV; For by grace you have been saved through faith, and that not of yourselves; *it is* the gift of God, not of works, lest anyone should boast. [10] For we are His workmanship, created in Christ Jesus for good works, which God prepared beforehand that we should walk in them. *The favorite scripture of many people, including my brother, Jim.*

3:19-21, KJV: Having been built on the foundation of the apostles and prophets, Jesus Christ Himself being the chief corner*stone*, [21] in whom the whole building, being fitted together, grows into a holy temple in the Lord. *(Jesus is the cornerstone upon which our lives should be built!)*

Ephesians 4:7, 11-14, 30-32, KJV: But unto every one of us is given grace according to the measure of the gift of Christ. [11] And he gave some, apostles; and some, prophets; and some, evangelists; and some, pastors and teachers; [12] For the perfecting of the saints, for the work of the ministry, for the edifying of the body of Christ: [13] Till we all come in the unity of the faith, and of the knowledge of the Son of God, unto a perfect man, unto the measure of the stature of the fullness of Christ: [14] That we henceforth be no more children, tossed to and fro, and carried about with every wind of doctrine, by the sleight of men, and cunning craftiness, whereby they lie in wait to deceive; [15] But speaking the truth in love, may grow up into him in all things, which is the head, even Christ:

[30] And grieve not the holy Spirit of God, whereby ye are sealed unto the day of redemption.[31] Let all bitterness, and wrath, and anger, and clamors, and evil speaking, be put away from you, with all malice: [32] And be ye kind one to another, tenderhearted, forgiving one another, even as God for Christ's sake hath forgiven you.

Ephesians 5:1, KJV: [1] Follow God's example, therefore, as dearly loved children [2] and walk in the way of love, just as Christ loved us and gave himself up for us as a fragrant offering and sacrifice to God. [3] But among you there must not be even a hint of sexual immorality, or of any kind of impurity, or of greed, because these are improper for God's holy people.

[8] For you were once darkness, but now you are light in the Lord. Live as children of light[9] (for the fruit of the light consists in all goodness, righteousness and truth) [10] and find out what pleases the Lord. [15] Be very careful, then, how you live—not as unwise but as wise, [16] making the most of every opportunity, because the days are evil. [17] Therefore do not be foolish, but understand what the Lord's will is. [18] Do not get drunk on wine, which leads to debauchery. Instead, be filled with the Spirit, [19] speaking to one another with psalms, hymns, and songs from the Spirit. Sing and make music from your heart to the Lord, [20] always giving thanks to God the Father for everything, in the name of our Lord Jesus Christ.

The following is part of the scripture Dale and I read the first night of our honeymoon and always read it together on our wedding anniversaries.

Instructions for Christian Households

Ephesians 5:21-33, KJV; Submit to one another out of reverence for Christ. [22] Wives, submit yourselves to your own husbands as you do to the Lord. [23] For the husband is the head of the wife as Christ is the head of the church, his body, of which he is the Savior. [24] Now as the church submits to Christ, so also wives should submit to their husbands in everything.

[25] Husbands, love your wives, just as Christ loved the church and gave himself up for her[26] to make her holy, cleansing her by the washing with water through the word, [27] and to present her to himself as a radiant church, without stain or wrinkle or any other blemish, but holy and blameless. [28] In this same way, husbands ought to love their wives as their own bodies. . . .A man shall leave his father and mother and be united to his wife, and the two will become one flesh." [32] This is a profound mystery—but I am talking about Christ and the church. [33] However, each one of you also must love his wife as he loves himself, and the wife must respect her husband.

Pass the Baton of Faith to the Next Generation: Ephesians 6:1-4: KJV: Children, obey your parents in the Lord, for this is right. [2] "Honor your father and mother"—which is the first commandment with a promise—[3] "so that it may go well with you and that you may enjoy long life on the earth." [4] Fathers, do not exasperate your children; instead, bring them up in the training and instruction of the Lord.

The Whole Armor of God: Ephesians 6:10-1, KJV: I memorized this while I was teaching at East Central University and teaching the College and Career Sunday School Class at the Wayne First Baptist Church. Then, while teaching children at church, I purchased a child-sized armor. Toby Blair, our grandson, had his armor, also. I pray this will help our children remember to put on their spiritual armor every day.

6:10: Finally, my brethren, be strong in the Lord, and in the power of his might.[11] Put on the whole armour of God, that ye may be able to stand against the wiles of the devil. [12] For we wrestle not against flesh and blood, but against principalities, against powers, against the rulers of the darkness of this world, against spiritual wickedness in high places.[13] Wherefore take unto you the whole armor of God, that ye may be able to withstand in the evil day, and having done all, to stand.

[14] Stand therefore, having your loins girt about with truth, and having on the breastplate of righteousness; [15] And your feet shod with the preparation of the gospel of peace; [16] Above all, taking the shield of faith, wherewith ye shall be able to quench all the fiery darts of the wicked. [17] And take the helmet of salvation, and the sword of the Spirit, which is the word of God:

We must stand like a rock to defend our Christian Liberty! We can, if we put on the Whole Armor of God every day!

THE BOOK OF PHILIPPIANS
In Philippians, Jesus is the servant's heart.

<u>Theme:</u> The joy of knowing Jesus. Believers should disregard things of earth and count all things loss in order to win Christ.

Paul had founded the church after a vision during the night in which a Macedonian man pleaded with him to "Cross over to Macedonia and help us." I'm glad this happened. Philippi was the first place Paul visited in Western Europe. Had he not come there, the USA would probably have not been settled by Christians. Upon Paul's first visit to Philippi, he and his co-workers were beaten and thrown into prison. This prison became a place of revival, where God's saving grace was evidenced in a mighty way. Later, while in prison, Paul wrote this warm letter to his friends at Philippi. He told them to be joyful in the Lord even when in prison and when nothing around them is joyful. This can truly be a living letter for us today.

According to O. B. Greene (1965), in Philippians, Jesus is the center of Christianity — the point around which all of God's truth is centered. The key verse of Philippians is: Philippians 3:8: Yea doubtless, and I count all things but loss for the Excellency of the knowledge of Christ Jesus my Lord: for whom I have suffered the loss of all things, and do count them but dung, that I may win Christ,

Philippians 1: 1: Paul and Timothy, the servants of Jesus Christ, to all the saints in Christ Jesus which are at Philippi, with the bishops and deacons:

[2] Grace be unto you, and peace, from God our Father, and from the Lord Jesus Christ. [3] I thank my God upon every remembrance of you, [4] Always in every prayer of mine for you all making request with joy, [5] For your fellowship in the gospel from the first day until now;

I have taught nearly all grades in school and under graduate and graduates at the University, and when asked, "What is your favorite age to teach?" I always say, "The age I am teaching now." I loved all ages. The same is true with the Epistles written by Paul. I love all of them. But I do believe that Philippians is really my favorite!

I like this promise for my grandchildren and write it to them often:

Chapter 1:6, KJV Being confident of this very thing, that he which hath begun a good work in you will perform it until the day of Jesus Christ.

As I look at the life of each grandchild and great grandchild – from age 3 months to 31 years, I see a promise, a potentiality, and I see that God is working in them! When I think to myself about each of them and the reasons I love each so much, it seems that the one I love the most at the time is the one who seems to have the greatest needs for prayer at the time.

Paul was confident of his own salvation. He knew God's purpose for him; he knew God's purpose for the Church, and he knew God would work out and fulfill His purpose for each and every believer. (Greene, 1965)

As I get closer to Heaven, the following verse and poem are mine, and I pray they will be yours: 21: For to me to live is Christ, and to die is gain.

Philippians 1
Paul revealed the desire in his heart,
"For I am in a strait betwixt two,
To be with Christ I desire to depart,
But more I need to remain in the flesh with you."

My mother's favorite scripture, which she and I memorized, is Philippians 2:5-11, KJV
[5] Let this mind be in you, which was also in Christ Jesus: *(Note the two major parts of the "mind of Christ: humiliation and exaltation. He humbled himself to go to the cross. Then he is exalted.)* [6] Who, being in the form of God, thought it not robbery to be equal with God: [7] But made himself of no reputation, and took upon him the form of a servant, and was made in the likeness of men: [8] And being found in fashion as a man, he humbled himself, and became obedient unto death, even the death of the cross.

[9] Wherefore God also hath highly exalted him, and given him a name which is above every name: [10] That at the name of Jesus every knee should bow, of things in heaven, and things in earth, and things under the earth; [11] And that every tongue should confess that Jesus Christ is Lord, to the glory of God the Father.

What a wonderful revelation and promise! Think of every tongue praising God and confessing that Jesus Christ is Lord!

The "mind of Christ" reminds us of his humiliation and his exultation. He is a servant and a King. We are told to have this mind of Christ. He was exalted in Heaven and emptied himself to come to earth and die for us. But in all of his humiliation, he never ceased to be God.

Philippians 3:7-16
[7] But what things were gain to me, these I have counted loss for Christ. [8] Yet indeed I also count all things loss for the excellence of the knowledge of Christ Jesus my Lord, for whom I have suffered the loss of all things, and count them as rubbish, that I may gain Christ [9] and be found in Him, not having my own righteousness, which *is* from the law, but that which *is* through faith in Christ, the righteousness which is from God by faith; [10] that I may know Him and the power of His resurrection, and the fellowship of His sufferings, being conformed to His death, [11] if, by any means, I may attain to the resurrection from the dead.

Pressing Toward the Goal: [12] Not that I have already attained, or am already perfected; but I press on, that I may lay hold of that for which Christ Jesus has also laid hold of me. [13] Brethren, I do not count myself to have apprehended; but one thing *I do,* forgetting those things which are behind and reaching forward to those things which are ahead, [14] I press toward the goal for the prize of the upward call of God in Christ Jesus.

Paul often referred to sports to make his points about life. These Philippian Scriptures were very pertinent for youth. I sponsored the Fellowship of Christian Athletes (FCA), and then in later years used their principles when teaching children at church. FCA stresses these three points:

1. Christ is the Coach of Life. 2. The Bible is the Rulebook of Life.3. With these two, we can win in the game of life.

<u>Our Citizenship in Heaven:</u> Phil. 3:20: [20] For our citizenship is in heaven, from which we also eagerly wait for the Savior, the Lord Jesus Christ,[21] who will transform our lowly body that it may be conformed to His glorious body, according to the working by which He is able even to subdue all things to Himself.

Look at the promises of peace and comfort when we pray with Thanksgiving in our hearts as in Philippians 4:4-8, 11, 12, 13, and 19. Rejoice in the Lord always: and again I say, Rejoice. [5] Let your moderation be known unto all men. The Lord is at hand. [6] Be careful for nothing; but in everything by prayer and supplication with thanksgiving let your requests be made known unto God. [7] And the peace of God, which passeth all understanding, shall keep your hearts and minds through Christ Jesus

[8] Finally, brethren, whatsoever things are true, whatsoever things are honest, whatsoever things are just, whatsoever things are pure, whatsoever things are lovely, whatsoever things are of good report; if there be any want: for I have learned, in whatsoever state I am, therewith to be content. [12] I know both how to be abased, and I know how to abound: everywhere and in all things I am instructed both to be full and to be hungry, both to abound and to suffer need. [13] I can do all things through Christ which strengthens me.

[19] But my God shall supply all your need according to his riches in glory by Christ Jesus. [20] Now unto God and our Father be glory for ever and ever. Amen. [21] Salute every saint in Christ Jesus. The brethren which are with me greet you. [23] The grace of our Lord Jesus Christ be with you all. Amen.

THE BOOK OF COLOSSIANS
In Colossians, Jesus is the Godhead Trinity.

Theme: Fullness and freedom in Christ. Being right with God through faith in Jesus Christ.

Message: While in prison at Rome, Paul wrote this letter to Colosse to combat errors in the church and to show that believers have everything they need in Christ. Christ has absolute supremacy and is sufficient for all needs.

Jesus is the power,

Jesus is the glue.

In this trying hour

He holds all together with a bonding love so true.

Colossians 1:1: Paul, an apostle of Christ Jesus by the will of God, and Timothy our brother, [2] To God's holy people in Colossae, the faithful brothers and sisters in Christ. [3] We always thank God, the Father of our Lord Jesus Christ, when we pray for you,[4] because we have heard of your faith in Christ Jesus and of the love you have for all God's people—[5] the faith and love that spring from the hope stored up for you in heaven and about which you have already heard in the true message of the gospel. . . .We continually ask God to fill you with the knowledge of his will through all the wisdom and understanding that the Spirit gives, [10] so that you may live a life worthy of the Lord and please him in every way: bearing fruit in every good work, growing in the knowledge of God. . . .[13] For he has rescued us from the dominion of darkness and brought us into the kingdom of the Son he loves, [14] in whom we have redemption, the forgiveness of sins.

Verses 13-22 tell of the work of Christ. He is the exact likeness of God; he is the creator, he is the Head of his Church; his death on the cross makes it possible for us to stand in the presence of God. Because Christ is supreme, our lives should be centered on Christ. When our sins are forgiven, we are reconciled to God and have a union with Christ and can identify with his death, burial, and resurrection.

The Supremacy of the Son of God: **[15] The Son is the image of the invisible God, the firstborn over all creation. [16] For in him all things were created: things in heaven and on earth, visible and invisible, whether thrones or powers or rulers or authorities; all things have been created through him and for him. [17] He is before all things, and in him all things hold together. [18] And he is the head of the body, the church; he is the beginning and the firstborn from among the dead, so that in everything he might have the supremacy. [19] For God was pleased to have all his fullness dwell in him, [20] and through him to reconcile to himself all things, whether things on earth or things in heaven, by making peace through his blood, shed on the cross.**

Colossians 1:24-29 is the commission given to the Southern Baptist Foreign Missionaries.

24 Now I rejoice in what I am suffering for you, and I fill up in my flesh what is still lacking in regard to Christ's afflictions, for the sake of his body, which is the church. 25 I have become its servant by the commission God gave me to present to you the word of God in its fullness — 26 the mystery that has been kept hidden for ages and generations, but is now disclosed to the Lord's people. 27 To them God has chosen to make known among the Gentiles the glorious riches of this mystery, which is Christ in you, the hope of glory.

28 He is the one we proclaim, admonishing and teaching everyone with all wisdom, so that we may present everyone fully mature in Christ. 29 To this end I strenuously contend with all the energy Christ so powerfully works in me.

Suffering is unavoidable when we bring the Good news of Christ to the world. It is called Christ's suffering because of our relationship with Christ. When we suffer, Christ suffers with us. Colossians 2:6: [6] So then, just as you received Christ Jesus as Lord, continue to live your lives in him[7] rooted and built up in him, strengthened in the faith as you were taught, and overflowing with thankfulness.

[9] For in Christ all the fullness of the Deity lives in bodily form, [10] and in Christ you have been brought to fullness. He is the head over every power and authority.. . .[12] having been buried with him in baptism, in which you were also raised with him through your faith in the working of God, who raised him from the dead.

[13] When you were dead in your sins and in the uncircumcision of your flesh, God made you alive with Christ. He forgave us all our sins, [14] having canceled the charge of our legal indebtedness, which stood against us and condemned us; he has taken it away, nailing it to the cross. [15] And having disarmed the powers and authorities, he made a public spectacle of them, triumphing over them by the cross.

> Set your desires on things above,
> Not on things on earth.
> Jesus Christ dwells in us in love
> To direct us after our second birth.

Picture the New Earth

Yes, we can imagine the future New Earth when we picture our earth today without the sin of the present earth! Colossians 3:1: Since, then, you have been raised with Christ, set your hearts on things above, where Christ is, seated at the right hand of God. [2] Set your minds on things above, not on earthly things. [5] Whatever belongs to your earthly nature: sexual immorality, impurity, lust, evil desires and greed, which is idolatry. . . .Rid yourselves of all such things as these: anger, rage, malice, slander, and filthy language from your lips. [12] Therefore, as God's chosen people, holy and dearly loved, clothe yourselves with compassion, kindness, humility, gentleness and patience. [13] Bear with each other and forgive one another if any of you has a grievance against someone. Forgive as the Lord forgave you. [7] And whatever you do, whether in word or deed, do it all in the name of the Lord Jesus, giving thanks to God the Father through him.

Instructions for Christian Households: [18] Wives, submit yourselves to your husbands, as is fitting in the Lord. [19] Husbands, love your wives and do not be harsh with them. [20] Children, obey your parents in everything, for this pleases the Lord. [21] Fathers, do not embitter your children, or they will become discouraged.

Remember me here in jail.
Pray for me daily; don't fail.
I have opportunity here to preach the Good News,
I am comforted every day by Christian Jews.

Colossians 4:2: Devote yourselves to prayer, being watchful and thankful. [3] And pray for us, too, that God may open a door for our message, so that we may proclaim the mystery of Christ, for which I am in chains. [4] Pray that I may proclaim it clearly, as I should. [5] Be wise in the way you act toward outsiders; make the most of every opportunity. [6] Let your conversation be always full of grace, seasoned with salt, so that you may know how to answer everyone.

Christ, alone is the source of our spiritual life. The path to a deeper spiritual life comes through a clear connection with the Lord Jesus Christ.

THE BOOK OF I THESSALONIANS
In Thessalonians, Jesus is our coming King

Theme: The Second Coming of Our Lord

Paul founded the church at Thessalonica on his second missionary journey. He wrote the epistles to the church to encourage them during persecution and to answer questions concerning the second coming of Jesus. The book of I Thessalonians gives an excellent account of the Rapture. Jesus will come when we are least expecting it. The rapture is the first of the end-time events. It will happen before the millennial. (Halley, 2007)

Kyle Carson Blair, our grandson, called and excitedly told of the Bible Study he is having at the Second Baptist Church at Katy Texas about the End Events. He reminded me that I Thessalonians Chapters 4 and 5, along with I Corinthians 15 and Romans 8, give great hope of the future for us believers who will be alive when Jesus comes as well as for us who will already have gone to be with the Lord. Kyle also said we could always replace the word, "Hope" with the word, "confidence" any time we are talking about the hope we have in Jesus Christ.

Chapter 2: *Paul gave a profile of an effective ministry, as well as what our lives should be like. He said we should share the good news of the gospel even when persecuted for it. Our motive should be to please God and not to receive praise from men.*

[13] For this cause also thank we God without ceasing, because, when ye received the word of God which ye heard of us, ye received it not as the word of men, but as it is in truth, the word of God.

Chapter 4 contains a wealth of exhortations on how to live a Godly life in preparation of the Lord's coming. Abstain from Fornication and be Sanctified (*Set apart for the Lord's Service.*).

I Thess. 4:2-4, KJV: For ye know what commandments we gave you by the Lord Jesus. [3] For this is the will of God, even your sanctification, that ye should abstain from fornication: [4]That every one of you should know how to possess his vessel in sanctification and honour;

PEOPHECY: Paul wants the Thessalonians, whom he loves, to prepare for the second coming of Christ. The second coming of Christ is viewed as the culmination of Christ's redemptive work!

I Thessalonians 4:12: I would not have you to be ignorant, brethren, concerning them which are asleep, that ye sorrow not, even as others which have no hope. [14] For if we believe that Jesus died and rose again, even so them also which sleep in Jesus will God bring with him. [15] For this we say unto you by the word of the Lord, that we which are alive and remain unto the coming of the Lord shall not prevent them which are asleep. [16] For the Lord himself shall descend from heaven with a shout, with the voice of the archangel, and with the trump of God: and the dead in Christ shall rise first: [17]Then we which are alive and remain shall be caught up together with them in the clouds, to meet the Lord in the air: and so shall we ever be with the Lord.

<u>I Thess. 5: 1-23, KJV:</u> But of the times and the seasons, brethren, ye have no need that I write unto you. [2] For yourselves know perfectly that the day of the Lord so cometh as a thief in the night. [3] For when they shall say, Peace and safety; then sudden destruction cometh upon them, as travail upon a woman with child; and they shall not escape. [4] But ye, brethren, are not in darkness, that that day should overtake you as a thief.

[8] But let us, who are of the day, be sober, putting on the breastplate of faith and love; and for an helmet, the hope of salvation. [9] For God hath not appointed us to wrath, but to obtain salvation by our Lord Jesus Christ, [10] Who died for us, that, whether we wake or sleep, we should live together with him.

[11] Wherefore comfort yourselves together, and edify one another, even as also ye do. [12] And we beseech you, brethren, to know them which labour among you, and are over you in the Lord, and admonish you; [13] and to esteem them very highly in love for their work's sake. And be at peace among yourselves.

[14] Now we exhort you, brethren, warn them that are unruly, comfort the feebleminded, support the weak, be patient toward all men. [15] See that none render evil for evil unto any man; but ever follow that which is good, both among yourselves, and to all men. [16] Rejoice evermore. [17] Pray without ceasing. [18] In everything give thanks: for this is the will of God in Christ Jesus concerning you. [19] Quench not the Spirit.

[20] Despise not prophesying. [21] Prove all things; hold fast that which is good. [22] Abstain from all appearance of evil. [23] And the very God of peace sanctify you wholly; and I pray God your whole soul and body be preserved blameless unto the coming of our Lord Jesus Christ.

THE BOOK OF II THESSALONIANS
In Thessalonians, Jesus is our Coming King

Theme: Further teachings about the coming of the Lord.

Paul emphasized in this book that the Day of the Lord would be a day of terror for those who have rejected God and the Gospel of Jesus Christ.

Chapter 1:4-8: KJV: [4] So that we ourselves glory in you in the churches of God for your patience and faith in all your persecutions and tribulations that ye endure: [5] Which is a manifest token of the righteous judgment of God, that ye may be counted worthy of the kingdom of God, for which ye also suffer:

[6] Seeing it is a righteous thing with God to recompense tribulation to them that trouble you; [7] And to you who are troubled rest with us, when the Lord Jesus shall be revealed from heaven with his mighty angels, [8] In flaming fire taking vengeance on them that know not God, and that obey not the gospel of our Lord Jesus Christ: [9] Who shall be punished with everlasting destruction from the presence of the Lord, and from the glory of his power; [10] When he shall come to be glorified in His saints, and to be admired in all them that believe (because our testimony among you was believed) in that day.

[11] Wherefore also we pray always for you, that our God would count you worthy of this calling, and fulfill all the good pleasure of his goodness, and the work of faith with power: [12] That the name of our Lord Jesus Christ may be glorified in you, and ye in him, according to the grace of our God and the Lord Jesus Christ.

II Thessalonians 2:3-4, KJV: [3] Let no man deceive you by any means: for that day shall not come, except there come a falling away first, and that man of sin be revealed, the son of perdition; [4] Who opposeth and exalteth himself above all that is called God, or that is worshipped; so that he as God sitteth in the temple of God, shewing himself that he is God.

Therefore, brethren, stand fast, and hold the traditions which ye have been taught, whether by word, or our epistle. 17: Comfort your hearts, and establish you in every good word and work.

Verse 10: KJV: For even when we were with you, this we commanded you, that if any would not work, neither should he eat. 13: But ye, brethren, be not weary in well-doing. *According to Halley, (2007), Paul was an advocate for those who were truly in need. He spent much time collecting for the needy. But he condemns the person who could work but would not. This is where the saying originates, "If you don't work, you don't eat."*

Then Paul, always loving and longing to be with the flock, ends with Verse 16, KJV: Now the Lord of peace himself give you peace always by all means. The Lord be with you all.

BOOK OF I TIMOTHY
In Timothy, Jesus is our mediator and our faithful pastor.

Theme: A faithful ministry

I and II Timothy are called the Pastoral Letters. They were written by Paul to Timothy about AD 63-65. Timothy, the child of a Gentile and a Jew, was taught the Gospel as a small child and matured so fast in the Lord that the local church recommended Timothy to Paul as a traveling companion. Paul called him "My faithful and beloved child in the Lord." I love to use Timothy as an example when teaching children and youth. God can use young people in magnificent ways!

Paul wrote this letter telling the work that Timothy was to do at the churches of Ephesus. Timothy is to tell pastors not to teach doctrines other than that of Jesus Christ.

Timothy is charged to oppose false teachers: I Timothy 1:3: [3]As I urged you when I went into Macedonia, stay there in Ephesus so that you may command certain people not to teach false doctrines any longer [4]or to devote themselves to myths and endless genealogies. Such things promote controversial speculations rather than advancing God's work—which is by faith. [5]The goal of this command is love, which comes from a pure heart and a good conscience and a sincere faith. [6]Some have departed from these and have turned to meaningless talk. [7]They want to be teachers of the law, but they do not know what they are talking about or what they so confidently affirm.

The Lord's Grace to Paul: *(Paul always felt unworthy, though he had perhaps done more for Christ than all others put together. It seems that the closer we walk with Christ, the more humble we will feel. Paul felt his conversion was intended by God to be an everlasting example of God's patience with sinners. Yet Paul said many times that he was the chief of sinners.)*

[12]I thank Christ Jesus our Lord, who has given me strength, that he considered me trustworthy, appointing me to his service. [13]Even though I was once a blasphemer and a persecutor and a violent man, I was shown mercy because I acted in ignorance and unbelief.[14]The grace of our Lord was poured out on me abundantly, along with the faith and love that are in Christ Jesus.

[15]Here is a trustworthy saying that deserves full acceptance: Christ Jesus came into the world to save sinners—of whom I am the worst. [16]But for that very reason I was shown mercy so that in me, the worst of sinners, Christ Jesus might display his immense patience as an example for those who would believe in him and receive eternal life.

The Charge to Timothy Renewed: [18]Timothy, my son, I am giving you this command in keeping with the prophecies once made about you, so that by recalling them you may fight the battle well, [19]holding on to faith and a good conscience, which some have rejected and so have suffered shipwreck with regard to the faith.

(At the time of this writing, Nero was the ruler of the Roman Empire. Under him, Paul had been imprisoned and will soon be executed. Paul, in I Timothy 2, tells us to pray for our leaders, whether they are good or bad leaders.)

I urge, then, first of all, that petitions, prayers, intercession and thanksgiving be made for all people — [2] for kings and all those in authority, that we may live peaceful and quiet lives in all godliness and holiness. [3] This is good, and pleases God our Savior, [4] who wants all people to be saved and to come to a knowledge of the truth. [5] For there is one God and one mediator between God and mankind, the man Christ Jesus, [6] who gave himself as a ransom for all people.

[8] Therefore I want the men everywhere to pray, lifting up holy hands without anger or disputing. [9] I also want the women to dress modestly, with decency and propriety, adorning themselves, not with elaborate hairstyles or gold or pearls or expensive clothes, [10] but with good works.

I Timothy 2: Instructions concerning Church Administration: Verses 1-8 gives instruction for public prayer. Verses 9-15 tell about Women in public worship.

I Timothy 2
Adam was formed first, then Eve.
The origin of sin on earth began
When the woman in transgression was deceived.
She now is to learn from the man. By Marilyn Kay Paddack Gage

I Timothy 3:1-3: gives Qualifications for Church Officers.

3 Here is a trustworthy saying: Whoever aspires to be an overseer desires a noble task. [2] Now the overseer is to be above reproach, faithful to his wife, temperate, self-controlled, respectable, hospitable, able to teach, [3] not given to drunkenness, not violent but gentle, not quarrelsome, not a lover of money. [4] He must manage his own family well and see that his children obey him, and he must do so in a manner worthy of full respect. [5] (If anyone does not know how to manage his own family, how can he take care of God's church?) [6] He must not be a recent convert, or he may become conceited and fall under the same judgment as the devil. [7] He must also have a good reputation with outsiders, so that he will not fall into disgrace and into the devil's trap.

[11] In the same way, the women are to be worthy of respect, not malicious talkers but temperate and trustworthy in everything.

(The above tells the qualifications for pastors and their wives for our churches today. It is followed by very similar qualifications for deacons.)

[12] A deacon must be faithful to his wife and must manage his children and his household well. [13] Those who have served well gain an excellent standing and great assurance in their faith in Christ Jesus.

I Timothy 4 addresses the latter times. I and II Timothy are truly Living Letters that speak to us today because all indicators show we may be living in the last days. Today, as in the day of Paul, unbiblical doctrines are appearing. The best way to combat error is by constantly restating the simple Gospel truth. The Bible, itself, will do the job if we will read and share it.

I Tim. 4:1: The Spirit clearly says that in later times some will abandon the faith and follow deceiving spirits and things taught by demons. [2] Such teachings come through hypocritical liars, whose consciences have been seared as with a hot iron.

[6] If you point these things out to the brothers and sisters you will be a good minister of Christ Jesus, nourished on the truths of the faith and of the good teaching that you have followed.

I Timothy 4

I must never despise one's youth

If he be an example of purity and truth.

God can give a gift regardless of age,

Experience, or monetary advantage.

[12] Don't let anyone look down on you because you are young, but set an example for the believers in speech, in conduct, in love, in faith and in purity. [13] Until I come, devote yourself to the public reading of Scripture, to preaching and to teaching. [14] Do not neglect your gift, which was given you through prophecy when the body of elders laid their hands on you.

[15] Be diligent in these matters; give yourself wholly to them, so that everyone may see your progress. [16] Watch your life and doctrine closely. Persevere in them, because if you do, you will save both yourself and your hearers.

I Timothy 5: *(We are told to treat older men and women with respect, to help those widows who are really in need, and to pay our preachers well.)*

Do not rebuke an older man harshly, but exhort him as if he were your father. Treat younger men as brothers, [2] older women as mothers, and younger women as sisters, with absolute purity. [3] Give proper recognition to those widows who are really in need. We are told how to discern which are "widows indeed."

[16] If any woman who is a believer has widows in her care, she should continue to help them and not let the church be burdened with them, so that the church can help those widows who are really in need.

[17] The elders who direct the affairs of the church well are worthy of double honor, especially those whose work is preaching and teaching. [18] For Scripture says, "Do not muzzle an ox while it is treading out the grain," and "The worker deserves his wages"

I Timothy 6: *(On several occasions Paul said to become free of slavery if you can, but if not, become a good slave. Christianity abolished slavery by teaching the doctrine of human brotherhood.)*

All who are under the yoke of slavery should consider their masters worthy of full respect, so that God's name and our teaching may not be slandered. ²Those who have believing masters should not show them disrespect just because they are fellow believers. Instead, they should serve them even better because their masters are dear to them as fellow believers and are devoted to the welfare of their slaves.

False Teachers and the Love of Money: ⁶But godliness with contentment is great gain. ⁷For we brought nothing into the world, and we can take nothing out of it. ⁸But if we have food and clothing, we will be content with that. ⁹Those who want to get rich fall into temptation and a trap and into many foolish and harmful desires that plunge people into ruin and destruction. ¹⁰For the love of money is a root of all kinds of evil. Some people, eager for money, have wandered from the faith and pierced themselves with many griefs.

Final Charge to Timothy

¹¹But you, man of God, flee from all this, and pursue righteousness, godliness, faith, love, endurance and gentleness. ¹²Fight the good fight of the faith. Take hold of the eternal life to which you were called when you made your good confession in the presence of many witnesses. ¹³In the sight of God, who gives life to everything, and of Christ Jesus. . .I charge you ¹⁴to keep this command without spot or blame until the appearing of our Lord Jesus Christ. . . .¹⁷Command those who are rich in this present world not to be arrogant nor to put their hope in wealth, which is so uncertain, but to put their hope in God, who richly provides us with everything for our enjoyment. ¹⁸Command them to do good, to be rich in good deeds, and to be generous and willing to share. ¹⁹In this way they will lay up treasure for themselves as a firm foundation for the coming age, so that they may take hold of the life that is truly life.

²⁰Timothy, guard what has been entrusted to your care.

(With what love Paul admonished Timothy! And I, with love to all you Young People that I love, have taught, and have admired, I beg you to guard that which God has entrusted to your care! Only you, with the talents God has given you, can do what God has for you to do.)

THE BOOK OF II TIMOTHY
Jesus is our Mediator and our Faithful Pastor

<u>Theme:</u> Guard the Gospel

Message: The Epistle of II Timothy is the triumphant cry of a dying conqueror. Paul, the author, is awaiting martyrdom in a Roman Prison. He and other Christians are scapegoats for Emperor Nero. In AD 64 much of Rome was destroyed by fire, which was set by Nero, himself. He blamed Christians. Peter, also, was executed at about this time by the Romans. While awaiting execution, Paul wrote to Timothy with urgency, urging him to "keep ablaze the gift of God that is in you" and to "not be ashamed of the testimony of our Lord." Paul told the young man to "Proclaim the Gospel, whether it is convenient or not." He writes Timothy to carry on the work of the Gospel despite persecution.

(I quoted from the New International Version of the Bible in I Timothy, but because I am going to use scriptures I've memorized when reviewing II Timothy, I will return to my beloved King James Version. II Timothy is rich in memorable verses! Young people, (You are all young to me.) this letter to Timothy is for you.)

II Timothy 1:5, KJV: When I call to remembrance the unfeigned faith that is in thee, which dwelt first in thy grandmother Lois, and thy mother Eunice; and I am persuaded that in thee also. 1:6 Wherefore I put thee in remembrance that thou stir up the gift of God, which is in thee by the putting on of my hands. 1:7: For God hath not given us the spirit of fear; but of power, and of love, and of a sound mind.

II Timothy 1
Grandmother, mother, and son – m –
An unfeigned faith dwelt in each one.
God gave them a spirit of power and a strong mind
Keeping them forever through the love of Jesus kind.

1:8 Be not thou therefore ashamed of the testimony of our Lord, nor of me his prisoner: but be thou partaker of the afflictions of the <u>Gospel</u> according to the power of God; 1:9 Who hath saved us, and called us with an holy calling, not according to our works, but according to his own purpose and grace, which was given us in Christ Jesus before the world began, 1:10 But is now made manifest by the appearing of our Saviour Jesus Christ, who hath abolished death, and hath brought life and immortality to light through the gospel: 1:11 Whereunto I am appointed a preacher, and an <u>apostle</u>, and a teacher of the Gentiles.

1:12: For the which cause I also suffer these things: nevertheless I am not ashamed: for I know whom I have believed, and am persuaded that he is able to keep that which I have committed unto him against that day. 13 Hold fast the form of sound words, which thou hast heard of me, in faith and love which is in Christ Jesus.

II Timothy 2
Work hard so God can say,
"My child, well done."
I could not in this life time repay
The debt I owe his son.

If I suffer and am put in chains,
The word of God ever remains.
I must study to be approved when found.
The word of truth cannot be bound.

Advice to Timothy: II Timothy 2:1-2, KJV: Thou therefore, my son, be strong in the grace that is in Christ Jesus. 2 And the things that thou hast heard of me among many witnesses, the same commit thou to faithful men, who shall be able to teach others also.

Isn't it wonderful that we and our children can receive teaching from the greatest missionary of all time! I would not willingly disobey him, would you? But then, the whole Bible is written by one who has greater authority than Paul!

2:3 Thou therefore endure hardness, as a good soldier of Jesus Christ.

2:11 It is a faithful saying: For if we be dead with him, we shall also live with him: 2:12 If we suffer, we shall also reign with him: if we deny him, he also will deny us: 2:13 If we believe not, yet he abideth faithful: he cannot deny himself.

(Emphasis is always put upon studying the word of God so we can share it with others.) II Timothy 2:15: Study to shew thyself approved unto God, a workman that needeth not to be ashamed, rightly dividing the word of truth.

2:22 Flee also youthful lusts: but follow righteousness, faith, charity, peace, with them that call on the Lord out of a pure heart.

II Timothy 3:1: This know also, that in the last days perilous times shall come. 3:2 For men shall be lovers of their own selves, covetous, boasters, proud, blasphemers, disobedient to parents, unthankful, unholy, 3:3 Without natural affection, trucebreakers, false accusers, incontinent, fierce, despisers of those that are good, 3:4 Traitors, heady, high-minded, lovers of pleasures more than lovers of God; 3:5 Having a form of godliness, but denying the power thereof: from such turn away.

3:10 But thou hast fully known my doctrine, manner of life, purpose, faith, longsuffering, charity, patience, 3:11 Persecutions, afflictions, which came unto me at Antioch, at Iconium, at Lystra; what persecutions I endured: but out of them all the Lord delivered me. 3:12 Yea, and all that will live godly in Christ Jesus shall suffer persecution. 3:13 But evil men and seducers shall wax worse and worse, deceiving, and being deceived.

3:14 But continue thou in the things which thou hast learned and hast been assured of, knowing of whom thou hast learned them; 3:15 And that from a child thou hast known the holy scriptures, which are able to make thee wise unto salvation through faith which is in Christ Jesus. 3:16 All scripture is given by inspiration of God, and is profitable for doctrine, for reproof, for correction, for instruction in righteousness: 3:17 That the man of God may be perfect, throughly furnished unto all good works.

II Timothy 3
Do you learn your Bible in a way that is glib,
Quoting verses easy to say?
Would you have to ad lib
The scripture message you wish to convey?

II Timothy 4
Don't preach the word only when it is convenient
But preach when it is not.
If you wait for a willing recipient,
You may have no audience your message to allot.

1: I charge thee therefore before God, and the Lord Jesus Christ, who shall judge the quick and the dead at his appearing and his kingdom; 4:2 Preach the word; be instant in season, out of season; reprove, rebuke, exhort with all longsuffering and doctrine. 4:3 For the time will come when they will not endure sound doctrine; but after their own lusts shall they heap to themselves teachers, having itching ears; 4:4 And they shall turn away their ears from the truth, and shall be turned unto fables.

4:5 But watch thou in all things, endure afflictions, do the work of an evangelist, make full proof of thy ministry. 4:6 For I am now ready to be offered, and the time of my departure is at hand. 4:7 I have fought a good fight, I have finished my course, I have kept the faith: 4:8 Henceforth there is laid up for me a crown of righteousness, which the Lord, the righteous judge, shall give me at that day: and not to me only, but unto all them also that love his appearing.

(What wonderful assurance of the hope we have when we finish our course of life here on Earth! I have recently been with those who have died or have gone to memorial services, and I feel that even greater is the assurance that those Saints who have gone on before us are receiving their glorious reward. Paul also asked Timothy to come to him shortly and told him to bring the books and parchments. His sharing of the Gospel was more important than his having his physical needs met.)

4:9 Do thy diligence to come shortly unto me: 4:13 The cloak that I left at Troas with Carpus, when thou comest, bring with thee, and the books, but especially the parchments.

4:17 Notwithstanding the Lord stood with me, and strengthened me; that by me the preaching might be fully known, and that all the Gentiles might hear: and I was delivered out of the mouth of the lion. 18 And the Lord shall deliver me from every evil work, and will preserve me unto his heavenly kingdom: to whom be glory for ever and ever. Amen.

(Paul summed up what we should be doing until the Lord returns. What is the whole Gospel?

1. Love God and love your neighbor. (When you do this you will keep the Ten Commandments.)
2. Keep the Golden Rule: Do to others as you want them to do to you.
3. Always be ready to give an answer and tell others why you have The Hope within You. *(All of these are the Gospel of Jesus Christ.)*

THE BOOK OF TITUS

Theme. Be devoted to what is good.

Message: Paul wrote to Titus, who, like Timothy, is his "son in Jesus Christ." After Paul's first imprisonment in Rome, the three of them went to Crete on a mission tour. Titus stayed to firmly establish the new churches in Crete, and Timothy went to Ephesus. Paul wrote letters from Macedonia to Titus and Timothy. Paul reminds Titus of his role: To appoint good leaders who will guide the church wisely and to combat the false teachers found on the Island of Crete.

Like the epistles to Timothy, this letter to Titus emphasizes good works. We are saved by God's grace but because of this we are under strict obligation to do good in order to live productive lives. He tells the qualifications of an elder or bishop. He talks of the power of beautiful lives as the older women and men teach the younger; of obedience to civil authorities, and of the blessed hope; we have in Jesus Christ.

Titus 1:1, KJV: Paul, a servant of God, and an apostle of Jesus Christ, according to the faith of God's elect, and the acknowledging of the truth which is after godliness;. . .[4] To Titus, mine own son after the common faith: I left thee in Crete so that you might set in order the things that are wanting, and ordain elders in every city, as I had appointed thee:

[6] If any be blameless, the husband of one wife, having faithful children not accused of riot or unruly. [7] For a bishop must be blameless, as the steward of God; not self-willed, not soon angry, not given to wine, no striker, not given to filthy lucre; [8] But a lover of hospitality, a lover of good men, sober, just, holy, temperate; [9] Holding fast the faithful word as he hath been taught, that he may be able by sound doctrine both to exhort and to convince the gainsayers.

15. Unto the pure all things are pure: but unto them that are defiled and unbelieving is nothing pure; but even their mind and conscience is defiled. [16] They profess that they know God; but in works they deny him, being abominable, and disobedient, and unto every good work reprobate.

The Importance of Mentors and Sound Teaching

Titus 2, KJV: But speak thou the things which become sound doctrine: [2] That the aged men be sober, grave, temperate, sound in faith, in charity, in patience. [3] The aged women likewise, that they be in behavior as becometh holiness, not false accusers, not given to much wine, teachers of good things; [4] That they may teach the young women to be sober, to love their husbands, to love their children, [5] To be discreet, chaste, keepers at home, good, obedient to their own husbands, that the word of God be not blasphemed.

[6] Young men likewise exhort to be sober minded. [7] In all things shewing thyself a pattern of good works: in doctrine shewing incorruptness, gravity, sincerity, [8] Sound speech,

that cannot be condemned; that he that is of the contrary part may be ashamed, having no evil thing to say of you shewing all good fidelity; that they may adorn the doctrine of God our Saviour in all things.[11] For the grace of God that brings salvation hath appeared to all men, [12] Teaching us that, denying ungodliness and worldly lusts, we should live soberly, righteously, and godly, in this present world; [13] Looking for that blessed hope, and the glorious appearing of the great God and our Saviour Jesus Christ; [4] Who gave himself for us, that he might redeem us from all iniquity, and purify unto himself a peculiar people, zealous of good works. [15] These things speak, and exhort, and rebuke with all authority.

The Fellowship of Christian Athlete's Bible, <u>God's Game Plan</u>, has a lesson on Titus 2, entitled "Just Say 'No.'" It emphasizes the importance of determining the areas in which we need more self-control in today's society. It asks, "What difference can our salvation make in our behavior and our ability to say, "No?" Titus 2:11-12: [11] For the grace of God that bringeth salvation hath appeared to all men, [12] Teaching us that, denying ungodliness and worldly lusts, we should live soberly, righteously, and godly, in this present world;

Titus 3, KJV: The Importance of Good Works:

Put them in mind to be subject to principalities and powers, to obey magistrates, to be ready to every good work, [2] To speak evil of no man, to be no brawlers, but gentle, shewing all meekness unto all men. [3] For we ourselves also were sometimes foolish, disobedient, deceived, serving divers lusts and pleasures, living in malice and envy, hateful, and hating one another.

[4] But after that the kindness and love of God our Saviour toward man appeared, [5] Not by works of righteousness which we have done, but according to his mercy he saved us, by the washing of regeneration, and renewing of the Holy Ghost; [6] Which he shed on us abundantly through Jesus Christ our Saviour;

[7] That being justified by his grace, we should be made heirs according to <u>the hope of eternal life</u>. [8] They which have believed in God must be careful to maintain good works. These things are good and profitable unto men.

Hope of Eternal Life: Paul, as he neared the end of his life, kept his eyes fixed on heaven. See II Corinthians 5:1-2; Romans 8:18, 23; Philippians 3:20-21; II Timothy 4:6-9. As we near the end of life, we think more of Heaven. Doesn't heaven get nearer and dearer as more of our loved ones are there? When we were younger, Heaven may have seemed like a fairy-tale kingdom, but when our loved ones are there, it becomes so real. Also, when our precious family is there, it is our connection to them. It is the thread of hope that we hang on to knowing that our relationship is not over. The wonderful old hymns about heaven have a greater impact.

Sing the wondrous love of Jesus, Sing His mercy and His grace.
In the mansions bright and blessed He'll prepare for us a place.
When we all get to heaven, What a day of rejoicing that will be!
When we all see Jesus, We'll sing and shout the victory.

THE BOOK OF PHILEMON
Theme: Radical Forgiveness

Message: Paul wrote this private letter to a friend, Philemon, on behalf of a Onesimus, a run-away slave. At this time in the Roman Empire, runaway slaves were subject to severe punishment or death. We see Christian compassion in action as Paul deprives himself of help from Onesimus and promises to pay Philemon for any loss caused to him.

Philemon 1, KJV: Paul, a prisoner of Jesus Christ, and Timothy our brother, unto Philemon our dearly beloved, and fellow laborer, [3] Grace to you, and peace, from God our Father and the Lord Jesus Christ. [4] I thank my God, making mention of thee always in my prayers, [5] Hearing of thy love and faith, which thou hast toward the Lord Jesus, and toward all saints; [6] That the communication of thy faith may become effectual by the acknowledging of every good thing which is in you in Christ Jesus.

[10] I beseech thee for my son Onesimus, whom I have begotten in my bonds:..

[15] For perhaps he therefore departed for a season, that thou should receive him forever; [16] Not now as a servant, but above a servant, a brother beloved, specially to me, but how much more unto thee, both in the flesh, and in the Lord? [17] If thou count me therefore a partner, receive him as myself. [18] If he hath wronged thee, or oweth thee ought, put that on mine account;

[19] I Paul have written it with mine own hand, I will repay it: [21] Having confidence in thy obedience I wrote unto thee, knowing that thou wilt also do more than I say..

[25] The grace of our Lord Jesus Christ be with your spirit. Amen.

Remember that in Philemon, we see Jesus as our mediator. Paul is a mediator for Onesimus. We have much that must be forgiven, and Jesus is High Priest, our mediator, if we will accept Him.

Philemon, By MK Gage

This one wish for me grant,
That you will lovingly receive your run-away servant.
Remember, you owe me
For your very soul.

THE BOOK OF HEBREWS
In Hebrews, Jesus is the everlasting covenant

Theme: The superiority of Jesus

Message: Hebrews is written to Christian Jews who are suffering constant injustices for being Christians. The author (probably Paul) fears they are tempted to give up. He told them to persevere and hold unswervingly to the hope we possess lest they compromise Christ and lose all the enormous blessings of the new covenant.

Purpose: *Paul prepared Jewish Christians for the destruction of Jerusalem. They had thought their Messiah, Jesus, would reign over Jerusalem. They were zealous in continuing temple rites and sacrifices. This letter to the Hebrew people was to explain that animal sacrifices were no longer needed. They had been a picture of the coming sacrifice of Jesus. God's people must look now only to Christ for redemption and salvation. Christ would become our high priest. We need no priest to approach God. We are priests and Jesus is our high priest, who makes intercession for us.*

<u>The Deity of Christ:</u> *H*ebrews 1, KJV: In the past God spoke to our forefathers through the prophets at many times and in various ways, [2] but in these last days he has spoken to us by his Son, whom he appointed heir of all things, and through whom he made the universe.[3] The Son is the radiance of God's glory and the exact representation of his being, sustaining all things by his powerful word. After he had provided purification for sins, he sat down at the right hand of the Majesty in heaven. *As humans, we are to reflect God's glory and praise his glory. (*Warren*: The Purpose-Driven Life.)*

Hebrews 2:3: How shall we escape if we ignore such a great salvation? This salvation, which was first announced by the Lord, was confirmed to us by those who heard him.

Why did God allow Jesus to become human? "What is man that you are mindful of him, the son of man that you care for him?[ ] You made him a little lower than the angels; you crowned him with glory and honor [8] and put everything under his feet[9] But we see Jesus, who was made a little lower than the angels, now crowned with glory and honor because he suffered death, so that by the grace of God he might taste death for everyone.

[17...] .he had to be made like his brothers in every way, in order that he might become a merciful and faithful high priest in service to God, and that he might make atonement for the sins of the people. Because he himself suffered when he was tempted, he is able to help those who are being tempted.

Hebrews 3:12, KJV: See to it, brothers, that none of you has a sinful, unbelieving heart that turns away from the living God. [13] But encourage one another daily, as long as it is called Today, so that none of you may be hardened by sin's deceitfulness. [14] We have come to share in Christ if we hold firmly till the end the confidence we had at first.

Unity of the Scriptures [15] As has just been said: "Today, if you hear his voice, do not harden your hearts as you did in the rebellion."[16] Who were they who heard and rebelled?

Were they not all those Moses led out of Egypt? [17.] And with whom was he angry for forty years? Was it not with those who sinned, whose bodies fell in the desert? [18.] And to whom did God swear that they would never enter his rest if not to those who disobeyed? [19.] So we see that they were not able to enter, because of their unbelief. *(So the author of Hebrews did not want them to lose all their promised blessings like the Israelites did under the first covenant.)*

Hebrews 4:1:[KJV;] Therefore, since the promise of entering his rest still stands, let us be careful that none of you be found to have fallen short of it. [2.] For we also have had the gospel preached to us, just as they did; but the message they heard was of no value to them, because those who heard did not combine it with faith. "Today, if you hear his voice, do not harden your hearts."

[12.] For the word of God is living and active. Sharper than any double-edged sword, it penetrates even to dividing soul and spirit, joints and marrow; it judges the thoughts and attitudes of the heart. [13.] Nothing in all creation is hidden from God's sight. Everything is uncovered and laid bare before the eyes of him to whom we must give account.

Christ is our High Priest.

[14.] Therefore, since we have a great high priest who has gone through the heavens, Jesus the Son of God, let us hold firmly to the faith we profess. [15.] For we do not have a high priest who is unable to sympathize with our weaknesses, but we have one who has been tempted in every way, just as we are—yet was without sin. [16.] Let us then approach the throne of grace with confidence, so that we may receive mercy and find grace to help us in our time of need.

Christ Compared to the Levitical Priests: Hebrews 5:1: Every high priest is selected from among men and is appointed to represent them in matters related to God, to offer gifts and sacrifices for sins. [2.] He is able to deal gently with those who are ignorant and are going astray, since he himself is subject to weakness.[3.] This is why he has to offer sacrifices for his own sins, as well as for the sins of the people. [4.] No one takes this honor upon himself; he must be called by God, just as Aaron was. [5.] So Christ also did not take upon himself the glory of becoming a high priest. But God said to him, "You are my Son; today I have become your Father. You are a priest forever, in the order of Melchizedek."

[8.] Although he was a son, he learned obedience from what he suffered.[9.] and, once made perfect, he became the source of eternal salvation for all who obey him and was designated by God to be high priest in the order of Melchizedek.

The Hebrews are encouraged by the fact that God kept his promise to Abraham:

Hebrews 6:10: God is not unjust; he will not forget your work and the love you have shown him as you have helped his people and continue to help them. [11.] We want each of you to show this same diligence to the very end, in order to make your hope sure. [13.] When God made his promise to Abraham, since there was no one greater for him to swear by, he swore by himself, saying, "I will surely bless you and give you many descendants." [15.] And so after waiting patiently, Abraham received what was promised.

[19.] We have this hope as an anchor for the soul, firm and secure. It enters the inner sanctuary behind the curtain, where Jesus, who went before us, has entered on our behalf. He has become a high priest forever, in the order of Melchizedek.

(The greatness of Melchizedek, who met Abraham, who was without father or mother and without beginning of days or end of days is described in Hebrews 7:1-4.). If perfection could have been attained through the Levitical priesthood (for on the basis of it the law was given to the people), why was there still need for another priest to come—one in the order of Melchizedek, not in the order of Aaron?

Jesus has become the guarantee of a better covenant. Now there have been many of those priests, since death prevented them from continuing in office; [24.] but because Jesus lives forever, he has a permanent priesthood. [25.] Therefore he is able to save completely those who come to God through him, because he always lives to intercede for them.[26.] Such a high priest meets our need—one who is holy, blameless, pure, set apart from sinners, exalted above the heavens. [27.] Unlike the other high priests, he does not need to offer sacrifices day after day, first for his own sins, and then for the sins of the people. He sacrificed for their sins once for all when he offered himself. [28.] For the law appoints as high priests men who are weak; but the oath, which came after the law, appointed the Son, who has been made perfect forever.

In Hebrews 7 we find the Levitical Priesthood was temporary, but Christ's Priesthood is Eternal.

Hebrews 8:1, KJV: The point of what we are saying is this: We do have such a high priest, who sat down at the right hand of the throne of the Majesty in heaven, and who serves in the sanctuary, the true tabernacle set up by the Lord, not by man.

Chapter 8 reviews why God made a new covenant with Israel. The old covenant was centered around the tabernacle, the Ten Commandments, and blood sacrifices. The first covenant was written on stone. Christ's laws would be written on the heart.

Hebrews 8:6: The ministry Jesus has received is as superior to theirs as the covenant of which he is mediator is superior to the old one, and it is founded on better promises. I will make a new covenant with the house of Israel and with the house of Judah, not be like the covenant I made with their forefathers when I took them by the hand to lead them out of Egypt, because they did not remain faithful to my covenant, and I turned away from them, declares the Lord. [10.] This is the covenant I will make with the house of Israel after that time, declares the Lord. I will put my laws in their minds and write them on their hearts. I will be their God, and they will be my people. [12.] For I will forgive their wickedness and will remember their sins no more."

Christ and the Tabernacle: Hebrews 9:1: Now the first covenant had regulations for worship and also an earthly sanctuary. [2.] A tabernacle was set up. In its first room were the lampstand, the table and the consecrated bread; this was called the Holy Place. [7.] But only the high priest entered the inner room, and that only once a year, and never without blood, which he offered for himself and for the sins the people had committed in ignorance.

[11.] When Christ came as high priest of the good things that are already here, he went through the greater and more perfect tabernacle that is not man-made, that is to say, not a part of this creation. [12.] He did not enter by means of the blood of goats and calves; but he entered the Most Holy Place once for all by his own blood, having obtained eternal redemption.

Christ became the sacrificial lamb and offered His own blood as redemption for all of mankind. [13.] The blood of goats and bulls and the ashes of a heifer sprinkled on those who are ceremonially unclean sanctify them so that they are outwardly clean. [14.] How much more, then, will the blood of Christ, who through the eternal Spirit offered himself unblemished to God, cleanse our consciences from acts that lead to death, so that we may serve the living God!

[15.] For this reason Christ is the mediator of a new covenant, that those who are called may receive the promised eternal inheritance—now that he has died as a ransom to set them free from the sins committed under the first covenant. [18.] This is why even the first covenant was not put into effect without blood.

[25.] Nor did he enter heaven to offer himself again and again, the way the high priest enters the Most Holy Place every year with blood that is not his own. [25.] So Christ was sacrificed once to take away the sins of many people; and he will appear a second time, not to bear sin, but to bring salvation to those who are waiting for him

Hebrews 10:1: The law is only a shadow of the good things that are coming—not the realities themselves. For this reason it can never, by the same sacrifices repeated endlessly year after year, make perfect those who draw near to worship.

[12.] But when this priest had offered for all time one sacrifice for sins, he sat down at the right hand of God. [15.] The Holy Spirit also testifies to us about this. First he says: [16.]"This is the covenant I will make with them after that time, says the Lord. I will put my laws in their hearts, and I will write them on their minds."

(The Hebrews are encouraged during persecution because of the superiority of the new covenant: Better hope, better promises, better possessions in heaven, better country: heaven, better resurrection.)

21. . . .since we have a great priest over the house of God, [22] let us draw near to God with a sincere heart in full assurance of faith, having our hearts sprinkled to cleanse us from a guilty conscience and having our bodies washed with pure water. [23.] Let us hold unswervingly to the hope we profess, for he who promised is faithful. [24.] And let us consider how we may spur one another on toward love and good deeds. [25.] Let us not give up meeting together, as some are in the habit of doing, but let us encourage one another—and all the more as you see the Day approaching.

26. If we deliberately keep on sinning after we have received the knowledge of the truth, no sacrifice for sins is left, 27. but only a fearful expectation of judgment and of raging fire that will consume the enemies of God. 28. Anyone who rejected the Law of Moses died without mercy on the testimony of two or three witnesses.

29. How much more severely do you think a man deserves to be punished who has trampled the Son of God under foot, who has treated as an unholy thing the blood of the covenant that sanctified him, and who has insulted the Spirit of grace? 30. For we know him who said, "It is mine to avenge; I will repay," and again, "The Lord will judge his people." It is a dreadful thing to fall into the hands of the living God.

36. You need to persevere so that when you have done the will of God, you will receive what he has promised.

Hebrews Chapter 11 is the Faith Chapter of the Bible.

Because it contains a review of the lives of great Heroes of the faith, it is a favorite of mine and of many students of the Bible. In this chapter, we find The Hall of Faith.
What is faith? Verse 1: Now faith is confidence in what we hope for and assurance about what we do not see. ²This is what the ancients were commended for. ³By faith we understand that the universe was formed at God's command, so that what is seen was not made out of what was visible.

(I*t was by faith that all the mighty men of God, such as Able, Enoch, and Noah accomplished what they did. HEROES OF THE FAITH are in chapter 11!)*
Hebrews 11: 8: By faith Abraham, when called to go to a place he would later receive as his inheritance, obeyed and went, even though he did not know where he was going. ⁹By faith he made his home in the Promised Land like a stranger in a foreign country; he lived in tents, as did Isaac and Jacob, who were heirs with him of the same promise. ¹⁰For he was looking forward to the city with foundations, whose architect and builder is God¹²And so from this one man came descendants as numerous as the stars in the sky and as countless as the sand on the seashore.¹³All these people were still living by faith when they died. They did not receive the things promised; they only saw them at a distance.

By faith Abraham, when God tested him, offered Isaac as a sacrifice. He who had embraced the promises was about to sacrifice his one and only son, ¹⁸even though God had said to him, "It is through Isaac that your offspring will be reckoned."

²²By faith Joseph, when his end was near, spoke about the exodus of the Israelites from Egypt and gave instructions concerning the burial of his bones.

²⁴By faith Moses, when he had grown up, refused to be known as the son of Pharaoh's daughter. ²⁵He chose to be mistreated along with the people of God rather than to enjoy the fleeting pleasures of sin.²⁶He regarded disgrace for the sake of Christ as of greater value than the treasures of Egypt, because he was looking ahead to his reward. ²⁷By faith he left

Egypt, not fearing the king's anger; he persevered because he saw him who is invisible. [28] By faith he kept the Passover and the application of blood, so that the destroyer of the firstborn would not touch the firstborn of Israel.

[29] By faith the people passed through the Red Sea as on dry land; but when the Egyptians tried to do so, they were drowned. [30] By faith the walls of Jericho fell, after the army had marched around them for seven days.

[32] And what more shall I say? I do not have time to tell about Gideon, Barak, Samson and Jephthah, about David and Samuel and the prophets, [33] who through faith conquered kingdoms, administered justice, and gained what was promised; who shut the mouths of lions, [34] quenched the fury of the flames, and escaped the edge of the sword; whose weakness was turned to strength; and who became powerful in battle and routed foreign armies. [35] Women received back their dead, raised to life again. There were others who were tortured, refusing to be released so that they might gain an even better resurrection. [36] Some faced jeers and flogging, and even chains and imprisonment.[37] They were put to death by stoning; they were sawed in two; they were killed by the sword. *Don't these verses say volumes!*

[39] These were all commended for their faith, yet none of them received what had been promised, [40] since God had planned something better for us so that only together with us would they be made perfect.

The people in the Hall of Faith did not live to see the Promised Messiah! How much more faith should we have who are under the covenant of Grace!

Keep your eyes on Jesus: Hebrews 12: 1: Therefore, since we are surrounded by such a great cloud of witnesses, let us throw off everything that hinders and the sin that so easily entangles. And let us run with perseverance the race marked out for us, [2] fixing our eyes on Jesus, the pioneer and perfecter of faith. For the joy set before him he endured the cross, scorning its shame, and sat down at the right hand of the throne of God. *(What motivation this should be! We should run this race in the game of life with all we have!)*

My son, do not make light of the Lord's discipline,
and do not lose heart when he rebukes you,
[6] because the Lord disciplines the one he loves,
and he chastens everyone he accepts as his son."

[22] But you have come to Mount Zion, to the city of the living God, the heavenly Jerusalem. You have come to thousands upon thousands of angels in joyful assembly. *Jerusalem will be the city capital.*

(Our good Lord disciplines us who are His children) [7] Endure hardship as discipline; God is treating you as his children. For what children are not disciplined by their father? [8] If you are not disciplined—and everyone undergoes discipline—then you are not legitimate, not true sons and daughters at all. [11] No discipline seems pleasant at the time, but painful. Later on, however, it produces a harvest of righteousness and peace for those who have been trained by it.

[14] Make every effort to live in peace with everyone and to be holy; without holiness no one will see the Lord. . . .[28] Therefore, since we are receiving a kingdom that cannot be shaken, let us be thankful, and so worship God acceptably with reverence and awe, [29] for our "God is a consuming fire."[f]

Concluding Exhortations: *This is truly a living letter, because this is for all of us today.* Hebrews 13:1: Keep on loving one another as brothers and sisters. [2] Do not forget to show hospitality to strangers, for by so doing some people have shown hospitality to angels without knowing it. [3] Continue to remember those in prison as if you were together with them in prison, and those who are mistreated as if you yourselves were suffering.

[4] Marriage should be honored by all, and the marriage bed kept pure, for God will judge the adulterer and all the sexually immoral. [5] Keep your lives free from the love of money and be content with what you have, because God has said, "Never will I leave you; never will I forsake you."

[15] Through Jesus, therefore, let us continually offer to God a sacrifice of praise—the fruit of lips that openly profess his name. [16] And do not forget to do good and to share with others, for with such sacrifices God is pleased. [17] Have confidence in your leaders and submit to their authority, because they keep watch over you as those who must give an account.

Benediction and Final Greetings: [20] Now may the God of peace, who through the blood of the eternal covenant brought back from the dead our Lord Jesus, that great Shepherd of the sheep, [21] equip you with everything good for doing his will, and may he work in us what is pleasing to him, through Jesus Christ, to whom be glory for ever and ever. Amen.

(These final words were written shortly before Jerusalem was destroyed and the Jewish state was swept away.)

THE BOOK OF JAMES
In James, Jesus is the one who heals the sick

Theme: Christianity in Action

James has the following concerns: The relationship between the rich and poor; the use and abuse of speech, ethical behavior and how it affects the Day of Judgment, and the relationship of faith and works. James asserted that works are the outward evidence of inner faith. Works make faith visible to others.

I taught James to youth as the January Bible Study when our daughter, Lolly, and Jay Dale Posey were juniors in high school. I learned so much, and the large group of youth did well in a program for the church, as we used problems from their lives to demonstrate the teachings in James.

James 1, KJV: My brethren, count it all joy when ye fall into divers temptations; [3] Knowing this, that the trying of your faith worketh patience. [4] But let patience have her perfect work, that ye may be perfect and entire, wanting nothing.

[5] If any of you lack wisdom, let him ask of God, that giveth to all men liberally, and upbraideth not, and it shall be given him. Let the brother of low degree rejoice in that he is exalted: [10] But the rich, in that he is made low: because as the flower of the grass he shall pass away.

[12] Blessed is the man that endureth temptation: for when he is tried, he shall receive the crown of life, which the Lord hath promised to them that love him.

[13] Let no man say when he is tempted, I am tempted of God: for God cannot be tempted with evil, neither tempteth he any man: [14] But every man is tempted, when he is drawn away of his own lust, and enticed. [15] Then when lust hath conceived, it bringeth forth sin: and sin, when it is finished, bringeth forth death.

But be ye doers of the word, and not hearers only, deceiving your own selves.

[26] If any man among you seem to be religious, and bridleth not his tongue, but deceiveth his own heart, this man's religion is vain. [27] Pure religion and undefiled before God and the Father is this, To visit the fatherless and widows in their affliction, and to keep himself unspotted from the world.

My brethren, have not the faith of our Lord Jesus Christ, the Lord of glory, with respect of persons. [2] For if there come unto your assembly a man with a gold ring, in goodly apparel, and there come in also a poor man in vile raiment;

[3] And ye have respect to him that weareth the gay clothing, and say unto him, Sit thou here in a good place; and say to the poor, Stand thou there, or sit here under my footstool: Harken, my beloved brethren, Hath not God chosen the poor of this world rich in faith, and heirs of the kingdom which he hath promised to them that love him?

[8] If ye fulfill the royal law according to the scripture, Thou shalt love thy neighbour as thyself, ye do well: [9] But if ye have respect to persons, ye commit sin, and are convinced of the law as transgressors.

[10] For whosoever shall keep the whole law, and yet offend in one point, he is guilty of all. [17] Even so faith, if it hath not works, is dead, being alone.

[18] Yea, a man may say, Thou hast faith, and I have works. shew me thy faith without thy works, and I will shew thee my faith by my works. [19] Thou believest that there is one God; thou doest well: the devils also believe, and tremble. [20] But wilt thou know, O vain man, that faith without works is dead? And the scripture was fulfilled which saith, Abraham believed God, and it was imputed unto him for righteousness: and he was called the Friend of God.

James 3:5, KJV Even so the tongue is a little member, and boasteth great things. Behold, how great a matter a little fire kindleth! 6 And the tongue is a fire, a world of iniquity: so is the tongue among our members, that it defileth the whole body, and setteth on fire the course of nature; and it is set on fire of hell. But the tongue can no man tame; it is an unruly evil, full of deadly poison.

10 Out of the same mouth proceedeth blessing and cursing. My brethren, these things ought not so to be. 11 Doth a fountain send forth at the same place sweet water and bitter? 12 Can the fig tree, my brethren, bear olive berries? either a vine, figs? 13. Who is a wise man and endued with knowledge among you? let him shew out of a good conversation his works with meekness of wisdom.

14 But if ye have bitter envying and strife in your hearts, glory not, and lie not against the truth. 15 This wisdom descendeth not from above, but is earthly, sensual, devilish. 17 But the wisdom that is from above is first pure, then peaceable, gentle, and easy to be entreated, full of mercy and good fruits, without partiality, and without hypocrisy.

James 4, KJV [3] Ye ask, and receive not, because ye ask amiss, that ye may consume *it* upon your lusts. [4] Ye adulterers and adulteresses, know ye not that the friendship of the world is enmity with God? Whosoever therefore will be a friend of the world is the enemy of God.

[7] Submit yourselves therefore to God. Resist the devil, and he will flee from you. [8] Draw nigh to God, and he will draw nigh to you.. . .10 Humble yourselves in the sight of the Lord, and he will lift you up.

14b: For what is life? It is a vapor that appears for a little time, and then vanishes away. *Yes, life on this earth is but a vapor. This life is just preparation for eternity. We were made to last forever. When we realize life is preparation for eternity, we will start living a Purpose Driven Life (Rick Warren, 2002). Our purpose is to glorify God. We glorify God by loving him, by learning to love other people, and by becoming like Christ. We glorify God when we serve others and when we tell others about Him. Our relationship to God now will determine our relationship to him in eternity. Everything we do now has eternal implications. In eternity, we must be prepared to answer 2 crucial questions that God will ask:*

1. *What did you do with my Son, Jesus Christ?*
2. *What did you do with your life?*
   The answer to the first question will determine <u>where</u> you spend eternity.
   The answer to the second question will determine <u>what you will do</u> in eternity.

17. Therefore to him that knoweth to do good, and doeth it not, to him it is sin.

James 5: 26, KJV Confess your faults one to another, and pray one for another, that you may be healed. The effectual fervent prayer of a righteous man availeth much. (*Herein is a wonderful promise accompanied by action on our part?*)

BOOKS OF I & II PETER
In I & II Peter, Jesus is our Shepherd.

Theme: Hope in the midst of suffering

In the year 64 AD Rome was burned. The Christians were blamed for it, and persecution resulted. The Apostle Peter wrote to Christians encouraging them and telling them to rejoice in persecution. In Peter, we can find the purpose of life's trials.

The Unity of the Bible: Peter is familiar with Paul's writings, and we see parallels to Romans, Hebrews, and Ephesians. Also quotes from the Old Testament, especially from Isaiah, exist.

I Pater 1:3-25, KJV 3 Blessed be the God and Father of our Lord Jesus Christ, which according to his abundant mercy hath begotten us again unto a lively hope by the resurrection of Jesus Christ from the dead, 4 To an inheritance incorruptible, and undefiled, and that fadeth not away, reserved in heaven for you, 5 Who are kept by the power of God through faith unto salvation ready to be revealed in the last time.

6 Wherein ye greatly rejoice, though now for a season, if need be, ye are in heaviness through manifold temptations: 7 That the trial of your faith, being much more precious than of gold that perisheth, though it be tried with fire, might be found unto praise and honor and glory at the appearing of Jesus Christ: 8 Whom having not seen, ye love; in whom, though now ye see him not, yet believing, ye rejoice with joy unspeakable and full of glory: 9 Receiving the end of your faith, even the salvation of your souls.

18 Forasmuch as ye know that ye were not redeemed with corruptible things, as silver and gold, from your vain conversation received by tradition from your fathers; 19 But with the precious blood of Christ, as of a lamb without blemish and without spot:

23 Being born again, not of corruptible seed, but of incorruptible, by the word of God, which liveth and abideth for ever. 24 For all flesh is as grass, and all the glory of man as the flower of grass. The grass withereth, and the flower thereof falleth away: 25 But the word of the Lord endureth for ever. And this is the word which by the gospel is preached unto you.

(What words of wisdom are in I Peter, chapter 1. Then in Chapter 2, verses 1-8, we are told to grow in Christ and to become as lively stones, with Jesus as the chief cornerstone of our lives. Peter also tells strangers and pilgrims scattered throughout Asia, as well as Europe, to abstain from fleshly lusts.)

11 Dearly beloved, I beseech you as strangers and pilgrims, abstain from fleshly lusts, which war against the soul; 12 Having your conversation honest among the Gentiles: that, whereas they speak against you as evildoers, they may by your good works, which they shall behold, glorify God in the day of visitation.

13 Submit yourselves to every ordinance of man for the Lord's sake: whether it be to the king, as supreme. . . .7 Honour all men. Love the brotherhood. Fear God. 21. . . .because Christ also suffered for us, leaving us an example, that ye should follow his steps, who did

315

no <u>sin</u>, neither was guile found in his mouth: 24 Who his own self bare our sins in his own body on the tree, that we, being dead to sins, should live unto <u>righteousness</u>: by whose stripes ye were healed.

I Peter 3:1, KJV Likewise, ye wives, be in subjection to your own husbands; that, if any obey not the word, they also may without the word be won by the <u>conversation</u> of the wives.

7 Likewise, ye husbands, dwell with them according to knowledge, giving honour unto the wife, as unto the weaker vessel, and as being heirs together of the <u>grace</u> of life; that your prayers be not hindered. 8 Finally, be ye all of one mind, having compassion one of another, love as brethren, be pitiful, be courteous: 9 Not rendering evil for evil, or railing for railing: but contrariwise blessing; knowing that ye are thereunto called, that ye should inherit a blessing.

15 But sanctify the Lord God in your hearts: <u>and be ready always to give an answer to every man that asketh you a reason of the hope that is in you</u> with <u>meekness</u> and fear: *Yes, this is the reason we "Hide God's Word in our hearts!*

17 For it is better, if the will of God be so, that ye suffer for well doing, than for evil doing.

I Peter 4:1, KJV: Forasmuch then as <u>Christ</u> hath suffered for us in the <u>flesh</u>, arm yourselves likewise with the same mind: for he that hath suffered in the <u>flesh</u> hath ceased from <u>sin</u>;

12. Beloved, think it not strange concerning the fiery trial which is to try you, as though some strange thing happened unto you: 13 But rejoice, inasmuch as ye are partakers of Christ's sufferings; that, when his <u>glory</u> shall be revealed, ye may be glad also with joy. . .16 Yet if any man suffer as a Christian, let him not be ashamed; but let him <u>glorify</u> God on this behalf. Wherefore let them that suffer according to the will of God commit the keeping of their souls to him in well doing, as unto a <u>faithful</u> Creator.

I Peter 5:1—To the elders among you, I appeal as a fellow elder and a witness of Christ's sufferings who also will share in the glory to be revealed: [2] Be shepherds of God's flock that is under your care, watching over them—not because you must, but because you are willing, as God wants you to be; not pursuing dishonest gain, but eager to serve; [3] not lording it over those entrusted to you, but being examples to the flock. [4] And when the Chief Shepherd appears, you will receive the crown of glory that will never fade away.

[5] In the same way, you who are younger, submit yourselves to your elders. All of you clothe yourselves with humility toward one another, because, "God opposes the proud but shows favor to the humble." [6] Humble yourselves, therefore, under God's mighty hand, that he may lift you up in due time. [7] Cast all your anxiety on him because he cares for you. [8] Be alert and of sober mind. Your enemy the devil prowls around like a roaring lion looking for someone to devour. [9] Resist him, standing firm in the faith, because you know that the family of believers throughout the world is undergoing the same kind of sufferings.

24 "The God who made the world and everything in it is the Lord of heaven and earth and does not live in temples built by human hands. 25 And he is not served by human hands, as if he needed anything. Rather, he himself gives everyone life and breath and everything else. 26 From one man he made all the nations, that they should inhabit the whole earth; and he marked out their appointed times in history and the boundaries of their lands. 27 God did this so that they would seek him and perhaps reach out for him and find him, though he is not far from any one of us. 28 'For in him we live and move and have our being.

How I love Peter, the impetuous one who once denied Jesus but became powerful after he was endowed with the Holy Spirit on the day of Pentecost! We, too, have the Holy Spirit to empower us!

THE BOOK OF II PETER

Theme. Be Eager and on your guard:

This book is important for us because it deals with similar issues confronting us today. Peter says we must remain true to the truths we learned from the prophets and from Jesus, our Lord. Chapter 1 is an exhortation to grow in Christian virtues. Written shortly before the Martyrdom of Peter around AD 67.

II Peter 1, KJV Whereby are given unto us exceeding great and precious promises: that by these ye might be partakers of the divine nature, having escaped the corruption of the world through <u>lust</u>.

5 And beside this, giving all diligence, add to your faith virtue; and to virtue knowledge; 6 And to knowledge temperance; and to temperance patience; and to patience godliness; 7 And to godliness brotherly kindness; and to brotherly kindness charity. 8 For if these things be in you, and abound, they make you that ye shall neither be barren nor unfruitful in the knowledge of our Lord Jesus Christ. 10 Therefore, my brothers. Be all the more eager to make your calling and election sure, Fore if you do these things, you will never fall.

13 Yea, I think it meet, as long as I am in this <u>tabernacle</u>, to stir you up by putting you in remembrance; 14 Knowing that shortly I must put off this my <u>tabernacle</u>, even as our Lord <u>Jesus Christ</u> hath shewed me. *(Because Peter refused to stop speaking in the name of Jesus, he was hung on a cross upside down to die shortly after in the year AD 68.)*

<u>Apostasy:</u> *In Chapter 2, Peter warns against false prophets and says those who follow their ways will not be spared from punishment. He said that God did not spare angels who sinned, nor did he spare those in Noah's day. Neither will he spare them (or us) who have heard the truth and turned away from it. But there is hope when we are delivered from temptation. The way the church is to combat apostasy and keep itself pure is to hold fast to the Word of God as given in the Prophets and Apostles.*

II Peter 2:9, KJV The Lord knoweth how to deliver the godly out of temptations, and to reserve the unjust unto the day of judgment to be punished.

II Peter 3:3, KJV Knowing this first, that there shall come in the last days scoffers, walking after their own lusts,

8 But, beloved, be not ignorant of this one thing, that one day is with the Lord as a thousand years, and a thousand years as one day. 9 The Lord is not slack concerning his promise, as some men count slackness; but is longsuffering to us-ward, not willing that any should perish, but that all should come to <u>repentance</u>. 10 But the day of the Lord will come as a thief in the night; in the which the heavens shall pass away with a great noise, and the <u>elements</u> shall melt with fervent heat, the earth also and the works that are therein shall be burned up. 11 Seeing then that all these things shall be dissolved. . . .13 Nevertheless

we, according to his promise, look for new heavens and a new earth, wherein dwelleth righteousness.

18/ But grow in <u>grace</u>, and in the knowledge of our Lord and <u>Savior</u> <u>Jesus</u> <u>Christ</u>. To him be <u>glory</u> both now and forever. <u>Amen</u>.

BOOKS OF I, II, & III JOHN
In John and in Jude, Jesus is the lover coming for his bride.

THE BOOK OF I JOHN

Theme: Walking in the Light

In his old age, John, the Beloved Disciple, said, "This is what it all boils down to: God is light; God is love: Jesus is the Messiah, the Son of God, who came in the flesh; we are God's children; we do not continue in sin, but we love one another

I John 1:1, KJV That which was from the beginning, which we have heard, which we have seen with our eyes, which we have looked upon, and our hands have handled, of the Word of life;

2 (For the life was manifested, and we have seen it, and bear <u>witness</u>, and shew unto you that eternal life, which was with the Father, and was manifested unto us;) 3 That which we have seen and heard declare we unto you, that ye also may have <u>fellowship</u> with us: and truly our <u>fellowship</u> is with the Father, and with his Son <u>Jesus</u> <u>Christ</u>. 4 And these things write we unto you, that your joy may be full.

God is Light: 5 This then is the message which we have heard of him, and declare unto you, that God is light, and in him is no <u>darkness</u> at all. 6 If we say that we have <u>fellowship</u> with him, and walk in <u>darkness</u>, we lie, and do not the truth: 7 But if we walk in the light, as he is in the light, we have <u>fellowship</u> one with another, and the <u>blood</u> of <u>Jesus</u> <u>Christ</u> his Son cleanseth us from all <u>sin</u>.

8 If we say that we have no <u>sin</u>, we deceive ourselves, and the truth is not in us. 9 If we confess our sins, he is <u>faithful</u> and just to forgive us our sins, and to cleanse us from all unrighteousness. 10 If we say that we have not sinned, we make him a liar, and his word is not in us.

I John 1:1, KJV: My little children, these things write I unto you, that ye <u>sin</u> not. And if any man <u>sin</u>, we have an <u>advocate</u> with the Father, <u>Jesus</u> <u>Christ</u> the righteous: 2 And he is the <u>propitiation</u> for our sins: and not for ours only, but also for the sins of the whole world.

3 And hereby we do know that we know him, if we keep his commandments. 4 He that saith, I know him, and keepeth not his commandments, is a liar, and the truth is not in him. . . .9 He that saith he is in the light, and hateth his brother, is in <u>darkness</u> even until now. 10 He that loveth his brother abideth in the light, and there is none occasion of stumbling in him.

15 Love not the world, neither the things that are in the world. If any man love the world, the love of the Father is not in him.

21 I have not written unto you because ye know not the truth, but because ye know it, and that no lie is of the truth. 22 Who is a liar but he that denieth that <u>Jesus</u> is the <u>Christ</u>? He

is <u>antichrist</u> that denieth the Father and the Son. 23 Whosoever denieth the Son, the same hath not the Father: he that acknowledgeth the Son hath the Father also.

Love: I John 3:1, KJV: Behold, what manner of love the Father hath bestowed upon us, that we should be called the sons of God: therefore the world knoweth us not, because it knew him not.

14 We know that we have passed from death unto life, because we love the brethren. He that loveth not his brother abideth in death. . . .16 Hereby perceive we the love of God, because he laid down his life for us: and we ought to lay down our lives for the brethren.

22 And whatsoever we ask, we receive of him, because we keep his commandments, and do those things that are pleasing in his sight. 23 And this is his commandment, that we should believe on the name of his Son <u>Jesus</u> <u>Christ</u>, and love one another, as he gave us commandment. 24 And he that keepeth his commandments dwelleth in him, and he in him. And hereby we know that he abideth in us, by the <u>Spirit</u> which he hath given us.

I John 4:4, KJV Ye are of God, little children, and have overcome them: because greater is he that is in you, than he that is in the world.

Here is the great test. Do we know God? John 4:7-8 Beloved, let us love one another: for love is of God; and every one that loveth is born of God, and knoweth God. 8 He that loveth not knoweth not God; for God is love. 10 Herein is love, not that we loved God, but that he loved us, and sent his Son to be the <u>propitiation</u> for our sins. 11 Beloved, if God so loved us, we ought also to love one another.

15 Whosoever shall confess that <u>Jesus</u> is the Son of God, God dwelleth in him, and he in God. 20 If a man say, I love God, and hateth his brother, he is a liar: for he that loveth not his brother whom he hath seen, how can he love God whom he hath not seen? 21 And these commandments have we from him, That he who loveth God love his brother also.

I John 5:2: By this we know that we love the children of God, when we love God and keep his commandments.

<u>Assurance of Eternal Life:</u> I John 5:4, KJV For whatsoever is born of God overcometh the world; and this is the victory that overcomes the world, even our faith. 5. Who is he that overcometh the world, but he that believeth that that Jesus is the Son of God. 12. He that hath the son hath life; and he that hath not the Son of God hath not life.

THE BOOK OF II JOHN

Theme: Hospitality for traveling missionaries

In II John, the author worries about false prophets who are teaching erroneous doctrine, and in III john, he addresses the problem of Christians who failed to provide hospitality for genuine teachers, John is the only apostle left, and he calls himself <u>The Elder</u>.

II John 7: For many deceivers are entered into the world, who confess not that <u>Jesus</u> <u>Christ</u> is come in the <u>flesh</u>. This is a deceiver and an <u>antichrist</u>. 9 Whosoever transgresseth, and abideth not in the doctrine of <u>Christ</u>, hath not God. He that abideth in the doctrine of <u>Christ</u>, he hath both the Father and the Son. 10 If there come any unto you, and bring not this doctrine, receive him not into your house, neither bid him God speed:

THE BOOK OF III JOHN

Theme: <u>Truth</u>

Truth as in verse 1, is a favorite word of John, the Beloved. He used it 20 times in the Gospel of John and 5 times in this very short letter.

III JOHN 1:1-4: The elder unto the well-beloved Gaius, whom I love in the truth. . . . .3 For I rejoiced greatly, when the brethren came and testified of the truth that is in thee, even as thou walkest in the truth. 4 I have no greater joy than to hear that my children walk in truth.

8. We ought to receive such, that we might be fellow-helpers to the truth.

12. Demetrius hath good report of all men, and of the truth itself, yea, and we also bear record, and ye know that our record is true.

Also, John prayed that God would prosper those to whom he wrote. This man who was very close to Christ prayed for temporal as well as spiritual gifts. But this same John warned against loving things of the world in I John 2:15-17.

THE BOOK OF JUDE

In Jude, Jesus is the lover coming for his bride.

Theme: Contend for the faith

Teachers who rejected all moral standards and indulged in all kinds of immoral sexual behavior went from church to church, seeking hospitality. Jude, a brother of James and of Jesus, makes two points: Christians are to contend for the faith and to contend with false Christians.

The Sin and Doom of Ungodly People

Jude 2- 4: Dear friends, although I was very eager to write to you about the salvation we share, I felt compelled to write and urge you to contend for the faith that was once for all entrusted to God's holy people. For there are certain men crept in unawares, who were before of old ordained to this condemnation, ungodly men, turning the <u>grace</u> of our God into lasciviousness, and denying the only Lord God, and our Lord <u>Jesus</u> <u>Christ</u>.

20 But ye, beloved, building up yourselves on your most holy faith, praying in the Holy <u>Ghost</u>, 21 Keep yourselves in the love of God, looking for the <u>mercy</u> of our Lord <u>Jesus</u> <u>Christ</u> unto eternal life. 22 And of some have compassion, making a difference:23 And others save with fear, pulling them out of the fire; hating even the garment spotted by the <u>flesh</u>. 24 Now unto him that is able to keep you from falling, and to present you faultless before the presence of his <u>glory</u> with exceeding joy, 25 To the only <u>wise</u> God our <u>Savior</u>, be <u>glory</u> and majesty, dominion and power, both now and ever. <u>Amen</u>.

THE BOOK OF REVELATION
In the Revelation, Jesus is King of Kings and Lord of Lords!

Theme: Grand Finale of the Bible Story. Christ shall overcome! The New Heavens and the New Earth

Revelation is the only book in the New Testament that is prophetic in nature. Revelation is an explanation of Christ's teachings of things to come. It includes references to the prophets of the Old Testament. It is an apocalyptic book, unveiling future events.

<u>When talking with children</u>, we can stress the wonders that await us in heaven. What will it be like when Jesus begins His reign and His faithful followers join Him there? We will witness with John, the Beloved Disciple, the world that is to come. How wonderful to be a child of God!

History is divided into three ages: The past when God created all things good, the present day of evil, and the future that is characterized by God's presence and power. The day Adam sinned was the turning point when the past era gave way to the present. The *Day of the Lord* is the turning point when the present age will give way to the new age. Christ will return, not as an infant, but as a king before whom the whole creation would bow. Revelation is a book with Christ as the center. The Messiah will be the central figure in The Day of the Lord.

Author, Background, and Setting: Revelation was written by John, the Beloved Disciple, when he was exiled all alone on the Island of Patmos because he wouldn't stop telling about Christ. Persecution of Christians was very severe. Many oppressed people had learned to communicate in cryptograms. John used figures and symbols, which to the enemies were meaningless jargon. But to the suffering Christians, these visions and symbols had much meaning.

John was told by Jesus, himself, what to write. Yes, when John was there on the Island of Patmos to die of exposure and hunger, the Lord Jesus put His right hand on the shoulder of the beloved disciple and said, "Fear not." He then gave him the great outline of the Apocalypse of Jesus Christ: "Write the things that you've seen, and write the things which are, and the things which shall be after these things that are."

According to Hester (1950), The Book of Revelation is made up of seven visions and their messages.

The first vision (Chapters 1 to 3) is that of the triumphant, living Lord who moves among his churches with assurance. The second vision in chapters 4 through 7 is that of the slain Lamb controlling the events of history. The third is that of the seven angels with the seven trumpets in which devastation is visited upon unrepentant people, but at last, victory comes and men worship God. The fourth, found in chapters 12-14, tells of the seven symbolic figures that represent the conflict between good and evil, which ends with victory for righteousness. In Chapters 15-16, we have a fifth vision of the seven angels who came to pour divine wrath upon the earth. Chapters 17-19 give the sixth vision of the judgment of "the great harlot that sits upon many waters." In Chapter 20, we are told of the capturing and the binding of Satan. The seventh vision is a picture of the "consummation of the historical process." (Chapters 21-22.) Here we see the New Heaven and the New Earth and the New Jerusalem coming down out of heaven from God. (pp. 349-350).

Revelation speaks to both the first century struggle of Christians and also to the future when the Lord will return. Some of the passages are the most superb and precious in the Bible. Its glorious visions make it a roadway into the human soul.

Greetings to the Seven Churches: The main emphases of the whole book are included in the greeting. He Who Is, and Who Was and Who Is To Come. Verses 1-4; Jesus the Ruler of the Kings of the Earth (1:5); He Who Freed us from Our Sins with His Blood (1:5); To Him Be Glory and Power for Ever and Ever (1:6); He Is Coming in the Clouds. (1:7)

Some years after Jesus' death, John was brought as a prisoner to be exiled on the Isle of Patmos.

John might have thought about Jesus, his guide, teacher, and friend, when suddenly Jesus, himself appeared to him:

Revelation 1:1: <u>The Revelation of Jesus Christ, which God gave unto him, to show unto his servants things which must shortly come to pass; and he sent and signified *it* by his angel unto his servant John:</u> 4. John, to the seven churches in Asia. The Revelation of Jesus Christ, which God gave Him to show His servants—things which must shortly take place. And He sent and signified *it* by His angel to His servant John, [2] who bore witness to the word of God, and to the testimony of Jesus Christ, to all things that he saw. [3] Blessed *is* he who reads and those who hear the words of this prophecy, and keep those things which are written in it; for the time *is* near.

Greeting the Seven Churches and the first vision

[4] John, to the seven churches which are in Asia: Grace to you and peace from Him who is and who was and who is to come, and from the seven Spirits who are before His throne, [5] and from Jesus Christ, the faithful witness, the firstborn from the dead, and the ruler over the kings of the earth. To Him who loved us and washed us from our sins in His own blood, [6] and has made us kings and priests to His God and Father, to Him *be* glory and dominion forever and ever. Amen.

[7] Behold, He is coming with clouds, and every eye will see Him, even they who pierced Him. And all the tribes of the earth will mourn because of Him. [8] "I am the Alpha and the Omega, *the* Beginning and *the* End," says the Lord, "who is and who was and who is to come, the Almighty."

⁹ I, John, both your brother and companion in the tribulation and kingdom and patience of Jesus Christ, was on the island that is called Patmos for the word of God and for the testimony of Jesus Christ. ¹⁰ I was in the Spirit on the Lord's Day, and I heard behind me a loud voice, as of a trumpet, ¹¹ (*Note that Jesus, himself, is talking.*) saying, "I am the Alpha and the Omega, the First and the Last," and, "What you see, write in a book and send *it* to the seven churches which are in Asia: to Ephesus, to Smyrna, to Pergamum, to Thyatira, to Sardis, to Philadelphia, and to Laodicea."

¹² Then I turned to see the voice that spoke with me. . . . ¹⁷ And when I saw Him, I fell at His feet as dead. But He laid His right hand on me, saying to me, "Do not be afraid; I am the First and the Last. ¹⁸ I *am* He who lives, and was dead, and behold, I am alive forevermore. Amen. And I have the keys of Hades and of Death. ¹⁹ Write the things which you have seen, and the things which are, and the things which will take place after this. ²⁰ The mystery of the seven stars which you saw in My right hand, and the seven golden lampstands: The seven stars are the angels of the seven churches, and the seven lampstands which you saw are the seven churches.

"I am the Alpha and the Omega, the First and the Last," and, "What you see, write in a book and send *it* to the seven churches which are in Asia: to Ephesus, to Smyrna, to Pergamos, to Thyatira, to Sardis, to Philadelphia, and to Laodicea."

Rev. 1:12-19: *John sees his friend and Lord, Jesus Christ* ¹² Then I turned to see the voice that spoke with me. And having turned I saw seven golden lampstands, ¹³ and in the midst of the seven lampstands *One* like the Son of Man, clothed with a garment down to the feet and girded about the chest with a golden band.

. ¹⁷ And when I saw Him, I fell at His feet as dead. But He laid His right hand on me, saying to me, "Do not be afraid; I am the First and the Last. ¹⁸ I *am* He who lives, and was dead, and behold, I am alive forevermore. Amen. And I have the keys of Hades and of Death. ²⁰ The mystery of the seven stars which you saw in My right hand, and the seven golden Write the things which you have seen, and the things which are, and the things which will take place after this.

He wrote the Apocalypse, the Apocalypse of Jesus Christ, which God gave unto him. So, John took up his pen, and he began to write the unveiling of the Lord Jesus Christ in His glory and in His majesty and in His kingdom. He wrote the things that he'd seen, the vision of the glorified Lord walking in the midst of the seven golden lamp stands, Jesus among His churches. And then second, he wrote the things that are, His churches.

John wrote to seven churches, rebuking or complimenting them for those things they did.
Rev. 2:1: To the angel of the church in Ephesus write:
These are the words of him who holds the seven stars in his right hand and walks among the seven golden lampstands. ² I know your deeds, your hard work and your perseverance. I know that you cannot tolerate wicked people, that you have tested those who claim to be

apostles but are not, and have found them false. [3] You have persevered and have endured hardships for my name, and have not grown weary.

[4] Yet I hold this against you: You have forsaken the love you had at first. [5] Consider how far you have fallen! Repent and do the things you did at first. If you do not repent, I will come to you and remove your lampstand from its place.

[8] "To the angel of the church in Smyrna write:

These are the words of him who is the First and the Last, who died and came to life again. [9] I know your afflictions and your poverty—yet you are rich! I know about the slander of those who say they are Jews and are not, but are a synagogue of Satan. [10] Do not be afraid of what you are about to suffer. I tell you, the devil will put some of you in prison to test you, and you will suffer persecution for ten days. Be faithful, even to the point of death, and I will give you life as your victor's crown.

Rev. 3:5, KJV: He that overcometh, the same shall be clothed in white raiment; and I will not blot out his name out of the book of life, but I will confess his name before My Father, and before His angels. (*The Book of Life is spoken of in Daniel 12:1 and in Malachi 3:16. It is referred to as a divine ledger in Exodus 32:32-33. Heaven is inhabited by those written in the Book of Life.*)

Read about other churches in Revelation chapters 2 and 3. It seems that the Church at Laodicea speaks the most to today's churches: [14] "To the angel of the church in Laodicea write:

These are the words of the Amen, the faithful and true witness, the ruler of God's creation. [15] I know your deeds, that you are neither cold nor hot. I wish you were either one or the other! [16] So, because you are lukewarm—neither hot nor cold—I am about to spit you out of my mouth. [17] You say, 'I am rich; I have acquired wealth and do not need a thing.' But you do not realize that you are wretched, pitiful, poor, blind and naked. . . . [19] Those whom I love I rebuke and discipline. So be earnest and repent. [20] Here I am! I stand at the door and knock. If anyone hears my voice and opens the door, I will come in and eat with that person, and they with me. [21] To the one who is victorious, I will give the right to sit with me on my throne, just as I was victorious and sat down with my Father on his throne. Whoever has ears, let them hear what the Spirit says to the churches."

Revelation chapter 1: Poem by MKPG
In your church, is Christ in the midst?
Does the congregation follow as He bidest?
Is it as a candlestick?
With a love light glowing from a trimmed and ready wick?

Revelation Chapter 3:
I know thy works are neither cold nor hot.

For your being lukewarm, I want you not.
If you overcome, you may sit with me on my throne.
If I may come in your heart, I won't leave you alone.

(In the Second Vision, the setting changes from the seven churches to God's throne in heaven.)

In Revelation 4: 1 to 5:15, Jesus is pictured as a victorious Lion.

John heard the great voice saying, "I will show you these things that must be hereafter."

And he showed him the great throne room in which all of creation was worshipping Jesus, saying, "Holy, holy, holy, Lord God Almighty. Who was, and is, and is to come."

[9] Whenever the living creatures give glory, honor and thanks to him who sits on the throne and who lives for ever and ever, [10] the twenty-four elders fall down before Him who sits on the throne and worship him who lives for ever and ever. They lay their crowns before the throne and say:

[11] "You are worthy, our Lord and God, to receive glory and honor and power, for You created all things, and by Your will they were created and have their being."

(We know our purpose is to give glory to Jesus, our Lord, our creator, who is worthy of all praise.)

The Unity of the Bible: *Note in Revelation 5 that Jesus is called the Lion of the Tribe of Judah and the Root of David and is also called a lamb. One of the elders called Christ, "the Lion of the tribe of Judah" and John saw Christ as "a Lamb, looking as if it had been slain." The prophet Isaiah, years before Christ's birth, referred to our Savior as a Lamb. (Isaiah 53) He came as a lamb for the slaughter. One to be sacrificed, to spill His blood, to atone for the sins of the world. John called Him, "the Lamb of God Who takes away the sins of the world."*

Rev. 5:3: Then I saw in the right hand of him who sat on the throne a scroll with writing on both sides and sealed with seven seals. [2] And I saw a mighty angel proclaiming in a loud voice, "Who is worthy to break the seals and open the scroll?" [3] But no one in heaven or on earth or under the earth could open the scroll or even look inside it. [4] I wept and wept because no one was found who was worthy to open the scroll or look inside. [5] Then one of the elders said to me, "Do not weep! See, the Lion of the tribe of Judah, the Root of David, has triumphed. He is able to open the scroll and its seven seals."

[6] Then I saw a Lamb, looking as if it had been slain, standing at the center of the throne, [7] He went and took the scroll from the right hand of Him who sat on the throne. [8] And when He had taken it, the four living creatures and the twenty-four elders fell down before the Lamb. Each one had a harp and they were holding golden bowls full of incense, which are the prayers of God's people. [9] And they sang a new song, saying:

"You are worthy to take the scroll and to open its seals, because You were slain, and with your blood you purchased for God persons from every tribe and language and people and nation. [10] You have made them to be a kingdom and priests to serve our God, and they will reign on the earth."

[11] Then I looked and heard the voice of many angels, numbering thousands upon thousands, and ten thousand times ten thousand. They encircled the throne and the living creatures and the elders. [12] In a loud voice they were saying:

"Worthy is the Lamb, who was slain, to receive power and wealth and wisdom and strength and honor and glory and praise!"

[13] Then I heard every creature in heaven and on earth and under the earth and on the sea, and all that is in them, saying: "To him who sits on the throne and to the Lamb be praise and honor and glory and power, for ever and ever!"

Chapter 5
The lamb that was slain
Was worthy to break the book's seal.
He made us kings and priests to reign.
Before Him the elders sing and kneel.

The Lamb Opens the Seven Seals. The Lamb will now open the seven seals from the scroll, one at a time, and John will tell us what he sees. The period of time John will be observing in Revelation is also spoken of in the prophecies of Daniel and by Jesus in the Olivet discourse (Matthew chapters 24-25). This trilogy of passages from Daniel, Matthew, and Revelation should be studied and correlated by the wise student when seeking truth about these end time events.

Revelation 6:1: And I saw when the Lamb opened one of the seals, and I heard, as it were the noise of thunder, one of the four beasts saying, come and see. 2 And I saw, and behold a white horse: and He that sat on him had a bow; and a crown was given unto Him: and he went forth conquering, and to conquer.

(Each of the 7 seals is opened in chapter 6. In verse 9, we see the fifth seal includes the souls of all of those who were slain for the word of God, and white robes were given to all of them. This should be a scripture of assurance to the millions of Christians who are today being persecuted around the world.)

Revelation 6:9: When he opened the fifth seal, I saw under the altar the souls of those who had been slain because of the word of God and the testimony they had maintained. [10] They called out in a loud voice, "How long, Sovereign Lord, holy and true, until you judge the inhabitants of the earth and avenge our blood?" [11] Then each of them was given a white robe, and they were told to wait a little longer, until the full number of their fellow servants, their brothers and sisters, were killed just as they had been. *From just these 3 verses, we can see much of what the* <u>Present</u> *Heaven will be like!*

According to Alcorn (2004), when the martyrs died on Earth, they relocated in Heaven. They are the same people killed for Christ. Personal history extends back to their lives on earth. They are aware of each other and of their situation on Earth. They asked God to intervene on earth and to act on their behalf. People in the present heaven know what is happening on earth. Those in the present Heaven live in anticipation of the future fulfillment of God's promises. The present Heaven coexists with and watches over an Earth under the Curse, and suffering. These three verses demonstrate a vital connection between the events and people in Heaven and those on Earth. Our sovereign God knows the name and story of every martyr; the same is true of every one of us.

Alcorn believes departed saints currently in the present Heaven do intercede in prayer for those of us who are still on the Earth. (Ephesians 3:15) This is a comfort for me. We all depended upon my mother's prayers. Now I believe Mama is still praying for us! Of course we grieve for our departed loved ones who are in the presence of Christ, we are not to grieve as those who have no hope. Our parting is not the end of our relationship!

When he opened <u>the fifth seal</u>, I saw under the altar the souls of those who had been slain because of the word of God and the testimony they had maintained. 10 They called out in a loud voice, "How long, Sovereign Lord, holy and true, until you judge the inhabitants of the earth and avenge our blood?" 11 Then each of them was given a white robe, and they were told to wait a little longer, until the full number of their fellow servants, their brothers and sisters, were killed just as they had been.

According to Halley's (2007) Bible Handbook, "The Lamb" is Revelation's favorite name for Christ:

The lamb took the sealed book and opened it. The living creatures and elders worshipped the Lamb. 100,000,000 angels worshipped The Lamb. Multitudes from all nations worshipped the lamb. The Lamb leads them to living waters. They overcame Satan by the blood of the lamb. The 144,000 followed the lamb. The lamb is Lord of Lords and King of Kings. The Lamb will be married to his bride, the church. The 12 foundations of the city are named for the 12 apostles of the Lamb. Only those written in the Lamb's book of life shall enter.

Revelation Chapter 7
Water can never wash you clean
And make your heart snow and bright.
When you were sinful and mean,
Only the red blood of the Lamb can bleach your robes white.

Revelation chapters 8-11 include the third vision of the seven angels with the seven trumpets. Here we see calamity and devastation brought upon unrepentant people, but victory comes, and men worship God.

Chapter 8
The smoke of Incense
Is offered with all the saint's prayers.
Together as aromas dispense
Through Heaven, God knows our trials and cares. [3.]

Another angel, who had a golden censer, came and stood at the altar. He was given much incense to offer, with the prayers of all the saints, on the golden altar before the throne. [4.] The smoke of the incense, together with the prayers of the saints, went up before God from the angel's hand.

In chapter 9, the fifth angel opened the seal to the bottomless pit. The description is gruesome. Why will people choose darkness rather than light?

Chapter 9
The men who did not die would not repent
After the terrible plagues God sent.
They continued to worship the work of their hand,
And murder, theft, and sorcery still stand.

There is still one woe left, and it contains the seven vial judgments. We will be told about that later, but before that happens, a mighty angel takes possession of Earth in the name of the Lord. Then John is given additional background information on the events that John saw and heard. According to prophecy in Daniel, this angel is Michael.

Revelation 10:1: And I saw another mighty angel come down from heaven, clothed with a cloud: and a rainbow was upon his head, and his face was as it were the sun, and his feet as pillars of fire:

Just after the blowing of the sixth trumpet that unleashed an army that kills one third of the men on the earth, John sees a mighty angel come down from heaven. His face was as the sun and his feet as pillars of fire

2 And he had in his hand a little book open: and he set his right foot upon the sea, and his left foot on the earth,

The little book has more information about end time prophetic events. The angel puts one foot on the sea and the other on the land. This could mean the angel is proclaiming control over all the Gentile Nations (the sea) as well as the land of Israel. The angel apparently is claiming authority over the whole earth in the name of Jesus.

Revelation 11
A trumpet the seventh angel blew,
And from heaven loud voices did shout.
The kingdom for this world belongs to the Lord we knew.
He is Christ. His reign will never be in doubt.

His servants and prophets shall be given
Rewards if they feared his name.
From the opened temple in Heaven,
Those who destroyed the earth will be put to shame.

Revelation 11:15: And the seventh angel sounded; and there were great voices in heaven, saying, The kingdoms of this world are become the kingdoms of our Lord, and of his Christ; and he shall reign for ever and ever. *(The Hallelujah Chorus!)*

In chapters 12 to 14, we see the fourth vision, which includes the seven symbolic figures that represent the conflict between good and evil. This includes the fall of Satan, who wars against Michael and his angels. It concludes when opposition ceases with victory for righteousness.

Rev. 12:9, KJV The great dragon was cast out, that old serpent, called the Devil, and Satan, which deceiveth the whole world: he was cast out into the earth, and his angels were cast out with him.

12:17: And the dragon was wroth with the woman, and went to make war with the remnant of her seed, which keep the commandments of God, and have the testimony of Jesus Christ.

Chapter 12
How do you slay the dragon?
Not by jumping on a politician's band wagon.
By the blood of the Lamb Satan met defeat.
From heaven's glory he was forced to a fast retreat.

Rev. 13:1, KJV And I stood upon the sand of the sea, and saw a beast rise up out of the sea, having seven heads and ten horns, and upon his horns ten crowns, and upon his heads the name of blasphemy. And they worshipped the dragon which gave power unto the beast: and they worshipped the beast, saying, "Who *is* like unto the beast? Who is able to make war with him?" And there was given unto him a mouth speaking great things and blasphemies; and power was given unto him to continue forty *and* two months. And it was given unto him to make war with the saints, and to overcome them: and power was given him over all kindreds, and tongues, and nations. . . .8 And that dwell upon the earth shall worship him, whose names are not written in the book of life of the Lamb slain from the foundation of the world must be killed with the sword. Here is the patience and the faith of the saints. . . .

14 And deceiveth them that dwell on the earth by *the means of* those miracles which he had power to do in the sight of the beast; saying to them that dwell on the earth, that they should make an image to the beast, which had the wound by a sword, and did live.

And he had power to give life unto the image of the beast, that the image of the beast should both speak, and cause that as many as would not worship the image of the beast should be killed.

16 And he causeth all, both small and great, rich and poor, free and bond, to receive a mark in their right hand, or in their foreheads: And that no man might buy or sell, save he that had the mark, or the name of the beast, or the number of his name.

18 Here is wisdom. Let him that hath understanding count the number of the beast: for it is the number of a man; and his number *is* Six hundred threescore *and* six. (666)

Revelation chapter 13
In the world's future politics
Unless you have the mark of the beast,
Six hundred three score and six,
On your forehead, your buying power will cease.

Revelation 14: John saw a Lamb standing on Mount Zion with 144,000 who had the Father's name written on their foreheads. John heard great music being sung before the throne. [3] And they sang a new song before the throne and before the four living creatures and the elders. No one could learn the song except the 144,000 who had been redeemed from the earth. [6] Then I saw another angel flying in midair, and he had the eternal gospel to proclaim to those who live on the earth—to every nation, tribe, language and people. [7] He said in a loud voice, "Fear God and give him glory, because the hour of his judgment has come. Worship him who made the heavens, the earth, the sea and the springs of water." [8] A second angel followed and said, "'Fallen! Fallen is Babylon the Great, which made all the nations drink the maddening wine of her adulteries.'"

[9] A third angel followed them and said in a loud voice: "If anyone worships the beast and its image and receives its mark on their forehead or on their hand,[10] they, too, will drink the wine of God's fury, which has been poured full strength into the cup of his wrath. They will be tormented with burning sulfur in the presence of the holy angels and of the Lamb.[11] And the smoke of their torment will rise for ever and ever. There will be no rest day or night for those who worship the beast and its image, or for anyone who receives the mark of its name."

Life's Final Beatitude: *Remember the Beatitudes that Jesus gave in the Sermon on the Mount. Here is a final beatitude – for those who die knowing Christ:* Revelation 14:13: Then I heard a voice from heaven say, "Write this. Blessed are the dead who die in the Lord from now on." "Yes," says the Spirit, "they will rest from their labor, for their deeds will follow them."

Vision Five in chapters 15-16 includes a picture of seven angels who came to pour the bowls of wrath upon the earth.

Revelation 15 By Marilyn Paddack Gage
Since I have never sung accompanied by a harp,
I hope I don't sound flat nor sharp,
The songs of Moses and the Lamb I'll sing,
"Just and true are thy ways, my King.:

Revelation 16
Do punishments make men repent?
This question is fuel for argument.
With blood to drink, hail, and heat which didn't relent,
Stiffnecked men blasphemed God for the plagues he sent.

Vision #6 in chapters 17-19 is one of judgment of "the great harlot that sits upon many waters." In chapter 20, we are told of the capturing and the binding of Satan.

Revelation 17
John saw a woman drunk with the blood of the saints,
She had committed fornication with no restraints.
She sat upon a beast full of blasphemy,
On her forehead was written, "MYSTERY."

Revelation 18
Babylon, Alas.
Your proud sinful days are past.
No more shall music be heard.
She will be violently thrown down without a word.

Revelation 19: *The Best is yet to come: The wedding feast of the Lamb. Jesus, the Lamb of God, is the groom, and the church is the bride of Christ.*

The bride will dress in linen white
To be wed to Faithful and True with eyes flaming bright.
In blood the groom's vesture had been dipped.
Blessed are those called to the marriage fellowship.

Make the roar of rushing waters and like loud peals of thunder, shouting:
"Hallelujah! For our Lord God Almighty reigns.
[7] Let us rejoice and be glad and give him glory!
For the wedding of the Lamb has come, and his bride has made herself ready.
[8] Fine linen, bright and clean, was given her to wear."
(Fine linen stands for the righteous acts of God's holy people.)

[9] Then the angel said to me, "Write this: Blessed are those who are invited to the wedding supper of the Lamb!" And he added, "These are the true words of God."

The Heavenly Warrior Defeats the Beast (*The Beast is the Anti-Christ.*) *I* saw heaven standing open and there before me was a white horse, whose rider is called Faithful and True. With justice he judges and wages war. [12] His eyes are like blazing fire, and on his head are many crowns. He has a name written on him that no one knows but he himself. [13] He is dressed in a robe dipped in blood, and his name is the Word of God. [14] The armies of heaven were following him, riding on white horses and dressed in fine linen, white and clean. [15] Coming out of his mouth is a sharp sword with which to strike down the nations. "He will rule them with an iron scepter." He treads the winepress of the fury of the wrath of God Almighty. [16] On his robe and on his thigh he has this name written: King of kings and lord of lords.

[17] And I saw an angel standing in the sun, who cried in a loud voice to all the birds flying in midair, "Come, gather together for the great supper of God, [18] so that you may eat the flesh of kings, generals, and the mighty, of horses and their riders, and the flesh of all people, free and slave, great and small." [19] Then I saw the beast and the kings of the earth and their armies gathered together to wage war against the rider on the horse and his army. [20] But the beast was captured, and with it the false prophet who had performed the signs on its behalf. With these signs he had deluded those who had received the mark of the beast and worshiped its image. The two of them were thrown alive into the fiery lake of burning sulfur.

Revelation 20
At the great white throne,
The dead are judged for their wrong.
If in the book of life their names are not found,
They are cast into a lake of fire where death and hell abound.

Revelation 21
I'm homesick for heaven
When I think of what I'm given,
Gates of pearl, streets of gold,
And foundations of jewels my eyes can't wait to behold.

PROPHECY: *The Day of the Lord is a special term referring to the time when God directly intervenes in human affairs. The day we are waiting for is the rapture of the church, the tribulation period, and the reign of Christ on earth. Jesus, the Son of God, is the center of prophecy, past, present, and future. He is the Bible's supreme fascination. Therefore, it is impossible to hold to Christ and reject the Bible—and vice versa—it is impossible to hold to the Bible and reject Christ. (Greene, 1970)*

Vision Number 7 is the consummation of the historical process. Revelation 21 is that very familiar chapter that we love to read. Jesus comes back for his bride, the church. Also, we read that all tears will be wiped away. All things are made new. John was shown the holy Jerusalem. And Jesus, the lamb, will be the light of it!

The New Heaven and the New Earth

Revelation 21:1: Then I saw "a new heaven and a new earth,"for the first heaven and the first earth had passed away, and there was no longer any sea. [2] I saw the Holy City, the new Jerusalem, coming down out of heaven from God, prepared as a bride beautifully dressed for her husband. [3] And I heard a loud voice from the throne saying, "Look! God's dwelling place is now among the people, and he will dwell with them. They will be his people, and God himself will be with them and be their God. [4] 'He will wipe every tear from their eyes. There will be no more death or mourning or crying or pain, for the old order of things has passed away." [5] He who was seated on the throne said, "I am making everything new!" Then he said, "Write this down, for these words are trustworthy and true." [6] He said to me: "It is done. I am the Alpha and the Omega, the Beginning and the End. To the thirsty I will give water without cost from the spring of the water of life. [7] Those who are victorious will inherit all this, and I will be their God and they will be my children.

Revelation 22
On earth we may have limited energy,
But in heaven the Lord will forever provide
The light and warmth for eternity,
No electricity bills will plague where I will reside.

The City of Gold

The great street of the city was of gold, as pure as transparent glass. [22] I did not see a temple in the city, because the Lord God Almighty and the Lamb are its temple. [23] The city does not need the sun or the moon to shine on it, for the glory of God gives it light, and the Lamb is its lamp. [24] The nations will walk by its light, and the kings of the earth will bring their splendor into it.[25] On no day will its gates ever be shut, for there will be no night there. [26] The glory and honor of the nations will be brought into it. [27] Nothing impure will ever enter it, nor will anyone who does what is shameful or deceitful, but only those whose names are written in the Lamb's book of life.

The Tree of Life: *The Garden of Eden is restored in the midst of the city of Gold.*

Paradise and immortality: Revelation 22:1: Then the angel showed me the river of the water of life, as clear as crystal, flowing from the throne of God and of the Lamb [2] down the middle of the great street of the city. On each side of the river stood the tree of life, bearing twelve crops of fruit, yielding its fruit every month. And the leaves of the tree are for the healing of the nations. [3] No longer will there be any curse. The throne of God and of the Lamb will be in the city, and his servants will serve him. [4] They will see his face, and his name will be on their foreheads.[5] There will be no more night. They will not need the light of a lamp or the light of the sun, for the Lord God will give them light. And they will reign for ever and ever.

[12] "Look, I am coming soon! My reward is with me, and I will give to each person according to what they have done. [13] I am the Alpha and the Omega, the First and the Last, the Beginning and the end. Blessed are those who wash their robes, that they may have the right to the tree of life and may go through the gates into the city. [15] Outside are the dogs, those who practice magic arts, the sexually immoral, the murderers, the idolaters and everyone who loves and practices falsehood.

[16] "I, Jesus, have sent my angel to give you this testimony for the churches. I am the Root and the Offspring of David, and the bright Morning Star."

The wonderful storybook for children by Calvin Miller (1999), My Friend & My King, says that when John's vision of heaven and the last days was completed, John probably found himself again in his little cell on the lonely island. He probably said, "But all was changed. The wonder of heaven fell like new sunlight on my soul. He who had changed my life so long ago had changed it once again. I can never describe what it was like to be in the presence of my best friend, Jesus. But I must declare His great love to all, so that you may anticipate the joy of living in His grace forever. Amen and hallelujah to Jesus—to our friend, the King! (p. 31)"

The Final Invitation: Jesus' last recorded word contains an invitation to sinners to come to him that they may be ready when he comes. [17] The Spirit and the bride say, "Come!" And let the one who hears say, "Come!" Let the one who is thirsty come; and let the one who wishes take the free gift of the water of life. [20] He who testifies to these things says, "Yes, I am coming soon."

Amen. Come, Lord Jesus.

[21] The grace of the Lord Jesus be with God's people. Amen.

John has seen and said to the hearts of the Christians who are in persecution that God is on the throne of the universe and is in control of history and that He will be victorious. According to Hester (1950), "The conflict between righteousness and wickedness is bitter; the living Christ is present in the conflict with his people, and He dominates every stage of history. The outcome will be a righteous order which the redeeming God will rule in loving presence." God's people will reign with Him and will glorify Him on the New Earth forever and ever."

God's Plan in Genesis to Revelation is for _you_: God loves you and has a wonderful plan for your life, when you give your life to Him. The wonders of Heaven are for you. You can know for sure that you will go to Heaven. John said, "I write these things to you who believe in the name of the Son of God so that you may know that you have eternal life" (I John 5:13).

For what is life? It is a vapor that appears for a little time, and then vanishes away. *This life is just preparation for eternity. We were made to last forever. When we realize life is preparation for eternity, we will start living a Purpose Driven Life (Rick Warren, 2002). Our purpose is to glorify God. We glorify God by loving him, by learning to love other people, and by becoming like Christ. We glorify God when we serve others and when we tell others about Him. Our relationship to God now will determine our relationship to him in eternity. Everything we do now has eternal implications. In eternity, we must be prepared to answer 2 crucial questions that God will ask:*

1. *What did you do with my Son, Jesus Christ?*
2. *What did you do with your life?*
   The answer to the first question will determine _where_ you spend eternity.
   The answer to the second question will determine _what you will do_ in eternity.

But what about the problem of sin? Sin is what ended Eden's paradise. The Bible says, "All have sinned and fall short of the glory of God" (Romans 8:23). *Sin has terrible consequences, but God provided the solution.* "The wages of sin is death, but the gift of God is eternal life through Jesus Christ our Lord" (Romans 6:23.) *Only when our sins are dealt with through Jesus Christ can we enter Heaven.* "Salvation is found in no one else but

Jesus, for there is no other name under heaven given to men by which we must be saved" (Acts 4:12).

To be forgiven of our sins, we must repent of and confess our sins. "If we confess our sins, he is faithful and just and will forgive us our sins and cleanse us from all unrighteousness." (I John 1:9). *It is not by any good of works that we do that we are saved.* "For it is by grace you have been saved, through faith—not from yourselves, it is the gift of God—not of works lest any man should boast (Ephesians 2:8-9.) As Randy Alcorn, author of *Heaven* said, "If you will call upon Christ to save you, you'll have all eternity in the New Heaven and on the New Earth to be glad you did." And I'll look forward to seeing you there!

PART SIX

Heaven

The New Heaven and the New Earth

Randy Alcorn (2004) talks about the Present Heaven, or the Intermediate Heaven as the Heaven to which we resurrect when we leave this earth now. He also talks of the New Heaven and the New Earth that will last forever in the Future Era. <u>First,</u> we will discuss the New Heaven and the New Earth, <u>then</u> we will look into the Present Heaven where our loved ones are now.

"What will the New Earth be like? Look around you. It will be Earth, as God originally created it. The New Earth with natural beauty untainted by sin and destruction. The New Earth is an invention of a transcendent God, who made physical human beings to live on a physical Earth, and who chose to become a man himself on that same Earth. He did this that he might redeem mankind and Earth. Why? In order to glorify himself and enjoy forever the company of men and women in a world he's made for us." (Alcorn, 2004, page 81)

What will heaven be like? The Eden we long for will return. The Bible tells us this. We are now in the present era. Look at the three eras of the Earth. We have the future era to which to look forward.

<u>Three Eras of Mankind and Earth</u>: (Alcorn's *Heaven, 2004; pages 82-85).*

Note that Genesis 3, when Adam and Eve sinned, ended the first era. The second (the present) era will end and the third era will begin when God comes down from Heaven to rule with the redeemed on the New Earth. Yes, the redeemed of the Lord will win!

<u>Past:</u> Genesis 1-2: The original earth. God delegated reign to innocent mankind. No curse, no shame, universal perfection and blessing. God is in heaven, and visits the earth. The Tree of Life and the River of Life existed. No death, no sin, God walks with humans in

the garden. God's glory is evident in all. The first Adam reigns. It was before redemption. Creation and mankind are perfect: vegetation lush; abundant food and water; satisfaction in labor; Paradise; mankind is able to make choice to sin or not to sin; naked in innocence; one marriage, which is perfect; beginning of human culture; mankind learns, creates in purity; mankind rules and expands Paradise; God's plan for mankind is revealed.

Present: Genesis 3 – Revelation 20. Fallen mankind. Fallen earth. A disputed reign with God, Satan, and fallen mankind exists. God is in heaven, separate, yet active (indwells believers by his Spirit). Sin, curse, and shame are present. Mankind is cut off from the Tree of Life in Paradise. Sin corrupts; Death permeates all. First Adam falls, mankind reigns corruptly; second Adam (Jesus) comes; the drama of redemption unfolds. Sin corrupts; its power and penalty are assaulted and defeated by Christ, but worship is hampered by sin. Humans are cut off from God; God's goodness is known by some, doubted by others. Creation, mankind, and animals hurt each other; ground is cursed and vegetation is diseased; Hunger and thirst are present; man toils for food and water; sin alienates from God; some are declared righteous in Christ. Paradise is lost and sought; foretastes of future paradise by some; mankind is enslaved to sin, or empowered not to sin; marriage is flawed by sin; the culture is contaminated; mankind is banished from Paradise but longs to return to Paradise; God's plan is delayed and enriched.

Future: Revelation 21-22: Mankind is resurrected. A resurrected Earth exists. God delegates reign to righteous mankind; Redeemed stewardship of Earth exists. God lives forever with mankind on the New Earth. There is more curse, and grace is unending. The Tree of Life is in New Jerusalem, and mankind eats forever. The River of life flows from the throne; after redemption, sin and death are forever removed; mankind is resurrected from the earth to live on the New Earth; Last Adam (Jesus) reigns as God-man, with mankind as co-heirs and delegated kings. The Serpent, Satan, is removed from Earth and is thrown into eternal fire. God dwells face-to-face with humans; God's glory is forever celebrated and manifested in all. Creation and mankind are restored to perfection; Animals and mankind live in complete harmony. Vegetation thrives. Plentiful food and pure water exists. Man finds joy in labor; righteousness complete in Christ; Paradise is regained and magnified. Mankind is permanently empowered not to sin and clothed with righteousness. Only one marriage (Christ and the church) exists; purification and eternal expansion of culture exists; Man learns, is created in wisdom and purity; Mankind has unlimited, free access to Paradise; God's plan for Mankind and Earth is realized.

How exciting! There are many things about our earth that we love: the beautiful lush trees and landscape after a rain, the sunrise and sunsets, the mountains, the streams and rivers, the animals, beautiful people, the different cultures, our own hobbies. These will continue. Perhaps I will be a good writer, teacher, speaker, basketball player, swimmer, runner, singer, or piano player on this New Earth. These are all things I've loved and tried in the past. I will be able to sing praises to God in a beautiful, high soprano voice. I will be a story teller. I've loved telling the stories of Jesus as best I could as I have taught Sunday School, Bible School, etc. for 63 years. I want to continue telling the stories of Jesus.

My sister, Kay, will get to make beautiful quilts with tiny stitches like Mama did. She will constantly eat all the ethnic foods at banquets while catching up on news from her friends, Kay will walk in marathons; and her poetry will be readable and awesome. She will enjoy Southern Gospel music even more than while on earth and will be able to sing like Vestal Goodman and play the organ and piano as well as Raymond Berger, Like David, she can say, "I will sing praise to my God as long as I live."

Ronald, my brother, will be able to see every part of every country on Earth, while at present, he has seen only 182 countries. He will learn more and more about every culture and people. While his health is so bad here that he may not complete his autobiography as he wanted, he will have health to accomplish as he did when he was young! Great will be the reward for all he and his wife, Haw Yun, have done for people on this earth!

My brother, Jim, who has a servant's heart, has looked forward to Heaven a long time and has dedicated his life to helping people get there. He will have great rewards in heaven. The Bible says, "The Meek shall inherit the Earth." Jim is humble. He loves talking about "The Word" on this Earth, and he will actually see The Word, Jesus, on the New Earth. I'm sure he will continue to play basketball and will again be able to dunk the basketball. Perhaps he will be able to sing as beautifully in heaven as his wife, Sharon does on earth. Won't it be fun when they can sing together for Jesus!

My husband, Dale, will fish in all the wonderful lakes of the world; he will cook dishes never dreamed of before and will serve great banquets for the redeemed community; and he will find new ways of making God's flowers and nature even more beautiful than he does on the present earth.

Dayla, our daughter, will paint masterpieces with all kinds of mixed media, will study and learn much more about all the arts, and will teach and help children even more than while on this earth. She will have the time to do all she longs to do now. Dayla's husband, Steve, who enjoyed the children very much while being a school principal, will be able to not only talk in Donald Duck language to the kids, but will entertain them in ingenious ways. They will both love talking with Moses, Abraham, and Joshua!

Lolly, our daughter, will continue to be both a Martha and a Mary as she has compassion and helps others. She will continue to be a wonderful mother and grandmother. Her creativity with the computer and technology will soar. Lolly will no longer be allergic to cats, and she will enjoy the animals to the fullest. Eddie will continue singing, not at funerals as he did so much on the present Earth, but to glorify and praise God

And the grandchildren! They are serving the Lord every day. Great will be their service, talents, and creativity. Toby has loved telling the stories of Bible Heroes who foreshadow Jesus to his daughter, Landry and to son, Henry. Toby's wife, Sarah, will get to read and read to her heart's content, all the wonderful books of history "His story." I'm sure Toby's brother, Kyle, like he already does on this earth, will love telling stories of all the Lord has done for him, especially since the birth of his and Sara's son, Carson. Kyle's wife, Sara, will continue excelling in everything she does, as she has done on Earth.

Our granddaughter, Jordan, may be a teacher because she loves children, or she may be a nurse, not one who heals the sick, but an angel of light who will care for babies. On earth, she has loved all the babies, especially her daughter, Londyn! Her sister, Brooke, will sky dive in the whole of the new heavens and the new earth! Brooke's fiancé, Jacob, will surely soar as the navigator and the pilot of all kinds of newly invented planes. Just as on earth, he will have a heavenly job. Halle Grace, the six-year-old, loves to sing all the hymns, fun Christian songs, patriotic songs, etc. I know she will sing to the praise of God because she loves to do that now. Halle and her cousin, Landry Kate, love to play "Princess," and they will truly be more than princesses. They will be redeemed saints and joint heirs with Jesus, the King.

Yes, I have used Biblically inspired imagination to show that every Christian's life work will continue on the New Earth. Our calling to glorify God will never end. *In The Biblical Doctrine of Heaven,* Wilbur Smith suggests, "In heaven we will be permitted to finish many worthy tasks we dreamed of doing while on earth, but which neither time nor strength nor ability allowed us to achieve." What will we achieve when we have resurrected bodies and resurrected minds, undiminished by sin? We will create and innovate at unprecedented levels, to the Glory of God the Father, God the Son, and God the Holy Spirit!

And what about Xander Moore, the one to whom I dedicated my book? His mother, Ricki Lea, wrote about him shortly after he recently went to heaven at age 11 years:

"Xander was an amazing child. Xander was always mature well beyond his years. He learned to interact with adults at such a young age when he was diagnosed with cancer at the age of 2 1/2 years old. From that time, until Xander's death at age 11 on August 22, 2013, Xander lived his life to the fullest. Xander never let Satan steal his joy or rob him of the abundant life God wanted him to live. Xander had faith in The Lord that never wavered. Xander loved everything about life, His Lord and Savior, family, school, and sports."

How Xander loved his sisters and his brother, Carter. Carter and Xander probably shared more than any two brothers. Carter, usually in a Xander T-shirt, was there for the many fund-raisers done for Xander's benefit; he went with him for many kinds of painful experimental treatments; he played on the Xander Teams. When a basketball game was held for a fund raiser when Xander was 9 years old, Carter and their cousins played and watched as Xander's hair fell out and he was hurting, but Xander still played in it and scored many points, some of them long shots! Through pain, Xander was hailed by some as the best athlete and the best student at Lexington School. Carter is also a wonderful student, and he is now lonely without Xander, but he, too, can look forward to a wonderful future in heaven!

We know Xander spent his life telling others about the Lord, in hospitals across the United States during sports competitions, at church, and at school. What will Xander do on the New Earth? We are sure that Jesus will tell him that he will rule over much with Him. Xander will also have time to really excel in all the sports he loved. He loved basketball, track and baseball more than any kid, and I'm sure that when Jesus rewards him for all the great things he did for him on this earth that he will continue his leadership role in sports.

Jesus not only said to Xander, "Well done, thou good and faithful servant." But he also said, "You have been faithful in a few things. I will make you ruler over much." When Xander left this earth, he didn't say, "My Work is done." He just said, "This Day's work is done."

We're told that in Heaven, we will set goals, devise plans, and share ideas, Can't you just see Xander doing these things! Xander was the leader everywhere he went. God also said the humble, the meek shall inherit the kingdom of God. Never have I heard of a child who was such a combination of humility and leadership. Xander's lifework will continue. It seems his lifework was telling the story of Jesus. He will have eternity to tell stories of Jesus.

The Present or the Intermediate Heaven

But according to the book, *Heaven,* Xander is now in the Present Heaven. If God delays the coming of Jesus, we will go to the Intermediate Heaven, where Xander and my mother and daddy are now. I can see him in the following song, "I Bowed on My Knees and Cried, 'Holy.' Because of the resurrection, Xander's death was swallowed up in victory!

I Bowed on My Knees and Cried Holy

I dreamed of a city called Glory,
So bright and so fair.
When I entered the gates I cried, "Holy"
The angels all met me there:
They carried me from mansion to mansion,
And oh the sights I saw,
But I said, "I want to see Jesus,
The One who died for all."

As I entered the gates of that city,
My loved ones all knew me well.
They took me down the streets of Heaven;
Such scenes were too many to tell;

I saw Abraham, Jacob and Isaac
Talked with Mark, and Timothy
But I said, "I want to see Jesus,
'Cause He's the One who died for me."

Chorus
Then I bowed on my knees and cried,
"Holy, Holy, Holy."
I clapped my hands and sang, "Glory,
Glory, Glory."
I clapped my hands and sang, "Glory"
"Glory to the Son of God!"

We know he spent his life telling others about the Lord, in hospitals across the United States, during sports competition, at church, and at school. What will Xander do on the New Earth? We are sure that Jesus will tell him that he will rule over much with Him. Xander will also have time to really excel in all the sports he loved. He loved basketball, track and baseball more than any kid, and I'm sure that when Jesus rewards him for all the great things he did for him on this earth that he will continue his leadership role in sports. Jesus not only said to Xander, "Well done, thou good and faithful servant." But he also said, "You have been faithful in a few things. I will make you ruler over much." When Xander left this earth, he didn't say, "My Work is done." He just said, "This Day's work is done."

We're told that in Heaven, we will set goals, devise plans, and share ideas, Can't you just see Xander doing these things! Xander was the leader everywhere he went. God also said the humble, the meek shall inherit the kingdom of God. Never have I heard of a child who was such a combination of humility and leadership. Xander's lifework will continue. It seems his lifework was telling the story of Jesus. He will have eternity to tell stories of Jesus.

The Present or the Intermediate Heaven

But according to the book, *Heaven,* Xander is now in the Present Heaven. If God delays the coming of Jesus, we will go to the Intermediate Heaven, where Xander and my mother and daddy are now. I can see him in the following song, "I Bowed on My Knees and Cried, 'Holy.' Because of the resurrection, Xander's death was swallowed up in victory!

I Bowed on My Knees and Cried Holy, by Sola Dei Gloria

I dreamed of a city called Glory,
So bright and so fair.
When I entered the gates I cried, "Holy"
The angels all met me there:
They carried me from mansion to mansion,
And oh the sights I saw,
But I said, "I want to see Jesus,
The One who died for all."

As I entered the gates of that city,
My loved ones all knew me well.
They took me down the streets of Heaven;
Such scenes were too many to tell;
I saw Abraham, Jacob and Isaac

346

Talked with Mark, and Timothy
But I said, "I want to see Jesus,
'Cause He's the One who died for me."

Chorus
Then I bowed on my knees and cried,
"Holy, Holy, Holy."
I clapped my hands and sang, "Glory,
Glory, Glory."
I clapped my hands and sang, "Glory"
"Glory to the Son of God!"

References

Alcorn, R. 2004. *Heaven*. Carol Stream, Il: Tyndale

Carson, Dr. Shirley. A. 2002. *Rising Millennials Face Worldview Conflict*. Norman, OK: Hooper Printing.

Carson, Dr. S. A. & Paddack, M. A. (2006) Pass the Baton of Faith to the Next Generation. Self-published, 2006.

Carson, Dr. S. A. 2008. *Putting the Pieces Together: The Worldview Built on the Truth*. Noble, OK: The Creation Truth Foundation

Constable, Thomas L. 2013 Edition. *Notes on Malachi*. Google.

Criswell, Dr. W. A. 1961. *The Scarlet Thread through the Bible*. www.wacriswell.com. *A New Year's Eve Sermon*.

Fellowship of Christian Athletes. 2008. *God's Game Plan*, The Athlete's Bible. Nashville, TN: FCA Press, Serendipity

Got Questions.org 2013. Google Internet.

Greene, O. B. 1970. *Bible Prophecy*. Greenville, SC: The Gospel Hour, Inc.

Greene, O. B. 1965. *The Epistle of Paul the Apostle to the Philippians*. Greenville, SC: The Gospel Hour, Inc.

Greene, O. B. 1963. *The Epistle of Paul the Apostle to the Colossians*. Greenville, SC: The Gospel Hour, Inc.

Greene, O. B. 1962. *The Epistle of Paul the Apostle to the Romans*. Greenville, SC: The Gospel Hour, Inc.

Halley, Henry H. 2007. *Halley's Bible Handbook*: Grand Rapids, MI: Zondervan.

Ham, K., Sarfati, J; & Wieland, C. 2000. *The Revised and Expanded Answers Book*. Green Forest, AR, Aster Books, Inc.

Heston, Charles. 1997. *Charleton Heston Presents the Bible*. New York: GTPublishing.

Hymers, R. L. The Scarlet Thread through the Bible. Sermon preached 2002. Www/wacriswell.com.

Jones, *S. L. 2007. Jesus Story Book Bible*. Grand Rapids Michigan: Zondervan.

Kennedy, Dr. D. J. & J. Newcombe. 1994. *What if Jesus Had Never Been Born?* Nashville: Thomas Nelson Publishers. The King James Version of the Bible. 1976. Nashville: Thomas Nelson, Inc.

MacArthur, John. 2005. *The MacArthur Bible Commentary*. Dallas: Thomas Nelson.

The New International Version of the Bible (NIV). Grand Rapids, MI: Zondervan

McGee, Dr. R. L. 2012. From Bibles to Bullets to Bankruptcy. Dissertation.

Michelson, A. U. 1059. *The Trial of Jesus*. Los Angeles, CA: The Jewish Hope Publishing House.

Miller, Calvin. 1999. *My Friend & My King, 1999*. Chariot Victory Publishing.

Moore, Beth. 2003. *Praying God's Word*. Nashville, TN: Broadman & Holmon Publishers.

Morrison, Henry. 1984. *The Resurrection: The Most Proved Event in History*. The Institute of Creation Research.

Parker, G. . .1994. *Creation Facts of Life*. Green Forests, AR: Master Books, Inc.

Pink, A. W. 1922. *Gleanings in Genesis*, (Not in copyright. Can be downloaded or purchased on-line.)

Shepperson, F. & Horton, Beka. 1986. *Judges Flash-a-Card*. Pensacola, FL: Christian Bible College.

Smith, F. LaGard. 1984. *The Daily Bible in Chronological Order*. Eugene, OR: Harvest House.

Warner, Rick. 2004. *What on Earth Am I Here For?* Grand Rapids, MI: Zondervan.

Warner, Rick. 2002. *The Purpose Driven Life*. Grand Rapids, MI: Zondervan.

Wilkinson, Dr. Bruce. 2000. *The Prayer of Jabez*. Multnomah Books.

CPSIA information can be obtained at www.ICGtesting.com
Printed in the USA
BVOW06s1842251113

337303BV00004B/98/P